THOMAS HARDY

A STUDY OF HIS WRITINGS AND THEIR BACKGROUND

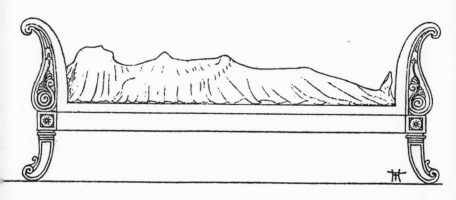

Drawings by Hardy in *Wessex Poems*.

THOMAS HARDY

A Study of his Writings and their Background

By William R. Rutland, B.Litt., D.Phil. (Oxon.).

NEW YORK

RUSSELL & RUSSELL · INC

FIRST PUBLISHED IN 1938
REISSUED, 1962, BY RUSSELL & RUSSELL, INC.
L. C. CATALOG CARD NO: 62-13851

PRINTED IN THE UNITED STATES OF AMERICA

CONTENTS

INTRODUCTION

THIS book is an attempt to bring something more than purely general criticism to the study of a great English author, the centenary of whose birth will fall two years hence. More than fifty publications concerned with Thomas Hardy have appeared; but, as far as I know, only one goes beyond general discussion, and that one confines itself to the very special field of folklore. This abundance of commentary has absolved me from the task of making yet another; for there are now at least half a dozen excellent general critical studies of Hardy. It has been my endeavour in the pages that follow to deal with facts rather than with impressions, even though the two cannot always be entirely separated. Only in the case of *The Dynasts*, to the better comprehension of which not all Hardy critics have contributed, have I allowed myself a personal critical interpretation.

My work falls into two parts. The first three chapters are concerned with what may be called the background to Hardy's writings. In the first two chapters an outline is attempted of the reading which formed Hardy's education in his self-chosen career of letters. In the third chapter I have tried to trace his spiritual development. The inadequacy of several previous attempts at discussing his 'philosophy' seemed to leave the field clear for me here. Whether or not I have succeeded in giving it, some understanding of the thought of the period outlined in this chapter is essential to the full appreciation of Hardy's art.

The last four chapters are devoted to the writings themselves, which are considered historically. In view of the present bulk of Hardy literature, it is surprising how little *information* about his books has been forthcoming; and I believe that some things in these pages will be new to students of Hardy; particularly with regard to the first

INTRODUCTION

three books which he wrote, and also to *The Dynasts*. That masterpiece, indeed, has as yet scarcely been approached by critical scholarship. If my treatment of Hardy's use of historical sources, in the latter, fails in any respect, I would plead in extenuation that the first pioneer in such a field has before him no light task. Of my attempted critical appreciation of *The Dynasts*, which forms the last section of this book, I would only repeat that it is a personal interpretation, as all pure criticism must be in the last analysis, at least until critical theory has advanced far beyond its present state; and as far as I know, I have taken none of it elsewhere than out of my own head.

Perhaps I should offer a word of excuse for having devoted less than a twentieth part of my book to Hardy's lyrical poems. The reason is to be sought in the nature of my undertaking. There is very little information concerning them available, other than such as is obvious to anyone who knows his Hardy. To chronicle the changes of words from one edition to another would be a weary business in the doing, and a still wearier business in the reading. Nearly all the Manuscripts are fair copies; should the originals ever become available, matters may be altered. Meanwhile the late Arthur Macdowall has absolved me from trying to write a general critical commentary to the poems.

I have availed myself impartially of all the sources of information open to me; but to the second Mrs. Hardy I owe a special debt. Upon two occasions she gave me access to Hardy's library at Max Gate; and in the two volumes of her biography of Hardy, *The Early Life* and *The Later Years*, there is much accurate information. The pages that follow were written before her death, and in the hope that she would read them. It has seemed best to leave them as they stood; some passages, however, which invite an answer upon questions where we differed, would have been phrased differently had I known that she could never reply.

One further word of self-justification. Hardy hated being

quizzed. In a private letter, which was on sale last year by a London bookseller, he wrote: 'The habit of critics in getting behind the work at the author is a vicious practice, and should be stopped' (I quote from memory). To the charge of this vicious practice I must plead guilty, up to a point. It is true that I have neither given an account of how the great man paused in his discourse to throw a piece of cheese to the favourite dog under the table; nor have I exercised my wit in making insinuations against his first wife. But of 'getting at the author' I am not wholly innocent. For I believe that the work of a great artist proceeds out of his inmost life; and that it can only be fully understood and appreciated in so far as we know and understand the living thought out of which it came. If I have ever succeeded in these pages in giving a glimpse of the inner life of a great man, my book will not be useless. I will not, after the fashion of authors, say 'in vain'; for to me, at least, the close communion with genius which the writing has entailed has been its own great reward.

It is a privilege, as well as a pleasure, to acknowledge the help which I have received from several eminent scholars. Without the kindly interest and advice of Professor D. Nichol Smith, the book might never have been written. Miss Helen Darbishire, Dr. Lascelles Abercrombie, Mr. C. S. Lewis and Mr. C. H. Wilkinson have all given me valuable counsel; without them, my work would have had more faults than it still has. To each of them individually, and to the Faculty of English at Oxford as a whole, I owe a debt beyond my power to repay.

My thanks are due to the executors of Mrs. F. E. Hardy and to Macmillan & Co. for kind permission to quote from copyright material, and to reproduce the drawings in the frontispiece; also to the proprietors of *The Sunday Times* for permission to quote from the article by Sir Edmund Gosse on Hardy's lost novel.

Oxford, February 1938.

CHAPTER I

THE INFLUENCE OF EARLY READING

TO carry out the Johnsonian advice, and read the books which your author had read, was a counsel of perfection even in the days of Malone; and, if the ideal was hard of attainment when dealing with an Elizabethan in the eighteenth century, it becomes an impossible one when dealing with a Victorian in the twentieth. The possible extent of Shakespeare's reading cannot have been one tenth part of the probable extent of Hardy's. Discussing this very question of Hardy's reading, a French scholar wrote a few years ago: 'La rareté des moyens d'information . . . ne permet point d'entrer dans le détail de ses lectures.'[1] But the case is not quite so hopeless as this. It is true that we cannot read all that Hardy read, for we cannot know all with any certainty. But we can, at least, discern the main lines of his reading during that early period which often so deeply influences the whole of a man's life; and the evidence is sufficient for a sketch in outline.

The first book with which Hardy became thoroughly familiar was the Authorized Version of the Bible. As child and boy he heard it read every Sunday in Stinsford Church. It was certainly read to him at home from early childhood; and we cannot doubt that he read it himself as soon as he could read. The natural and inevitable result was that his imagination was taken captive by the greatest book in our language. Nearly every great English author during the last three centuries has been influenced by the Authorized Version. It gripped Hardy with a grip which never relaxed. The fascination, indeed, seemed to grow with the years; and long after he had lost all religious faith, he continued to read the Bible as literature. The matchless writings,

[1] M. Cazamian: *Le Roman et les Idées en Angleterre*, p. 376.

I

which had cast the spell of their power and their con-
summate English upon him as a child, lost nothing of their
hold until his dying day. The Wessex novels contain
Biblical allusions by the hundred, and end upon the whispered quotation of the dying Jude: 'Let the day perish
wherein I was born.' The first poem in the last volume of
verse which Hardy published was suggested by the Book of
Job. The best known of his short poems is called, in a
phrase from Jeremiah, 'In Time of the Breaking of Nations.'
The Ancient Spirit of the Years, in *The Dynasts*, quotes from
that part of the ninth chapter of Isaiah which is the first
lesson for Christmas day. The last of his poems which
Hardy ever saw in print, in the *Times* a fortnight before his
death, fittingly enshrines two of the dominant influences in
his life. The Gods of Hellas, come to Borean exile in the
British Museum, ask of each other:

> What is the noise that shakes the night,
> And seems to soar to the pole-star height?
> > Christmas bells,
> > The Watchman tells
> Who walks this hall that blears us captives with its blight.

> And what, then, mean such clangs, so clear?
> —'Tis said to have been a day of cheer
> > And source of grace
> > To the human race
> Long ere their woven sails winged us to exile here.

Many who were moved to see that poem amid the barren
chronicle of the day's events, must have looked away from
the breakfast table, while they listened again in memory to
the music of another great Victorian poet:

> Thou hast conquered, O pale Galilean, the world has
> grown grey from thy breath.

It would be a not unprofitable study to compile a complete Biblical lexicon to Hardy's writings. The Biblical
references in the Wessex novels might be classified as

quotations, allusions, metaphors and similes; such a classification would show that the deliberate quotations are few, while the metaphors and similes are innumerable. This is another way of saying that Hardy's use of the Authorized Version was not ordinarily a deliberate, or even a conscious, practice. Its language and its stories had become so much a part of himself that they were a portion of his natural speech. In *Desperate Remedies* the Biblical allusions are few in number compared to those of the later novels, for they barely number a dozen, of which five are deliberate quotations. As time went on, the proportion of quotations declined; while the number of allusions increased. *Far from the Madding Crowd* has over thirty, several being due to the comical 'scripture manner' of Joseph Poorgrass. Hardy again put Holy Writ to humorous use in 'The Respectable Burgher on the Higher Criticism' (in *Poems of the Past and Present*). *The Return of the Native*, with about an equal number of Biblical references, provides this pen portrait of Eustacia:

> Had she been a mother, she would have christened her boys such names as Saul or Sisera in preference to Jacob or David, neither of whom she admired. At school she had used to side with the Philistines in several battles, and had wondered if Pontius Pilate were as handsome as he was frank and fair.

The interest of that passage is not confined to its portraiture of Eustacia's character; it has about it a flavour of the 'rationalism' in which, as will be seen in a later chapter, Hardy steeped himself in the 'seventies. Here he is no longer using Biblical allusions without *arrière pensée*; he is trying to suggest hidden meanings; and this is the difference between his use of Holy Scripture in his early and in his late novels. The Biblical allusions in *The Mayor of Casterbridge*, in *Tess* and in *Jude* are even more effective than those in *Far from the Madding Crowd*. Seldom has an allusion to the Bible been put to happier use than in the words which Angel Clare whispered to Tess as he took her in his arms to carry her over the flood: 'Three Leahs to get one Rachel'.

But too often, in the late novels, Hardy's references to Scripture are bitterly ironical; and when they are not ironical, they are terrible. Sue describes the doom hanging over her family as being like that which hung over the House of Atreus, and Jude replies: 'Or the House of Jeroboam'. That allusion to the two great literatures which were the food of Hardy's younger years brings to mind the words of Swinburne concerning: 'that jealousy which the Hebrews acknowledged and that envy which the Greeks recognized in the divine nature'.[1]

There are, in the Wessex novels, a number of places where passages from the Bible are deliberately used as artistic devices to produce a great climax. The most memorable of these is the death of Jude. Another, less known and less striking, but not less significant, passage is to be found in the short story 'What the Shepherd Saw' (reprinted in *A Changed Man and other Tales*); where the shepherd boy is made to kneel and swear a great oath clearly suggested by the twenty-eighth chapter of Deuteronomy. A third is in the thirty-third chapter of *The Mayor of Casterbridge*, where Henchard, in the Three Mariners Inn, forces the choir to sing the hundred and ninth psalm. In that Tate and Brady psalm we have a reminiscence of Hardy's youth at Stinsford, and a parallel to *Under the Greenwood Tree*: but the difference in the character of what is sung is eloquent. It is highly suggestive that in every one of these passages where a Biblical quotation is used as a climax, the words quoted are from the great curses in the Old Testament.

Hardy's favourite reading in the Bible were the narratives, whether the historical records of the Old Testament, the narrative portions of the prophets, such as Daniel, or the Gospels. After Genesis, his favourite single books were Job, the Psalms and Ecclesiastes. There is no doubt that, as well as reading the Bible all his life as a masterpiece of literature, he made a deliberate study of parts of it as models

---

[1] *Essay on Blake.*

for narrative prose[1]; and his style was deeply influenced by the Authorized Version, both in prose and in poetry.[2] The poems, indeed, are often Biblical in subject as well as in language. Two of Hardy's most personal utterances are poems suggested by the Bible. They both reveal the man behind the writer with poignant intensity; and show, more clearly than any critical exposition, what both the writer and the man owed to life long study of the greatest book in English, the book which Hardy first knew when he was a child at his mother's knee.

The first poem is called 'Quid Hic Agis?' (in *Moments of Vision*). It was first published in 1916. In it, Hardy recalls the days when, in Stinsford Church, he used to listen to the passages from the story of Elijah which form the first lessons for the tenth, eleventh and twelfth Sundays after Trinity. He remembers the days when he himself used, at St. Juliot's, to read the nineteenth chapter of the first book of Kings, and 'watched for her smile across the sunned aisle', and knew not that Time was devouring the prime of him and her. And here is the end:

> But now, at last
> When our glory has passed
> And there is no smile
> From her in the aisle,
> But where it once shone
> A marble, men say,
> With her name thereon
> Is discerned to-day;
> And spiritless
> In the wilderness
> I shrink from sight
> And desire the night
> (Though, as in old wise,
> I might still arise,

[1]Two passages prove this. See the note on 'Evidences of art in Bible narratives' in *Early Life*, pp. 222–3; and the conversation about David and Jonathan in *The Life and Letters of Leslie Stephen*, p. 227.

[2]What are perhaps Hardy's happiest Biblical allusions are to be found in the short story 'The Spectre of the Real,' reprinted in *In Scarlet and Grey*.

Go forth, and stand
And prophesy in the land)
I feel the shake
Of wind and earthquake,
And consuming fire
Nigher and nigher,
And the voice catch clear
'What doest thou here?'

It is on account of this poem that the memorial window to
Hardy in Stinsford Church depicts Elijah in the Wilderness.

The second poem is a work of his old age; it is the first
piece in the volume called *Human Shows*, published in 1925
when Hardy was in his eighty-sixth year. The Book of Job
had been favourite reading with him throughout four-score
years. In the fourteenth chapter, Job laments over the lot of
man born of woman, and many times must Hardy have
read that lament:

> As the waters fail from the sea, and the flood decayeth and
> drieth up: so man lieth down and riseth not: till the heavens be
> no more, they shall not awake, nor be raised out of their sleep.
> O that thou wouldest hide me in the grave, that thou wouldest
> keep me secret until thy wrath be past, that thou wouldest
> appoint me a set time and remember me! If a man die, shall he
> live again? All the days of my appointed time will I wait, till
> my change come.

Hardy wrote

A star looks down at me
And says: 'Here I and you
Stand, each in our degree:
What do you mean to do,—
        Mean to do?'

I say: 'For all I know,
Wait, and let Time go by,
Till my change come.'—'Just so,'
The star says: 'So mean I:—
        So mean I.'

A word must be said here of another very early influence

which profoundly affected Hardy. His mother was greatly attached to the Church of England, and her boy 'was kept strictly at Church on Sundays till he knew the morning and evening services by heart'.[1] The rubrics, observances and doctrines of the Church of England continued to occupy a place in Hardy's mind throughout his life. There are continual references to them throughout the Wessex Novels; indeed, it would be possible to write a pamphlet wholly upon the subject of the Church of England in his writings. By way of illustration, take the rustics in *Far from the Madding Crowd*, of whose everyday life Church festivals form such a part that events are, for example, dated by their relation to 'Sexajessamy Sunday'. Of these worthies, Joseph Poorgrass, with his extensive knowledge of the Bible, is the most striking; as witness his adventure at Lambing Down Gate:

> My heart died within me, at that time; but I kneeled down and said the Lord's Prayer, and then the Belief right through, and then the Ten Commandments, in earnest Prayer. But no, the gate wouldn't open; and then I went on with Dearly Beloved Brethren, and, thinks I, this makes four, and 'tis all I know out of book, and if this don't do it nothing will, and I'm a lost man. Well, when I got to Saying After Me, I rose from my knees and found the gate would open. Yes, neighbours, the gate opened the same as ever. (Ch. VIII.)

In Chapter XLII there is an even more entertaining, and perhaps more significant, passage, too long for quotation, and similar instances abound in Hardy.[2] There is also copious evidence of his personal reactions to Church services and doctrines. 'Afternoon Service at Mellstock' in *Moments of Vision* refers to his early experiences. Such a moving and very characteristic poem as 'Apostrophe to an Old Psalm Tune' (in *Moments of Vision*) proves how deep and how lasting were the traces which early experiences and associations left. It was in 1916 that he wrote:

[1] *Early Years*, p. 23.
[2] (E.g., in the short story 'The Three Strangers' the constable shouts 'Prisoner at the Bar, surrender in the name of the Father—I mane the Crown.')

I rose and went as a ghost goes,
And said, eyes full, 'I'll never hear it again!
It is overmuch for scathed and memoried men
When sitting among strange people
Under their steeple.'
So your quired oracles beat till they make me tremble
As I discern your mien in the old attire,
Here in these turmoiled years of belligerent fire
Living still on—and onward, may be,
Till Doom's great day be.

To a different, albeit no less personal, category belong the musings of Tess on the Benedicite, or of Sue Bridehead on the Marriage Service. It would here be out of place to discuss Hardy's attitude to the Church of England, of which he once, for a short time, even thought of becoming an ordained priest.[1] But, although we are not justified in taking the beginning of the eighth chapter of *Tess* as being autobiographical, Hardy made no attempt to conceal his personal concern with the affairs of the Church of England in his Preface to *Late Lyrics and Earlier*. All these things were certainly the result of his early training and associations.

It seems probable that the first poet whose work Hardy knew intimately was William Barnes. The first of his characteristic novels, which contains, if only in embryo, many of the elements of them all, *Under the Greenwood Tree*, owes a considerable debt to the Dorset poet. Hardy must have known both Barnes and his poems from a very early date. When he was an apprentice to Hicks at No. 39 South Street, Dorchester, the architect and his pupils used to argue over points of classical grammar:

> At this time the Rev. William Barnes, the Dorset poet and philologist, was keeping school next door. Knowing him to be an authority upon grammar, Hardy would often run in to ask Barnes to decide some knotty point in dispute.[2]

This was before 1860. Barnes' first collection, *Poems of Rural Life in the Dorset Dialect*, had appeared in 1844. We

[1] *Early Life*, p. 66.   [2] *Early Life*, p. 36.

cannot doubt that Hardy had read this local classic, probably in his early 'teens. The second collection was published when Hardy was nineteen, many of its contents having previously appeared in local periodicals which he would probably see. He certainly read the *Dorset County Chronicle* during the years of his apprenticeship, when he either went to Dorchester every day or lived there all the week (as he did towards the end of his term). A little later, he even became a contributor to it himself.[1] Throughout the first nine months of 1859 the *Dorset County Chronicle* published a poem by William Barnes regularly every week, most of which were reprinted in the third collection of *Poems in the Dorset Dialect* in 1862. That Hardy, with his appetite for poetry and his interest in the lives of country folk, would fasten on these is certain. One of his favourites among Barnes' poems, included both in his own selections from Barnes and in the selection which he made for Ward's English poets, 'Woak Hill', which he pronounced to be immortal, and quotes in the fifty-sixth chapter of *Far from the Madding Crowd*, first appeared in the *Dorset County Chronicle* on March 6th, 1862. It was during these years, also, that the readings from his own poems, which were important events locally, were periodically given by Barnes in Dorchester and the neighbourhood. From the description of these occasions which Hardy included in his obituary article on Barnes, no one can doubt that he himself had often been present.

> The poet's own mild smile at the boisterous merriment provoked by his droll delivery of such pieces as 'The Shy Man,' 'A Bit o' Sly Coorten' and 'Dick and I' returns upon the memory as one of the most characteristic aspects of a man who was nothing if not genial.

So wrote Hardy twenty years later.

The early debt which he himself owed to the Dorset poet is considerable, and, indeed, obvious. After the failure of his first two attempts at fiction, Hardy bethought him of the

[1] See *Early Life*, p. 43.

life he knew best and wrote a novel entirely of rural Dorset life; in so doing, he remembered the only other writer who had dealt with that life, whom, moreover, he knew well and loved, and with whom he found himself largely in sympathy. He did not plagiarize Barnes; he did in prose fiction what Barnes had done in lyric poetry; and the result was *Under the Greenwood Tree*. By way of illustration, take the episodes and scenes in that novel which have close parallels among the pieces in the first collection of *Poems of Rural Life*. The passages between Dick and Fancy in the chapter called 'Driving out of Budmouth' are a rather more polished version of 'A Bit o' Sly Coorten'. The delightful scene between them in the chapter 'A Confession' is a fairly close parallel to 'Meaken up a Miff'. Both scenes, and other similar ones, in Hardy are only superficially different from those in Barnes. Dick and Fancy are metamorphosed from the Dorset peasants of Barnes into the educated persons of fiction; in the process, the humour has become less broad, and the passions more refined. But essentially the same situation is reproduced on another plane. To take other instances of a different kind: the *Poems of Rural Life* include two on 'Bees a-zwarmen' and 'Out a-Nutten'. One of the most effective chapters in *Under the Greenwood Tree* is that describing the honey taking; and another deals with 'going nutting'. Barnes' description of 'The Zettle an' the Girt Wood Vire' irresistibly recalls Hardy's description of Geoffrey Day's Chimney Corner. The Christmas scenes in the novel may well have been suggested by the Christmas pieces in the first collection of *Poems of Rural Life*. And many other parallels might be drawn. The temptation, indeed, is to carry the comparison too far. For, while Hardy's debt to Barnes is obvious enough, it is also very limited. In all the essentials of his art, the greater Dorset poet owes nothing to the lesser. The personalities of the two men, and their views of the realities of life, were as different as well could be.

It is, perhaps, in the form of Hardy's verse that the

influence of the elder poet is most clearly to be seen. Among his many experiments in stanzaic form, Barnes had adapted to English a number of poetic forms from some of the many languages which he had studied—among them Persian and Welsh.[1] Hardy, who was a great experimenter in poetic forms and rhyme schemes, not only took from Barnes many hints concerning the use of assonances, refrains and feminine rhymes, with results which are to be found throughout his poetry; he also wrote a number of poems which are clearly imitations of Barnes. Among Barnes' poems in ordinary English is one called 'The Knoll', which begins as follows:

O home, people tell us, is home be it never so homely,
And Meldon's the home where my fathers all sleep by the knoll.
And there they have kept me a living, in land, where in summer
My hay, withered gray, awaits hauling in heap by the knoll.

In *Poems of the Past and Present* there is a poem called 'The Mother Mourns', the first two stanzas of which will serve as specimen:

> When mid-autumn's moan shook the night time,
>   And sedges were horny,
> And summer's green wonderwork faltered
>   On leaze and in lane,
>
> I fared Yell'ham firs way, where dimly
>   Came wheeling around me
> Those phantoms obscure and insistent
>   That shadows unchain.

Comment is needless. Other examples of poems in which Hardy has adopted the 'pearl' or identical end-rhyme throughout the poem, are 'My Cecily' in *Wessex Poems*, and 'The Flirt's Tragedy' in *Time's Laughingstocks*. The latter, beginning

> Here alone by the logs in my chamber,
>   Deserted, decrepit—
> Spent flames limning ghosts on the wainscot
>   Of friends I once knew—

[1] There is an account of these in *The Life of William Barnes*, p. 247.

is an imitation of 'Woak Hill':

> When sycamore leaves wer a-spreaden
> Green-ruddy in hedges,
> Bezide the red doust o' the ridges
> A-dried at Woak Hill:—

For the assonances and the initial 'pearl' rhyme in the last lines of the stanzas of 'Woak Hill,' Hardy substituted ordinary end rhyme; but the imitation is obvious.

The personal relationship between Hardy and Barnes would provide matter for an interesting little study, but it is outside the scope of these pages. From private letters at Max Gate it is clear that Hardy, like Coventry Patmore, Palgrave and others, did his best to spread the fame of the Dorset poet; Hardy early gave private readings in London; and in later years, when his own fame was secure, he edited for the Oxford University Press a selection from the Dorset Poems. The letters in which Sir Walter Raleigh coaxed him to write a Preface make, it need hardly be said, very good reading; they are still unpublished. This Preface was actually the third article on Barnes that Hardy wrote. The most picturesque and authoritative of the obituary notices of Barnes came from his pen, in the *Athenæum* of October 16th, 1886; and this itself was an amplification of an unsigned review of the *Collected Poems of Rural Life* which he had contributed to the *New Quarterly Magazine* of October 1879. He also made selections from Barnes for the fifth volume of Ward's English Poets. *Moments of Vision* contains some lines on the funeral of the Dorset poet.

Another poet of country life whom Hardy studied at a very early date, and to whom in later years he acknowledged a debt, was George Crabbe. Hardy's edition of Crabbe was the one-volume *Life and Poetical Works* edited by Crabbe's son and published in 1861 by John Murray. It is probable that this was one of the few books which Hardy bought, or was given, while still in Dorchester. He twice makes reference to Crabbe, each time in connection with Barnes. The first is in the obituary of Barnes which he contributed to the *Athenæum* on October 16th, 1886, where he writes of the Dorset poet:

> His rustics are, as a rule, happy people, and very seldom feel the sting of the rest of modern mankind—the disproportion between the desire for serenity and the power of obtaining it. One naturally thinks of Crabbe in this connection; but though they touch at points, Crabbe goes much further than Barnes in questioning the justice of circumstance.

The second is in the preface to the Barnes selections in vol. 5 of Ward's English poets, where Hardy writes of Barnes:

> 'he holds himself artistically aloof from the ugly side of things . . . and we escape in his pictures the sordid miseries that are laid bare in Crabbe, often to the destruction of charm.'

In a review of Canon Ainger's *Life of Crabbe* which appeared in the *Sphere* on October 24th, 1903, Clement K. Shorter, an intimate friend of Hardy in later years, wrote:

> Crabbe was a great and successful story teller in poetry, a great realist before the French realists were in being. To drag in the name of the laborious effortful George Eliot is quite beside the point. It is to the point that a much greater novelist than George Eliot, I mean Mr. Thomas Hardy, told me that his earliest influence in the direction of realism was obtained from Crabbe's work.

Mrs. Hardy tells me that the first time she ever spoke to Hardy, when, as Miss Dugdale, she was taken by a friend and introduced to the Hardys as a distant connection of the family, Hardy, in the course of a conversation with her on literary matters, asked her if she had ever read Crabbe; to whom, he said, he himself owed a debt.

One book, which we know Hardy to have possessed before he left Dorchester, was Walter Bagehot's *Estimates of Some Englishmen and Scotchmen*, published in 1858.[1] It is noteworthy that three of the articles in this volume deal with authors who were among Hardy's favourites, Gibbon, Shakespeare and Shelley. His reading of the first two must

[1] *Early Life*, p. 43.

be considered in later chapters. Whether he had read Shelley before he was eighteen we cannot know; but he certainly read him much thereafter. During his first visit to Italy in March 1887 he wrote a poem called 'Shelley's Skylark.' In the second stanza, Hardy, probably for the first and last time, writes with a movement and a phrasing which are those of Shelley:

> The dust of the lark that Shelley heard,
> And made immortal through times to be:—
> Though it only lived like another bird
> And knew not its immortality.

The concluding couplet has a flavour and a lilt like those of 'The Sensitive Plant', which are as unlike Hardy's stark and sometimes rugged language as they well could be. He *must* have been reading Shelley when he wrote that. The same Italian journey produced the poem written near the Pyramid of Cestius, outside Rome, in which Keats and Shelley are referred to, although not mentioned by name. In *Jude the Obscure* (Ch. IV, v), Sue Bridehead quotes *Epipsychidion*. The quotation of such a poem in such a context might almost please the Ironic Spirit. *Epipsychidion* seems to have been a favourite with Hardy. Three lines from it are quoted in the twenty-third chapter of *The Woodlanders* (which also contains several other quotations from Shelley):

> Towards the loadstar of my one desire
> I flitted like a dizzy moth, whose flight
> Is as a dead leaf in the owlet light.

The special interest of this quotation is that Hardy used it for one of the chapter headings in *An Indiscretion in the Life of an Heiress* (Pt. II, ch. 2). Another of these chapter headings is from Shelley—'When the lamp is shattered——'. That poem is also introduced, as a song sung by Elfride, in the eighteenth chapter of *A Pair of Blue Eyes*. There are three quotations from Shelley in *Desperate Remedies*, more than from any other, except Shakespeare, of the many poets there quoted. There is a quotation from the Ode to the

West Wind in the forty-fourth chapter of *Far from the Madding Crowd*:

> Bathsheba shook her dress to get rid of them (the leaves that had settled upon her in her sleep), when multitudes of the same family lying round her rose and fluttered away in the breeze thus created 'Like pale ghosts from an enchanter fleeing.'

In *The Hand of Ethelberta*—of all places—Hardy quotes *Adonais*; and the Epigraph of *The Well Beloved* is from *Prometheus Unbound*.

Hardy early possessed a copy of Keats, one of a cheap uniform edition of English poets published by Moxon in the 'sixties.[1] The 'Ode to a Nightingale' is quoted in *Desperate Remedies*, in *Far from the Madding Crowd* and in *A Pair of Blue Eyes*. The latter also contains a very striking use of a quotation from *La Belle Dame sans Merci*. The epigraph of *The Return of the Native* is from the song in *Endymion*; and in *Far from the Madding Crowd* Hardy borrows, in order to describe the sobered Bathsheba, the lovely simile which Keats used of the sleeping Madeleine in 'The Eve of St. Agnes':

> 'As though a rose should shut and be a bud again.'

At the other end of his life, Hardy visited Keats' house in Hampstead and wrote a beautiful poem, afterwards published in *Late Lyrics*.

Another great English poet figured in the reading of Hardy's boyhood and early manhood. Wordsworth certainly influenced him profoundly at one period. His earliest surviving poem 'Domicilium'[2] provides abundant proof of this. It was some years later that he bought for himself an edition of Wordsworth published in 1864, in which he wrote 'Thomas Hardy, 16 Westbourne Park Villas.' The volume is still at Max Gate. Writing to Edmund Gosse in

---

[1] Other volumes of this series still at Max Gate are: Spenser, Thomson, Milton, Herbert, Percy's *Reliques* and *Hudibras*. There is also an undated edition of Young's *Night Thoughts* (one of the books which Bathsheba takes into retirement with her, in Ch. XLIV) which contains a very early signature; and an 1859 edition of Coleridge signed 'Thomas Hardy 1865.'

[2] See p. 258.

1918 about a poem 'The Widow Betrothed' (in *Poems of the Past and Present*) he said:

> Though I thought of it about 1867 when looking at the house described. . . . it must have been written after I had read Wordsworth's famous Preface to Lyrical Ballads, which influenced me much and influenced the style of the poem, as you can see for yourself.[1]

In the forty-ninth chapter of *Far from the Madding Crowd* we may read of Bathsheba:

> Her exuberance of spirit was pruned down; the original phantom of delight had shown herself to be not too bright for human nature's daily food.

But there are not many quotations from Wordsworth in Hardy's writings until we come to *Tess*; and there may be found two very significant ones; describing the shiftless house of Durbeyfield:

> Some people would like to know whence the poet whose philosophy is in these days deemed as profound and trustworthy as his song is breezy and pure, gets his authority for speaking of 'Nature's holy plan.'

And in the fifty-first chapter:

> To Tess, as to not a few millions of others, there was a ghastly satire in the poet's lines
>
> > Not in utter nakedness
> > But trailing clouds of glory do we come.

The man who wrote those two bitter passages had, as a boy, written a poem redolent of Wordsworth, in which he referred to

> 'my father's mother, who is now
> Blest with the blest——'

Hardy had indeed turned and rent the hand which fed him.

The comparison, and contrast, between the two great poets of English earth has been made once for all by

---

[1] This letter has never been published. It is in the Ashley Library (Catalogue Vol. X, p. 131).

THE INFLUENCE OF EARLY READING

Lionel Johnson, in the fifth chapter of *The Art of Thomas Hardy*:

> Both writers love to deal with the spiritual magnificence of men in a humble station; with the unadorned majesty of natural lives; with things immemorial, the oldest signs and tokens of an ancient world; with great passages of time, dissolutions, vanishings and vicissitudes; both impress upon us the 'magnalities' of the universe . . . both are obedient to the vision of forms, laws, powers, ideas, awful and august, among which men walk, themselves mysterious and tragic.

There is much more besides, in the admirable passage from which this is taken. Johnson, moreover, is not the only good critic who has made the comparison.[1] But, writing in Hardy's lifetime, he was not able to see the whole matter. If it be not presumptuous to attempt to complete his comparison; the fundamental difference between Hardy and Wordsworth arises from the different ages into which they were born, with all that that implies. It will be seen in a later chapter how completely Hardy belonged to his day. Had he had the mental food of Wordsworth's youth, his work might have been more like the work of his great predecessor in spirit. As it was, he developed along other lines, until it came about that he could write such passages as those quoted from *Tess*. Late in life he could write to a friend: 'The more we know of the laws and nature of the Universe, the more ghastly a business one perceives it to be.'[2] For his own sake, if not for that of English literature, we must profoundly regret that Hardy, who learnt much from Wordsworth, could not also have learnt the lesson which human life taught to the greater man:

> Enough if something from our hands have power
> To live, and act, and serve the future hour;
> And if, as toward the silent tomb we go,
> Through love, through hope and faith's transcendent dower,
> We feel that we are greater than we know.

[1] Arthur Macdowall: *Thomas Hardy, a critical study* (1931).
[2] See p. 64.

17

THOMAS HARDY

It would seem logical to seek the antecedents of a great novelist in the previous history of the novel; but everything which we know of Hardy combines to suggest that he read far more poetry than fiction, and was more deeply influenced by it. Mrs. Hardy writes that for two years (i.e., about 1865–7) he did not read a word of prose except the daily papers.[1] Although doubtless an overstatement, this indicates a state of affairs which is also very strongly suggested by the large number of poetical allusions in *Desperate Remedies*, written in 1868. If, as is possible, the chapter headings in *An Indiscretion in the Life of an Heiress* originally appeared in *The Poor Man and the Lady*, they would provide further confirmation; for only one of them is in prose, from Thackeray's *Book of Snobs*.

There is little evidence to show what novels Hardy read at any time. On two of the rare occasions when he put aside creative work for a moment to turn critic, he wrote about the novel. The first of his articles on his own craft, 'The Profitable Reading of Fiction,' appeared in an American publication, *The Forum*, in March 1888. We cannot assume that the reading in fiction here displayed was all done in Hardy's youth; and even here there is more reference to poetry than to fiction. It is no revelation to be told that at forty-eight he had read *Tom Jones*, *The Bride of Lammermoor*, *Kenilworth*, *Tristram Shandy*, *Vanity Fair*, *Clarissa Harlowe* and *Pelham*. In the same place he refers more than once to Shakespeare, and to Æschylus; he quotes Horace, and illustrates a point, not with instances from fiction, but with a stanza from Herrick. As to Scott, it is characteristic that Hardy 'never ceased to regret that the author of the most Homeric poem in English, "Marmion," should later have declined on prose fiction.'[2] In his early years in London, he read the popular novelists of the day, such as Trollope and Wilkie Collins; the influence they had upon him was, however, very slight; and, at least in the case of Collins, he would have been better without it.

[1] *Early Life*, p. 64.   [2] *Early Life*, p. 64.

Hardy's reading in London in the 'sixties was greatly facilitated by the system of lending libraries, then becoming established. Mudie had started in a small way in 1842 in King Street, Holborn. By the end of the 'fifties he had absorbed most of the small booksellers, in the West End, and become a 'leviathan.'[1] Smith very soon afterwards inaugurated his system of book lending and selling at railway stations. The success of Mudie brought into being a rival, the Library Company, which had a meteoric career for a few years until it went bankrupt; Mudie's terms were a guinea a year, for which he supplied the newest books, and the Library Company did the same for half the sum. It was therefore an easy matter for the young and impecunious architect to read current literature; from Mudie or the Library Company he got *Barchester Towers* and *The Woman in White*; but he also got *Atalanta in Calydon* and *Poems and Ballads*. Writing to Swinburne in 1897, he spoke of

'the buoyant time thirty years ago when I used to read your early works walking along the crowded London streets, to my imminent risk of being knocked down.'[2]

Of the books which he read in that buoyant time, the fiction was soon forgotten. Had Hardy not read Wilkie Collins, we should have been without *Desperate Remedies*. Had he not read Swinburne, we should certainly be without a chapter in *Jude the Obscure*; but this takes us to the influences which formed the thought of his maturity; these claim a separate chapter.

[1] There is a very interesting account of the London book trade and lending library system in William Tinsley's *Random Recollections of an old Publisher*, Vol. I, p. 64.
[2] The letter is in the Ashley Library (Catalogue, Vol. II, p. 169).

CHAPTER II

HARDY AND THE CLASSICS

SEVERAL of Hardy's critics have remarked upon the appearance in his work of allusions to the classics, and more particularly to Greek drama. Madame Cazamian goes so far as to say that the Attic dramatists 'restèrent une de ses sources d'inspiration favorites.'[1] A careful examination of all Hardy's classics still remaining at Max Gate, made possible by the courtesy of Mrs. Hardy, has shown that in the most impressionable years of his early manhood he very closely studied Sophocles and Æschylus. The degree of minuteness with which this study was carried out, and the nature of the influence resulting, are very clearly shown by the annotations in his classics. It seems no exaggerated claim that if any purely literary influence could be held responsible for what has been called Hardy's 'twilight view of life,'[2] it would be that great and sombre art whose *leit motif* is 'call no man happy while he lives.' In Hardy's copy of the *Antigone* in Bohn's series, a line is drawn against the words 'For the future, and the instant and the past this law will suffice: nothing comes to the life of mortals far removed at least from calamity'; and in the margin, the hand that was to write *Tess* and *The Dynasts* has added the words of Sophocles νόμος ὅς ἀνδρος αἰσαν κ.τ.λ.

Hardy was not educated at a public school; and he did not therefore receive as a matter of course the thorough classical drilling which, in the middle of the last century, was the main item of instruction in every public school in England; such, for example, as Swinburne had received at Eton; although it should be added that the scholarship

---

[1] *Le Roman et les Idées en Angleterre*, p. 393. F. A. Hedgcock, *Thomas Hardy, Penseur et Artiste*, also notices Greek influence.
[2] R. E. Zachrisson, *Thomas Hardy's Twilight View of Life*. Upsala, 1931.

HARDY AND THE CLASSICS

which produced *Atalanta in Calydon* seems to have owed little either to Eton or to Oxford.[1] At the school which Hardy attended, Greek was not taught at all and Latin was an 'extra.' This extra Hardy began to receive at the age of twelve or thereabouts, as Mrs. Hardy relates.[2]

There is no further record of the classical studies of his school days. As is often the case, the growth of his real interest in the severer humanities probably coincided with the approach of more reflective, if still youthful, years. When he began to be interested in the Latin classics, he was removed from school to an architect's office where it was his duty to trace drawings and study elevations and perspective; and there he seems to have become thoroughly interested in the classics. To judge from Mrs. Hardy's description of it, which is entirely constructed from Hardy's own recollections, that architect's office in South Street, Dorchester, in the years 1856–8 seems to have been a veritable nursery of potential Bentleys and Porsons.[3] At this time, we are told, Hardy read the Aeneid, Horace and Ovid; and also took up Greek, 'getting on with some books of the Iliad.' Hardy's Iliad is still upon his shelves at Max Gate. It was an edition by Samuel Clarke, published in 1818, containing the text and a Latin translation upon opposite pages, obviously selected purposely by Hardy, who had learnt Latin for six years and was only now learning Greek. The volume, which is inscribed 'Thomas Hardy 1858,' shows how very thoroughly he studied the Iliad for two years. The text throughout is full of little notes in pencil; and the following list inside the cover seems to be one of favourite passages:

> Speech of Phoenix, 9, 434–601.
> Fight of Hector and Ajax 14, 388–432.
> Appearance of Achilles unarmed 18, 202–26.
> Heavenly armour for A (chilles) 18, 468–612.
> Funeral games in honour of Patroclus 23, 700.

[1] Georges Lafourcade: *La Jeunesse de Swinburne* (1928), Vol. I, *passim*.
[2] *Early Life*, p. 29.
[3] *Early Life*, pp. 36–7.

Beneath is written 'Left off. Bockhampton 1860.' At the end of the volume a piece of paper is stuck in, on which is written, in an early hand in pencil, a note on the Greek dialects.

Hardy's studies in this volume date from before his twentieth year. As will be seen in a later chapter, his last novel, *Jude the Obscure*, contains the history of many of Hardy's studies. It is remarkable that, when writing *Jude* more than thirty years later, he should have looked up the Iliad which he studied at Bockhampton in his 'teens, and should have put into Jude's mouth a list of the very passages which he had noted in his own youth:

> I have read two books of the Iliad, besides being pretty familiar with passages such as the speech of Phoenix in the ninth book, the fight of Hector and Ajax in the fourteenth, the appearance of Achilles unarmed and his heavenly armour in the eighteenth, and the funeral games in the twenty-third. (*Jude*, Ch. VI.)

Another very interesting parallel occurs in the same chapter. Hardy writes of Jude's Latin that he possessed

> a facility in that language which enabled him with great ease to himself to beguile his lonely walks by imaginary conversations therein.

When telling his second wife about his own classical studies in the days when he was an apprentice to Hicks, and walked into Dorchester, Hardy had no doubt forgotten that passage in *Jude*. It says much for the accuracy of Mrs. Hardy's transcription of his reminiscences, that her account of this habit tallies so exactly with Hardy's own. She writes:

> He grew so familiar with his authors that in his walks to and from the town he often caught himself soliloquizing in Latin on his various projects.[1]

Hardy's knowledge of Latin seems to have been considerable. Stinsford Church contains the Latin inscription with which, in 1903, he commemorated the connection of his

[1] *Early Life*, p. 36.

family with the building. Mrs. Hardy's statement that his choice of language was guided by the consideration that Latin would remain unchanged whatever variations English might undergo, is no doubt correct.[1] But such an explanation does not apply to his considerable fondness for Latin titles for poems, among which, to take them at random, may be named 'Plena Timoris,' 'Inter Sepulchrum,' 'In Tenebris,' 'Jubilate,' 'Exeunt Omnes,' 'Quid hic agis.' Most of these have an ecclesiastical, if not actually Biblical, flavour, and point to mediæval rather than classical Latin. It is possible that Hardy's architectural connection with, as well as personal predilection for, churchyards and churches is partly responsible. Such is clearly the origin of the inscription 'Ostium sepulchri antiquae familiae d'Urberville' which Tess read at Kingsbere on the terrible day when her seducer told her that the little finger of the sham d'Urberville could do more for her than the whole dynasty of the real beneath.[2] On the whole, however, Hardy's love of mediæval Latin seems to have been a growth of later years. Mrs. Hardy records that about 1900

> he spent time in hunting up Latin hymns at the British Museum, and copies that he made of several have been found of dates ranging from the thirteenth to the seventeenth century. . . . That English prosody might be enriched by adapting some of the verse forms of these is not unlikely to have been his view.[3]

Human Shows contain two such poems, which confirm Mrs. Hardy's conjecture, 'Sine prole' and 'Genetrix Laesa.'

In addition to his very extensive study of it in English, Hardy also read the Bible in Latin, and—at least the New Testament—in Greek. His acquaintance with the Latin Bible doubtless dated from the winning of Beza's Latin Testament as a prize at school; his quotations from the Latin Bible, however, appear to be always from the Old Testament. Examples are the quotations from the Psalms prefixed to the three parts of 'In Tenebris,' in *Poems of the Past and*

[1] *Later Years*, p. 102.   [2] *Tess*, Ch. LII.   [3] *Later Years*, p. 85.

Present. There is a certain wail in Jerome's Latin, 'Percussus sum sicut foenum et aruit cor meum,' which Hardy considered as a fitting prelude to his own lament:

Wintertime nighs;
But my bereavement-pain
It cannot bring again;
Twice no one dies.

Another example is the title 'Quid hic Agis?', which proves that Hardy had read in Latin, as well as from the lectern at St. Juliot's in the far-off days, that tremendous

tale of a seer
Which came once a year

in the nineteenth chapter of the first Book of Kings.

Among the Latin classics, Hardy's favourite was the Aeneid.[1] We know that he was reading it in July 1868[2]; so that we are not surprised to find two quotations from it in *Desperate Remedies*. The first is in chapter sixteen, where he speaks of a Dutch clock fixed against a wall, 'its entrails hanging down beneath its white face and wiry hands, like the faeces of a Harpy,' and adds the words in which Virgil described the Harpies in the third book of the Aeneid (1, 216 *et seq*.)

Virginei volucrum vultus, foedissima ventris
Proluvies, uncaeque manus, et pallida semper
Ora fame.

The other is in chapter nineteen, where he applies to Anne Seaway words from the seventh book of the Aeneid (1, 805 *et seq*.)

non illa colo calathisve Minervae
Foemineas assueta manus—

That he should, in the same novel, have given the Christian name Aeneas to one of the chief characters, Manston, is a slight point, but not unworthy of mention. As will be seen later, *Desperate Remedies* is especially interesting for the number of literary allusions which it contains and for the

[1] *Early Life*, pp. 36, 40, 41–2, 76, 78, 247.　　[2] *idem*, p. 76.

light which it throws on Hardy's reading during the 'sixties. To the Virgilian quotations already given there must be added another particularly interesting one. Dryden's Virgil was one of the first books which he possessed, having been given it by his mother when ten years old.[1] In the twelfth chapter of *Desperate Remedies*, Hardy applies to Manston some lines which are taken from Dryden's translation of the Aeneid (bk. 5); but, in addition to the interest of their being taken from one of the earliest books which Hardy ever knew, these lines also form one of the quotations which probably figured as chapter headings in the lost novel, *The Poor Man and the Lady*, and which certainly so figure in the revised form of that novel, published in 1878 under the title *An Indiscretion in the Life of an Heiress*. This and other quotations in a similar case must be discussed in a later chapter.

After Virgil, Hardy appears to have read Horace. Here again, *Jude the Obscure* provides the most striking instance of Hardy's own studies. No one who has read it is likely to forget the passage in the fifth chapter in which Jude, studying the classics as he drives his bread-cart, notices the full moon rising in the east, and bethinks him of the 'Carmen Saeculare':

> His mind had become so impregnated with the poem that
> . . . he stopped the horse, alighted, and, glancing round to see
> that nobody was in sight, knelt down on the roadside bank
> with open book. He turned first to the shiny goddess, who
> seemed to look so softly and critically at his doings, then to
> the disappearing luminary on the other hand, as he began:
> Phoebe silvarumque potens Diana!

There are other references to Horace in Hardy's writings, but none so striking as that.

In an article which appeared in a New York periodical, *The Forum*, in March 1888, entitled 'The Profitable Reading of Fiction,' Hardy quoted the *De Arte Poetica*. Speaking of style, he said, 'A writer who is not a mere imitator looks

---

[1] *Early Life*, p. 21.

upon the world with his personal eyes, and in his peculiar moods; thence grows up his style in the full sense of the term

Cui lecta potenter erit res
Nec facundia deseret hunc, nec lucidus ordo.[1]

Hardy also read Catullus, although perhaps only at a later period. *Poems of the Past and Present* contains, among the 'Imitations,' two stanzas headed 'Catullus XXXI. After passing Sirmione, April 1887.' A dictionary of Classical Quotations (published in 1860), which Hardy doubtless bought when it came out, as an adjunct to his classical studies, contains a number of annotations. It was, possibly, after some experience of trying to publish his early verse that Hardy marked the quotation from Horace 'Aut insanit homo, aut versus facit.' It might have been expected that in later years Hardy would read Lucretius. The only direct evidence that he did so appears to be the quotation from Lucretius 'Vitae post scenia celant' on the title page of *The Hand of Ethelberta*. His library contains a text of this poet, *Titi Lucreti Cari de rerum natura. Libros sex interpretatione et notis illustravit Michael Favus. Paris.* 1680. This volume contains no annotations. That a parallel between the two poets should have been drawn by the first, and still one of the most illuminating, of Hardy's formal critics is hardly surprising. Lionel Johnson, in his last and best chapter on 'Sincerity in Art', wrote:

> Various critics (of life) have various ways; Lucretius, whose argument is much that of Mr. Hardy, has no hesitation in stating his plain reasons in unadorned language, one by one, orderly and simply; that done, the spirit of poetry leaps from its restraint and chants the dirge of worlds and men.[2]

Hardy, we have seen, seems to have taught himself Greek during the first two or three years of his apprenticeship; and the first Greek text which he studied extensively was the

[1] Hardy's copy of Smart's translation of Horace has the Latin inserted in many places, proving his close knowledge of the original.

[2] *The Art of Thomas Hardy* (published 1894, reprinted 1923), p. 229. The same chapter contains further parallels to Lucretius.

Iliad. Donnegan's Greek Dictionary, still in his library, was doubtless bought at this time. An amusing poem, only published after his death, in *Winter Words*, appears to contain reminiscences of his Greek studies. It is entitled 'Liddell and Scott on the completion of their Lexicon (written after the death of Liddell in 1898)' and consists of an imaginary and highly diverting conversation between the lexicographers:

> I've often, I own,
> Belched many a moan
> At undertaking it,
> And dreamt forsaking it.
> —Yes, on to Pi,
> When the end loomed nigh,
> And friends said 'you've as good as done',
> I almost wished we'd not begun.
> Even now, if people only knew
> My sinkings, as we slowly drew
> Along through Kappa, Lambda, Mu,
> They'd be concerned at my misgiving
> And how I mused on a College living
> Right down to Sigma,
> But feared a stigma
> If I succumbed, and left old Donnegan
> For weary freshmen's eyes to con again;
> And how I often, often wondered
> What could have led me to have blundered
> So far away from sound theology
> To dialects and etymology,
> Words, accents not to be breathed by men
> Of any country ever again—

Hardy probably began to dip into Attic drama as soon as he was able. But a curious combination of circumstances at this time, about 1859, while it diverted his immediate attention for a while from Greek literature, also provided him with a more complete training in Greek than he would otherwise have obtained; and, indeed, may have exerted no unimportant influence upon him by leading him to a detailed study of the New Testament, traces of which are clearly to be seen throughout his work. Mrs. Hardy describes how the young Hardy was for a time diverted from his studies in classical literature by the necessity of having to conduct a doctrinal controversy with his fellow apprentice, one Bastow, an ardent Baptist. The subject of it was paedo-baptism; and Hardy bought himself Griesbach's Greek Testament to be the better equipped for the fray.[1]

This Testament is still in Hardy's library. An interesting volume it is in view of Mrs. Hardy's statements, which it most fully bears out. It is the Greek Testament in Griesbach's text, with (to quote the title page) 'the various readings of Mill and Scholz, marginal references to parallels, and a critical introduction. Third edition, revised and corrected, 1859.' On the half title is written

'Thos. Hardy. Feb. 7th 1860.

κaὶ ἡ ἀλήθεια
ἐλευθερώσει ὑμας   μώροι καὶ τυφλοί

Bockhampton, & 39 South Street, Dorchester.'

To hold this volume, and to reflect by whom it was so diligently studied, while he remembered his Creator in the days of his youth before the years drew nigh in which he said 'I have no pleasure in them,' is a not unmoving experience. Against the thirteenth chapter of the first Epistle to the Corinthians, verse five,[2] there is drawn a line, and in the margin is written T.H. That his controversies with Bastow were over baptism is clearly borne out by the seventh chapter of the same epistle; verse fourteen[3] has written against it in the margin 'Argument for Paedo baptism.'

Once again, this early study of Hardy's appears in *Jude the Obscure*. Already in chapter five Jude has got himself Griesbach's Greek Testament, which he studies for a long

---

[1] *Early Life*, pp. 37–40.
[2] 'Doth not behave itself unseemly, seeketh not her own . . .', etc.
[3] 'For the unbelieving husband is sanctified by the wife . . .', etc.

while to the exclusion of the classics. In chapter fourteen there is, indeed, a quotation from this same Epistle to the Corinthians:

> Just then he was earnestly reading from his Griesbach's text. At the very time that Sue was tossing and staring at her figures, the policeman and belated citizens passing along under his window might have heard, if they had stood still, strange syllables mumbled with fervour within—words that had for Jude an indescribable enchantment; inexplicable sounds something like these:—
>
> > 'All hemin heis Theos ho Pater, ex hou ta panta,
> > kai hemeis eis auton'
>
> Till the sounds rolled with reverent loudness, as a book was heard to close
>
> > 'Kai heis Kurios Iesous Christos, di hou ta panta
> > kai hemeis di autou!'[1]

One of Hardy's most characteristic poems, which does much more than foreshadow the *Dynasts*, although first published in *Poems of the Past and Present*, takes its title from the Greek Testament. Hardy wrote upon his apostrophe to 'the Immanence that reasoneth not' the words which St. Paul had found upon the altar of the Athenians (Acts xvii, 23) $A\Gamma N\Omega\Sigma T\Omega\iota$ $\Theta E\Omega\iota$.

Despite Mrs. Hardy's assertion that the putting aside of Homer for the Greek Testament for a while was a misfortune for Hardy, the thorough drilling in New Testament Greek which he thereby gave himself was certainly no misfortune, but quite otherwise. For, when his controversies with his fellow apprentice came to an end with Bastow's departure, Hardy returned to his classics; and he now possessed enough Greek for the masterpieces of Greek literature to become living to him. Bastow had emigrated to Tasmania; and Hardy must have written to him at the end of 1860 or early in 1861 and given him an account of his studies; for in May of that year, Bastow replied[2]

---

[1] *Jude the Obscure*, Ch. II, iii.   [2] *Early Life*, p. 41.

Really you are a plodding chap to have got through such a lot of Homer and all the rest. I am not a bit farther than I was in Dorchester; indeed, I think I have scarcely touched a book —Greek, I mean,—since. I see you are trying all you can to cut me out!

As we have seen, Hardy's studies in Homer are outlined in his Iliad, in which is also written 'Left off Bockhampton 1860.' This would fit perfectly with his sending Bastow an account of them at the end of that year. The point of greatest interest is—what were 'all the rest'? The evidence goes to show that this was Greek drama, more particularly Aeschylus and Sophocles.

It is not possible now to determine exactly at what periods of his life Hardy studied the masterpieces of Greek dramatic literature with such minuteness; for, as will be seen, he even went to the length of comparing different texts in passages which specially appealed to him. Mrs. Hardy is quite categorical that it was during his last years as an apprentice in Dorchester:

It seems that he had also set to work on the Agamemnon or the Oedipus; but on his enquiring of Moule—who was a fine Greek scholar and was always ready to act the tutor in any classical difficulty—if he ought not to go on reading some Greek plays, Moule's reluctant opinion was that if Hardy really had to make an income in some way by architecture in 1862, it would be hardly worth while for him to read Aeschylus or Sophocles in 1859-61. He had secretly wished that Moule would advise him to go on with Greek plays, in spite of the serious damage it might do his architecture; but he felt bound to listen to reason and prudence. So, as much Greek as he had got he had to be content with, the language being almost dropped from that date; for though he did take up one or two of the dramatists again some years later, it was in a fragmentary way only. Nevertheless his substantial knowledge of them was not small.[1]

To an enquiry as to the evidence upon which the above paragraph is based, Mrs. Hardy replied that it was supplied

[1] *Early Life*, p. 43.

verbally by her husband. This would, of course, have been in the last years of his life, when memory of exact dates had faded; and it is quite in the nature of things that he should refer all his classical studies to his early manhood, when first the new planet had swum into his ken. Two things, how-ever, are certain. Whether or no he was dissuaded from further study in 1859 or 1860 when he 'had set to work' on the *Agamemnon* or the *Oedipus*, he certainly at some period studied both these plays most thoroughly, and came to know them inside out. And, while it may be true that his most persistent study of Greek drama dated from his early manhood, and while he may—even for some years—have dropped it almost entirely, he not only never forgot what he had read, but he also returned to it. The conclusive evidence for this is that the references—and direct debts—to Greek drama are much more frequent in his later than in his earlier works; as will be seen. None of his earliest writings, indeed, nothing before the 'seventies, seems to contain direct refer-ences to Greek literature.[1] *Far from the Madding Crowd* con-tains one Greek reference, but it is a Biblical one; in chapter forty-three he wrote of the cry that came from Bathsheba's lips when Troy kissed the dead Fanny Robin, 'It was the τετέλεσται of her union with Troy.' But even Mrs. Hardy's own volumes contain strong evidence that Hardy's Greek was not 'almost dropped' after 1860. On July 24th, 1889, Hardy's diary contained this entry:

Εἰ᾽ δέ τι πρεσβύτερον etc. Soph. *Oed. Tyr.* 1365 ('and if there be a woe surpassing woes, it hath become the portion of Oedipus'—Jebb, cf. Tennyson 'a deeper deep').[2]

It was at this time, in the late 'eighties, that *Tess* was taking shape in his mind. As the most famous of all Hardy's allusions, at the end of *Tess*, was to an Æschylean original, so it was natural that other parts of his best known story

---

[1] If we exclude the reference to the Odyssey in *An Indiscretion* already mentioned, which we cannot prove to have been in *The Poor Man & The Lady*, although the probability that it was is strong.
[2] *Early Life*, p. 289.

should have been linked with Æschylus in the mind of its creator. During August 1889, Hardy wrote in his diary:

> When a married woman who has a lover kills her husband, she does not really wish to kill the husband; she wishes to kill the situation. Of course in Clytaemnestra's case it was not exactly so since there was the added grievance of Iphigenia, which half justified her.[1]

There are two other quotations from his diary given by Mrs. Hardy, both dating from the year 1891, which show that the Greek classics were in his mind at that time.[2] The first is dated January 30th:

> Somebody says that the final dictum of the Ion of Plato is 'inspiration, not art.' The passage is θειὸν καὶ μὴ τεχνικόν. And what is really meant by it is, I think, more nearly expressed by the words 'inspiration, not technicality'—'art' being too comprehensive in English to use here.

Hardy was not a Platonist, and it is rather surprising to find him quoting Plato in the original. At the present time, there is no Plato in Greek at Max Gate, although this entry proves that Hardy knew the original of the Ion. A letter which Hardy wrote to the *Academy* following a review of *The Well Beloved* in 1897 suggests that if he had ever been much interested in Plato, it was in his youth:

> After reading your review of *The Well Beloved* (more appreciative in feeling and generous towards its faults than such a slight story deserves) I think it would not be amiss to account for the ultra romantic notion of the tale, which seems to come slightly as a surprise to readers. Not only was it published serially five years ago, but it was sketched many years before that date when I was comparatively a young man and interested in the Platonic Idea, which, considering its charm and its poetry, one could well wish to be interested in always.[3]

It is more than likely that any vestiges of platonic ideas in that curious phantasy come, not from Hardy's reading of Plato, but from his reading of Shelley. The epigraph of

[1] *Early Life.* pp. 289–90.   [2] *Later Years*, p. 58.
[3] *The Academy*, Vol. LI, p. 381.

The Well Beloved is a quotation from the most platonic of English poets; and if Hardy read Plato at all, it was probably owing to Shelley's devotion to Plato. Even so, it seems unlikely that he read Plato extensively.

The other entry in Hardy's Diary for 1891 is of very much greater significance. On March 1st he wrote:

> Make a lyric of the speech of Hyllus at the close of the Trachiniae.

Mrs. Hardy need not have added in parenthesis 'It does not appear that this was ever carried out'; for, if he did not use it as the material for an isolated lyric, Hardy incorporated that famous impeachment into a scene in the *Dynasts*; where it forms one of the most cogent passages in all his writings.

What has been said will show the impossibility of accurately dating any particular portions of Hardy's Greek studies. Having once drunk at that fountain from which has sprung all Western literature, he could not keep away. Nor is that surprising. For, if the fundamental basis of Greek drama be religious, whereas Hardy's was essentially an agnostic nature, the true subject of every drama in ancient Greek which has come down to us is some aspect of the mystery of human existence; and more especially of the problem of suffering. There is no writer of the first rank in English literature, not even excepting the author of *Lear* and *Hamlet*, who has wrestled in spirit more arduously with that same problem than Thomas Hardy.

The extent of Hardy's studies in Attic drama can be deduced from the evidence in his own volumes at Max Gate. A few examples of this may be given, selected because Hardy's own writings prove the interest these passages had for him. A word of caution should be added: it would seem, on a cursory glance, that Hardy's studies were chiefly carried out, not with the Greek texts, but with the English of Bohn's translations. While there is no doubt that Hardy owed much to the rapidity which an English version gave him, closer examination shows that he was sufficiently familiar with the original to add it in pencil when any particular passage retained his attention, and even, on occasion, to compare variant Greek readings.

One of the two early *texts* now at Max Gate is Paley's Æschylus (1855), which contains a very early signature. An interesting and direct proof that Hardy read Æschylus at widely different periods of his life is to be found in the *Agamemnon* in this volume. The abridged argument of the trilogy, written in pencil at the beginning, is in an early hand, certainly not later than 1870. The word 'dynasts' written in the margin against λάμπρους δυνάστας is in a much later hand. If it be objected that one word is insufficient evidence, an Aeschylean reference in the *Dynasts*, shortly to be instanced, proves the same point.[1]

The other early text still in Hardy's library is the *Poetae Scenici Graeci* edited by Dindorf (Leipzig, 1841). Among the very few annotations in this volume is one of surpassing interest. At the beginning of the *Prometheus Vinctus*, against 'Kratos kai Bia' in the list of dramatis personæ, is written in pencil: 'This might be called the Will.' Were there any means of dating this pencil note, it would tell us how early Hardy had attained the conception of the Immanent Will. For reasons to be given in the next chapter, it seems unlikely that this was before the end of the 'seventies, at the earliest. This note does show, however, that the conception of the Immanent Will, besides what it owed to Herbert Spencer, J. S. Mill, Schopenhauer and others, may also have owed something to Æschylus. That it owed very much to the author of the *Prometheus* is unlikely; the note itself would seem to suggest that it was written at a reading of the play after Hardy had already formed his conception of 'the Will.' But the very fact that he should write such a note in such a place is interesting.

[1] The exact origin of the title 'Dynasts' is not quite clear. Hardy created the English word by simply anglicizing δυνάστας, but whether he got it from Aeschylus, as the above suggests, or from the original of the Magnificat, as he indicates in a note to the Afterscene of the Dynasts, cannot be determined.

Hardy's early studies in Sophocles were doubtless conducted in Dindorf's volume. There is at any rate no other early text of Sophocles remaining at Max Gate. The volume of Jebb's Sophocles containing the *Oedipus Rex*, which appeared in 1893, sufficiently proves by its presence in his library that Hardy was at that date enough interested in the play to buy the latest text. It is very little marked; but there is heavy underlining of the great lament over Oedipus

τίς γάρ, τίς ἀνὴρ πλέον, κ.τ.λ.

(*Oed. Rex.* 1190 *et seq.*)

The English versions of the Greek dramatists which Hardy possessed were those in Bohn's classical series translated by Buckley. Mrs. Hardy has told the present writer that her husband well remembered having exchanged an architectural prize which he won during his early years in London for volumes of Bohn's classics. The Euripides, which is in three volumes, was published in 1850. The Sophocles and the Aeschylus are undated. Both contain points of much interest. On the first leaf of the Aeschylus is written in pencil in Hardy's hand:

Isaiah and Ezekiel were timid, costive, hidebound in the way of 'imagery' compared to Pindar and Aeschylus—the two Greeks whom if I must not say I have tried to follow, I must say I have always read with the most passionate sympathy and magnetic attraction to the thought and utterance alike that any poet ever puts into me.'

Swinburne. (I don't quite agree.)

On the first leaf of the first volume of Euripides is written:

'It is far easier to overtop Euripides by the head and shoulders than to come up to the waist of Sophocles or the knee of Aeschylus.' Swinburne.

(An old opinion but not true.)

Both these passages are quotations from a private letter which Swinburne wrote to Edmund Gosse in 1876.[1] This

---

[1] The occasion was the publication of *Erechtheus* and a review of it: see William R. Rutland: *Swinburne, a 19th Century Hellene* (1931), p. 200 *et seq.* The letter is published in *The Letters of A. C. Swinburne*, edited by Gosse & Wise (2 vols., 1918).

letter was not published until 1918. We are therefore left with one of two alternative conclusions. Either Hardy discussed the Greek dramatists with Gosse, who showed him Swinburne's letter; or else Hardy added the quotations during the last ten years of his life. The handwriting does not help us, for Hardy could still write in 1920 the hand which he wrote in 1890. In either case, however, his continued interest in Greek drama is apparent. But there is much stronger proof of the fact than this.

To take the *Agamemnon* first. The great chorus with its refrain αἴλινον αἴλινον εἰπέ, τὸ δ'εὖ νικάτω (l. 120 *et seq.*) seems particularly to have appealed to Hardy. That he should have written the derivation of the word αἴλινον in the margin is little. That the refrain 'Sorrow, sing sorrow But good prevail, prevail!' (as Gilbert Murray renders it) should have greatly appealed to him is not surprising; for the words almost exactly sum up his own creed: that of the tragic poet acutely conscious of universal suffering, and yet deeply resenting the accusation of 'pessimist' on the ground that 'if a way to the better there be, it exacts a full look at the worst,'[1] and believing himself to be a 'meliorist.' Hardy has several times used this Aeschylean phrase. The best example is perhaps the last stanza of 'Compassion,' a very characteristic poem which Hardy wrote in January 1924 in celebration of the centenary of the Royal Society for the prevention of cruelty to animals. The last stanza runs thus:

> Cries still are heard in secret nooks,
> Till hushed with gag or slit or thud;
> And hideous dens whereon none looks
>   Are sprayed with needless blood.
> But here, in battlings, patient, slow,
> Much has been won—more, maybe, than we know—
> And on we labour hopeful. 'Ailinon!'
> A mighty voice calls: 'But may the good prevail!'
> And 'Blessed are the merciful'
>   Calls a yet mightier one.

[1] 'In Tenebris.'

HARDY AND THE CLASSICS

Another passage of a totally different sort, which found an echo in Hardy's mind, were some lines at the end of the second stasimon in the *Agamemnon*, in which the chorus ask whether the happy news of Agamemnon's impending return announced by the beacon fires can indeed be true. The passage is corrupt, and various Greek readings are preferred by various editors. The general sense is given in Gilbert Murray's version:

The fire of good tidings it hath sped the city through,
But who knows if a god mocketh? Or who knows if all be true?

Against Paley's reading of this passage, Hardy wrote 'Who knows if it be true, or some delusion of the gods?'; and both in his text and his Bohn he gives the line references to Dindorf's edition. When he first became interested in this passage cannot be known. In the afterscene of the *Dynasts* the phantom Intelligences discuss among themselves the meaning of the drama which they have witnessed. The whole scene is justly famous as one of the summits of Hardy's art. After the Chorus of the Pities have sung their hymn in praise of an understanding and merciful Omnipotence, the unconvinced Intelligences continue their questioning:

SEMICHORUS I OF THE YEARS
    O Immanence, that reasonest not
    In putting forth all things begot,
    Thou build'st thine house in space—for what?

SEMICHORUS II
    O Loveless, Hateless!—past the sense
    Of kindly-eyed benevolence,
    To what tune danceth this Immense?

SPIRIT IRONIC
    For one I cannot answer. But I know
    'Tis handsome of our Pities so to sing
    The praises of the dreaming, dark, dumb Thing
    That turns the handle of this idle show!

THOMAS HARDY

As once a Greek asked I would fain ask too,
Who knows if all the spectacle be true,
Or an illusion of the gods (the Will
to wit) some hocus-pocus to fulfil?

Very few students of the *Agamemnon* would maintain that
Aeschylus considered the world to be an illusion. But such
was clearly Hardy's interpretation. Moreover, there is striking
evidence that he held such an opinion of the significance of
the art of Aeschylus long before he wrote the *Dynasts*. It is
to be found in *The Return of the Native*, written a quarter of
a century earlier. That book has many claims to be considered his most perfect novel, almost entirely free as it is
from the insinuated argument which mars the later work.
But *The Return of the Native* contains a paragraph (at the
beginning of Book III) which is very considerably illuminated by the lucubrations of the Ironic Spirit. These, indeed,
furnish the key to what Hardy really meant by a passage
which, without such illumination, is by no means clear:

> The truth seems to be that a long line of disillusive centuries
> has permanently displaced the Hellenic idea of life, or whatever
> it may be called. What the Greeks only suspected, we know
> well; what their Aeschylus imagined our nursery children feel.
> That old-fashioned revelling in the general situation grows
> less and less possible as we uncover the defects of natural laws,
> and see the quandary that man is in by their operation.

If we can, by a very large stretch of the imagination, conceive of Aeschylus making àny sense whatever of that
passage, we can conjecture that he would have been as
much stupefied by it as would Milton by Shelley's pronouncement that Satan is the hero of *Paradise Lost*. But it
matters little that Hardy read into Aeschylus meanings of
which Aeschylus never dreamed. What matters is that it
was Aeschylus who provided him with mental stimulus.

It was to be expected that Hardy would study the
Prometheus Vinctus. At the end of the text of that masterpiece in his Paley is written the English of the closing

words and his name: 'Thou seest the wrongs I endure. T. Hardy.' The *Prometheus* in his Bohn volume is full of underlinings, and in many cases he has added the Greek text. Especially heavily underlined is the immortal speech: 'Ω διός αἰθὴρ καὶ ταχύπτεροι πνοάι — (L. 88 *et seq.*) in which Prometheus appeals to the elements to witness the wrongs which he, a god, suffers at the hands of gods. Hardy added the Greek of the last sentence:

$$\text{τὴν πεπρωμένην δὲ χρή}$$
$$\text{αἶσαν φέρειν ὡς 'ρᾶστα, γιγνώσκουθ' ὅτι}$$
$$\text{τὸ τῆς ἀνάγκης ἔστ' ἀδήριτον σθένος}$$

(ll. 103–5).

'The fate which is ordained must be borne as best it may, knowing that the might of Necessity may not be contended with.'

The most discussed sentence which Hardy ever wrote, at the end of *Tess*, contains a phrase which he took from the *Prometheus*; there can be few sentences in fiction which have produced more commentary. When the black flag went up on the tower of Winchester prison:

' "Justice" was done, and the President of the Immortals, in Aeschylean phrase, had finished his sport with Tess.'

The words 'President of the Immortals' are a translation of μακάρων πρύτανις (*Prom. Vinct.* 169). It will be more convenient to consider the implications of this famous sentence later.

Of Sophocles Hardy seems to have been a very close student. The pedestrian translation in Bohn's series is, in his copy, full of pencil marks; and he has even added a few stage directions, and the strophe and antistrophe marks of the choruses. Fortunately for him, he was able to read them in the Greek; for no one could have found Mr. Buckley's translation inspiring. It is not hard to imagine Hardy's response to such Sophoclean musings over the estate of man as these (to give them in Gilbert Murray's version):

Nothingness, nothingness, ye children of man, and less
  I count you, waking or dreaming.
None among mortals, none, seeking to live hath won
  More than to seem, and to cease
  Again from his seeming.[1]

When we consider how well Hardy must have known such choruses as this, or the earlier one in the same play:

Towards God's great mysteries, O let me move
Unstained till I die—[2]

we can see that his study of Greek drama was not without direct influence upon the spirit choruses in the *Dynasts*. As will be seen later, they owe an indirect debt to the same source through Shelley. Hardy's volume of Buckley's translation confirms that the text of Sophocles which he studied in the 'sixties was that of Dindorf; for after the two Oedipus plays the Bohn translator went on with the *Electra*, and at the head of this Hardy wrote: 'Antigone should have followed here, as in Dindorf.' It is hard to resist the conjecture—conjecture though it must remain—that it was especially of the *Antigone* that Hardy was thinking when he described Little Hintock thus at the beginning of the *Woodlanders*:

One of those sequestered spots outside the gates of the world ... where, from time to time, dramas of a grandeur and unity truly Sophoclean are enacted in the real, by virtue of the concentrated passions and closely knit interdependence of the lives therein.

That Hardy was as fully appreciative of the form and technique of the masterpieces of Greek dramatic literature as he was of their emotional and intellectual significance would be sufficiently evident, even if he had not definitely paid tribute to them in his article on 'The Profitable Reading of English Fiction' in *The Forum* of March 1888; where, writing of Richardson, he says:

[1] *Oed. Rex.*, 1172 *et seq.*   [2] *Oed. Rex.*, 848 *et seq.*

HARDY AND THE CLASSICS

No person who has a due perception of the constructive art shown in Greek tragic drama can be blind to the constructive art of Richardson.

When all is said, the significance for English literature of Hardy's study of Greek drama lies in the effect which that study had in confirming the cast of his thought; and this it would be hard to over-estimate. The criticism which points to the studies in pessimistic philosophy of his middle life, and finds therein the origin of his later works, is stating truth; but only half the truth. That Hardy read Schopenhauer and Von Hartmann, and that the influence of these is perceptible in *Tess* and *Jude* and the *Dynasts* is incontrovertible. But he had read Aeschylus and Sophocles long before. And to the poet Hardy, the poetry of the Attic stage—which is capable of partially surviving even the dry-as-dust translations of pedants—must have spoken at least as powerfully as did the ratiocination of German metaphysics. Whether what he, in the later nineteenth century, read into the words of Greek drama was what the authors had meant when they wrote them in the fourth century before Christ, is quite another matter. The interpretation of Greek drama by modern minds has been discussed in connection with another great poet of the nineteenth century, Swinburne, with whom Hardy in some ways had no little in common; and to whom he also owed something.[1] Having read his works, we understand what was in Hardy's mind when he marked such passages in his Bohn's Sophocles as this, in the *Oedipus Rex*:

> Thou hast rightly spoken. But to compel the gods to that which they shall not be pleased to do could no man have power (p. 11) ;

or this, in the *Antigone*:

> . . . wrongs that by day and by night I see continually budding rather than withering (p. 118);

or the opening sentences of the *Trachiniae*:

[1] *Swinburne, a nineteenth-century Hellene*, Chap. II, *passim*.

THOMAS HARDY

There is an ancient saying, renowned among men, that you cannot fully judge of the life of mortals, whether it has been good or bad, to an individual, before his death.

The close of the *Trachiniae* furnishes the most striking example of all. We know from his diary that Hardy meditated making a poem of the last words of Hyllus, the passage which Swinburne described as

> the haughty and daring protest or appeal in which Sophocles, speaking through the lips of the virtuous Hyllus, impeaches and denounces the iniquity of Heaven with a steadfast and earnest vehemence unsurpassed in its outspoken rebellion by any modern questioner or blasphemer of divine providence.[1]

In Hardy's Bohn Sophocles, a piece of paper has been stuck into the volume at the last page of the *Trachiniae*, and on it Hardy has written in ink the words of the original. Moreover, he has corrected Buckley's translation by deleting the personal pronouns, thus giving to the words οἱ φύσαντες καὶ κληζομένοι πατέρες a universal significance. What that significance was in his own mind, the *Dynasts* leaves us in no doubt. We shall see in the next chapter that the conception of the Immanent Will owes a debt, upon the intellectual plane, to *Die Welt als Wille und Vorstellung* and to *Die Philosophie des Unbewusstes*. But the cogency of great literature lies upon another plane than the purely intellectual. The Spirit of the Pities, when it cries out against the hours of Nelson's useless suffering after his spine was shot through, does not quote Schopenhauer. It quotes Sophocles (*Dynasts*, Pt. 1, Act v, Sc. iv):

CHORUS OF THE PITIES
> His thread was cut too slowly! When he fell
>   And bade his fame farewell,
> He might have passed, and shunned his long drawn pain,
>   Endured in vain, in vain!

SPIRIT OF THE YEARS
> Young Spirits, be not critical of That
> Which was before, and shall be after you.

[1] *The Age of Shakespeare*, apropos Heywood's *Brazen Age*.

HARDY AND THE CLASSICS

SPIRIT OF THE PITIES
>But out of tune the Mode, and meritless
>That quickens sense in shapes whom, thou hast said
>Necessitation sways! A life there was
>Among these self-same frail ones—Sophocles—
>Who visioned it too clearly, even the while
>He dubbed the Will 'the gods.' Truly said he
>*Such gross injustice to their own creation*
>*Burdens the time with mournfulness for us*
>*And for themselves with shame.* Things mechanised
>By coils and pivots set to fore-framed codes
>Would, in a thorough-sphered melodic rule
>And governance of sweet consistency,
>Be cessed no pain, whose burnings would abide
>With That Which holds responsibility,
>Or inexist.

CHORUS OF THE PITIES
>Yea, yea, yea!
>Thus would the Mover pay
>The score each puppet owes,
>The Reaper reap what His contrivance sows!
>Why make Life debtor when it did not buy?
>Why wound so keenly Right that it would die?

With such evidence before us, it is easy to see the nature of the influence which the study of Sophocles exercised upon Hardy. In the Preface to his translation of the *Oedipus Rex*, Gilbert Murray writes that that play depicts human beings as the playthings of Gods strangely and incomprehensibly malignant, whose ways there is no attempt to explain or justify. This play it was, among others, which the future author of *Tess*, *Jude* and the *Dynasts* studied lovingly before he was twenty.

It might have been expected that Hardy would find even more affinity with Euripides than with Sophocles, if he was obsessed by the purposelessness of life and the injustice of circumstance; for, for every such passage in Sophocles, there are a dozen in Euripides. But Euripides he appears to have studied much less closely. There appears to be no reference to Euripides in all his writings. The extent to which he read Euripides in translation is indicated from the marks in his Bohn volumes, which seem to show that while he read the English version with close attention in the case of several plays, he did not read the originals. The two plays which especially attracted him appear to have been the *Trojan Women* and the *Hippolytus*. In the former, he has marked the prayer of Hecuba:

> Whoever thou art, hard to be known even by conjecture, Jove, whether thou art the necessity of nature or the mind of mortals, I pray to thee.[1]

What appealed to him in the *Hippolytus* was clearly the treatment of the theme of love; and his underlining of the words

> Whosoever has chastity, not that which is taught in schools, but that which is by nature.[2]

carries the mind at once to *Tess*. Hardy might have used the Greek of that passage as an epigraph for his most moving, if not his greatest book; and it is likely that, if he had, he would have had no occasion to have written in a later preface what he wrote of 'A pure woman faithfully presented,' 'Melius fuerat non scribere.' Hardy's treatment of love does not derive from the classics. But it is surprising that so subtle a connoisseur in women's hearts, and at one period of life so persistent a student of the problem of marital relationships upon the emotional, rather than the intellectual, plane, who was withal a student of Greek drama, should not have shown more devotion to the author of the *Medea*.

Having tried to show what Hardy owed to the study of Greek drama, we must enter a *caveat* against going too far. One critic light-heartedly compares 'the philosopher of Wessex' to the author of the *Prometheus Vinctus*, and con-

---

[1] *Troades*, 884 *et seq.*   [2] *Hippolytus*, 79 *et seq.*

tends that Hardy's work is Aeschylean.[1] If by Aeschylean be meant that Hardy's art has the same significance, philosophically, as have the remains of the art of Aeschylus that have come down to us, then the comparison hardly bears examination. That Hardy's art, taken as a whole, has an ethical significance, a 'tendency' in popular phraseology, no one except Hardy himself has ever seriously denied. So has the art of Aeschylus. There is no more ethically significant work in all literature, not excepting the Book of Job, than the *Oresteia*. But the *Oresteia* belongs to one period in the history of human thought; the period when the growth of the consciousness of moral responsibility was making possible the emergence of civilization out of tribal barbarism. And the work of Hardy belongs to a very different period; one to which we are yet so near that we cannot see it in perspective, but which may be described as the first stage of flux resulting from the overthrow by science of standards accepted for many generations. The period of Hardy's mental development came at a time of intellectual upheaval; and we shall see in the next chapter how largely his thought belonged to the day and generation into which he was born. It was the age, not of the *Oresteia*, nor of the *Prometheus Vinctus*, but of *Essays and Reviews* and Herbert Spencer's *First Principles*; of *Atalanta in Calydon*, and of *The City of Dreadful Night*.

[1] E. Brennecke: *The Life of Thomas Hardy*.

CHAPTER III

THE BACKGROUND TO HARDY'S THOUGHT

IT has been the fashion to write books about Hardy's philosophy. Patrick Braybrooke's *Thomas Hardy and his Philosophy* is little more than a discursive essay lacking either philosophical or literary background, in which the *Dynasts* is disposed of in one astounding sentence.[1] There are two American theses, of widely divergent character. Helen Garwood's well-written Essay was the earliest attempt at a systematic comparison of Hardy with Schopenhauer,[2] of which more hereafter. George Swann's dissertation[3] is devoted to the drawing of real or imagined parallels between Defoe and Aristotle, Richardson and Kant, Fielding and Hume, Dickens and J. S. Mill, Meredith and Hegel, and Hardy and von Hartmann. It calls in the aid of mathematical formulæ, and states that 'the starting point of Hardy's thought was Schopenhauer,' ignoring the fact that Hardy did not read Schopenhauer until he was over forty. Ernest Brennecke's *Thomas Hardy's Universe: A Study of a Poet's Mind* is a very thorough exposition of *Die Welt als Wille und Vorstellung* and an anthology of quotations from the *Dynasts*, in alternate chapters. The correlation of the two is not always happy; as for example when Mr. Brennecke writes 'Particularly in his treatment of the theme of love does Mr. Hardy follow the disillusioned Schopenhaurian view of the dominant will,' the illustration chosen is the ditty sung by the Ironic Spirits on the betrothal of Napoleon to Marie Louise:

[1] 'It would, I suppose, be absurd to ask whether there is any philosophy in the *Dynasts*.'

[2] *Thomas Hardy: An Illustration of the Philosophy of Schopenhauer*. Philadelphia. Winston, 1911.

[3] G. R. Swann: *Philosophical Parallelisms in Six English Novelists*. Pennsylvania, 1931.

46

(Part 2, Act v, Sc. vii)

> First 'twas a finished coquette,
> And now 'tis a raw ingenue—
> Blonde instead of brunette,
> An old wife doffed for a new.
> She'll bring him a baby
> As swiftly as maybe
> And that's what he wants her to do,
>   Hoo, hoo!
> And that's what he wants her to do.

Hardy himself repeatedly disclaimed the title of philosopher.[1] If the word is to be taken in its strictly technical sense, he was justified in so doing. For he was before all things an artist: if his work endures, it will endure as art. But that his art owes something of its greatness to his thought can hardly be denied. That he was a thinker in the sense that all great artists are thinkers, he tacitly admitted in the Apology prefixed to *Late Lyrics and Earlier*; when he rounded upon the critics, who accused him of pessimism, with this question: 'Should a shaper of such stuff as dreams are made on disregard considerations of what is customary and expected, and apply himself to the real function of poetry, the application of ideas to life (in Matthew Arnold's familiar phrase)?' That Hardy applied ideas to life needs no demonstration. So far did he go in the process that, to one reader of it at least, his last novel seems to be constructed wholly for the sake of ideas, round which is draped the insufficient and transparent fabric of a thin romance. The point must be amplified in another chapter. It has been generally agreed that even *Tess*, his most powerful although not his best, novel, is partly marred by the protrusion of arguments into the artistic illusion, like girders through ill-fitting scenery. It is significant that neither in *Tess* nor in *Jude*, nor in the *Dynasts*, in which Hardy carried the applica-

---

[1] The preface to *Winter Words* concludes 'I also repeat what I have often stated, that no harmonious philosophy is attempted in these pages—or in any bygone pages of mine, for that matter.' Cf. the paragraph devoted to the Spirits in the Preface to the *Dynasts*.

tion of ideas to life so far that he created a new form of literature in the process, are the 'ideas' wholly of the intellect. With the artist, especially the poet, arguments continued by the mind are apt to be initiated by the heart. And with Hardy himself, if the mind argued when the question was once raised, it was often the heart which first questioned. The Ancient Spirit of the Years is the mind in the *Dynasts*. But there would be no *Dynasts*, and no Wessex novels, for that matter, without the Pities.

It would seem a truism that every man is the product of his age. Hardy was most certainly the product of the age in which he lived. And yet scarcely any of those who have attempted to examine his thought, have even glanced at the thought of that age in which Hardy came to maturity. An almost perfect example of the manner in which *not* to approach an investigation of Hardy's intellectual formation is provided in the latest American thesis upon him; in which the writer quotes very unfavourable comments by him upon Nietzsche and Bergson, and says of them: 'They completely refute the usual concept that the trend of Hardy's ideas was shaped by the authors he read.'[1] Leaving out of account that there is no such 'usual concept' except with regard to Schopenhauer, it needs small proof that Hardy can have read not one word of either Nietzsche or Bergson until he was well on in middle life. Hardy did not read German easily: Nietzsche was not available in English until the 'nineties; that Hardy read him later is proved by a letter which appeared in the *Manchester Guardian* on October 12th, 1914, in which he said of Nietzsche:

> He used to seem to me (I have not looked into him for years) an incoherent rhapsodist who jumps from Macchiavelli to Isaiah as the mood seizes him, whom it is impossible to take seriously as a mentor.

Bergson was nineteen years younger than Hardy, and only began to assume importance when the bulk of Hardy's work was written. Neither of these philosophers can pro-

[1] A. P. Elliott: *Fatalism in the Works of Thomas Hardy*. Philadelphia, 1935.

vide the smallest shred of evidence as to the shaping of Hardy's ideas by the authors he read. For that we must look to the authors whom he read, not after he was sixty, but before he was thirty-five. The point is worth making only because this apparently obvious course has not been taken by any of Hardy's critics. The only approach to it is made in the last chapter of Dr. de Ridder Barzin's excellent analysis of Hardy's ideas; and even this chapter, entitled 'Hardy et le Courant des Idées en Angleterre au XIX Siècle' is only intended as a sketch, and is based upon textbooks of English literature, not upon original knowledge.[1]

To give long quotations of passages, detached from their contexts, out of Hardy's works, as specimens of his thought, is unscientific. If it be not clear from the works themselves what Hardy thought about, there is an admirable and fully documented summary entitled *Le Pessimisme de Thomas Hardy* in which his ideas are set forth with Latin clarity and precision. Assuming these to be known, it remains to give an account of the most important influences which may have helped to mould his intellect. When all is said, an artist of the calibre of Hardy remains himself, trace influences as we may. Some things which were absorbed into his consciousness may be pointed out; they do not explain the happily inexplicable mystery of creative genius.

It is fashionable at the present time to regard the 'mid-Victorian' years as a period of barren complacency and intellectual stagnation. In point of fact, the 'sixties witnessed a crisis in English intellectual life to which our times offer no parallel. The twentieth year of Hardy's life produced two events which are landmarks; he entered upon the threshold of manhood at the moment when there began what has probably been the most rapid change in our cultural history. This period can conveniently be dated from the publication of two books. The first edition of Charles Darwin's *Origin of Species* appeared on November 24th, 1859, and was sold out on the day of publication; the

[1] Louise de Ridder Barzin: *Le Pessimisme de Thomas Hardy*. Brussels, 1932.

second edition became available in January 1860. In 1860 there also appeared a volume entitled *Essays and Reviews*. It is hardly too much to say that these books shook England to its centre.

Writing long afterwards of the appearance of *Essays and Reviews*, Leslie Stephen said, 'Nobody who remembers the time can doubt that it marked the appearance of a very important development of religious and philosophical thought.'[1] We have Mrs. Hardy's testimony that Hardy read this book shortly after its publication, and that it impressed him much.[2] Small wonder that it impressed him. It should be remembered that he was at this time seriously considering ordination,[3] and that he was deeply interested both in the Bible (in which he remained interested always), and in the Church; and the special significance of *Essays and Reviews* has been thus described:

> The importance of this book in the history of religious thought in England lies in the proclamation of a view of Scripture which, at the time of its publication, seemed, as put forward by ordained ministers of the national church, nothing less than revolutionary. This view would not have excited surprise if found in the writings of opponents of orthodoxy or even of scholars unpledged to any particular position; it was in the enunciation of it by clergymen that the startling novelty lay.[4]

The effect which the thorough study of this book produced upon young Hardy, who, while he had been devoutly brought up in strict orthodoxy, was at this very time in what may be called a state of intellectual renaissance effected by study of the classics, can best be suggested by passages from the book itself. One of the most powerful articles in it was that 'On the Interpretation of Scripture' from the pen of Benjamin Jowett, who had then for some years been Regius Professor of Greek at Oxford. In the course of this

[1] *Studies of a Biographer*, vol. 2, p. 129.
[2] *Early Life*, p. 43.
[3] *Early Life*, p. 66.
[4] C. C. J. Webb: *A Study of Religious Thought in England since* 1850, p. 72.

article, which was in the main a piece of textual criticism, Jowett made a potent attack upon the stupidity of conventional orthodoxy.

'Consider, for example, the extraordinary and unreasonable importance attached to single words, sometimes of doubtful meaning, in reference to any of the following subjects: Divorce; Marriage with a Wife's Sister; Inspiration; The Personality of the Holy Spirit; Infant Baptism; Episcopacy; Divine Right of Kings; Original Sin.'

Jowett examined the orthodox bases of each of these dogmas with devastating effect, and continued:

There is indeed a kind of mystery in the way in which the chance words of a simple narrative, the occurrence of some accidental event, the use even of a figure of speech or a mistranslation of a word in Latin or English, have affected the thoughts of future ages and distant countries. Nothing so slight that it has not been caught at, nothing so plain that it may not be explained away.

This insistence upon doctrines often scarcely supported by Biblical authority was contrasted with the entire neglect of other precepts repeatedly and clearly given by our Lord; e.g., the blessedness of poverty. The close of this section ran thus:

The conduct of our Lord to the woman taken in adultery affords a painful contrast to the excessive severity with which even a Christian society punishes the errors of women.

The conclusion of the article contained a paragraph to which it is not hard to imagine young Hardy's vibrant response; it is at the same time eloquent concerning the atmosphere in which he was growing to maturity:

'It is a mischief that critical observations which any intelligent man can make for himself should be ascribed to atheism or unbelief. It would be a strange and almost incredible thing that the Gospel which at first made war only on the vices of mankind should now be opposed to one of the highest and rarest of human virtues—the love of truth. And that in the present day the great object of Christianity should be, not to change the lives of men, but to prevent them from changing their opinions; that would be a singular inversion of the purposes for which Christ came into the world.'

It has sometimes been asked why Hardy chose Oxford as the type of intellectual obscurantism and obstructionism, and said, in the most bitter of all his works, that if Christ-minster could not move with the times, Christminster must go.[1] It might be remembered that most of the collaborators to *Essays and Reviews* were Oxford scholars; their position may be illustrated by the case of the most conspicuous of them. On February 20th, 1863, Benjamin Jowett was prosecuted for heresy in the Vice-Chancellor's Court. The prosecution was ultimately dropped on the advice of counsel against application to the Court of Queen's Bench. Foiled in their attempt to eject him from the University, Jowett's enemies next tried to ruin him. Of the four Regius Professorships, his was the only one whose salary had not been adjusted to modern conditions, but had remained the forty pounds granted under the mediæval foundation. A measure was introduced to endow the chair, and upon February 4th, 1864, there was a debate in Congregation upon it. The proposal ultimately went through; despite a memorial drawn up by Jowett's enemies, in the course of which they said:

'The Regius Professor of Greek in this University is charged —and that not hastily, or by a few persons, or a single party, but by the general voice of Christian people in Oxford and throughout the land—with holding and affirming doctrines subversive of the Church's faith. The fact of that faith having lost its hold upon the minds of the generality of those who have been brought within the sphere of his influence is but too evident.'[2]

Hardy, who was still in Dorchester, had an opportunity of witnessing the working of obscurantism nearer home.

---

[1] *Jude the Obscure*, Pt. 3, Chap. IV.
[2] The memorial is preserved in a collection of Oxford pamphlets in the Bodleian. Gough. Adds. Oxon 8⁰. 179.

THE BACKGROUND TO HARDY'S THOUGHT

Early in 1861, Rowland Williams, who, in the review of Bunsen's Biblical Researches in *Essays and Reviews*, had written that the command to Abraham to sacrifice his son Isaac had been given 'by the fierce ritual of Syria with the awe of a divine voice,' was indicted for heresy before the Court of Arches by William Kerr Hamilton, Bishop of Salisbury. He was condemned in that court, and suspended. But the decision was reversed by the Judicial Committee of the Privy Council. This case, being of great local interest—for Dorchester is in the Diocese of Salisbury—almost filled the *Dorset County Chronicle* during several weeks with polemical correspondence and controversy. It produced at least one leading article, in which the Editor gave as an example of the blasphemy of the new heretics the view that the whole of the book of Daniel was not written by Daniel, which, he said, amounted to a charge of forgery against the Almighty.[1] Hardy was then reading the *Dorset County Chronicle* every day.

What must have impressed Hardy even more than the conclusions in *Essays and Reviews* was the method, which was imported from science, and was at that date new to theology. An excellent example is to be found in the article on the Mosaic Cosmogony, by C. W. Goodwin. The author there refers to the attempt made to reconcile the recent findings of science with the traditional interpretations of the Bible:

'In a text book of theological instruction widely used (Horne's Introduction to the Holy Scriptures, 10th ed., 1856) we find it stated in broad terms: "Geological investigations, it is now known, all prove the perfect harmony between Scripture and Geology in reference to the history of creation." In truth, however, if we refer to the plans of conciliation proposed, we find them at variance with each other and mutually destructive. The conciliators are not agreed among themselves, and each holds the view of the other to be untenable and unsafe. The ground is perpetually shifted, as the advance of geological science may require. The plain meaning

[1] *Dorset County Chronicle*, May 2, 1861.

53

of the Hebrew record is unscrupulously tampered with, and in general the pith of the whole process lies in divesting the text of all meaning whatever.'

The writer of that was not a geologist but a Doctor of Divinity.

To pursue the history of the controversy further would here be out of place. Another *cause célèbre* resulted in 1862 from the publication, by John William Colenso, first Bishop of Natal, of a book entitled *Introduction to the Pentateuch*; for which, in the following year, his metropolitan, Robert Gray, Bishop of Capetown, deposed him from his see as an heretic. Although the deposition had no legal force and was disregarded by Colenso, it caused a storm at the time. And the young Hardy was not the only writer who was interested. Browning's *Dramatis Personæ*, when it appeared in 1864, contained a poem called 'Gold Hair: A Story of Pornic in Brittany,' the penultimate stanza of which runs:

> The candid incline to surmise of late
> That the Christian faith proves false, I find;
> For our Essays-and-Reviews debate
> Begins to tell on the public mind,
> And Colenso's words have weight.

Of even greater influence upon the whole of English thought in the later nineteenth century was the theory of evolution propounded in Darwin's epoch-making book, *The Origin of Species*, and in its sequel, *The Descent of Man* (1871). When Darwin died in 1882, Hardy attended his funeral in Westminster Abbey on April 26th. 'As a young man,' says Mrs. Hardy, 'he had been among the earliest acclaimers of *The Origin of Species*.'[1] Writing the Preface to *Late Lyrics* in February 1922, Hardy, in his eighty-third year, lamented that he had fallen upon a period 'when belief in witches of Endor is displacing the Darwinian theory, and "the truth shall make you free." ' The famous book, which became the gospel of so many in Hardy's youth, does not

[1] *Early Life*, p. 198.

itself contain any philosophical speculation. It is a strict work of science, the contents of which may be concisely described in one sentence from the famous third chapter, 'The Struggle for Existence': 'I should infer from analogy,' wrote Darwin, 'that probably all the organic beings which have ever lived on this Earth have descended from some one primordial form, into which life was first breathed.' That this conclusion, if true, destroyed at one stroke the cosmogony of the Pentateuch and with it the doctrine of the infallibility of Holy Writ, was much; but still more were the further implications, which are described by Professor C. C. J. Webb:

The importance to religious thought of the introduction of the idea of evolution was of course far greater than it would have been, had it merely, in its application in a particular form to a particular case, led to a questioning of the claim of Scripture to be considered as possessing infallible authority in respect of its statements regarding matters which fall within the domain of natural science. Regarded as the enunciation of a principle valid throughout the Universe, it seemed, at any rate to some minds, to explain by processes going on *within* the universe what it had previously been commonly maintained that an intelligent Power *beyond* and *above* the Universe was required to account for. If this use of the idea of evolution was to be reconciled with religion at all, it must plainly be by some doctrine of divine *immanence*, which should replace an instantaneous operation of *transcendent* divine power, calling the world into existence out of nothing in a form substantially the same from the first as it wears to-day, such as was then commonly supposed to be implied by the term 'creation,' by a gradual operation of God whereby some simple germ or seed might be developed into an ever progressively richer variety of forms. Moreover, if the world process were thus to be conceived after the analysis of the known facts of organic life, it would almost inevitably follow that individual members of any species, and therefore individual human beings among the rest, would come to be envisaged rather as transitory embodiments of relatively abiding types than as themselves the supremely important realities for the sake of which the whole process exists.[1]

This, then, was the intellectual atmosphere into which Hardy entered as he entered manhood; the two dominant ideas were, firstly that the Primal Cause was Immanent in the Universe, not transcendent to it; and, secondly, that the individual human being was of very small significance in the scheme of things. All the critics are agreed that these two conceptions are those which dominate all Hardy's work. Such of them as have sought the sources of this thought at all have gone to Schopenhauer and von Hartmann. It will be shown later in this chapter that Hardy studied both these philosophers in the 'eighties, and did in fact owe something to them in his last novels and in the *Dynasts*; but Hardy grew to manhood in the 'sixties. It was in the spring of 1862 that he came to make his fortune in London; and it was in those early, lonely, years in London that his personality was formed.

The speculative writer whose name is especially associated with the doctrine of the *immanence* of the Primal Cause as a means of reconciling religion and science, is Herbert Spencer (1820–1903). Spencer, who was a friend of Darwin and Huxley, and who coined the phrase 'survival of the fittest,' had already published four works by 1860. It was in 1862 that there appeared the first instalment of the great system of philosophy which is Spencer's monument in the history of thought. *First Principles* is almost certainly the earliest work of Spencer with which Hardy became acquainted. The metaphysical part of this work is that which has found least favour with either science or religion, and is generally regarded as the least important part of Spencer's philosophy. But to the student of Hardy, who, it is certain, was deeply impressed by this book in his early twenties, it is intensely interesting. The first part of the book is called 'The Unknowable'; and at the conclusion of the second chapter Spencer writes:

[1] *Religious Thought in England since* 1850, p. 12.

> If Religion and Science are to be reconciled, the basis of reconciliation must be this deepest, widest and most certain of all facts—that the Power which the Universe manifests to us is utterly inscrutable.

The third chapter on Ultimate Scientific Ideas consists of a 'reductio ad absurdum.' 'What,' asks Spencer, 'are Space and Time?', and proceeds to show that Space, Time, Matter, and, indeed, any ultimate scientific idea, are all representative of realities that cannot be comprehended. At which a reader of the *Dynasts* cannot but recall the ditty of the Spirits:

> What are space and Time? A Fancy—(Pt. 3, Act i, Sc. iii)

or the chorus of the Intelligences (at the close of the fore-scene) considering

> . . . the Prime that willed ere wareness was,
> Whose brain, perchance, is Space, whose thought its laws,
> Which we as threads and streams discern,
> We may but muse on, never learn.

Or the sarcasm of the Spirit of the Years at the end of Sc. viii, Act vii, Part 3:

> 'Your knowings of the Unknowable declared,
> Let the last Picture of the Play be bared.'

The conclusion of the fifth chapter of *First Principles* contains a passage, not hitherto mentioned by a single critic of Hardy, which Hardy must have known by heart when he was two-and-twenty; and which, if he had chosen, he might have written in 1903 upon the title-page of his greatest contribution to our literature:

> Thus the consciousness of an inscrutable Power, manifested to us through all phenomena, has been growing ever clearer; and must eventually be freed from its imperfections. The certainty that on the one hand such a power exists, while on the other hand its nature transcends intuition and is beyond imagination, is the certainty towards which intelligence has from the first been progressing.

Hardy's biography provides a piece of external evidence

that he knew Herbert Spencer, which, taken with the above, is most significant. In 1888 a certain Rev. Dr. Grosart wrote to Hardy asking him if he could suggest any explanation of certain terrible facts of life which could reconcile them to the hypothesis of the absolute goodness and non-limitation of God. To which Hardy replied that he could suggest no such explanation, but that 'Perhaps Dr. Grosart might be helped to a provisional view of the Universe by the recently published Life of Darwin, and the works of Herbert Spencer.'[1]

The man who, more than any other, was the active champion of the theory of evolution was Thomas Henry Huxley (1825–1895). While Darwin remained in comparative seclusion, Huxley, one of the most agile intellects of the century and one of the most fearless men who ever lived, resolutely set out to secure fair public hearing for the new theories. At the beginning he fought the battle almost single-handed against formidable odds. For ten years, at least, he was popularly considered as the personification of the new doctrines; and it is hardly too much to say that no inconsiderable portion of the orthodox public regarded him as Antichrist.

There is about Huxley something which captures the imagination, even at this distance. To the men who were then young, and who, like Hardy, had acclaimed the new dawn of truth, he must have seemed a very Ajax striding into the ranks of obscurantism and scattering them before him. It was not until the 'seventies that Hardy met this champion face to face. Then, says Mrs. Hardy, 'For Huxley he had a liking which grew with the knowledge of him—though that was never great—speaking of him as a man who united a fearless mind with the warmest of hearts and the most modest of manners.'[2] But from the written word he knew him long before.

The review in the *Times* of *The Origin of Species*, although nominally by the *Times* critic, was in fact by Huxley; the

[1] *Early Life*, p. 269. [2] *Early Life*, p. 159.

critic having applied to him for help in a matter beyond his own competence, and having complied with the letter of the law by prefixing a paragraph of his own to Huxley's article.[1] Entirely from Huxley's pen was the review in the *Westminster Review* for April 1860. This was in the main a carefully reasoned and dispassionate scientific review. But it contained two paragraphs which have a ring as of trumpet calls, and which are even more eloquent of the conditions in which it was possible to write them than they are in themselves:

> The myths of paganism are as dead as Osiris and Zeus, and the man who should revive them, in opposition to the knowledge of our time, would be justly laughed to scorn; but the coëval imaginations current among the rude inhabitants of Palestine, recorded by writers whose very name and age are admitted by every scholar to be unknown, have unfortunately not yet shared their fate, but, even at this day, are regarded by nine-tenths of the civilised world as the authoritative standard of fact and the criterion of the justice of scientific conclusions, in all that relates to the origin of things, and among them, of species. In this nineteenth century, as at the dawn of modern physical science, the cosmogony of the semi-barbarous Hebrew is the incubus of the philosopher and the opprobrium of the orthodox. Who shall number the patient and earnest seekers after truth, from the days of Galileo until now, whose lives have been embittered and their good name blasted by the mistaken zeal of bibliolaters? Who shall count the host of weaker men whose sense of truth has been destroyed in the effort to harmonize the impossibilities—whose life has been wasted in the attempt to force the generous new wine of science into the old bottles of judaism, compelled by the outcry of the same strong party?

> It is true that if philosophers have suffered, their cause has been amply avenged. Extinguished theologians lie about the cradle of every science as the strangled snakes beside that of Hercules; and history recalls that whenever science and orthodoxy have been fairly opposed, the latter has been forced to retire from the lists, bleeding and crushed, if not annihilated;

[1] *Life and Letters of T. H. Huxley*, by L. Huxley, Vol. I, p. 176.

scotched, if not slain. But orthodoxy is the Bourbon of the world of thought. It learns not, neither can it forget; and though at present bewildered and afraid to move, it is as willing as ever to insist that the first of Genesis contains the beginning and end of sound science, and to visit with such petty thunderbolts as its half-paralyzed hands can hurl those who refuse to degrade nature to the level of primitive Judaism.

Orthodoxy picked up the glove thrown into the lists with such superb audacity. In June 1860 there was held in Oxford the annual meeting of the British Association for the Advancement of Science. To this meeting there came, besides the men of science from all countries, Samuel Wilberforce, Bishop of Oxford; whose First Class in Mathematics in his youth gave him, in some orthodox eyes, standing in matters of science as well as in those of doctrine. Whatever he may have been in his youth, Wilberforce was an experienced and formidable controversialist; and he came to Oxford fully primed by the palaeontologist, Richard Owen, whom Huxley had demolished some little time before. On Saturday, June 30th, Dr. Draper, of New York, read a paper: 'On the intellectual development of Europe considered with reference to the views of Mr. Darwin and others that the progression of organisms is determined by law.' At the conclusion of this paper, there followed a general discussion, which soon became tempestuous. One speaker, who went to the blackboard and began 'Let the point A be Man, and let the point B be the mawnkey . . .' was howled down with cries of 'mawnkey!' The President demanded that the discussion be confined to scientific matters only. After a short speech by another scientist, the Bishop rose and began to ridicule Darwin, savagely attacking Huxley:

'The Bishop spoke thus for full half an hour with inimitable spirit, emptiness and unfairness. In a light, scoffing tone, florid and fluent, he assured us there was nothing in the idea of evolution; rock pigeons were what rock pigeons had always been. Then, turning to the antagonist with a smiling insolence, he begged to know, was it through his grandfather or through his grandmother that he claimed his descent from a monkey.'[1]

Huxley, who was at this point heard to remark 'The Lord hath delivered him into my hand,' sat patiently till the Bishop had said his say; and even refused to rise until repeatedly called for. He then made a speech in which he showed that the Right Reverend Father did not know what he was talking about when it came to physiology.

'But if this question is treated, not as a matter for the calm investigation of science, but as a matter of sentiment, and if I ask whether I would choose to be descended from the poor animal of low intelligence and stooping gait, who grins and chatters as we pass, or from a man, endowed with great ability and a splendid position, who should use these gifts to discredit and crush humble seekers after truth, I hesitate what to answer.'

The conclusion of the sentence was drowned in cheers.

It was in such an atmosphere as this that Hardy came of age. It was, not improbably, with a memory of the events of the 'sixties that, when he was finishing *Jude the Obscure*, he wrote in his notebook:

'Never retract. Never explain. Get it done, and let them howl.'[2]

By a curious coincidence, the most sensational episode in the storm over *Jude* was provided by a Bishop, who wrote to the *Yorkshire Post* that he had thrown the novel into the fire: 'probably,' said Hardy, 'in his despair at not being able to burn me.' In the rather bitterly ironical second Preface to *Jude* he added:

'To do Bludyer and the conflagratory bishop justice, what they meant seems to have been only this: "We Britons hate

[1] *Life and Letters of T. H. Huxley*, vol. 1, p. 180 *et seq.* There was no official report of the meeting issued, and the versions of the speeches given by eye-witnesses, in the *Life of Huxley* and in the *Life and Letters of Charles Darwin* by F. Darwin, vol. 2, p. 320 *et seq.*, have slight verbal differences. But the substance is common to all. The meeting had resounding publicity, in Press and from pulpit, all over the country.

The allusion to rock pigeons refers to Darwin's example that the four varieties of domestic pigeon all derive from the rock pigeon.

[2] *Later Years*, p. 38.

ideas, and we are going to live up to that privilege of our native country. Your picture may not show the untrue or the uncommon, or even be contrary to the canons of art; but it is not the view of life that we who thrive on conventions can permit to be painted."

There is in *Wessex Poems* a sonnet addressed 'To a Lady, offended by a book of the Writer's,' which is of a higher seriousness:

Now that my page is exiled—doomed, maybe,
Never to press thy cosy cushions more,
Or wake thy ready yeas as heretofore,
Or stir thy gentle vows of faith in me:

Knowing thy natural receptivity,
I figure that, as flambeaux banish eve,
My sombre image, warped by insidious heave
Of those less forthright, must lose place in thee.

So be it, I have borne such. Let thy dreams
Of me and mine diminish day by day,
And yield their space to shine of smugger things;
Till I shape to thee but in fitful gleams,
And then in far and feeble visitings,
And then surcease. Truth will be truth alway.

It is possible wholly to understand Hardy, both as a man and as a writer, only if we understand in what school he was brought up. Of the masters whose example inspired him in early manhood and whose principles he never forgot, Huxley was not the least. By the time he was thirty-five, Hardy had lost all religious faith. No one has regretted that loss more bitterly than he (as can be seen by such a moving poem as 'The Impercipient' in *Wessex Poems*). It was the inevitable result of an evolution of character conditioned by the age. In the volume of Essays called *Lay Sermons* which Huxley published in 1870, there is one upon Descartes. After describing Descartes's condition for the assent to any proposition, Huxley wrote:

'The enunciation of this first great commandment of science

consecrated doubt. It removed doubt from the seat of penance among the grievous sins to which it had long been condemned, and enthroned it in that high place among the primary duties which is assigned to it by the scientific conscience of these later days.'

What Hardy and those whom he followed lost, irreparable as it was, was at least lost in no ignoble quest. Huxley himself thus described the principles that had guided him:

'To promote the increase of natural knowledge and to further the application of scientific methods of investigation to all the problems of life to the best of my ability, in the conviction, which has grown with my growth and strengthened with my strength, that there is no alleviation for the sufferings of mankind except veracity of thought and action, and the resolute facing of the world as it is, when the garment of make-believe, by which pious hands have hidden its ugly features, is stripped off.'[1]

That lesson Hardy learnt well and truly. All his novels and all his poetry are permeated with it. He was over eighty when he wrote, looking back upon his life:

'If I may be forgiven for quoting my own old words, let me repeat what I printed in this relation more than twenty years ago, and wrote much earlier, in a poem entitled "In Tenebris."

If a way to the Better there be, it exacts a full look at the Worst:

that is to say, by the exploration of reality, and its frank recognition stage by stage along the survey, with an eye to the best consummation possible.'[2]

The nature of Huxley's influence upon Hardy's thought is shown most clearly in a letter written by the latter on February 27th, 1902, to Edward Clodd, thanking him for his book on Huxley. This letter is in Mr. T. J. Wise's Ashley Library,[3] and has not been published. In it Hardy wrote:

[1] Quoted in the article on Huxley by W. F. R. Weldon in the *Dictionary of National Biography*.
[2] Preface to *Late Lyrics*. The poem is in *Poems of the Past and Present*.
[3] Catalogue of the Ashley Library, vol. 10.

THOMAS HARDY

What is forced upon one again after reading such a life as Huxley's, is the sad fact of the extent to which Theological lumber is still allowed to discredit religion, in spite of such devoted attempts as his to shake it off. If the doctrines of the supernatural were quickly abandoned to-morrow by the church, and 'reverence and love for an ethical ideal' alone retained, not one in ten thousand would object to the readjustment, while the enormous bulk of thinkers excluded by the old teaching would be brought into the fold, and our venerable old churches and cathedrals would become the centres of emotional life that they once were.

Well: what we gain by science is, after all, sadness, as the Preacher saith. The more we know of the laws and nature of the Universe the more ghastly a business one perceives it all to be—and the non-necessity of it. As some philosopher says, if nothing at all existed, it would be a completely natural thing; but that the world exists is a fact absolutely logicless and senseless.

In that letter we have the concise history of Hardy's mental and emotional development, and an illustration of the results to which it led.

Huxley, although the outstanding figure in the battle over evolution, was not alone as a fearless thinker in his day. In 1864 there was published a small volume which has become one of the major classics of English philosophy. The third chapter of it treats of Individuality as one of the elements of well-being; and in this we may read, as all the young men of that day, Hardy among the rest, read:

There is now scarcely any outlet for energy in this country except business. The energy expended in this may still be regarded as considerable. What little is left from that employment, is expended on some hobby, which may be a useful, even a philanthropic, hobby, but is always some one thing, and generally a thing of small dimensions. The greatness of England is now all collective; individually small, we only appear capable of anything great by our habit of combining; and with this our moral and religious philanthropists are perfectly contented. But it was men of another stamp than this that made

England what it has been; and men of another stamp will be needed to prevent its decline.

The writer of those words was John Stuart Mill (1806–73), and the book is the famous treatise *On Liberty*, the appearance of which raised Mill to the zenith of his fame. This was two years after Hardy had come to London; in the following year, Mill was elected to Parliament as Member for Westminster. Among the tributes called forth forty years later by the centenary of Mill's birth, there was a letter in the *Times* of May 21st, 1906, in which Hardy described a personal experience of that election:

This being the hundredth anniversary of J. Stuart Mill's birth, and as writers like Carlyle, Leslie Stephen and others have held that anything, however imperfect, which affords an idea of a human personage in his actual form and flesh, is of value in respect of him, the few following words on how one of the profoundest thinkers of the last century appeared forty years ago to the man in the street may be worth recording as a footnote to Mr. Morley's admirable estimate of Mill's life and philosophy in your impression of Friday.

It was a day in 1865, about three in the afternoon, during Mill's candidature for Westminster. The hustings had been erected in Covent Garden, near the front of St. Paul's Church; and when I—a young man living in London—drew near to the spot, Mill was speaking. The appearance of the author of the treatise *On Liberty* (which we students of that date knew almost by heart) was so different from the look of persons who usually address crowds in the open air that it held the attention of people for whom such a gathering in itself had little interest. Yet it was, primarily, that of a man out of place. The religious sincerity of his speech was jarred on by his environment—a group on the hustings who, with few exceptions, did not care to understand him fully, and a crowd below who could not. He stood bareheaded, and his vast pale brow, so thin-skinned as to show the blue veins, sloped back like a stretching upland, and conveyed to the observer a curious sense of perilous exposure. The picture of him as personified earnestness surrounded for the most part by careless curiosity derived an added piquancy—if it can be called such—from the fact that the cameo clearness of his face chanced to be in relief against the blue shadow of a church, which on its transcendental side, his doctrines antagonized. But it would not be right to say that the throng was absolutely unimpressed by his words; it felt that they were weighty, though it did not quite know why.

The peculiar value of this most suggestive letter—and who but an artist could convey what is given by that touch of the cameo clear face against the blue shadow of a church? —is the direct testimony it affords of Mill's influence upon Hardy when the younger writer was just becoming a man. He knew the treatise *On Liberty* almost by heart. To get that treatise by heart is an experience which could leave no intellectual man quite as he was before it. In the second chapter on the Liberty of Thought and Discussion, the young Hardy read:

> No one can be a great thinker who does not recognise that as a thinker it is his first duty to follow his intellect to whatever conclusions it may lead. Truth gains even more by the errors of one, who, with due study and preparation, thinks for himself, than by the true opinion of those who only hold them because they do not suffer themselves to think.

It is not too much to say that the whole of Hardy's life, and all his writings, were profoundly influenced by thoughts that had come out of that vast pale brow, which he glimpsed on an afternoon in 1865. Thirty years later, in the third chapter of the fourth part of *Jude the Obscure*, he made Sue Bridehead quote to Phillotson a passage out of the third paragraph of the third chapter of the treatise *On Liberty*:

> She or he who lets the world, or his own portion of it, choose his plan of life for him, has no need of any other faculty than the ape-like one of imitation.

As must be shown in another chapter, *Jude the Obscure* occupies a place by itself among Hardy's writings in that it was primarily written for the sake of propagating certain ideas. The whole attitude of mind in which the book was written bears traces of Hardy's early studies in John Stuart

Mill; although it may be conjectured that the result would have considerably startled Mill himself. When the storm broke upon Hardy after the publication of *Jude*, a far more effective reply than that which he actually made, would have been supplied by Mill's words:

> If any opinion is compelled to silence, that opinion may, for aught we can certainly know, be true. To deny this is to assume our own infallibility. Though the silenced opinion be an error, it may, and very commonly does, contain a portion of truth; and since the general and prevailing opinion on any subject is rarely or never the whole truth, it is only by the collision of adverse opinions that the remainder of the truth has any chance of being supplied.[1]

Hardy's first study in Mill was doubtless the treatise *On Liberty* in the 'sixties. But it would not be hard to show that his reading extended further also. As a brief example, we may take the *Three Essays on Religion* which first appeared in 1874 after Mill's death. The first of these, the Essay on Nature, written between 1850 and 1858, contains the following paragraph:

> That much applauded class of authors, the writers on natural theology, have, I venture to think, entirely lost their way and missed the sole line of argument which could have made their speculations acceptable to any who can perceive when two propositions contradict one another. They have exhausted the resources of sophistry to make it appear that all the suffering in the world exists to prevent greater—that misery exists, for fear lest there should be misery; a thesis which, if ever so well maintained, could only avail to explain and justify the works of limited beings, compelled to labour under conditions independent of their own will; but can have no application to a Creator assumed to be omnipotent, who, if he bends to a supposed necessity, himself makes the necessity which he bends to. If the maker of the world *can* all that he will, he wills misery, and there is no escape from the conclusion.

No reader of *Tess* or of the *Dynasts* will require further comment. There are a few passages in the novel, and

[1] *On Liberty*, Chap. II.

several in the drama, so exactly corresponding to this that, given the knowledge that Hardy was a devoted admirer of Mill, the possibility of pure coincidence in the resemblance is practically ruled out. Simply because it is less generally known than his creative work, a passage may also be quoted from a letter which Hardy wrote concerning an essay in Maeterlinck's *Le Temple Enseveli*, that appeared in *The Academy* of May 17th, 1902 (at the time when he was putting the finishing touches to *The Dynasts*):

> Far be it from my wish to disturb any comforting phantasy, if it be barely tenable. But alas, no profound reflection can be needed to detect the sophistry in M. Maeterlinck's argument, and to see that the original difficulty recognised by thinkers like Schopenhauer, Hartmann, Haeckel, etc., and by most of the persons called pessimists, remains unsurmounted.
>
> Pain has been, and pain is: no new sort of morals in Nature can remove pain from the past and make it pleasure for those who are its infallible estimators, the bearers thereof. And no injustice, however slight, can be atoned for by her future generosity, however ample, so long as we consider Nature to be, or to stand for, unlimited power. The exoneration of an omnipotent Mother by her retrospective justice becomes an absurdity when we ask, What made the foregone injustice necessary to her omnipotence?

No comment upon this is needed, except that Hardy was perfectly familiar with the idea expressed in the last paragraph quoted, at least ten years before he had read a word of Schopenhauer or of von Hartmann (who were not translated into English until the 'eighties). It is true that three books by Haeckel were translated during the 'seventies, of which more hereafter. But it seems superfluous to invoke Haeckel when we know how Hardy studied Mill.

Before leaving Mill, there is one exceedingly suggestive point to be made, which has never, as far as I am aware, been made hitherto. It is commonly supposed and stated that the Doctrine of the unconscious Immanent Will, which forms the great theme of Hardy's greatest work, owes a debt to the writings of Schopenhauer and von Hartmann. This must later be discussed. But in the second of the *Essays on Religion*, that on Theism, written between 1868 and 1870, which is Mill's last important work, there is in the third chapter dealing with the Evidences of Theism a discussion of the theory of Will as the Prime Cause. Mill, who is of course combating the argument of those who use Will as synonymous with Personality, rejects this; but he makes a comment upon it which, in conjunction with the known facts of Hardy's attitude, is highly suggestive; Mill himself is dissenting from the proposition which he describes:

> The assertion is that physical nature must have been produced by a will because nothing but will is known to us as having the power of originating the production of phenomena. . . . That nothing can *consciously* produce Mind but Mind is self-evident, being involved in the meaning of the words; but that there cannot be *unconscious* production must not be assumed.

It need hardly be said that the theory of the production of conscious mind by unconscious process is the very kernel and heart of the *Dynasts*. Says the Ancient Spirit of the Years:

> The cognisance ye mourn, Life's doom to feel,
> If I report it meetly, came unmeant,
> Emerging with blind gropes from impercipience
> By listless sequence—luckless, tragic chance,
> In your more human tongue.

To which the Pities reply:

> And hence unneeded
> In the economy of Vitality,
> Which might have ever kept a sealed cognition
> As doth the Will itself.
>
> (Pt. 1, Act v, Sc. iv.)

Until further evidence is forthcoming, the first place in which Hardy can have found the germ of that idea would seem to be the writings of John Stuart Mill, which he studied long and lovingly.

Among the writers whom Hardy studied in his twenties, and whose work left upon him a deep and lasting impression, there remains to be mentioned a poet whose name rings strangely in the porch of the philosophers. And yet a dispassionate consideration of the evidence suggests that no writer whom he read in the 'sixties impressed young Hardy more than Algernon Charles Swinburne. The nature of the impression was obviously very different from that made by the philosophers and rationalists mentioned hitherto. If J. S. Mill influenced Hardy by an appeal to his intellect, Swinburne influenced him by an appeal to his emotions. Now Hardy, for all his claims to be scientific and rational, was primarily a being of emotion, as are most great creative artists. His stature as an artist is, indeed, the measure of the depth and intensity of his emotional nature; for intellectually he is smaller than many great writers have been; smaller, to make an obvious comparison, than Browning. Even his response to philosophical stimulus was largely emotional; as may be seen in the *Dynasts*; where his broodings upon the suggestions of thinkers, from Mill to Schopenhauer and von Hartmann, issue in the cry of the Pities:

> O, the intolerable antilogy
> Of making figments feel!

> (Pt. 1, Act iv, Sc. v.)

To the young architect-poet adrift in London, and still more perilously adrift upon the strange seas of thought into which the loss of religious convictions had launched him, the appearance of *Atalanta in Calydon* in 1865, of *Poems and Ballads* in 1866, of *Songs Before Sunrise* in 1871 must have been events that stirred him to his depths. There is in the Ashley Library a letter which he wrote thirty years later, in reply to a letter from Swinburne praising *The Well-Beloved*, which gives a glimpse of what those experiences must have been:

THE BACKGROUND TO HARDY'S THOUGHT

Max Gate, Dorchester. April 1st, 1897.

DEAR MR. SWINBURNE,

I must thank you for your kind note about my fantastic little tale, which, if it can make, in its better parts, any faint claims to imaginative feeling, will owe something of such feeling to you, for I often thought of lines of yours during the writing; and indeed was not able to resist the quotation of your words now and then.

And this reminds me that one day, when examining several English imitations of a well-known fragment of Sappho, I interested myself in trying to strike out a better equivalent for it than the commonplace 'Thou, too, shalt die,' which all the translators had used during the last hundred years. I then stumbled upon your 'Thee, too, the years shall cover,' and all my spirit for poetic pains died out of me. Those few words present, I think, the finest *drama* of Death and Oblivion, so to speak, in our tongue. Having rediscovered this phrase, it carried me back to the buoyant time of thirty years ago, when I used to read your early works walking along the crowded London streets to my imminent risk of being knocked down.

Believe me to be,

Yours very sincerely,

THOMAS HARDY.[1]

Beside this letter must be placed one written when he heard of Swinburne's death in 1912, which is printed by Mrs. Hardy on pp. 135-6 of *Later Years*:

For several reasons I could not bring myself to write on Swinburne immediately I heard that, to use his own words, 'Fate had undone the bondage of the gods' for him.

No doubt the press will say some good words about him now he is dead and does not care whether it says them or no. Well, I remember what it said in 1866, when he did care, and how it made the blood of some of us young men boil.[2]

Was there ever such a country—looking back at the life, work and death of Swinburne—is there any other country in Europe whose attitude towards a deceased poet of his rank would have been so ignoring and almost contemptuous? I

[1] Catalogue of the Ashley Library, Vol. 2, p. 169.
[2] One of the epithets was 'an unclean fiery imp from the pit.' The famous article by Morley appeared in the *Saturday Review* of August 4th, 1866.

except the *Times*, which has the fairest estimate I have yet seen. But read the *Academy* and the *Nation*.

The kindly cowardice of many papers is overwhelming him with such toleration, such theological judgments, hypocritical sympathy and misdirected eulogy that, to use his own words again, it makes one sick in a corner—or, as we say down here in Wessex, it is enough to make every little dog run to mixen.

However, we are getting on in our appreciativeness of poets. One thinks of those other two lyricists, Burns and Shelley, at this time for obvious reasons, and of how much harder it was with them. We know how Burns was treated at Dumfries, but by the time that Swinburne was a young man Burns had advanced so far as to be regarded as no worse than 'the glory and the shame of literature' (in the words of a critic of that date). As for Shelley, he was not tolerated at all in his lifetime. But Swinburne has been tolerated—at any rate since he has not written anything to speak of. And a few months ago, when old and enfeebled, he was honoured by a rumour that he had been offered a complimentary degree at Oxford. And Shelley, too, in these latter days of our memory, has been favoured so far as to be considered no lower than an ineffectual angel beating his luminous wings in vain.

I was so late in getting my poetical barge under way, and he was so early with his flotilla—besides my being between three and four years younger, and being nominally an architect (an awful imposter at that, really)—that though I read him as he came out I did not personally know him till many years after the *Poems and Ballads* year.

Three days later, Hardy wrote in his diary that it was the day of Swinburne's funeral, to which he could not go because of his rheumatism; and he thought of some of Swinburne's lines: that on Shelley: 'O sole thing sweeter than thine own songs were'; two out of *Songs Before Sunrise* (one of which, on Man, 'Save his own soul he hath no star' was used as a chapter heading in *Jude*); and one from the sonnet on Newman and Carlyle. The latter is perhaps the most significant to the present purpose. This sonnet first appeared in the *Athenaeum* of January 8th, 1876, under the title of 'Two Leaders,' who were Newman and Carlyle.

In it, Swinburne bade farewell, in the words of the Athenians' Farewell to the Eumenides, to two men who represented that older order of thought which he and Hardy were the most conspicuous English writers to discard. It is significant of the influence which his older contemporary had exercised upon him that on the day of Swinburne's funeral, Hardy should have thought of this sonnet:

> With all our hearts we praise you whom ye hate,
> High souls that hate us; for our hopes are higher,
> And higher than yours the goal of our desire,
> Though high your ends be as your hearts are great.
> Your world of gods and kings, of shrine and state,
> Was of the night when hope and fear stood nigher,
> Wherein men walked by light of stars and fire
> Till man by day stood equal with his fate.
> Honour, not hate, we give you, love, not fear,
> Last prophets of past kind, who fill the dome
> Of great dead gods with wrath and wail, nor hear
> Time's word and Man's: 'Go honoured hence, go home,
> Night's childless children; here your hour is done;
> Pass with the stars and leave us with the sun.'[1]

It is highly significant that in both the letters reproduced here, Hardy should have quoted from the same famous poem in the notorious volume of 1866. 'Anactoria' was, indeed, after 'Dolores,' the most famous of the 'pièces damnées.' And 'Anactoria,' besides what Hardy considered the finest drama of death and oblivion in our language, contained one of the most frenzied denunciations of Providence which English poetry had produced:

> Were I made as he
> Who hath made all things, to break them one by one,
> If my feet trod upon the stars and sun
> And souls of men as his have alway trod,
> God knows I might be crueller than God.
>
> . . . . .
>
> Is not his incense bitterness? His meat
> Murder? His hidden face and iron feet
> Hath not man known, and felt them on their way

[1] This sonnet was republished in *Poems and Ballads*, Second Series.

Threaten and trample all things and every day?
Hath he not sent us hunger? Who hath cursed
Spirit and flesh with longing? Filled with thirst
Their lips who cried unto him? Who bade exceed
The fervid will, fall short the feeble deed,
Bade sink the spirit and the flesh aspire,
Pain animate the dust of dead desire,
And life yield up her flower to violent fate?

Although Hardy could not go to Swinburne's funeral, he went the year after to see the grave at Bonchurch; and in memory of the 'Singer Asleep' he wrote what is by common consent one of the most beautiful of all his poems (published in *Satires of Circumstance*). To quote this poem partially is to spoil it. The allusion to Sappho is perhaps the most exquisite touch in Hardy's poetry. One stanza alone must be quoted from the poem for our present purpose:

O that far morning of a summer day
When, down a terraced street whose pavements lay
Glassing the sunshine into my bent eyes,
I walked and read with a quick glad surprise
New words, in classic guise—

What were those words that went so near to the heart of the young poet masquerading as an architect as he walked down Adelphi Terrace? 'Anactoria,' with its drama of death and oblivion, and its astonishing blasphemy; and the 'Hymn to Proserpine.' In the third chapter of the second part of *Jude*, Sue Bridehead comes home with statuettes of Apollo and Venus (whom she describes to Miss Fontover as St. Peter and St. Mary Magdalen); she places them in her bedroom, and enacts a strange and significant scene:

Placing the pair of figures on the chest of drawers, a candle on each side of them, she withdrew to the bed, flung herself down thereon, and began reading a book she had taken from her box, which Miss Fontover knew nothing of. It was a volume of Gibbon, and she read the chapter dealing with the reign of Julian the Apostate. Occasionally she looked up at the statuettes, which appeared strange and out of place, there happening to be a Calvary print hanging between them, and,

as if the scene suggested the action, she at length jumped up
and withdrew another book from her box—a volume of verse—
and turned to the familiar poem—

> Thou hast conquered, O pale Galilean:
> The world has grown grey from thy breath. . . .[1]

It is certain that Hardy's memory of the 'words in
classic guise' which moved him so in his youth included
another volume, published the year before *Poems and
Ballads*, which he perhaps came to know through them.
The copy of *Atalanta in Calydon*, which is still in the Library
at Max Gate, dates from the 'eighties, for in the 'sixties Hardy
could not afford to buy books that he could get from Mudie.
But that he knew *Atalanta* in the 'sixties is certain. In the
copy still to be seen in his library, there is a pencil line
drawn against the fourth Stasimon:

> For now we know not of them; but one saith
> The Gods are gracious, praising God; and one,
> When hast thou seen? or hast thou felt his breath
> Touch, nor consume thine eyelids as the sun,
> Nor fill thee to the lips with fiery death?
>   None hath beheld him, none;
> Seen above other gods and shapes of things,
> Swift without feet and flying without wings,
> Intolerable, not clad with death or life,
> Insatiable, not known of night or day,
> The lord of love and loathing and of strife
> Who gives a star and takes a sun away:
> Who shapes the soul and makes her a barren wife
> To the earthly body and grievous growth of clay;
> Who turns the large limbs to a little flame
> And binds the great sea with a little sand;
> Who makes desire, and slays desire with shame;
> Who shakes the heaven as ashes in his hand;
> Who, seeing the light and shadow for the same,
> Bids day waste night as fire devours a brand,
> Smites without sword and scourges without rod;
>   The supreme evil, God.

---

[1] The 'Hymn to Proserpine' is also quoted in Chap. IV of Part 3 of *Jude*.

Hardy was twenty-five or twenty-six when first he read that. Simultaneously, he was steeping himself in the writings of agnostics—to use the phrase coined by Huxley—who proved to his satisfaction that the omnipotence of a First Cause was incompatible with its goodness. In the light of these facts, it is easy to understand *Tess of the d'Urbervilles*, with its famous ending:

> Upon the cornice of the tower a tall staff was fixed. Their eyes were riveted on it. A few minutes after the hour had struck something moved slowly up the staff, and extended itself upon the breeze. It was a black flag.
>
> 'Justice' was done, and the President of the Immortals, in Aeschylean phrase, had ended his sport with Tess.[1]

By the time that Hardy entered his thirties, the rationalism which had made so determined an onslaught in his twentieth year, had practically gained the day. Some conception of the prodigious change which had taken place in opinion inside the church itself within twenty years may be gathered by a comparison. It was in 1853 that Frederick Denison Maurice, one of the most influential figures of the religious world in his generation, was expelled from his Professorship at King's College, London, for pointing out the inconsistency between the assertion that God is love, and the assertion that the majority of the human race must, for failure to repent during the earthly life, be doomed to everlasting damnation. It was to this expulsion that Tennyson alluded in the poem addressed to Maurice. The views upon this question expressed twenty-five years later by Canon Farrar, afterwards Dean of St. Paul's, in a volume of sermons called *Our Eternal Hope* published in 1878, were thus described by Leslie Stephen:

> Canon Farrar does not deny the existence of hell; he only thinks that fewer people will go there and perhaps find it much less disagreeable than is generally supposed.[2]

---

[1] One of the choruses of *Atalanta* is quoted in *Tess*, Chap. XXXV.

[2] In the essay 'Dreams and Realities,' reprinted in *An Agnostic's Apology*; like the other contents of that volume, it had first appeared in a periodical.

But it was not only the severer doctrines of the Church which had lost their hold upon the intellect and conscience of Christian people. The Church itself, and the religion for which it stood, had lost their hold upon a large section of the English public. The position is described by Matthew Arnold in the Preface to *Literature and Dogma*. How much Arnold's own beliefs had been shaken is evident in such a poem as 'Dover Beach.' But he never became a complete agnostic; his plea, in *Literature and Dogma*, is that the assertion concerning a Great Primal Cause, which is unverifiable, must be replaced by that of 'an enduring Power, not ourselves, that makes for righteousness.' Thus far, Arnold himself remained in agreement with the church. But he wrote in 1873:

And yet, with all this agreement, both in words and in things, when we behold the clergy and ministers of religion lament the neglect of religion and aspire to restore it, how much one must feel that to restore religion as they understand it, to re-enthrone the Bible as explained by our current theology, whether learned or popular, is absolutely and forever impossible!—as impossible as to restore the predominance of the feudal system, or the belief in witches. Let us admit that the Bible cannot possibly die; but then the churches cannot even conceive the Bible without the gloss they at present put upon it; and this gloss, as certainly, cannot possibly live. And it is not a gloss which one church or sect puts upon the Bible and another does not; it is the gloss they all put upon it, and call the substratum of belief common to all Christian churches, and largely shared by them even with natural religion. It is this so-called axiomatic basis which must go, and it supports all the rest; and if the Bible were really inseparable from this, and depended upon it, then Mr. Bradlaugh[1] would have his way, and the Bible would go too; for this basis is inevitably doomed. For whatever is to stand must rest upon something that is verifiable, and not unverifiable. Now the assumption with which all the churches and sects set out, that there is a great Personal First Cause, the moral and intelligent Governor of

---

[1] Charles Bradlaugh (1833–1891), militant atheist and republican, author of *A Plea for Atheism*.

the Universe, and that from Him the Bible derives its authority, can never be verified.[1]

While, upon one hand, a large proportion of the intellectual world of England was taking the direction which Matthew Arnold, the apostle of culture, took; on the other some misguided champions of orthodoxy took steps illjudged to conciliate thinking minds. One such step, which had very wide publicity at the time, may be described in the words used by Leslie Stephen, in an article entitled 'An Agnostic's Apology,' which first appeared in the *Fortnightly Review* in June 1876:

> Not long ago there appeared in the papers a string of propositions framed—so we were assured—by some of the most candid and most learned of living theologians. These propositions defined by the help of various languages the precise relations which exist between the persons of the Trinity. It is an odd, though far from an unprecedented, circumstance that the unbeliever cannot quote them for fear of profanity. If they were translated into the pages of the *Fortnightly Review* it would be impossible to convince anyone that the intention was not to mock the simple-minded persons who, we must suppose, were not themselves intentionally irreverent. It is enough to say that they defined the nature of God Almighty with an accuracy from which modest naturalists would shrink in describing the genesis of a black beetle.

There is a reference to this same manifesto in *Literature and Dogma*, where Arnold characterized it as 'the faiery tale of the three Lord Shaftesburys'; and the gentle Arnold was devout if compared to Leslie Stephen. It was because Stephen exercised no small influence over the mind of Hardy in the 'seventies that he is of importance to this inquiry.

It is the literary side of Leslie Stephen's activities which has proved the most enduring. We think of him to-day

[1] In 1888, Hardy noted in his diary 'When dogma has to be balanced on its feet by such hair-splitting arguments as the late M. Arnold's, it must be in a very bad way.' (*Early Life*, p. 281.)

primarily as the moving spirit of the *Dictionary of National Biography*, or as the author of *Hours in a Library*, rather than as a philosopher. If we connect him with philosophy at all, it is with the philosophy of an age not his own, as the author of the *History of English Thought in the Eighteenth Century*. But during the third quarter of the nineteenth century he was a militant rationalist, and proved himself one of the most acrimonious controversialists of that age of bitter controversy. His articles on questions of religion are mostly collected into two volumes: *Essays on Freethinking and Plain Speaking* and *An Agnostic's Apology*, published in 1873 and 1893 respectively. Nearly all of them first appeared during the 'seventies and early 'eighties in the pages of the *Fortnightly Review* or in those of *Frazer's Magazine*. Hardy first became acquainted with Stephen in 1871, when the latter was Editor of the *Cornhill Magazine*. The literary side of this relationship belongs to the history of *Far from the Madding Crowd*.[1] It was really to Stephen that Hardy owed the secure establishment of his reputation as a novelist. The two men remained close friends for some years. *The Hand of Ethelberta* came out under Stephen's command, following *Far from the Madding Crowd* in the *Cornhill*. Stephen refused *The Return of the Native* in 1877. They continued in correspondence until the early 'eighties, after which they lost sight of each other for many years. *The Life and Letters of Leslie Stephen*, by F. W. Maitland, contains half a chapter by Hardy (p. 270 *et seq.*), as well as the poem on the Schreckhorn 'With Thoughts of Leslie Stephen,' afterwards reprinted in *Satires of Circumstance*.

It is a curious thing that the writers on Hardy's philosophy should have overlooked Leslie Stephen. The probability is very strong that, given the known facts of their close friendship during Hardy's early thirties and Hardy's state of mind at that time, the older man would try to persuade the younger into his own rationalistic attitude. There is also unmistakable evidence of this influence in Hardy's

[1] See p. 167.

writings. But Mrs. Hardy puts the matter beyond possible doubt. She makes two definite statements:

> On a visit to London in the winter (of 1873) Hardy had made the personal acquaintance of Leslie Stephen, the man whose philosophy was to influence his own for many years, indeed, more than that of any other contemporary. (*Early Life*, p. 132.)
>
> Since coming into contact with Leslie Stephen about 1873, Hardy had been much influenced by his philosophy and also by his criticism. (*Early Life*, p. 167.)

The general tone of Stephen's rationalist essays can best be shown by quotations. The *Fortnightly Review* for March 1873, when Hardy was becoming personally intimate with him, contained an article by Stephen called 'Are we Christians?' In this he examined evidence of Christian attitude and conduct in England:

> Are we to look to those popular platitudes which bring down the applause of crowded audiences and sell cheap newspapers by the hundred thousand? From them we may learn, for example, that the British workman will not have the Bible excluded from his schools, and will not have the Sunday desecrated. Certainly these are two of the most definite points in the popular creed. Our reverence for the Bible is, as Dr. Newman tells us, the strong point of Protestantism; and our observance of the Sunday is the one fact which tells a foreigner that we have a religious faith. No one, whatever his opinions, should undervalue those beliefs, or, if they must so be called, superstitions. An English Sunday, with all its gloom and with all its drunkenness, is a proof that we do in fact worship something besides our stomachs.

The word 'agnostic' came into general use in the early 'seventies. It is said that it was suggested by Huxley at a party held previous to the formation of the Metaphysical Society at Mr. James Knowle's house on Clapham Common one evening in 1869. Huxley took it from St. Paul's mention of the altar to the Unknown God.[1] In the *Fortnightly Review*

[1] This is the account of the origin of the word given in the *New English Dictionary*.

for June 1876, Leslie Stephen published an article entitled 'An Agnostic's Apology,' already quoted, in which he contended that the position of Agnostic was the only one compatible with intellectual honesty, and in which he gave very short shrift to his opponents:

Let us then ask once more, does Christianity exhibit the ruler of the universe as benevolent or as just? If I were to assert that of every ten beings born into this world, nine would be damned, that all who refused to believe what they did not hold to be proved, and all who sinned from overwhelming temptation, and all who had not the good fortune to be the subjects of a miraculous conversion or the recipients of a grace conveyed by a magical charm, would be tortured to all eternity, what would an orthodox theologian reply? He could not say 'That is false'; I might appeal to the highest authorities for my justification; nor, in fact, could he on his own showing deny the possibility. Hell, he says, exists; he does not know who will be damned; though he does know that all men are by nature corrupt and liable to be damned if not saved by supernatural grace. He might, and probably would, now say: 'That is rash. You have no authority for saying how many will be lost and how many saved; you cannot even say what is meant by hell or heaven; you cannot tell how far God may be better than His word, though you may be sure that He won't be worse than His word.' And what is all this, but to say We know nothing about it? In other words, to fall back on Agnosticism. The difficulty, as theologians truly say, is not so much that evil is eternal as that evil exists. That is in substance a frank admission that, as nobody can explain evil, nobody can explain anything. Your revelation, which was to prove the benevolence of God, has proved only that God's benevolence may be consistent with the eternal and infinite misery of most of His creatures; you escape only by saying that it is also consistent with their not being eternally and infinitely miserable. That is, the revelation reveals nothing.

Of an attitude of mind savouring distinctly of Leslie Stephen there are many traces in *Tess*. Perhaps the clearest are to be found in the fourteenth and the eighteenth chapters, both in connection with ecclesiastics. The first is the parson to whom Tess comes to ask if her baptism of her baby Sorrow is as effective as his would have been:

> Having the natural feelings of a tradesman at finding that a job he should have been called in for had been unskilfully botched by his customers among themselves, he was disposed to say no.

And again, when he replies that it will be just the same whether the poor little body is buried in Christian burial or not:

> How the Vicar reconciled his answer with the strict notions he supposed himself to hold on these subjects it is beyond a layman's power to tell, though not to excuse.

Had Leslie Stephen written *Tess*, he would have made both answers 'no.' He might, however, have written the phrase describing Angel Clare's father:

> A firm believer—not as the phrase is now elusively construed by theological thimble-riggers in the church and out of it, but in the old and ardent sense of the Evangelical School.

The 'theological thimble-riggers' is an echo of Stephen's article on the Broad Church.[1] The whole matter of Angel's beliefs, however, is a particularly interesting one, as there seems reason to believe that Hardy is here giving a piece of his own spiritual autobiography. It must be remembered that Hardy had neither the asperity nor the pugnacity of Stephen.[2] Hardy, moreover, retained all his life a sort of affection for the English Church, of which he had once wished to become a priest, even though he no longer believed her creeds; and he used occasionally to go to a service almost until he died. It is significant that Stephen, who had started life as a tutor at Cambridge entitled 'The Reverend Leslie Stephen,' chose Hardy as witness to his deed renunciatory of Holy Orders.[3] But Hardy came in

---

[1] In *Freethinking and Plain Speaking*.

[2] To the Rev. Dr. Grosart, whom Hardy advised to read Herbert Spencer, Stephen, who had also been asked, replied that it was the Doctor's business to explain to him, not his to the Doctor.

[3] Hardy recounts the incident in *The Life of Leslie Stephen*.

later years to feel that 'rationalists err as far in one direction as Revelationists or Mystics in the other.' The same notes from which this is taken contain other entries, which are most revealing, and pathetic:

> 'We enter church, and we have to say "We have erred and strayed from thy ways like lost sheep," when what we want to say is "Why are we made to err and stray like lost sheep?" Then we have to sing "My soul doth magnify the Lord," when what we want to sing is "O that my soul could find some Lord that it could magnify!" Till it can, let us magnify good works, and develop all means of easing mortals' progress through a world not worthy of them.'[1]

A word must be said of a philosopher with whose writings Hardy certainly became acquainted during the 'seventies. Mrs. Hardy says that it was about 1873 that he read Comte.[2] She also reproduces an extract from his diary for 1880:

> If Comte had introduced Christ among the worthies in his calendar, it would have made Positivism tolerable to thousands who, from position, family connection or early education, now decry what in their heart of hearts they hold to contain the germs of a true system.[3]

There is also a reference to Comte in the Preface to *Late Lyrics*; and another in the article 'Candour in English Fiction,' written in 1889. It would have been strange had Hardy not read Comte; for, from the time when the writings of the French philosopher became available in English about the middle of the century,[4] 'Positivism' became a very popular word; although whether all those who so lightly bandied it about had ever looked into Comte's work may be doubted. To such an extent did this word enter into the popular vocabulary, that it caused great annoyance to other philosophers to whom it was applied indiscriminately. The Essays of Herbert Spencer contain a vigorous protest

[1] *Later Years*, p. 121.   [2] *Early Life*, p. 129.   [3] *Early Life*, p. 189.
[4] *La Philosophie positive* was translated by Harriet Martineau in 1853, and *Le Discours sur l'Ensemble* had been translated in 1852.

against this affiliatoin; and Huxley made an attack on Positivism in an essay 'The Scientific Aspects of Positivism' in *Lay Sermons* (1870), in which he wrote:

> It has been a source of periodical irritation to me to find M. Comte put forward as a representative of scientific thought; and to observe that writers whose philosophy had its legitimate parent in Hume or in themselves were labelled 'Comtists' or 'Positivists' by public writers, even in spite of vehement protests to the contrary. It has cost Mr. Mill hard rubbings to get that label off; and I watch Mr. Spencer as one regards a good man struggling with adversity, still engaged in eluding its adhesiveness, and ready to tear away skin and all rather than let it stick. My own turn might come next.

That the philosophy of Auguste Comte had no small influence in England in the latter half of the last century is undeniable. George Eliot was a student of Comte; and even many of those who were not were yet affected by ideas in the air which derived from him. For example, Swinburne, whom no one has yet accused of being a Comtist, was voicing the essential doctrine of the 'Philosophie positive' when he wrote in *Songs Before Sunrise*:

> Not each man of all men is God, but God is the fruit of the whole.

Comte did, in fact, attempt to devise an immanentist religion in which a transcendent God was displaced by Humanity, conceived as a single entity and advancing towards perfection:

> A deeper study of the great universal order reveals to us at length the ruling power within it of the true Great Being, whose destiny it is to bring that order continually to perfection by constantly conforming to its laws.

The lengths to which Comte developed his Religion of Humanity caused Huxley to describe it as 'ultramontane Christianity without Christ.' This doctrine can never have been very congenial to Hardy, who never had any such bent towards sociological idealism as had Shelley or Swinburne. He naturally read Comte; but it is doubtful whether

he took anything from him. The hope of the gradual perfection of the world order which is faintly suggested in the
Dynasts bears very little, if any, resemblance to anything
in Comte. As far as it was not Hardy's own, it was the fruit
of hints from J. S. Mill, and von Hartmann. Moreover,
cognate ideas were common enough in the later nineteenth
century; they are to be found, for instance in Renan.[1]
In many important respects, the ideas which Comte
entertained for the emergence of a better order of things were
diametrically opposed to those of Hardy.[2]

It was towards the close of the eighteen-seventies that
there crept over Hardy a deep and incurable nostalgia,
very clearly to be traced in his writing. He had never been
gay. The author of *A Pair of Blue Eyes* was a potential—
perhaps more than a potential—tragedian. There is tragedy
of a kind in *Far From the Madding Crowd*. But the tragedy
darkens in *The Return of the Native*; and, above all, it takes a
philosophical tinge of universality for which we should
seek vainly in the early writings. It can best be illustrated
by example. In the very first, famous, chapter of *The Return*
we may read:

> The new Vale of Tempe may be a gaunt waste in Thule;
> human souls may find themselves in closer and closer harmony
> with external things wearing a sombreness distasteful to our
> race when it was young. The time seems near, if it has not
> actually arrived, when the chastened sublimity of a moor, a
> sea, or a mountain will be all of nature that is absolutely in
> keeping with the moods of the more thinking among mankind.

In the fifth chapter of the second book, Yeobright's face is
described:

> He already showed that thought is a disease of the flesh,
> and indirectly bore evidence that ideal physical beauty is in-
> compatible with emotional development and a full recognition
> of the coil of things.

---

[1] Dr. de Ridder Barzin even suggests a comparison of Hardy with Renan, 'le
philosophe du devenir,' *Le Pessimisme de Hardy*, p. 71.

[2] For example, those on the relations between the sexes. Comte laid great stress
on marriage and the importance of its being indissoluble.

The beginning of the third book contains a still more significant passage:

> The truth seems to be that a long line of disillusive centuries has permanently displaced the Hellenic idea of life, or whatever it may be called. What the Greeks only suspected, we know well; what their Aeschylus imagined, our nursery children feel.[1] That old-fashioned revelling in the general situation grows less and less possible as we uncover the defects of natural laws, and see the quandary that man is in by their operation.

The Return of the Native was written in 1877. By that time, the first wave of enthusiasm over the theory of evolution had spent its force, and it was giving place to a profound disillusion. For such men as Hardy, science had utterly destroyed the basis of religion. And, at least in Hardy's case, it had not left him the permanent consolation of a perpetual 'progress' in its stead. It was inevitable that he should now be writing about 'the defects of natural laws and the quandary that man is in by their operation.'

Hardy was not the only writer who had come to despair over the plight of humanity. The 'seventies saw the appearance of one of the most profoundly sorrowful writings in the English language. On March 22nd, 1874, James Thomson's *City of Dreadful Night* began to appear in the pages of the *National Reformer*, a periodical which had been founded by a group of free-thinkers in 1860, and which was conducted for some thirty years by Charles Bradlaugh. This poem is a most eloquent illustration of the pessimism produced by the free-thinking crusaders of the mid-century, who had destroyed religion for many minds, and had given nothing in return but a deterministic nihilism. Without suggesting that Hardy was especially influenced by Thomson, it is interesting to show how Thomson expressed ideas which were later made more famous by Hardy. The substance of much of the philosophical argument in the *Dynasts* is given by the Preacher in the Church in the *City of Dreadful Night*:

[1]Hardy meant by this that Aeschylus suspected the world to be an illusion. See p. 37.

We bow down to the universal laws,
Which never had for man a special clause
Of cruelty or kindness, love or hate.
If toads and vultures are obscene to sight,
If tigers burn with beauty and with might,
Is it by favour or by wrath of fate?

All substance lives and struggles evermore
Through countless shapes continually at war,
By countless interactions interknit:
If one is born a certain day on earth,
All times and forces tended to that birth,
Nor all the world could change or hinder it.

I find no hint throughout the Universe
Of good or ill, of blessing or of curse;
I find alone Necessity supreme;
With infinite Mystery, abysmal, dark,
Unlighted ever by the faintest spark
For us the flitting shadows of a dream.

There is a famous passage in the fourth chapter of *Tess*,
in which Tess's little brother asks her if the stars are worlds;
and in which the girl is made to reply that they are worlds,
like apples on the stubbard tree, and that we live on a
blighted one. And in the fourth chapter of *Two on a Tower*,
St. Cleeve is expounding some of the mysteries of astronomy
to Lady Constantine. He says that twenty million stars are
visible in a powerful telescope; 'So that, whatever the stars
were made for, they were not made to please our eyes. It is
just the same in everything. Nothing was made for man.'
He then goes on to expound to her the size of the stellar
universe, which is of that order which reaches ghastliness:

And to add a new weirdness to what the sky possesses in its
size and formlessness, there is involved the quality of decay.
For all the wonder of these everlasting stars, eternal spheres,
and what not, they are not everlasting, they are not eternal;
they burn out like candles. You see that dying one in the body
of the great Bear? Two centuries ago it was as bright as the
others. The senses may become terrified by plunging among

them as they are, but there is a pitifulness even in their glory. Imagine them all extinguished, and your mind feeling its way through a heaven of total darkness, occasionally striking against the black invisible cinders of those stars. . . .

That could only have been written in the later nineteenth century. The theory of the universe upon which it is based is described by Sir James Jeans in the first chapter of *The Mysterious Universe*. But what were only theories concerning supposed physical facts to the scientists, became terrible to the artists who invested them with philosophical significance:

> With such a living light these dead eyes shine,
> These eyes of sightless heaven, that as we gaze
> We read a pity, tremulous, divine
> Or cold majestic scorn in their pure rays.
> Fond man! They are not haughty, are not tender;
> There is no heart or mind in all their splendour,
> They thread mere puppets all their marvellous maze.
>
> If we could near them with the flight unflown,
> We should but find them worlds as sad as this,
> Or suns all self-consuming like our own
> Enringed by planet worlds as much amiss:
> They wax and wane through fusion and confusion;
> The spheres eternal are a grand illusion,
> The empyrean is a void abyss.

When Edward Fitzgerald, in the 'fifties, was producing the remarkable poem, which is called a translation from Omar Khayyám, but which contains much that is so typical of the pessimism of the later nineteenth century in England, he was anticipating Thomson by twenty years. The first edition of his Rubáiyát in 1859 was stillborn. But by the 'eighties it had reached four editions; for then many had come to believe, with Hardy, that 'nothing is made for man.' And Fitzgerald bears the same burden as Thomson:

> And that inverted bowl we call the sky,
> Whereunder cooped we crawling live and die,
> Lift not thy hands to it for help—for it
> Rolls impotently on, as thou or I.

When the century had grown beyond its threescore years and ten, the strength of its thought indeed turned to labour and sorrow.

It is, then, against the whole background that has been outlined, that Hardy's later work must be regarded if we are to understand the deepening and darkening of his inspiration. If, in 1877, he wrote of the quandary in which man finds himself through the operation of defective natural laws, it was because the canker of thought had been at work. If, in 1880, he shuddered at the horrible abyss of heaven and grieved that nothing had been made for man, it was because he had eaten of the fruit of the Tree of Knowledge. Therefore, writing of the Dorsetshire labourer in *Longman's Magazine*, in July 1883, he wrote:

> It is among such communities as these that happiness will find her last refuge upon earth, since it is among them that a perfect insight into the conditions of existence will be longest postponed.

Therefore, the conclusion of *The Mayor of Casterbridge*, written in 1885, is that happiness is but an occasional episode in the general drama of pain.

Whether or no the physicists of the seventeenth century were right when they said that nature abhors a vacuum, it is certainly true that human nature does. Having reached a stage of spiritual vacuum by about 1880, Hardy seems to have set about trying to fill it by reading philosophy. As has already been shown, this was not the favourite of his younger years; and apart from such occasional allusions as might be found in the writing of any well-educated man, there is hardly a trace of philosophy, in the technical sense of the word, in his early works. Philosophy became the study of his middle life. On the last day of 1901 he wrote in his diary:

> After reading various philosophic systems, and being struck with their contradictions and futilities, I have come to this: Let every man make a philosophy for himself out of his own experience. He will not be able to escape using terms and

phraseology from earlier philosophers, but let him avoid adopting their theories if he values his own mental life. Let him remember the fate of Coleridge, and save years of labour by working out his own views as given him by his surroundings.[1]

When he was eighty, he composed a ditty which appears in *Winter Words*:

'Our Old Friend Dualism'

All hail to him, the Protean! A tough old chap is he:
Spinoza and the monists cannot make him cease to be.
We pound him with our 'Truth, Sir, please!' and quite appear to
    still him:
He laughs, holds Bergson up, and James; and swears we cannot
    kill him.
We argue them pragmatic cheats. 'Aye,' says he. 'They're
    deceiving:
But I must live; for flamens plead I am all that's worth believing!'

To this had the study of philosophy brought him in his old age. . . . It is, however, very interesting to trace the beginning of his philosophical studies in his writing in the mid-'eighties. They are very clearly visible in *The Wood-landers*, which was begun in 1885, and finished during 1886; where they are exemplified in the person of Fitzpiers, and his studies in philosophy. To avoid falling into the error of some of the earnest American thesis writers, it must be admitted that Hardy sometimes had his tongue in his cheek, even on the subject of philosophy. He makes Grammer Oliver describe Fitzpiers thus:

> And yet he's a projick, and says the oddest of rozums. 'Ah Grammer', he said at another time, 'Let me tell you that Everything is Nothing. There's only Me and Not Me in the whole world.' And he told me that no man's hands could help what they did, any more than the hands of a clock.

But Hardy was now too much sicklied o'er with the pale cast of thought to jest as he had jested in *Far from the Madding Crowd*. Two pages later we are made to follow

[1] *Later Years*, p. 91.

Melbury and his daughter into a wood which at once confronts us again with the problem of the Universe:

> Here, as everywhere, the Unfulfilled Intention, which makes life what it is, was as obvious as it could be among the depraved crowds of a city slum. The leaf was deformed, the curve was crippled, the taper was interrupted; the lichen ate the vigour of the stalk, and the ivy slowly strangled to death the promising sapling.

This could be compared to many of Hardy's poems. It was in an attempt to solve this riddle of the Unfulfilled Intention that he turned to the philosophers, with their enigmas of 'Me and Not Me.' That Fitzpiers quotes Spinoza (in Chap. XVI), and Schleiermacher (in Chap. XIX), is in itself little. What is significant is that Hardy should now be studying the problem of the 'ipsa hominis essentia,' and the riddle of Reality. How this study progressed could easily be illustrated out of *Tess* and *Jude*. But so many catalogues have already been made of the passages in which Tess is described as a 'psychological phenomenon', and what not, that time need not be wasted in repeating them. Moreover, they are largely misleading. The character of Marty South, the pity and the beauty of the life and death of Tess, which are great possessions in our literature, owe nothing to Hardy's wrestlings with the theories of the 'Thing-in-Itself.' The work which does owe something of its essential character to Hardy's speculations upon the nature of reality and the Universe, and to his philosophical studies during the last fifteen years of the century, is the *Dynasts*.

The subject of the philosophy of the *Dynasts* has by now been discussed almost *ad nauseam*. It was naturally pounced upon by the reviewers when the work first appeared, with its provocative preface about 'the wide prevalence of the Monistic theory of the Universe . . . and the abandonment of the masculine pronoun in allusions to the First or Fundamental Energy.' The author of the article on the *Dynasts* in the *Edinburgh Review* in 1908 took Hardy severely to task[1]; and all the critics since that date have had their say about the philosophy of the *Dynasts*. It would probably be difficult to improve upon the original verdict pronounced upon the First Part by Max Beerbohm:

> The book closes, and (so surely has it cast its spell upon us) seems quite a fugitive and negligible piece of work. We wonder why Mr. Hardy wrote it; or rather, one regrets that the Immanent Will put him to the trouble of writing it. 'Wot's the good of anythink? Wy, Nothink!' was the refrain of a popular coster song some years ago, and Mr. Hardy has set it ringing in our ears again. But presently the mood passes. And, even as in the stage directions of the *Dynasts* we see specks becoming mountain tops, so do we begin to realise that we have been reading a really great book.
>
> Cries Mr. Hardy's Spirit of the Pities:
>
> > This tale of Will,
> > And Life's impulsion by Incognisance
> > I cannot take.
>
> Nor can I. But I can take, and treasure with all gratitude, the book in which that tale is told so finely.[2]

The same thing was said more seriously by Dr. Lascelles Abercrombie when he wrote of the supernatural part of the *Dynasts*:

> 'It would be easy to say that as a philosophy of existence, this will not do. But as a tragedy of existence it is surely magnificent.'[3]

So much has been written about Hardy's real or supposed debt to Schopenhauer that there would appear little left to be said. While Gosse maintained that Hardy's philosophy was complete by 1874, that he had never then heard of Schopenhauer, and that he owed nothing to Schopenhauer whatever,[4] Brennecke in *Thomas Hardy's Universe*, derives the entire scheme of the *Dynasts* from *Die Welt als Wille und Vorstellung*, and wholly ignores everything that Hardy read

[1] *Edinburgh Review*, Vol. 207, p. 421.
[2] *Saturday Review*, Vol. 97, p. 136.
[3] *Thomas Hardy*: A Critical Study.
[4] A letter from Gosse to this effect is quoted at the end of Hedgcock's *Thomas Hardy: Penseur et Artiste*.

in the first forty-five years of his life. Both these positions are obviously untenable. In a well-written but rather slight essay published at Philadelphia in 1911, Helen Garwood discussed the resemblances between Hardy and Schopenhauer, and came to the conclusion that:

> The two men are not entirely alike in the details of their problem, not at all alike in their solution; they are alike in starting from the same basis, the basis of utter purposelessness. It might be possible to parallel many a passage in Schopenhauer with a like one in Hardy. Such a process is neither entertaining nor entirely trustworthy. It savours too much of seeing what we want to see. But without unduly stretching the material to fit the theory, it is possible to say that they are alike in the spirit which drives them to utterance.[1]

Without being dogmatic, it is possible by a few quotations to suggest what Hardy may have owed to Schopenhauer, as it has been suggested what he owed to Herbert Spencer and J. S. Mill. It is essential to remember, as critics in their haste for affiliations have not always done, that Hardy did not read German with ease; and that it can therefore only be a question of English translations when the subject of his debt to German philosophy is raised. There had been some talk of Schopenhauer in England during the 'seventies.[2] But the first English version of *Die Welt als Wille und Vorstellung* was that by Haldane and Kemp, which was published in three volumes in 1883. Hardy bought this book, and it is still in his library.

In the second book of *The World as Will and Idea*, which treats of the objectification of the Will, Schopenhauer defines Will, and explains his preference for the concept of Will to that of Force as the underlying Principle of the Universe. He then, in Section 23, continues:

> The *Will* as a thing in itself is quite different from its phenomenal appearance, and entirely free from all the forms of the phenomenal, into which it first passes when it manifests

---

[1] *Thomas Hardy: An Illustration of the Philosophy of Schopenhauer*, p. 40.

[2] A Life of Schopenhauer appeared in 1875, and the *Westminster Review*, published an article upon him.

itself, and which therefore only concern its objectivity. . . . The uncaused nature of will has been actually recognised, where it manifests itself most distinctly, as the will of man, and this has been called free, independent. But on account of the uncaused nature of the will itself, the necessity to which its manifestation is everywhere subjected has been overlooked, and actions are treated as free, which they are not. . . . The fact is overlooked that the individual, the person, is not will as a thing-in-itself, but is a phenomenon of will, is already determined as such, and has come under the form of the phenomenal, the principle of sufficient reason. Hence arises the strange fact that everyone believes himself *a priori* to be perfectly free, even in his individual actions and thinks that at every moment he can commence another manner of life. But *a posteriori*, through experience, he finds to his astonishment that he is not free, but subjected to necessity.

This is the doctrine which the Pities find so hard to accept in the Forescene of the *Dynasts*, even when shown the 'anatomy of the Immanent Will,' which, says the Spirit of Years, is:

> the while unguessed
> Of those it stirs, who (even as ye do) dream
> Their motions free, their orderings supreme;
> Each life apart from each, with power to mete
> Its own day's measures; balanced, self-complete;
> Though they subsist but atoms of the One
> Labouring through all, divisible from none;
> But this no further now. Deem yet man's deeds self-done.

In Section 25, Schopenhauer deals with the unity of the will:

The thing-in-itself is, as such, free from all forms of knowledge, even the most universal, that of being an object for the subject. In other words, the thing-in-itself is something altogether different from the idea.[1] If, now, this thing is the *will*, as I believe I have fully and convincingly proved it to be, then, regarded as such and apart from its manifestation, it lies outside time and space and therefore knows no multiplicity and is con-

[1] Schopenhauer has his own use of the word 'idea,' which he employs to mean 'phenomenon'; claiming this to be the Platonic, as opposed to the Kantian, sense.

sequently *one*.[1] Yet, as I have said, it is not one in the sense in which an individual or a concept is one, but as something to which the condition of the possibility of multiplicity, the *principium individuationis*, is foreign. The multiplicity of things in space and time, which collectively constitutes the objectification of the will, does not affect the will itself, which remains individual notwithstanding it.

In Section 28 there is a further remark upon the unity of the will:

> As the magic-lantern shows many different pictures which are all made visible by one and the same light, so in all the multifarious phenomena which fill the world together or throng after each other as events, only *one will* manifests itself, of which everything is the visibility, the objectivity, and which remains unmoved in the midst of this change; it alone is thing-in-itself; all objects are manifestations, or, to speak the language of Kant, phenomena.

In Section 29 Schopenhauer deals with the question:

> Every will is a will towards something, has an object, an end of its willing; what then is the final end, or towards what is that will striving that is exhibited to us as the being-in-itself of the world? This question rests, like so many others, upon the confusion of the thing-in-itself with its manifestations. The principle of sufficient reason, of which the law of motivation is also a form, extends only to the latter, not to the former. It is only of phenomena, of individual things, that a ground can be given, never of the will itself.

Schopenhauer's conclusion on the subject of the will is this:

> In fact, freedom from all aim, from all limits, belongs to the nature of the will, which is an endless striving. . . . Eternal becoming, an endless flux, characterizes the revelation of the inner nature of the will.

This is the constant burden of the Spirits in the *Dynasts*. As good an example as any is to be found in the antiphonal

---

[1] In Hardy, who was not so subtle at metaphysics, space and time are part of the 'laws' of Immanent Will. But Schopenhauer simply means that the will is not subject to the *principium individuationis*.

chant of the semichoruses of the Ironic Spirits during Waterloo (Pt. 3, Act vii, Sc. viii):

> Of Its doings if It knew
> What It does It would not do!
> Since It knows not, what far sense
> Speeds its spinnings in the Immense?
> None; a fixed foresightless dream
> Is Its whole philosopheme.
> Just so; an unconscious planning,
> Like a potter raptly panning!
> Are then Love and Light its aim—
> Good its glory, Bad its blame?
> Nay; to alter evermore
> Things from what they were before.

Although, as has been shown, he may have taken a hint from Herbert Spencer twenty years before, there cannot be any doubt that it was Hardy's reading in Schopenhauer after 1884 which determined the final form of the poem on the Napoleonic wars which he had long been meditating.[1] The correspondence between the presentation of the Immanent Will in the *Dynasts*, and Schopenhauer's discussion of the objectification of the Will in the second book of *The World as Will and Idea*, cannot be merely fortuitous. Brennecke rightly claims that the evidence of the language alone would refute such a theory. An interesting point of detail is the conception of Napoleon. In Section 26 of his second book, Schopenhauer, considering man as an objectification of the Will, writes:

> Motives do not determine the character of a man, but only the phenomena of his character, that is his actions; the outward fashion of his life, not its inner meaning and content. These proceed from the character which is the immediate manifestation of the will, and is therefore groundless. . . . Whether a man shows his badness in petty acts of injustice, cowardly tricks and low knavery which he practises in the narrow sphere of his circumstances, or whether as a conqueror he oppresses nations, throws a world into lamentation and sheds the blood

[1] See p. 275.

of millions; this is the outward form of his manifestation, that which is unessential to it, and depends upon the circumstances in which fate has placed him, upon his surroundings, upon external influences, upon motives, but his decision upon these motives can never be explained from them; it proceeds from the will, of which man is a manifestation.

It has often been brought as a criticism against the *Dynasts* that Napoleon is a mere puppet. Says the Spirit of the Years at Ulm:

> So let him speak, the while we clearly sight him
> Moved like a figure on a lantern slide.
> Which, much amazing uninitiate eyes,
> The all-compelling crystal pane but drags
> Whither the showman wills—
>
> (Pt. 2, Act iv, Sc. vi.)

Hardy, possibly partly under the influence of Haeckel (whose *Riddle of the Universe*, translated into English in 1900, he must have read just before writing the *Dynasts*), was a much more thorough determinist than Schopenhauer, who was born in the eighteenth century. In the chorus of the Spirits before Austerlitz, the Ironic Spirits ask:

> O Innocents, can ye forget
> That things to be were shaped and set
> Ere mortals and this planet met?

And Hardy would have said that the surroundings, external influences and motives which are the phenomena of a man's character, proceed as much from the 'All urging Will, raptly magnipotent,' as does the inner nature of the man himself—the *ipsa hominis essentia*, as Spinoza called it.

The fourth book of *The World as Will and Idea* deals with the assertion and denial of the will, and contains an elaborate exposition of the necessity of universal suffering. There is a close similarity between the tone of this and that of Hardy's last works on a large scale, especially *Jude*:

> It is really incredible how meaningless and void of signifi-
> cance when looked on from without, how dull and unen-
> lightened by intellect when felt from within, is the course of

the life of the great majority of men. It is a weary longing and complaining, a dreamlike staggering through the four ages of life to death, accompanied by a series of trivial thoughts. Such men are like clockwork, which is wound up, and goes it knows not why; and every time a man is begotten and born, the clock of human life is wound up anew to repeat the same old piece it has played innumerable times before, passage after passage, measure after measure, with insignificant variations. Every individual, every human being and his course of life, is but another short dream of the endless spirit of nature, of the persistent will to live; is only another fleeting form, which it carelessly sketches on its infinite page, space and time, allows to remain for a time so short that it vanishes into nothing in comparison with these, and then obliterates to make new room. And yet, and here lies the serious side of life, every one of these fleeting forms, these empty fancies, must be paid for by the whole will to live, in all its activity, with many and deep sufferings and finally with a bitter death.

In the nineteenth chapter of *Tess of the d'Urbervilles*, Tess says to Angel Clare:

> What's the use of learning that I am one of a long row only—finding out that there is set down in some old book somebody just like me and to know that I shall only act her part; making me sad, that's all. The best is not to remember that your nature and your past doings have been just like thousands' and thousands', and that your coming life and doings 'll be like thousands' and thousands'.

Such sentiment is depressing stuff. And there is a large quantity of it in Schopenhauer. The realization that Hardy steeped himself in such reading helps to an understanding of *Jude the Obscure*. The paragraph quoted might, indeed, be the text upon which *Jude* is a sermon; and it explains why, to many critics and readers, *Jude* is so much inferior to Hardy's great novels; for out of futility it is not possible to make anything great. That *Jude* was largely the result of Hardy's reading in Schopenhauer is, of course, only conjecture. The conjecture is, however, supported by one very significant piece of internal evidence. The last part of the fourth book of *The World as Will and Idea* is devoted to the denial of the will to live. Schopenhauer preaches that the overcoming of suffering and the attainment of peace can be achieved through the denial of the will to live by asceticism and self-denial. It is, he says, only by denying the will to live, of which his own body is the objectification, that man can pierce the veil of Maya and escape from the *principium individuationis*. In the horrible second chapter of the sixth part of *Jude the Obscure*, when Arabella's son Time has hanged Sue's children and himself, Jude says:

> It was in his nature to do it. The Doctor says there are such boys springing up amongst us—boys of a sort unknown in the last generation—the outcome of new views of life. They seem to see all its terrors before they are old enough to have staying power to resist them. *He says it is the beginning of the coming universal wish not to live.*

Now, although Schopenhauer devotes an entire section (69) to suicide, which he demonstrates to be actually the strongest possible assertion of the will to live, and which he calls 'the masterpiece of Maya,' it can hardly be denied that the man who wrote the words just quoted from *Jude* had been reading the chapter on the denial of the will to live. His speech betrays him.

In connection with the metaphysics of the *Dynasts*, there is another philosopher to be mentioned to whom Hardy once acknowledged that he owed something. The nature of the debt is not difficult to show, although the only attempt hitherto made to draw a 'parallelism' between Hardy and Eduard von Hartmann is most unsatisfactory.[1] In a volume entitled *Real Conversations* which William Archer published in 1904, there is one with Hardy. In the course of it he reports Hardy as saying:

> A ghost story that should convince me would make me a happier man. And if you come to that, I don't know that the grotesqueness, the incompleteness of the manifestations (of spiritualism) is at all conclusive against their genuineness. Is

[1] George R. Swann: *Philosophical Parallelisms in Six English Novelists.*

not this incompleteness a characteristic of all phenomena, of the universe at large? It often seems to me like a half-expressed, an ill-expressed, idea. Do you know Hartmann's philosophy of the Unconscious? It suggested to me what seems almost like a workable theory of the great problem of the origin of evil—though this, of course, is not Hartmann's own theory—namely, that there may be a consciousness, infinitely far off, at the other end of the chain of phenomena . . . ?

It is much to be regretted that Archer did not simply confess his ignorance of von Hartmann, and bring Hardy out a little further, instead of trying to cover it up, and drawing a red herring across the trail by talking about the Manichaean heresy. His further report of Hardy's words shows that he did not understand what Hardy was referring to. But there is enough to show that Hardy did speak of *The Philosophy of the Unconscious*.

Von Hartmann began to be discussed in England in the later 'seventies.[1] *Die Philosophie des Unbewusstes* was translated into English by W. C. Coupland, and published in three volumes in 1884. Even if Hardy had not said so, there would be no doubt that he had read this work; especially that part of it which deals with the metaphysics of the Unconscious. It is curious that he should have told Archer at the beginning of the century what is obviously true, namely, that Hartmann had suggested to him a working theory of the origin of evil, which he embodied in the *Dynasts* as the theory of the unconscious nature of the First Cause; and then that he should later have claimed entire originality for the theory of the gradual emergence of consciousness, which is an integral part of von Hartmann's philosophy. This theory peeps out in places elsewhere, but is adumbrated in set terms in the After Scene. The Spirit of the Pities says to the Spirit of the Years:

> Thou arguest still the Inadvertent Mind.
> But even so, shall blankness be for aye?
> Men gained cognition from the flux of time,

[1] See *Westminster Review* for 1876.

> And wherefore not the Force informing them,
> When far-ranged aions past all fathoming
> Shall have swung by, and stand as backward years?

And the *Dynasts* ends upon the hope of

'Consciousness the Will informing, till It fashion all things fair——'

In a letter on the *Dynasts* which Hardy wrote in 1914,[1] he said:

> The assumption of unconsciousness in the driving force is, of course, not new. But I think the view of the unconscious force as gradually *becoming* conscious; i.e., that consciousness is creeping further and further back towards the origin of force, had never (as far as I know) been advanced before the *Dynasts* appeared.

The third chapter of von Hartmann's *Metaphysics of the Unconscious* is on the origin of consciousness; and in it he says:

> We have seen (in the first chapter) how Will and Idea are united in the Unconscious as an inseparable unity, and we shall see further in the final chapters how the salvation of the world depends on the emancipation of the intellect from the Will, the possibility of which is given in consciousness, and how the whole world process is tending slowly towards this goal.

In order to appreciate what the metaphysic of the *Dynasts* may have owed—almost certainly did owe—to von Hartmann, it is necessary to glance at the seventh chapter of the *Metaphysics of the Unconscious*, which is entitled 'The Unconscious and the God of Theism.' Here von Hartmann writes:

> If hitherto theism has eagerly insisted on assigning to God a consciousness of his own in the sphere of his divinity, this has happened for two reasons, both of which had their justification, but from which an illegitimate conclusion was drawn, because the possibility of an unconscious intelligence had never been conceived. These two grounds are: firstly, as regards man, repugnance to the thought, in default of a conscious God,

[1] *Later Years*, p. 270.

of being a blind product of natural forces, an unintended, un-watched, purposeless and transient result of fortuitous necessity. Secondly, as regards God, the fear of thinking this supreme existence . . . to be destitute of that excellence which passes with the human mind for the highest, namely clear consciousness and distinct self-consciousness. Both scruples, however, disappear before a correct estimation of the principles of the Unconscious, which hold the golden mean between a theism constructed of the floating human ideal made absolute, and a naturalism in which the highest flowers of the mind and the eternal necessity of natural law from which they have sprung, are mere results of a casual actuality, imposing to us on account of our importance—the right mean between conscious teleology, which is conceived after the human prototype, and entire renunciation of final causes. This right mean just consists in the recognition of a final causality which, however, is not represented according to the pattern of conscious human purposive activity by discursive reflection, *but as immanent unconscious teleology of an intuitive unconscious intelligence is revealed in natural objects and individuals by means of the same activity, which, in the last chapter, we described as continual creation or conservation, or as real phenomenon of the All-One Existence.*

If there is such a thing as close resemblance between one abstract conception and another, surely we have an instance here. The sentences here italicised may be regarded as the immediate origin of Hardy's metaphysic of the Immanent Will.

What almost amounts to proof on internal evidence is provided by the next paragraph in the same chapter:

In our inability positively to apprehend the mode of perception of this intelligence, we are only able to indicate it through the contrast to our own form of perception (consciousness); thus, only to characterise it by the negative predicate of Unconsciousness. But we know from the previous enquiries that the function of this unconscious intelligence is anything but blind, rather far seeing, nay, even *clairvoyant*, although this seeing can never be aware of its own vision, but only of the world, and without the mirrors of the individual consciousness can also not see the seeing eye. Of this unconscious clairvoyant intelligence we have come to perceive that in its infallible purposive activity, embracing out of time all ends and means in one, and always including all necessary data within its ken, it infinitely transcends the halting, stilted gait of the discursive reflection of consciousness, ever limited to a single point, dependent on sense-perception, memory and inspirations of the Unconscious. *We shall then be compelled to designate this intelligence, which is superior to all consciousness, at once unconscious and super-conscious.*

In Scene iv, Act v of the First Part of the *Dynasts*, following the death of Nelson, there occurs one of the high-water marks of the supernatural debate. After the Spirit of the Pities has quoted Sophocles, and a chorus of Pities has reviled the morality of the Immanent Will, the Spirit of the Years replies:

> Nay, blame not! For what judgment can ye blame?
> In that immense unweeting Mind is shown
> One far above forethinking; processive,
> Yet super-conscious; a Clairvoyancy
> That knows not what It knows, yet works therewith.

As to Hardy's claim—which, it should in justice be said, was made when he was seventy-four and cannot have had perfect memory—that the idea of the becoming-conscious of the Will was his own, it hardly seems to stand; for in the same chapter of the Metaphysics of the Unconscious there occurs this passage:

> Unquestionably, besides its value for the individual as such, consciousness has also in addition a universal significance for the redemption of the world, i.e., for the conversion of the World Will. . . . For this final purpose the All-One does in fact need consciousness, and accordingly it possesses the same —namely in the sum of individual consciousnesses, whose common subject it is.

In the letter to the *Academy* in 1902, which has already been quoted, Hardy mentioned Haeckel; from which it is to be inferred that he had at least looked into that writer.

Ernst Haeckel (1834–1919) was primarily a scientist, and was, indeed, the most distinguished German zoologist of his generation. In the introduction to *The Descent of Man* in 1871, Darwin wrote of his *Natürliche Schöpfungsgeschichte*:

> If this work had appeared before my essay had been written, I should probably never have completed it.

One or two of Haeckel's works were translated into English fairly early. *Freedom in Science and Teaching*, which was largely concerned with a controversy over Evolution in the German scientific world, appeared in 1879 with a prefatory note by Huxley. It was followed by *The Pedigree of Man and Other Essays* in 1883. Both these books, however, were so largely scientific as to be unlikely to appeal to a layman like Hardy. That one of Haeckel's works which had the widest circulation among the ordinary public was *Die Welträtsel* (1899). This was translated into English and appeared in 1900 as *The Riddle of the Universe*. It was much discussed at the time, and provoked a reply from Sir Oliver Lodge; and Hardy would certainly have looked into it.[1] *The Riddle of the Universe* is a popular exposition, in rather provocative language, of an extreme form of materialism. Haeckel claims that science has conclusively established that there is no such thing as soul; that all deductions from the hypothesis of soul, including, of course, all religion, are mere delusions; and that the religion of the twentieth century will be "scientific monism." Reading *The Riddle of the Universe* with its cocksure assumptions, one can understand why Sir James Jeans in 1930 wrote at the end of *The Mysterious Universe*:

> Our main contention can hardly be that the science of to-day has a pronouncement to make. Perhaps it ought rather to be that science should leave off making pronouncements.

If Hardy had shared that view of science, he would have been a happier man; but he took the scientists of the nineteenth century at their own estimation. It is unlikely that he

[1] See p. 106.

took much from Haeckel, who in any case has no standing in philosophy; but it may be that a recent reading of *The Riddle of the Universe* was responsible for the phrase in the Preface to the *Dynasts*: 'The wide prevalence of the Monistic theory of the Universe in this twentieth century. . . .' The assumption is not necessary, for such a student of philosophy as Hardy had become must long since have been familiar with the term 'monism' and all that it implied, although it was chiefly popularized by Haeckel.[1]

Other writers might be added, who influenced Hardy's thought from 1860 onwards. Gibbon, for example, was certainly one. Like many other agnostics, Hardy had made a study of the famous fifteenth and sixteenth chapters of the *Decline and Fall*; and their author is one of the 'Christminster Ghosts' in *Jude*. The significant reference to the chapter on Julian the Apostate in *Jude* has already been quoted. There is an equally significant reference to Gibbon in the Preface to *The Woodlanders*.[2] The caustic poem in *Poems of the Past and Present*, inspired by Gibbon's garden at Lausanne, was written while Hardy was still smarting from the lash of the critics of *Jude*—episcopal and other; so that it is not surprising that he made the shade of the historian say to him:

> How fares the Truth now? Ill?
> Do pens but slyly further her advance?
> May one not speed her but in phrase askance?
> Do scribes aver the Comic to be Reverend still?
>
> Still rule those minds on earth
> At whom sage Milton's wormwood words were hurled:
> 'Truth like a bastard comes into the world
> Never without ill fame to him who gives her birth'?

The quotation is from Milton's *Doctrine and Discipline of Divorce*, which is also quoted for the chapter heading to the

---

[1] According to the N.E.D., the word 'monism' first appears in the eighteen-sixties. There is one instance of 'monist' in the writings of Sir W. Hamilton, in the 'thirties.

[2] 'As Gibbon blandly remarks on the evidence for and against Christian miracles, the duty of an historian does not call upon him to interpose his private judgment in this nice and important controversy.'

fourth part of *Jude*; so that we may add some of Milton's more daring prose works to Hardy's philosophical studies.

Another book which Hardy read was Strauss' *Life of Jesus* as translated by George Eliot. The edition of this book which is still in his library is that of 1892; and he must have studied it extensively if he went to the expense of buying it. It was certainly from here that he started upon the track which caused him to produce what is perhaps the only one of his productions that dishonours him, the offensive poem called 'Panthera,' in *Time's Laughingstocks*. Even David Strauss describes the subject of this poem as 'the ancient Jewish blasphemy, which we find in Celsus and the Talmud.'[1] From the note at the head of this poem (of which the references are taken out of Strauss), we have incidental proof that Hardy had read *The Riddle of the Universe*; for it is there that Haeckel describes the legend, one most congenial to him.

A work which it is interesting to find in Hardy's not very large library is the French translation of Leopardi in three volumes, by F. A. Aulard, which was published in Paris in 1880. It is not surprising that the greatest pessimistic poet of the nineteenth century should, even if only in translation, appear on Hardy's shelves; their names have been coupled more than once,[2] and there is a reference to Leopardi in *Tess* (Chap. XXV). Hardy, whose faith in God, in life and in happiness had been destroyed by 'rationalism,' might well have echoed the words of Leopardi:

> E figurato è il mondo in breve carta;
> Ecco tutto è simile, e discoprendo
> Solo il nulla s'accresce.[3]

For the one as for the other, nothing remained after that study except sorrow:

---

[1] Part 1, Chap. III, Section 28. (P. 139 in the edition of 1892.)
[2] By Hedgcock, and also by Abercrombie.
[3] Aulard renders: 'Voici maintenant que le monde est représenté dans une petite carte. Voici que tout est semblable et que les découvertes n'accroissent que notre néant.'

THE BACKGROUND TO HARDY'S THOUGHT

Il certo e solo
Veder che tutto è vano altro che il duolo.[1]

It seems unlikely that Hardy can have been materially
affected by reading Leopardi in French after he was forty.
And yet, if he wished to feel that others before him had
walked through the Slough of Despond, he could hardly
have found in the literature of Europe a poet more suitable
to his purpose:

Or poserai per sempre
Stanco mio cor. Perì l'inganno estremo
Ch'eterno io mi credei. Perì. Ben sento,
In noi di cari inganni,
Non che la speme, il desiderio è spento.
Posa per sempre. Assai
Palpitasti. Non val cosa nessuna
I moti tuoi, nè di sospiri è degna
La terra. Amaro e noia
La vita, altro mai nulla; e fango è il mondo.
T'acqueta omai. Dispera
L'ultima volta. Al gener nostro il fato
Non donò che il morire. Omai disprezza
Te, la natura, il brutto
Poter che, ascoso, a commun danno impera,
E l'infinita vanità del tutto.[2]

For three-quarters of a century, Hardy had studied
such writings as these, from the days when, as a child in
Stinsford church, he had heard read out the lamentation of
the Preacher—'Vanity of Vanities, all is vanity.' For him,
too, at last, the day drew nigh in which all the daughters of
music should be brought low. Some hours before he died,

[1] 'Rien, si ce n'est de savoir avec certitude que tout est vain, excepté la douleur,
vous reste.'

[2] Aulard renders thus: 'Maintenant tu te reposeras pour toujours, mon coeur
fatigué. Elle a péri, l'erreur suprême que j'ai crue éternelle pour moi. Elle a péri. Je
sens bien, qu'en nous des chères erreurs non seulement l'espoir, mais le désir est
éteint. Repose-toi pour toujours. Tu as assez palpité. Aucune chose ne mérite tes
battements, et de tes soupirs la terre n'est pas digne. Amertume et ennui, voila la
vie; elle n'est rien d'autre, le monde n'est que fange. Repose-toi désormais. Dés-
espère à jamais. A notre race le destin n'a donné que de mourir. Méprise désormais et
toi-même, et la nature, et le pouvoir honteux, qui, caché, régne pour la ruine com-
mune, et l'infinie vanité de ce tout.'

after long silence and as dusk was falling, he asked his wife to read to him a certain verse from Fitzgerald's Omar; and she read:

> O Thou who man of baser earth didst make,
> And even with Paradise devise the snake—
> For all the sin wherewith the face of man
> Is blackened, man's forgiveness give—and take!

He signed to her to close the book.[1]

[1] *Later Years*, p. 266.

CHAPTER IV

HARDY'S EARLY WRITINGS

D ESPITE the precocity recorded by Mrs. Hardy, Hardy does not seem to have written anything during childhood and youth. If he did, no trace of it has remained, nor is there any record of such literary activity as that which, for example, was a feature of Macaulay's childhood.[1] The earliest flowering of his genius was in poetry; and this must be discussed in a later chapter. About his first recorded production in prose there hangs a mystery. According to Mrs. Hardy, this was a skit which appeared in a Dorchester paper, and was in the form of a plaintive letter from the ghost of the Alms House clock, removed from its bracket in South Street, Dorchester. Mrs. Hardy has told the present writer that she has never seen this letter, having based her account of it on her husband's recollections.[2] A search has not discovered anyone who has seen it, nor can it be traced either in the *Dorset County Chronicle* or the *Dorset County Express*, the only two Dorset papers of the period preserved at the British Museum. The Editor of the *Chronicle* replied to an inquiry that he had never been able to trace anything from Hardy's pen to his paper during the 'sixties. The date of the letter must have been between 1856 and 1862. His biographer says that Hardy also wrote some prose articles, which were never printed, before leaving Dorchester in April 1862. No further information about these is available.

In one of the letters written to his sister Mary during his first year in London,[3] Hardy says that he used in the evenings to go and read in the reading room of the Kensington

[1] *Life and Letters of Lord Macaulay*, by C. O. Trevelyan, Vol. I, p. 30, *et seq.*
[2] *Early Life*, p. 43.
[3] *Early Life*, p. 50 *et seq.*

Museum. This was in preparation for an Essay for the competition organized yearly by the Royal Institute of British Architects. The *Sessional Papers* of the Institute for 1862–3 (No. 2, Pt. 5), record that at a special general meeting of members on March 16th, 1863, the medal was adjudicated 'To Mr. Thomas Hardy of 9 Clarence Place, Kilburn, for his Essay *On the application of coloured bricks and terra cotta in modern architecture*; Motto: "Tentavi quid in eo genere possem."' It has proved impossible to find this Essay, either in print, or in manuscript; its disappearance from the Library of the Institute may be due to Hardy's having borrowed it to make a copy and having failed to return it. We know all that probably ever will be known about it from its title, and from the regulation with which it presumably complied that 'The Essays are to be written very legibly on alternate pages and are to be accompanied by suitable illustrations.' In A. P. Webb's *Bibliography of Thomas Hardy* there is reproduced what is described as 'the text of the judges' criticism,' presumably preserved by Hardy himself. This is as follows:

> The author of this essay has scarcely gone sufficiently into the subject proposed, and that portion referring to moulded and shaped bricks has scarcely been noticed. The essay, as far as it is written, is a very fair one, and deserves the medal; but, for the above reason, we cannot recommend that the supplementary sum of £10 be given with it.

A suggestion made to Hardy at this time that he might combine literature with architecture by becoming an art critic[1] does not seem to have been followed up. But in *Chambers' Edinburgh Journal* for Saturday, March 18th, 1865, there appeared an unsigned article entitled 'How I built Myself a House,' which Hardy wrote for his own amusement, and that of his fellow assistants at Blomfield's. Mrs. Hardy suggests that 'it may have been the acceptance of this *jeu d'esprit* that turned his mind in the direction of prose.'[2] The article is the earliest of Hardy's surviving compositions

[1] *Early Life*, p. 61.   [2] *Early Years*, p. 62.

in prose. Apart from its being quasi-autobiographical, the interest of 'How I built Myself a House' is not great. There is a certain pawky humour; but the style is, on the whole, remarkably undistinguished for the work of a great novelist in his twenty-sixth year. Contrasted with the poems which he wrote at that age, it shows how late was the development of his power of self-expression in prose. There are, nevertheless, one or two touches which foreshadow the maturer Hardy: for example:

> ' "If it could only be in the Chinese style, with beautiful ornaments at the corners, like Mrs. Smith's only better," she continued, *turning to me with a glance in which a broken tenth commandment might have been seen.*'

The Chinese conservatory is foolery; but the broken tenth commandment in the woman's glance tells of a greater power to come.

Towards the end of July 1867, Hardy's health having for some time been giving way in London, he returned to Dorchester, 'leaving most of his books and other belongings behind him at Westbourne Park.'[1] Being determined to do something in literature, and having learnt by experience that no one would pay for poetry, he began to write a novel, searching his own experiences for material. The original title of this novel was:

THE POOR MAN AND THE LADY
A Story with no Plot
Containing some original Verses.

This was later abridged to

THE POOR MAN AND THE LADY
By the Poor Man.[2]

One point of interest about this title is that it seems to indicate that the narrative was written in the first person. This was a continuation of the method of 'How I Built Myself a House.' The writing of the novel was continued throughout the winter; when it was completed, Hardy made

[1] *Early Life*, p. 71. [2] *Early Life*, p. 75.

a fair copy of the MS., and this was finished on June 9th, 1868.[1] At this point it will be convenient to give a plain statement of the further events without reference to authorities. The evidence upon which the statement is based will then be given.

Hardy posted the MS. on July 25th to Alexander Macmillan. On August 12th he received a reply. The substance of this was that Macmillan thought it undesirable to publish the story as it stood, but was considering whether it might do with modifications. Meanwhile he had shown the story to a friend, who had written a criticism which Macmillan enclosed. The friend was John Morley. Nothing further seems to have happened until December, when Hardy went to London and called on Macmillan. He there met Morley in person. Macmillan said he could not publish the novel, but that Chapman and Hall might do so. Hardy took the MS. to Chapman. Nothing happened until January 1869, when Hardy again went to London and called on Chapman. Chapman said he would publish it if Hardy would guarantee him twenty pounds. This Hardy did, and the book was put in hand. After some weeks, Chapman wrote to Hardy asking him to come and meet 'the gentleman who read your MS.'[2] Hardy went in March and met the gentleman, who was George Meredith. Meredith talked to Hardy about his novel, and advised him not to publish it. Hardy took away his MS.

This closes the first chapter in the history of Hardy's first novel. It has not hitherto been known what became of the manuscript. Mrs. Hardy writes:

> What he did with the MS. is uncertain, and he could not precisely remember in after years, though he found a few unimportant leaves of it—now also gone. He fancied that he may have sent it to some other publisher just as it stood to get another opinion before finally deciding its fate.[3]

[1] *Early Life*, p. 76.
[2] All the foregoing paragraph is based on *Early Life*, p. 76 *et seq.*
[3] *Early Life*, p. 83.

Edmund Gosse reported Hardy as having said, in a discussion of this lost novel in 1921, that

> some time afterwards he destroyed, as he thought, the whole MS., but lately he had come upon four or five pages of it, spared by some accident.[1]

Mr. V. H. Collins, who in 1928 published a small book called *Talks With Thomas Hardy*, there reported that he had asked Hardy whether there was any chance of his first novel being published, to which Hardy replied:

> It no longer exists. When I was moving I got rid of it. It does not occur to authors when they are young that some day their early unsuccessful efforts may come to have value.[2]

It is clear that when he was over eighty, Hardy had actually forgotten what he had done with the MS. half a century before. All the above evidence, including that of Mrs. Hardy, simply derives from Hardy himself. It is the more remarkable that the MS. should have vanished because Hardy seems generally to have taken care of his MSS., almost all of which are extant. But the most remarkable feature of the whole business is that SOME of the MS. survived, and was found by Hardy towards the end of his life, although it now no longer exists. Had he destroyed his early novel, as he told Collins, this would have been impossible, for all of it would then have perished together.

Sir Sydney Cockerell was kind enough to give me an account of what actually happened concerning the discovery of some of the MS. at Max Gate. He wrote:

> Hardy showed me in the latter half of 1916 a good portion of the MS. of *The Poor Man and the Lady* and I undertook to get it handsomely bound in blue morocco. This I did at a cost of two pounds and he seemed very pleased. But about ten years later he came to the conclusion that it ought not to be preserved and he burnt it himself in his study fire.

It may be noted that this MS. which came to light in 1916 did not consist only of a few leaves, as Hardy told his wife

[1] *Sunday Times*, January 22nd, 1928, 'Hardy's Lost Novel.'   [2] p. 54.

and Gosse; also that the date of Hardy's decision to burn it coincided with that when, possibly as a result of American publications, he burnt his private papers and diaries, and erased inscriptions in some of his books.

There is one explanation which covers all the facts, and one only. It is a perfectly simple one; and, although proof is wanting, circumstantial evidence that this is the true explanation is overwhelmingly strong. What happened was this: Hardy did not destroy the MS. of *The Poor Man and the Lady* in 1869. He saved it up. Some years later, when he was becoming an established novelist, he took his first novel (parts of which he had already used in *Desperate Remedies* and *Under the Greenwood Tree*), recast it, excised some portions, rewrote others, and published it under another title. For the purpose of recasting, he used the old MS., only taking out of it the sheets which contained cancelled matter. These were the sheets which he found in 1916, having probably preserved them as a memento, possibly with an idea that he might still make use of some of them. The rest of the MS., with all the alterations, went to the publisher.

In 1878 the July number of the *New Quarterly Magazine*, published by Chatto and Windus, contained a story, filling some sixty-five pages, entitled *An Indiscretion in the Life of an Heiress*, signed by Hardy. The pages which follow will show that this story was a version of Hardy's first, lost, novel *The Poor Man and the Lady*. There is no doubt that if we could recover from Limbo the MS. which Hardy sent to Chatto and Windus for the *New Quarterly* in 1878, it would prove to be the revised and altered MS. of *The Poor Man and the Lady*.

An Indiscretion in the Life of an Heiress had not been reprinted until recently, when Mrs. Hardy privately printed one hundred copies at the Curwen Press, Plaistow. Facing the title page of this reprint is the following:

> An Indiscretion in the Life of an Heiress is an adaptation by the author of his first novel, The Poor Man and the Lady, which was never published. The manuscript of the latter was

destroyed by Thomas Hardy some years before his death and no copy remains. This version appeared in the *New Quarterly Magazine* for July 1878, but was not published in book form.

In the spring of 1935, the press of the Johns Hopkins University published the story as a volume in the United States, with an introduction and notes by Carl J. Weber, Professor of English Literature in Colby College, and the author of a number of articles on Hardy in American periodical publications. The source from which his text was taken is a copy of the *New Quarterly Magazine* for July 1878, in the possession of Mr. Paul Lemperly, an American collector. Professor Weber's introduction consists of an hypothetical reconstruction of *The Poor Man and the Lady* in the form of one hundred numbered items: this is then compared with *An Indiscretion* in which Prof. Weber finds forty of the hundred. He concludes his introduction with these words:

> Hardy's first attempt at fiction was obviously intended to meet the usual Victorian three volume requirement. It seems reasonably clear that the contents of one volume were destroyed, the contents of a second found their way into other novels by Hardy, and the contents of the third may be read, in a slightly revised form, in the story which is here presented for the first time to American readers.

Professor Weber's convenient disposal into volumes is a little too good to be true. How much of *The Poor Man* Hardy used in later novels we shall never know. Prof. Weber does not mention the fact that *Desperate Remedies*, which was written in 1870, shortly after *The Poor Man*, but eight years before the publication of *An Indiscretion*, contains three sentences, and two quotations, which are to be found in *An Indiscretion*, of which more anon.

The remaining evidence concerning *The Poor Man and the Lady* consists of three main items: the account given by Mrs. Hardy on pp. 75 to 83 of *Early Life*; an article by Sir Edmund Gosse which appeared in *The Sunday Times*[1] on January 22nd, 1928, just after Hardy's death; and the letter

---

[1] Incorrectly described as 'the *London Times*,' by Prof. Weber.

which Macmillan wrote to Hardy after reading his MS., which was published in *The Life and Letters of Alexander Macmillan*, by Charles L. Graves, in 1910. The second of these will be reproduced here, and the third in Appendix I.

Mrs. Hardy's account is easily accessible. She tells the genesis and early history of *The Poor Man and the Lady*, as already related, up to the interview which Hardy had with Macmillan (and perhaps Morley also) in December 1868. It is curious, in view of the fact that Mrs. Hardy's narrative must be wholly based upon her husband's recollections, that he told her nothing of the interview with Morley of which he gave an account to Gosse. Mrs. Hardy, however, gives something more valuable than a recollection; and that is an extract from a written criticism of *The Poor Man* by Morley, which, she says, was enclosed in Macmillan's letter:

> He said that the book was "A very curious and original performance; *the opening pictures of the Christmas Eve in the tranter's house* are really of good quality; much of the writing is strong and fresh."

From the sentence italicized in the above, it becomes apparent that one of the best scenes in *Under the Greenwood Tree* originally appeared in *The Poor Man*. We know that Hardy used bits of his rejected novel of 1868 in *Desperate Remedies* in 1871 (possibly more than bits, but this can only be guessed); so that nothing is more likely than that he used others in *Under the Greenwood Tree* in 1872. The second and third, and parts of the seventh and eighth, chapters of that book may, if we only knew, be taken almost word for word from *The Poor Man and the Lady*. Mrs. Hardy relates the interview in the offices of Chapman and Hall in March 1869 in some detail. The substance of Meredith's criticism was: that Hardy's story was a sweeping dramatic satire of the squirearchy and nobility, with a socialistic, not to say revolutionary tendency; the style was not argumentative, but affectedly simple, with a naïve realism which Hardy had imitated in part from Defoe; but this did not deceive Meredith, who said that if Hardy published so pronounced a piece of propaganda the press would be about his ears like hornets, and his future would be injured.[1]

The upshot of this interview was that Hardy took away the MS. with him to decide on a course. *Meredith had added that Hardy could rewrite the story, softening it down considerably;* or what would be much better, put it away altogether for the present and attempt a novel with a purely artistic purpose, giving it a more complicated "plot" than was attempted with *The Poor Man and the Lady*.

Hardy partly took both pieces of advice. The sentence here italicized is clearly the genesis of *An Indiscretion in the Life of an Heiress*. The complicated plot appears in *Desperate Remedies*.

Extract from an article entitled 'Thomas Hardy's Lost Novel,' by Sir Edmund Gosse, which appeared in *The Sunday Times*, January 22, 1928.

(The first five paragraphs of the article in question are prefatory, or refer to other matters. In the following transcript of the remainder, those details of the plot of *The Poor Man and the Lady* which are to be found in *An Indiscretion in the Life of an Heiress* are italicized):

It was on an earlier occasion that he volunteered some precious reminiscences of his earliest effort at fiction, *The Poor Man and the Lady*. He said that he wrote it in 1867, soon after he left London and went to Weymouth. It took him a long time to finish, and now and then he could not get the story to move; it "stuck," but he persevered and ended it early the next year. He sent the MS. to Messrs. Macmillan, and for some time he heard no more. Then came a letter declining the book, but asking him to call at the publishing office.[2] Hardy came up

---

[1] That Meredith's advice, probably dictated by his own experience with *Modern Love* a year or two earlier, was correct, was proved by the fate which *Desperate Remedies* met with at the hands of the *Spectator* in 1871.

[2] This is not in the letter of August 10th, 1868, as published in *The Life and Letters of Alexander Macmillan*. It may have been in a subsequent letter, as Hardy appears to have called on Macmillan in December (*Early Life*, p. 78); or possibly Hardy may have confused Macmillan with Chapman, at whose invitation he called in March 1869 to be given the opinion of Meredith, Chapman's reader. The parallelism between the interview with Morley, as related by Gosse, and that with Meredith as related by Mrs. Hardy, is striking.

to town and paid his visit. He was shown in to a gentleman whom he believed to be old Mr. Alexander Macmillan, who said that he would like to introduce him to their reader, Mr. Morley. This he did, to Hardy's perturbation, since he had lately read with great admiration the *Edmund Burke*, and since this was the first time he had ever met an author of distinction. John Morley received him very kindly, but said they could not possibly publish the story, because it was crudely put together, but that it had interested him very much, and, oddly enough, he made the suggestion that he thought Hardy would do well to get practice by writing reviews of books. He offered the young architect a letter to John Douglas Cook, the editor of the *Saturday Review*. Hardy, however, thought to himself 'there is nothing in the world I could do less well,' and declined the introduction. As Cook was even then a dying man, it would in no case have been very serviceable. Hardy formed, however, a very lively enthusiasm for John Morley, who seemed to him the greatest man he had ever met. He took his own MS. away, and sent it to Messrs. Chapman & Hall, where it was read by George Meredith, and rejected in circumstances which are already known.

The moment seemed favourable for further information, so I pressed Hardy to tell me something of the plot of *The Poor Man and the Lady*, which he proceeded to do as follows:

'*The scene was laid in Dorsetshire, in the nineteenth century, and the hero was the son of peasants working on the estate of the great local squire.*[1] *This squire had a beautiful and spirited daughter who was his heiress.* The hero showed remarkable talent at the village school, and was patronized by the people of the great house, who had him educated as a draughtsman. When he was just grown up, *he was thrown by accident much into the company of the squire's daughter, who took a romantic interest in him.* Her parents, discovering this, *forbade her to communicate with him*[2]— for they had begun to write letters to each other—and the lad was sent up to London, where he was taken into the office of an

[1] In *A Pair of Blue Eyes*, the fact that Stephen Smith is the son of local peasant parents is the cause of the whole calamity, without which there would have been no story.

[2] In *An Indiscretion*, the forbidding comes at a later stage, but the situation is fundamentally the same.

eminent architect, and made striking progress.[1] *The lovers, however, were not able to resist the temptations of letter writing, and considered themselves betrothed.*[2] The squire discovered his daughter's disobedience, and intervened again. The young man became very hostile to the father, and took up radical politics in pique. *The great Wessex family now came up to their town house,* and, The Lady and the Poor Man contriving to meet, their engagement was secretly renewed. But he took to addressing public meetings, and once, while he was speaking passionately to a crowd in Trafalgar Square, the Lady drove by in her carriage, recognized him, and stopped to hear what he was saying. (Hardy paused here to remark that this was a rather remarkable prophecy, because at that time no such meetings had ever been held in Trafalgar Square, and John Morley actually pointed out this scene to him as absurd and impossible.)

The Lady's Conservative feelings were deeply wounded by this radical speech, and she broke off all relations with the young architect. A short time afterwards, however, *there was given a public concert at which the Lady happened to be seated alone in the last row of the expensive places, and the Poor Man immediately behind her in the front row of the cheap seats. Both were extremely moved by the emotion of the music, and, as she chanced to put her hand on the back of her seat, he took it in his and held it till the close of the performance.* They walked away together, and all their affection was renewed. She asked him to call upon her openly, at the great town house, and he did so.[3] Unluckily the Lady was out, and her mother received him with much anger and arrogance. He lost his temper, and they both became so excited that the mother fainted away. He found some water, and flung it over

[1] Although the details are here different, the result achieved is the same; namely that the hero goes to London and begins to attain a success which places him upon a different footing. In *The Poor Man and the Lady*, he appears to have followed Hardy by becoming an architect, and in *An Indiscretion*, he follows Hardy by becoming an author, so that the very differences are interesting, as Hardy used the two experiences he had himself known as the two versions of his story.

[2] In *An Indiscretion*, the letter in which Geraldine tells Edward of her father's ban on their correspondence ends with a postscript 'Might we not write just one line at very rare intervals? It is too much never to write at all.'

[3] In *An Indiscretion* the proposal to call is the man's. This, and Gosse's version of the episode, show how Hardy's increased knowledge of the world induced him to soften down the wild impossibilities of *The Poor Man and the Lady* into the much more probable events of *An Indiscretion* without material alteration of the general situation.

her face, with the result that the rouge ran down her cheeks. On coming to she discovered this, with redoubled rage, and the squire himself now coming in, ordered the footman to turn the architect out of the front door. *The family returned to Dorset-shire*, and no more letters passed between the lovers. In the course of time, however, the Poor Man learned from his relatives in Wessex that *the squire's daughter was just about to marry* the heir of a wealthy neighbouring landowner. On *the night before the wedding, hanging about the churchyard, the church still being open, the architect saw a muffled figure steal into the church, and, following it, found himself alone with the Lady. They had a very emotional interview*, she being at first very angry, and *then confessing that she had never loved any man but him*'.[1]

The story then ended, but Hardy could not recollect whether she married the proposed bridegroom or no. He racked his brain to remember, but in vain; he could not tell at all. Some time afterwards, he continued, he destroyed, as he thought, the whole manuscript, but lately he had come upon four or five pages of it, spared by some accident. I should read them next time I came to Max Gate, but we both forgot it. Hardy said that they were from the least interesting part of the book. I recall one other scrap of information about *The Poor Man and the Lady*. At some quite different, and much earlier time, he spoke to me of the lost novel, and admitted that it was very crude. "The only interesting thing about it," he added, "was that it showed a wonderful insight into female character. I don't know how that came about!" He said this with the utmost detachment. When in 1921 he gave me the particulars which I have repeated as nearly as possible in his own words, I told him I should write down notes of what he had said. "Oh, very well!" he replied; "they may be amusing some day. But it is hunting very small deer!" The student of his mind in its early development will hardly, I think, agree with him.

The third piece of evidence as to the nature of *The Poor Man and the Lady* is the letter which Macmillan wrote to Hardy when he rejected it. This is published in *The Life*

[1] In *An Indiscretion* the woman's avowal of her love comes a little later, when Geraldine comes to Egbert in the night.

and Letters of Alexander Macmillan (p. 289 *et seq.*) Some of
Macmillan's allusions require brief comment:

The description of country life among working men,
which remained Hardy's own peculiar province, and of
which he had a mastery probably unique in English literature, was the particular which struck the first experienced
reader of his first novel. As will later be seen, even the author
of the review which killed *Desperate Remedies* paid tribute
to Hardy's power of describing country folk.

That the squire in *The Poor Man and the Lady* sent for
the hero in a desperate attempt to save his daughter's life,
and that this ran counter to his prejudices, corresponds
exactly to the dying scene in *An Indiscretion*. There, it was
only by the insistence of the Doctor that Geraldine's
husband was told of what had happened; and to Geraldine's
request that she might be left alone with Egbert, her father
replies: 'Anything you wish, child . . . and anything can
hardly include more.'

It is only *supposition* that the award by 'The Palace of
Hobbies Company' was an architectural one made to the
hero in an architectural competition. The probability not
only seems the only explanation which will cover all the
requirements, but is also greatly strengthened by the fact
of Hardy's own winning of the prize of the R.I.B.A.
Having drawn on personal experience so far as to make
his hero a budding architect, it was very natural that
Hardy should go even further. Although this particular
incident was removed from *An Indiscretion*, Hardy did not
refrain from introducing there another one, drawn from
his own architectural experience.

Although in the recasting of the early into the later
narrative, most of the satire of a political nature, to which
all the advisers objected so strongly in 1868-9, has disappeared, chap. IV of *An Indiscretion* retains traces of it.
Some sentences may well be the original ones of *The Poor
Man and the Lady*:

To further complicate his feelings, there was the sight, on

the one hand, of the young lady with her warm rich dress and glowing future, and on the other of the weak little boys and girls—some only five years old, and none more than twelve—going off in their different directions in the pelting rain, some for a walk of more than two miles, with the certainty of being drenched to the skin, and with no change of clothes when they reached their home. He watched the rain spots thickening upon the faded frocks, worn-out tippets, yellow straw hats and bonnets and coarse pinafores of his unprotected little flock. . . . Miss Allenville, too, was looking at the children, and unfortunately she chanced to say, as they toddled off, "Poor little wretches!" A sort of despairing irritation at her remoteness from his plane, as implied by her pitying the children so unmercifully impelled him to remark "Say poor little *children*, madam."

That Hardy's first story should contain extreme, not to say ridiculous, improbabilities is as characteristic as that it should contain masterly descriptions of country life and folk. These two characteristics seem like two strands of startlingly incompatible colour which are yet present all through the woof of his art. As has often been remarked, the former becomes particularly noticeable when Hardy tries to draw high society. The supreme examples of the two are probably the scenes in the malt house in *Far from the Madding Crowd*, and that truly amazing tale 'Barbara of the House of Grebe' in *A Group of Noble Dames*. They were evidently both present in embryo in *The Poor Man and the Lady*.

The scene in the churchyard at midnight which Mac-millan criticized seems, to judge by Gosse's report, to have been substantially the same in *The Poor Man* as it is in *An Indiscretion*. The only differences are that the time is changed to evening; whereas in the first version the meeting began with anger on the lady's part, in the second it begins with feigned indifference on the man's (probably due to Hardy's increased knowledge of life); and whereas in the early version the lady confessed that she had always loved him, at the end of the interview, in the second she runs away from her father's house in the middle of the night on purpose to tell him. The difference may be due to different endings, for it is this which precipitated the ending, and what the ending of *The Poor Man* was is not quite clear. The second version makes it impossible for the hero not to take her if he has the least feeling for her, which he might otherwise hesitate to do. In both versions, the incident is characteristically melodramatic, and equally unlikely. That Hardy did not agree with Macmillan's criticism 'Could it happen?' is abundantly clear from all his novels.

That he so often outrages what Macmillan called 'the modesty of nature' is the burden of all his critics, from Lionel Johnson to Macdowall.

Macmillan asked if any gentleman would pursue and strike his wife at midnight. It is very much to be regretted that he was so allusive and not a little more explicit here. There is no really decisive answer to any of the questions: Who was it who pursued his wife at midnight and struck her? Was the wife the heroine? Was she unhappily married? Was this before or after the church scene? If before, what was the outcome of the church scene? If after (which seems less likely), did the second meeting correspond to Geraldine's nocturnal visit in *An Indiscretion*, the difference between the two versions being in that case that in *The Poor Man* she was running away from a husband, whereas in *An Indiscretion* it was only from a prospective bridegroom? The suggestion of Professor Weber, that the husband was the Squire, and that he struck his wife, not only does not fit in with what Gosse's report suggests concerning the relationship between the parents of the heiress, but seems also to lack applicability of any kind; nor does Prof. Weber explain how it 'brought about a meeting of the lovers.' Had the Squire been at variance with his dame, the story of *The Poor Man and the Lady* would have been quite a different one.

All the evidence hitherto given primarily concerns *The Poor Man and the Lady*, written in 1868, and incidentally shows its resemblances to *An Indiscretion in the Life of an Heiress* published in 1878. To show in full how far the latter is a version of the former, it would be necessary to give a summary of *An Indiscretion* in great detail. This would demand more space than is available, and the plot must be taken as known. A number of points in the story demand notice, nevertheless.

Tollamore Church is obviously Stinsford, the Mellstock of *Under the Greenwood Tree*. Here Hardy came to church as child and boy; here there is a memorial window to him; and here his heart is buried near the grave of his first wife. Egbert Mayne, gazing at Geraldine during evening service, sees her face

> modified in his fancy till it almost seemed to resemble the carved marble skull immediately above her head.

That monument with the carved marble skull, which may be seen on the wall of Stinsford Church to this day, had often terrified Hardy as a child. It may be noted that although *An Indiscretion* was not published until 1878, the place names in it are not normalized to conform to the toponomy which Hardy first adopted in 1871 in *Under the Greenwood Tree*, as they were normalized in all editions of *Desperate Remedies* subsequent to 1896. Although not proof positive, this strongly suggests that *An Indiscretion* existed in some form before 1871.

In chapter three, when Egbert waylays Geraldine, she is reading *Childe Harold's Pilgrimage*. We know that Hardy was reading that poem in July 1865.[1] In the recital of the first love passages between the two, the general situation and the girlishness of Geraldine's character bear a close resemblance to the situation in *A Pair of Blue Eyes* and to the character of Elfride. All this part looks like having been written nearer to 1870 than to 1880. In chapter five, however, there is a later touch. Egbert chooses a strategic spot for his critical encounter with Geraldine:

[1] *Early Life*, p. 64.

having previously surveyed the spot and thought it suitable for the occasion, much as Wellington antecedently surveyed the field of Waterloo.

This passage seems the earliest reference in Hardy's writings to Napoleonic matters. With a view to the 'Drama of Kings' which was even then taking shape in his mind, he himself surveyed the field of Waterloo in 1876.[1]

Chapter seven contains an account of an incident which Hardy witnessed in 1865, that of the laying of the foundation stone:

> Geraldine laid down the sealed bottle with its enclosed memorandum . . . and taking a trowel from her father's hand, dabbled confusedly in the mortar, accidentally smearing it over the handle of the trowel. . . . The dainty-handed young woman was looking as if she would give anything to be relieved of the dirty trowel; but Egbert, the only one who observed this, was guiding the stone with both hands into its place, and could not receive the tool of her. Every moment increased her perplexity. "Take it, take it, will you?" she impatiently whispered to him, blushing with the consciousness that people began to perceive her awkward handling.

This incident almost certainly figured in *The Poor Man*, for Hardy had witnessed it in 1865. The account which he gave to Mrs. Hardy half a century later, and which appears in *Early Life* (p. 63), even preserves the same phrase:

> Subsequent historic events brought back to his (Hardy's) mind that this year (1865) he went with Blomfield to New Windsor, to the laying of the memorial stone of a church there by the Crown Princess of Germany (the English Princess Royal). She was accompanied by her husband the Crown Prince, afterwards the Emperor Frederick. Blomfield handed her the trowel, and during the ceremony she got her glove daubed with the mortar. In her distress she handed the trowel back to him with an impatient whisper of "Take it, take it!"

[1] See p. 274. Prof. Weber remarks on this passage that ' it helps to date the action in the nineteenth century.' Being an author's remark, it no more dates the action than would a reference to the siege of Troy; moreover, the introduction of a steam threshing machine sufficiently indicates the nineteenth century.

In chapter eight, apropos of the social disparity between Egbert and his beloved we are told:

> That the habits of men should be so subversive of the law of nature as to indicate that he was not worthy to marry a woman whose own instincts said that he was worthy, was a great anomaly, he thought with some rebelliousness.

This is a very striking foretaste of Hardy's quarrel with social conventions that run counter to the apparent laws of nature, which forms so great a part of *Tess*. The rôle of the sexes is reversed, but the attitude of mind is the same. We have here, indeed, a link between Hardy's earliest effort in fiction, and his most famous work. As a young man, his quarrel with 'this sorry scheme of things entire,' and more particularly with the organization of human society, seems to have taken a political tinge. There is no trace of politics in *Tess*; but there is a passionate indictment of the warping, contorting and trammelling of existence 'by those creeds which futilely attempt to check what wisdom would be content to regulate.'[1]

The descriptions of Egbert's experiences as a man of letters in London clearly owe something to Hardy's own experiences between 1862 and 1868. The scene at the concert of the *Messiah* (in Chap. II, of Pt. 2), is probably hardly, if at all, altered from the concert scene which we know to have been in *The Poor Man*. The meeting of the long parted lovers in such an atmosphere is very well done: 'They were like frail and sorry wrecks upon that sea of symphony.' The modifications which the church scene underwent with its transference from *The Poor Man* to *An Indiscretion* have been noted. Despite Macmillan's strictures, Hardy evidently considered this melodramatic situation a valuable means of bring about the *dénouement*, for a very similar device is used in *Desperate Remedies*. The scene in chapter thirteen of that novel, when Edward Springrove appears at the wedding of Cytherea, is at a further remove

[1] *Tess*, Chap. XXV.

from the original scene in *The Poor Man*, but clearly derives from it.

The ending of *An Indiscretion* is a fine one, and recalls those of much more mature work, for example that in *The Trumpet Major*. Of stately endings Hardy was especially fond. An account of the death of the heiress may well have figured in the early version; and the supposition is strengthened by the fact that the most memorable sentence occurs again in the description of the death of Miss Aldclyffe in the twenty-first chapter of *Desperate Remedies*; it may be noted that this sentence contains a suggestion which is repeatedly introduced, with very great effect, in *The Return of the Native*; that of the latent hostility of the external universe to human life. Its effectiveness lies largely in the artistry with which it is used, for it is never more than a suggestion.

We are now in a position to make a concise statement of the relationship between *The Poor Man and the Lady*, written in 1868 and only known to us by the evidence already quoted, and *An Indiscretion in the Life of an Heiress*, published in 1878.

(*a*) *An Indiscretion* is a version of *The Poor Man*, considerably shortened, partly simplified, but substantially the same novel.

(*b*) Some parts of *The Poor Man*, retained in *An Indiscretion*, have been partially rewritten; nevertheless, as will shortly appear even more conclusively, much of the later version remains verbatim as originally written.

(*c*) Three scenes, which we know to have been in the early novel, figure in the later one. The concert scene may be taken as being, with the alteration of two or three sentences, as it was first written. The church scene, while having undergone more modification, still bears many traces of its original state. The scene of the hero's call at the town house of the heiress has been rewritten, but retains its original purpose in the plot.

(*d*) The following features in the later novel were almost

certainly not in the early one. They were introduced in the late 'seventies, and their interest is their connection of Hardy's later work with his early writings:

(1) The stress laid upon the instinctive and uncalculating nature of love, and its fatal consequences.

(2) The quarrel with conventions of society which run counter to the apparent laws of nature. This was a transformation of the critical faculty, which seems first to have tended to a political complexion, and is psychologically most interesting.

(e) The following features of the early novel still to be found in the later one show how very far from general was the revision, and how close *An Indiscretion* must in many ways be to *The Poor Man*:

(1) Two events of Hardy's own life which occurred in 1865 are to be definitely traced, the episode of the laying of the foundation stone, and the reading of *Childe Harold*. A number of reminiscences of his early years in London are probably also present, but cannot be definitely identified.

(2) The place names in the story are not the place names of all the other Wessex Novels. This was also the case with the first edition of *Desperate Remedies* in 1871; but the familiar names first appeared in 1872 in *Under the Greenwood Tree*, and were thereafter Hardy's standard practice.

(3) Several touches of a sort which in a modern author would be called 'class-conscious' are clearly perceptible. There is no parallel to these in any of Hardy's later writings.

(4) There are certain analogies with *Desperate Remedies*, and possibly one or two with *A Pair of Blue Eyes*, in certain details of plot and treatment, which suggest a date of composition much nearer to 1870 than to 1880.

It has been suggested already that the Manuscript of

An Indiscretion, if it could now be found, would prove to be the MS. of *The Poor Man*, with excisions and alterations. How far the later version actually reproduces the wording of the early one, as this hypothesis would demand, cannot be known with certainty. That, for example, the concert scene dates almost entirely from 1868 is only very strong probability. It so happens, however, that there is even stronger circumstantial evidence to the probable verbal fidelity of *An Indiscretion* to *The Poor Man*. This is the fact that three rather striking phrases to be found in *An Indiscretion* are also to be found in *Desperate Remedies*. It might be argued that Hardy, in 1878, took them out of the novel in which he first wrote them in 1871. This cannot be positively disproved. But the onus of proof rests with those who would advance a theory for which there seems no reason; for Hardy can have had no motive for doing in this instance what he never did again, that is, borrowing from his own earlier work. Besides, if he had wanted to borrow in 1878 it seems probable that he would have gone to more finished work than *Desperate Remedies*. But the opposite theory, that the appearance of these sentences in the novel of 1871, is due to his having borrowed them from the suppressed story of 1868, provides not merely a plausible, but the only reasonable, explanation. Assuming that he was fond of these sentences, nothing is more likely than that, having had to suppress the story in which they appeared, he afterwards used them again in his next novel.

The following are the passages in question:

(1) In chapter seven (Pt. 1) of *An Indiscretion*, at the end of the love scene between Egbert and Geraldine on the night after Broadfoot's death, she again asks him, as they leave, whether he forgives her:

> 'Do you forgive me entirely?'
> 'How shall I say "Yes" without assuming that there was something to forgive?'
> 'Say "Yes." It is sweeter to fancy I am forgiven than to think I have not sinned.'

Towards the end of the twelfth chapter of *Desperate Remedies*, when Manston is pressing Cytherea to fix a date for their wedding, she at first refuses, then relents and asks forgiveness:

> 'Will you forgive me?'
> 'How shall I say "Yes" without judging you? How shall I say "No" without losing the pleasure of saying "Yes"?' He was himself again.
> 'I don't know' she absently murmured.
> 'I'll say "Yes"' he answered daintily. 'It is sweeter to fancy we are forgiven, than to think we have not sinned; and you shall have the sweetness without the need.'

(2) In chapter eight (Pt. 1) of *An Indiscretion*, when Egbert is just about to leave Geraldine to catch his boat, at the end of their interview through the window on the morning on which he sets out to seek his fortune, her parting words to him are these:

> 'If you cannot in the least succeed, I shall never think the less of you. The truly great stand on no middle ledge; they are either famous or unknown.'

In the third chapter of *Desperate Remedies*, Springrove is telling Cytherea of his ambitions, and that he has got to the stage of being content to aim at reasonable wealth sufficient for his needs:

> 'And if you should fail—utterly fail to get that reasonable wealth,' she said earnestly, 'don't be perturbed. The truly great stand upon no middle ledge; they are either famous or unknown.'

(3) The last paragraph of *An Indiscretion*, describing the death of Geraldine:

> Everything was so still that her weak act of trying to live seemed a silent wrestling with all the powers of the universe.

In chapter twenty-one of *Desperate Remedies* Cytherea comes to Knapwater House in answer to an urgent summons and finds Miss Aldclyffe dying:

In the room everything was so still, and sensation was as it were so rarified by solicitude, that thinking seemed acting, and the lady's weak act of trying to live a silent wrestling with all the powers of the universe.

It will be noticed that in all three instances, the version of *An Indiscretion* is the simpler as well as the more effective, whereas the version of *Desperate Remedies* is padded out. This fits in with the theory that the versions of *An Indiscretion* are the earlier; which amounts to saying that, in part at least, *An Indiscretion* retains the actual wording of *The Poor Man*. It is, of course, quite possible, that other parts of *Desperate Remedies* were transferred thither out of *The Poor Man*, although their absence from *An Indiscretion* leaves us without clues. Prof. Weber's conjecture, that the description of Knapwater House in chapter five of *Desperate Remedies* originally figured in *The Poor Man*, would fit in with this.

Two other, much less important, points of contact between *An Indiscretion* and *Desperate Remedies* remain to be mentioned. The quotations at the chapter headings of the former have already been referred to. There are four from Shakespeare, three from Browning, two from Shelley, one each from Tennyson, Thackeray, Ecclesiastes and Waller, and one from Dryden's translation of the *Aeneid*. Three of these are also used in *Desperate Remedies*. This of course proves nothing as to date; one of the Shelley quotations appears again in *The Woodlanders*; but it is worthy of mention.

The most interesting of them, from the point of view of the student of Hardy, is that from Dryden's *Aeneid*, for this was one of the first books Hardy ever possessed, having been given it by his mother about 1850. The lines at the head of the first chapter in the second part of *An Indiscretion*, where they apply to Egbert's tactics towards Geraldine, appear also in the twelfth chapter of *Desperate Remedies*, where they apply to Manston's tactics towards Cytherea:

He, like a captain who beleaguers round
Some strong-built castle on a rising ground,
Views all the approaches with observing eyes,
This and that other part in vain he tries,
And more on industry than force relies.

(*Aeneid*, Bk. V.)

Chapter eight of *An Indiscretion* is headed by four lines from
Browning's 'The Statue and the Bust':

The world and its ways have a certain worth,
And to press a point while these oppose
Were a simple policy; best wait,
And we lose no friends and gain no foes.

The poem was a favourite with Hardy. Cytherea quotes
three of these lines to Edward in the thirteenth chapter of
Desperate Remedies. Three other lines from the same poem
occur in the third chapter, where Hardy uses them of
Edward and Cytherea. In the sixth chapter of *Desperate
Remedies*, Miss Aldclyffe quotes to Cytherea a stanza from
Shelley's 'When the lamp is shattered.'

Love's passions shall rock thee
As the storm rocks the raven on high,
Bright reason will mock thee
Like the sun from a wintry sky.

The last two lines stand at the head of the third chapter in
the second part of *An Indiscretion*.

This last point of contact is a small, and by itself incon-
clusive, one. Taken with the other evidence it tends to
confirm that, despite the later date of its publication, *An
Indiscretion* is in the main the work of Hardy's late twenties
rather than of his late thirties.

Considered purely as literature, *An Indiscretion* is disappointing; it is easy to understand why Hardy never
reprinted it, and put off inquiries about his first novel from
Gosse and Mr. Collins with remarks that it 'was hunting
very small deer,' or that he 'got rid of it when moving.'
When we remember that by 1878, when it appeared,
Hardy had written *Far from the Madding Crowd* and *The*

Return of the Native, the conclusion that *An Indiscretion* had been written many years before is irresistible. This somewhat feeble composition belongs to the period of *Desperate Remedies*. That it happened to be first published in the same year as one of Hardy's masterpieces was a coincidence which does not confer upon it any distinction.

Desperate Remedies

The particular field of English letters in which Hardy, in the later 'sixties, set out to make himself a place, was already crowded almost to overflowing. There have been few decades in the whole history of English prose fiction when four novelists of the calibre of Thackeray, Dickens, Meredith and 'George Eliot' have all been in the field simultaneously, as they were then. And beside these four there were many other considerable novelists who are not forgotten to-day: Trollope, Charles and Henry Kingsley, Mrs. Gaskell, Mrs. Henry Wood, Mary Braddon, R. D. Blackmore; while Wilkie Collins hardly gets the credit for having virtually invented, in *The Woman in White*, what has become by far the largest branch of contemporary fiction. Hardy, in search of a popular method of treatment after the failure of *The Poor Man and the Lady* to achieve publication, chose as a model the work of Wilkie Collins; who was then, following the publication of *The Moonstone* in 1868, the most popular living novelist. The result was *Desperate Remedies*; but its debt to Collins does not seem to have been noticed by any of the critics except Madame Cazamian.[1] Detailed comparison of Hardy's book with certain aspects of *The Woman in White*, *No Name*, *Armadale* and *The Moonstone*, the most successful of Collins' novels in the 'sixties, will come more appropriately later. Only twice in his career did Hardy write a mystery novel. The second time was when circumstances compelled him, although desperately ill, to continue *A Laodicean*, upon which the success or failure of

[1] She calls it 'un sombre recit de terreur à la Wilkie Collins.' *Le Roman et les Idées en Angleterre*, p. 372.

the periodical in which it was appearing depended. But traces of his early apprenticeship to Wilkie Collins appear now and then throughout his work. His taste for coincidence, and the occasional lapses into the sensational which occur even in his late novels, are partly due to this influence. Even if the bloodstain on the ceiling in *Tess* be not indecent, as it was accused of being, it is highly sensational.

In April 1869, Hardy was working in Dorchester for an architect called G. R. Crickmay, who had purchased the practice of Hicks, lately deceased, and taken on various schemes of church restoration which Hicks had had in hand. Crickmay's business was in Weymouth, and during the summer Hardy went to his office there and lived in Weymouth until the following February. It was during these nine months in Weymouth that *Desperate Remedies* was written, all but the last chapters. Having returned to his father's house, Hardy sent the MS. on March 5th, 1870, to Alexander Macmillan, together with a synopsis of the final chapters. He then went on a commission for Crickmay to St. Juliot, near Boscastle in Cornwall, where he met Emma Lavinia Gifford, who later became his wife.[1]

There are a few clear traces of the Weymouth sojourn in the novel. Edward Springrove the younger was sketched, partly, from an assistant who came to Crickmay's office during the summer. But the history of the literary aspirations which he confesses to Cytherea in the course of the rowing expedition which concludes chapter three is Hardy's own:

> When I found all this out that I was speaking of, whatever do you think I did? From having already loved verse passionately, I went on to read it continually; then I went rhyming myself. If anything on earth ruins a man for useful occupation and for content with reasonable success in a profession, it is the habit of writing verses on emotional subjects, which had much better be left to die from want of nourishment.

Passages from the early parts of *Desperate Remedies*, the poem called 'The Dawn after the Dance,' dated 'Weymouth

[1] *Early Life*, p. 84 *et seq.*

1869,' in *Time's Laughingstocks*, and allusions by Mrs. Hardy to a 'quadrille class,' suggest that the Weymouth sojourn may not have been devoid of subjects for verses of the kind in question.

In April 1870 Hardy returned from Cornwall. On the 5th of that month he had received a letter from Macmillan declining to publish his MS. In May he went to London, and apparently got his MS. from Macmillan, and sent it to Tinsley Brothers.[1] This firm anticipated the publishers of the twentieth century in regarding MSS. submitted to it wholly from a commercial standpoint, and did not trouble itself with fine points of literary criticism. The policy had served it well; for the firm followed the guidance of its adviser in publishing *Lady Audley's Secret* in 1862, which had been such a success that it had made the fortunes, not only of its publishers, but even of its author. Tinsleys had also been fortunate enough to find another excellent investment in 'Ouida,' for whose first novel *Held in Bondage* they had paid £80 in 1863. Hardy, who was no fool, doubtless knew these things. What he wanted was to be published, not to receive sermons on his writings from Macmillan, Morley and Meredith. This seems to be the reason, which Mrs. Hardy cannot find, why he went to Tinsleys rather than to Chapman, after having been a second time refused by Macmillan.

On May 6th Tinsley wrote stating the terms upon which he would publish *Desperate Remedies* if Hardy would send him the concluding chapters. Mrs. Hardy, who gives this information,[2] does not say what those terms were. What happened during the next few months is not clear; except that during the autumn

There were passing between him and Miss Gifford chapters of the story for her to make a fair copy of, the original MS having been interlined and altered, so that it may have suffered, he thought, in the eyes of a publisher's reader by being difficult

[1] William and Edward Tinsley, whose offices were at 18 Catherine Street, Strand.
[2] *Early Life*, p. 100.

to read. He meanwhile wrote the three or four remaining chapters and the novel—this time finished—was packed off to Tinsley in December.[1]

Hardy marked the date December 15th, 1870, in his *Hamlet* against the words:

'Thou would'st not think how ill all's here about my heart.'

Tinsley again wrote his terms, which, says Mrs. Hardy, 'for some unaccountable reason were worse now than they had been in the first place.' What they were is evident from Hardy's reply[2]

> Bockhampton, Dorchester, December 20th, 1870.
>
> SIR,
>
> I believe I am right in understanding your terms thus—that if the gross receipts reach the costs of publishing I shall receive the £75 back again, and if they are more than the costs I shall have £75 added to half the receipts beyond the costs (i.e., assuming the expenditure to be £100 the receipt £200 I should have returned to me £75 plus £50—125). Will you be good enough to say too if the sum includes advertising to the customary extent, and about how long after my paying the money the book would appear?
>
> Yours faithfully,
> THOMAS HARDY.

These terms cannot be considered unfavourable by modern standards. Hardy accepted them, and the book appeared on March 25th, 1871. In reply to a request a year later, Tinsley sent Hardy an account according to which 500 copies of *Desperate Remedies* had been printed, of which 370 had been sold, and enclosed a cheque for £60. Mrs. Hardy says that Hardy was 'much gratified thereby.'[3]

Desperate Remedies was published anonymously on March 25th, 1871. It was well reviewed in the *Athenæum* of April 1st, and as 'an eminent success' in the *Morning Post* of the 13th. On the 22nd, in Mrs. Hardy's words:

[1] *Early Life*, p. 109.
[2] This letter was published in an article, 'Amenities of Book Collecting,' by A. Edward Newton, in *The Atlantic Monthly*, March 1915.
[3] *Early Life*, p. 110.

The *Spectator* brought down its heaviest-leaded pastoral staff on the prematurely happy volumes, the reason for this violence being mainly the author's daring to suppose it possible that an unmarried lady owning an estate could have an illegitimate child.[1]

In the absence of more adequate explanation, this seems possible; even in 'Victoria's formal middle time,' however, such situations were not absolutely without precedent in fiction which was not of the lowest order. A novel which Wilkie Collins published in 1862, *No Name*, opens with the far more unlikely situation of a country squire with grown-up daughters, whose mother has never been legally married, and continues with a plot much more objectionable than Hardy's, occasionally sugared with moralizing. Whatever his reasons, the anonymous critic in the *Spectator* applied the rod with vigour:

This absolutely anonymous story bears no assumption of a nom-de-plume which might, at some future time, disgrace the family name, and still more the Christian name, of a repentant and remorseful novelist—and very right too. By all means let him bury the secret in the profoundest depths of his own heart, out of reach, if possible, of his own conscience. The law is hardly just which prevents Tinsley Brothers from concealing their participation also.[2]

Were this review simply a piece of wrongheadedness, it would not be worth notice; but it contained rational criticism also. The substance of the critic's quarrel with Hardy was 'here are no fine characters, no original ones to extend one's knowledge of human nature, no display of passion except of the brute kind' (which is not true), 'no pictures of Christian virtue.' In view of subsequent developments, the notion of going to Hardy for pictures of Christian virtue is not without piquancy. But this critic was not quite blind:

But there is . . . an unusual and very happy facility in catching and fixing phases of peasant life, in producing for us, not the

[1] *Early Life*, p. 110.   [2] *Spectator*, April 22nd, 1871.

manners and language only, but the tone of thought . . . and the simple humour of consequential village worthies and gaping village rustics. . . . The scenes allotted to these humble actors are few and slight, but they indicate powers that might be and ought to be extended largely in this direction instead of being prostituted to the purposes of idle prying into the ways of wickedness. . . . This nameless author, too, has one other talent of a remarkable kind—sensitiveness to scenic and atmospheric effects, and to their influence on the mind, and the power of rousing similar sensitiveness in his readers.

The review contained long quotations from the descriptions of the cider pressing (Chap. VIII), the bell ringing (sequel) and Cytherea's vision of her father's accident in chapter one, by way of illustration, and the critic said 'we wish we had space' for more quotation. He concluded: 'We have said enough to warn our readers against this book, and, we hope, to urge the author to write far better ones.'

It was by largely extending the powers which this critic recognized that Hardy produced the scenes depicting Joseph Poorgrass and his cronies, or the description of Egdon Heath.

The review hurt Hardy badly when he read it. 'The bitterness of that moment,' says Mrs. Hardy 'was never forgotten; at the time he wished that he were dead.'[1] Some time later, the critic seems privately to have written a sort of apology.[2] On returning in June from a visit to Cornwall, Hardy saw his novel in Smith's surplus catalogue at Exeter Station for half a crown the three volumes. It cannot be said that *Desperate Remedies* marked the beginning of Hardy's reputation as a novelist. It was one of those false starts which seem to be almost the rule in the case of really great authors.

Before the attack by the *Spectator*, *Desperate Remedies* had also been reviewed in the *Morning Post*, on April 13th; and by the *Athenæum* on April 1st. The writer of the latter

[1] *Early Life*, p. 111.   [2] *Idem*, p. 112.

article indulged in speculation as to the sex of the author, and, while returning an open verdict, inclined to the opinion that it must be a man, on the ground that some of the expressions in the book were too coarse to have been written by a lady! He acknowledged, however, that it was 'a powerful novel.' *The Saturday Review*, in an article which appeared on September 30th, tried to bring Hardy's novel to life again. A review which ran to two and a half columns ended with the sentence:

> 'We sincerely hope to hear of him again, for his deserts are of no ordinary kind.'

Although this cannot be verified, it is possible that this review was written by Hardy's friend, Horace Moule, who reviewed *Under the Greenwood Tree* in the same paper the next year.

The novel contains occasional touches traceable to Hardy's own experiences. In addition to the Weymouth scenes, and the subject of poetical aspirations, there is the architectural motif. Both the young men in the story, Graye and Springrove, are architects. There is also the visit of Miss Aldclyffe to the Institute of Architects in chapter seven; and some touches clearly taken from Hardy's life in London. But there is nothing in the story itself which can be considered remotely autobiographical; it is an elaborate fiction *à la* Wilkie Collins. The chief light which it throws upon its author is in the astonishing number of its allusions to English literature, and particularly English poetry. If, as Mrs. Hardy says, Hardy read nothing except poetry for two years while in London, he made haste to unburden himself of some of his reading as soon as he got a pen into his hands. It is probable that *The Poor Man and the Lady* was, in its original state, rich in similar allusions, although they have all disappeared from *An Indiscretion*. Perhaps the poem to Eunice, which Springrove found among Manston's papers, was one of the 'original verses' alluded to in the discarded title of *The Poor Man*, although this is mere conjecture. However that may be, Hardy's reading is abundantly clear in *Desperate Remedies*. There are some forty allusions to, or quotations from, English literature; not including the Biblical ones already enumerated. Among them are four to Shakespeare, three to Shelley, two to Milton, two to Browning (both 'The Statue and the Bust'), two to Coleridge, one to Wordsworth, one to Keats ('Ode to a Nightingale'), one to Rossetti's 'Blessed Damosel,' one to Sterne's letters, one to de Quincey and one to Dryden's translation of the *Aeneid*. There are three quotations from Virgil in the original, one from Walt Whitman, and an allusion to a passage in Dante.

By way of example, a passage may be quoted from chapter three. In the previous chapter, Hardy has described Edward Springrove as:

> some years short of the age at which the clear spirit bids goodbye to the last infirmity of noble minds, and takes to house hunting and investments.

Just before his departure for London, Springrove asks Cytherea to go for a row round the bay at Budmouth (as Hardy so often went at Weymouth). The two are described in Browning's words:

> He looked at her as a lover can;
> She looked at him as one who awakes—
> The past was a sleep, and her life began.

When they are in the boat, Hardy returns to *Lycidas*, as witness their conversation:

> 'It doesn't matter to me now that I "meditate the thankless Muse" no longer—but . . .' He paused, as if endeavouring to think what better thing he did.
>
> Cytherea's mind ran on the succeeding lines of the poem, and their startling harmony with the present situation suggested the fancy that he was *sporting* with her, and brought an awkward contemplativeness to her face.
>
> Springrove guessed her thoughts. . . . 'If I had known an Amaryllis was coming here, I should not have made arrangements for leaving.'

This one example out of many will show how in his first published work Hardy was already addicted to the habit of literary allusion which is such a feature of his late novels.

There are other features in the novel which also anticipate what was to come after. Chapter three contains two passages descriptive of feminine nature which belong to that much discussed subject, Hardy's view of women[1]; and there is another in chapter twelve. There is a very characteristic remark about the short-lived bliss of love in the third chapter; and chapter twenty-two contains some sentences on sudden death which ought not to have been overlooked by those who have discussed Hardy's 'determinism':

> There's no such thing as a random snapping off of what was laid down to last longer. We only suddenly light upon an end—thoughtfully formed as any other—which has been existing at that very same point, though unseen by us to be so soon.

Desperate Remedies provides several instances of the delicate and minute use of nature which Hardy was to carry to a fine art; notably the description, in chapter seventeen, of the sound made by rain on various field surfaces.

Apart from such passages as these, the Hardy of the later Wessex Novels is to be seen in the descriptions of country life and folk, and especially in their conversation; in the scene of the cider pressing, and in that of the bell ringers. The rest is a very artificial dish, confectioned to a popular recipe perfected, if not invented, by Wilkie Collins.

What Hardy in *Desperate Remedies* owed to Wilkie Collins can best be seen by comparing the novel with Hardy's subsequent work, and by a glance at the novels which Collins published in the 'sixties. *Desperate Remedies* stands apart from the Wessex novels, chiefly by virtue of its construction. Much of Hardy's most characteristic work is

[1] At least two books have been entirely devoted to this subject: *La Femme dans le Roman de Thomas Hardy*, by A. Liron (Paris, 1919) and *Thomas Hardy's Frauen im Lichte seiner Weltanschauung*, by Gerda Salberg (Mulhouse, 1927).

constructed upon simple plots. Just as the story of Clarissa
Harlowe may, it is said, be told in two hundred words, so
may the stories of *Under the Greenwood Tree, A Pair of Blue
Eyes, The Return of the Native, Tess* and *Jude. Far from the
Madding Crowd* is hardly more complicated in plot, though
the wealth of incidents is greater. The most complicated of
Hardy's great novels is *The Mayor of Casterbridge*; which is,
nevertheless, most definitely a novel of character rather
than of incident. And even *The Mayor of Casterbridge* is
simple beside the involutions of *Desperate Remedies.*
Hardy's first published novel is a 'mystery novel'; one in
which the movement of the story and the final solution are
quite independent of character and humour, but result from
arbitrary combinations and devices such as the discovery
of a secret or the detection of a crime. *Desperate Remedies*
and *A Laodicean* are the only two such novels which Hardy
wrote.

Hardy did not take the plot of *Desperate Remedies* from
Wilkie Collins; he constructed it himself. But he took from
Collins all its essential elements, merely grouping them into
a different combination. The novels which Collins published
in the 'sixties were *The Woman in White* (1860), *No Name*
(1862), *Armadale* (1866) and *The Moonstone* (1868).[1] The last
two concern the student of Hardy least. Sergeant Cuff is a
prototype of Sherlock Holmes, even to some details; *The
Moonstone*, indeed might be a modern detective tale but for
the prolixity of its telling; while the sensational and involved
tale of the two Allen Armadales is too preposterous to have
originated any literary *genre*. But *The Woman in White*,
which is probably the first English detective story, and to a
slight extent *No Name*, contain all the elements of the plot
of *Desperate Remedies*. Apart from the matrimonial irre-
gularity of the elder Vanstone, which is the cause of the
whole story of *No Name*, and that of Miss Aldclyffe, which
is the cause of that of *Desperate Remedies*, there is no great

[1] All of them first appeared serially in *All the Year Round*, except *Armadale*, which
was in the *Cornhill*.

contact between the two novels. The trials of Magdalen have no close resemblance to those of Cytherea, nor is Captain Wragge any counterpart to Manston. But *The Woman in White* contains close parallels. There is the underlying mystery: Manston is a rather pale version of Sir Perceval Glyde. There is the sacrifice of the beautiful heroine, Cytherea Graye or Laura Fairlie, who loves and is loved by the virtuous but impecunious young hero, to this mysterious villain whose mystery and villainy only become apparent after the marriage. There is the elucidation of the mystery, not by Sergeant Cuff or Sherlock Holmes, but by the person chiefly interested in it, whether he be called Edward Springrove or Walter Hartright. This person is assisted, not by an obtuse if admirable Watson, but by the nearest relative of the distressed heroine; in one case her brother, in the other her half sister. In both cases this relative had in the first instance been instrumental in thwarting the true love of hero and heroine, and in assisting the marriage of the villain to the heroine. All these parallels with *The Woman in White* are very close. There are many others. Manston is finally driven into a corner by Springrove very much as Glyde is driven by Hartright. The deliberate confusion of the identity of one woman with another for criminal purposes is essentially the same in both novels, whether the woman be Lady Glyde and Ann Catherick, or Eunice and Ann Seaway.

Different as are the actual developments, it is hard to resist the conclusion that Hardy took all these elements of the plot of *Desperate Remedies* from *The Woman in White*. Hardy's novel, it is true, is a pale and feeble affair beside that of Collins. There is no Fosco; and in general there is little technique in the handling of the mechanics of a mystery story, of which Collins is an acknowledged master. But Hardy was recognizably imitating the manner of that master—whose manuscripts drew from his publishers, not literary lectures but substantial cheques. It ought not to be forgotten that Hardy was writing for his living, as he

reminded Gosse long afterwards.[1] Tinsley Brothers published *The Moonstone*; Tinsley, indeed, complained that
Collins had driven a hard bargain with him[2]; and Hardy
sent his MS. to Tinsley in the following year.

To a lesser degree than with the construction of the plot,
Desperate Remedies may even owe a certain element of style
to Collins. This is the manner of telling the story by building
up an effect of verisimilitude through the device of accumu-
lating minute realistic details. The first, and perhaps greatest, master of this method was Defoe, who carried it to
such perfection that, while we know the narratives of
Robinson Crusoe and Colonel Jack to be fictitious, the
exact proportion of fiction to history in such a narrative as
the *Journal of the Plague Year* can only be ascertained by
external evidence. The passage in which Mrs. Hardy
compares a similar style of narrative, adopted by Hardy in
The Poor Man and the Lady, to Defoe, was referred to in the
last chapter. She accounts for it as deliberate imitation of
Defoe. It is as certain that Hardy had read *Robinson Crusoe*
as it is that most boys read it[3]; and he doubtless read more
Defoe besides. But the circumstantial narrative of *Desperate
Remedies* may well have been imitated from Collins, as
was the construction of the plot. An editor of Collins has
pointed out that Collins himself owed something to Defoe:

> 'The inevitable comparison (of Collins' style) is with Defoe,
> for it was Defoe who first discovered this mechanical art of
> story telling.'[4]

In any case, the narrative style of much of *Desperate
Remedies* is indistinguishable from that of Collins. The
following paragraph taken at random (Chap. XIII) will
illustrate:

[1] In a letter dated February 18th, 1918, now in the Ashley Library, Hardy wrote
to Gosse: 'For the relief of my necessities, as the Prayer Book puts it, I began
writing novels and made a sort of trade of it.' Ashley Catalogue, Vol. X, p. 131.
[2] *Random Recollections of an Old Publisher*, Vol. I.
[3] *A Pair of Blue Eyes*, Chap. XII: 'Elfride had known no more about the stings of
evil report than the native wild fowl knew of the effects of Crusoe's first shot.'
[4] The introduction to W. A. Brockington's edition of *After Dark* (1900).

He hesitated as to the propriety of intruding upon her in Manston's absence. Besides, the women at the bottom of the stairs would see him—his intrusion would seem odd—and Manston might return at any moment. He certainly might call and wait for Manston with the accusation upon his tongue, as he had intended. But it was a doubtful course. That idea had been based upon the assumption that Cytherea was not married. If the first wife were really dead after all—and he felt sick at the thought—Cytherea as the steward's wife might in after years—perhaps at once—be subjected to indignity and cruelty on account of an old lover's interference now.

That is not Defoe, but it might be Collins. The 'propriety' and 'intrusion' and 'assumption' are as like Collins as they are unlike the style that was to give us Egdon Heath or the milking scene in Var Vale. It is true that even in *Desperate Remedies*, Hardy never descends to Collins' pseudo-grandiose; and that he can when he likes sketch a picture in a few words with a touch of which Collins was never capable. For example, that of the elder Springrove at the cider pressing:

He wore gaiters and a leather apron, and worked with his shirt sleeves rolled up, disclosing solid and fleshy rather than muscular arms. They were stained by the cider, and two or three brown apple pips from the pomace he was handling were seen to be sticking on them here and there.

Although Hardy does not adopt the method which Collins claimed to have invented in *The Woman in White*, of telling the story throughout in the persons of its characters, the narrative left by Manston at his death, which finally clears up all remaining mysteries, is exactly in the manner of Collins, while the occasional insertion of letters or extracts from letters to help on the narrative, which is sparingly used in *Desperate Remedies*, was a great favourite with Collins.

The deduction, from internal evidence, that Hardy made a deliberate study of *The Woman in White* as a preliminary to writing a novel which he hoped would be commercially successful, is strongly confirmed by the presence of Collins' novel in his library. The library at Max Gate does not now contain any of the fiction which Hardy must have read in the 'sixties. He certainly obtained the popular books of the time from Mudie, Smith or the Library Company. Such little money as he had for buying books went for poets, or Bohn classics, or a copy of a Rhyming Dictionary, which is marked 'Westbourne Park Villas 1865.' The earliest contemporary fiction which he *bought* seems to have been in the 'seventies, when he invested in Trollope's *The Eustace Diamonds*, which he admired for its construction. It is all the more noteworthy that his library *does* contain the very book to which *Desperate Remedies* owes its chief debt. There can be little doubt that Hardy invested in the one volume edition of *The Woman in White* published in 1861 because it was cheaper than the three volume edition, which he had probably got from Mudie; and because he wished to possess it as a text-book for the aspiring novelist, writing for the relief of his necessities, and to study it more minutely than would be possible in borrowed volumes.

The acceptance of *Desperate Remedies* by William Tinsley, whom Hardy long afterwards described as 'shrewd' in his dealings with young writers,[1] proves sufficiently that it had the elements necessary to popular fiction. Tinsley's remarks upon it, written thirty years later, are coloured by Hardy's subsequent career; but are none the less interesting:

> I read a good many MSS. almost every year during the time I was a publisher. One I read, and took an especial interest in, was Thomas Hardy's first novel called *Desperate Remedies*. In fact, I read the work twice, and even though I never thoroughly made up my mind that it was the sort of work to be a great success, I certainly thought that it contained some capital characters and character drawing. But Mr. Hardy had dragged into the midst of excellent humorous writing almost ultra

[1] V. H. Collins: *Talks with Thomas Hardy*, p. 55.

sensational matter, in fact, incidents unworthy of his pen and
the main portion of his work. Still, I quite thought that there
was enough of the bright side of human nature in it to sell at
least one fair edition. However, there was not, but for a first
venture I do not think Mr. Hardy had much to complain
about.[1]

Under the Greenwood Tree

Under the Greenwood Tree was written in the first half of
1871, and finished towards the end of the summer. The
original title on the first page of the manuscript was 'The
Mellstock Quire'; this was deleted because titles from poetry
were in fashion at the moment; it was restored as a sub-title
in later editions, but is not to be found in the two-volume
first edition, nor the one-volume second edition of 1876.
It appears that Hardy still had enough faith in the house of
Macmillan to send them the MS. during the autumn of 1871.
He received a letter in reply which he construed as refusing
his work; wrote, asking for the return of the MS.; and
'threw it into a box with his old poems, being quite sick of
all such.'[2] Macmillan had enclosed the opinion of his
critic (whose identity remains unknown), which is quoted
by Mrs. Hardy: but the letter seems to have been ambiguous
for she says:

> It was not till its acceptance and issue by another publishing
> house the year after that he discovered they had never declined
> it, and indeed would have been quite willing to print it a little
> later on.

Under the Greenwood Tree remained the copyright of Tinsley
Brothers until 1891, when it was published by Chatto and
Windus, with whom, as the publishers of the *New Quarterly
Magazine*, Hardy had connections. It was first published by
Macmillan in 1903, when that firm had become the pub-
lisher of all Hardy's works.

---

[1] *Random Recollections*, Vol. I, p. 127.
[2] *Early Life*, p. 114. The details of this and following paragraphs are taken from
Mrs. Hardy's account of *Under the Greenwood Tree* on p. 113 *et seq.*, unless otherwise
indicated.

The publication of the book seems to have been due to two chance meetings in London, to which Hardy returned in the spring of 1872. He first happened to meet in Trafalgar Square his friend Horace Moule, who advised him not to give up writing altogether in case his eyes should not be equal to the strain of architectural drawing. Some little while later, William Tinsley saw Hardy in the Strand, and persuaded him to produce the MS. of his new book. Hardy wrote home for it in the first week of April and:

> sent it on to Tinsley without looking at it, saying he would have nothing to do with any publishing accounts. This probably was the reason why Tinsley offered him £30 for the copyright, which Hardy accepted. It should be added that Tinsley afterwards sent him £10 extra, and quite voluntarily, being, he said, half the amount he had obtained from Tauchnitz for the continental copyright, of which transaction Hardy had known nothing.

Under the Greenwood Tree was published in two volumes in the last week in May 1872. The evidence as to its early fortunes is conflicting. The fact that Tauchnitz later published the book would seem to indicate considerable previous popularity in England. This would also appear from Tinsley's reluctance to part with the copyright only two years later. After the appearance of *Far from the Madding Crowd* in the *Cornhill Magazine* in 1874 had made Hardy's name, Smith, the *Cornhill* publisher, suggested that he should get back the copyright from Tinsley. Tinsley first said he would not part with it under any conditions; then he asked for £300. Hardy offered £150; Tinsley did not reply, and the negotiations ceased.

As might be expected, Tinsley's own account of the book he was so anxious to keep is rather less rosy:

> I purchased the copyright of Mr. Hardy's second novel, called *Under the Greenwood Tree*. In that book I felt sure I had got hold of the best little prose idyll I had ever read. By "little" I mean as regards the length of the book, in which there is not more than about four or five hours' reading; but

to my mind it is excellent reading indeed. I almost raved about the book; and I gave it away wholesale to pressmen and anyone I knew interested in good fiction. But, strange to say, it would not sell. Finding it hung on hand in the original two-volume form, I printed it in a very pretty illustrated one-volume form. That edition was a failure. Then I published it in a two shilling form, with paper covers, and that edition had a very poor sale indeed; and yet it was one of the best press-noticed books I ever published. But even though it is as pure and sweet as new mown hay, it just lacks the touch of sentiment that lady novel readers most admire. In fact, to my thinking, if Mr. Hardy could have imported stronger matter for love, laughter and tears in *Under the Greenwood Tree*, the book would have in no way been unworthy of the pen of George Eliot.[1]

In later years, *Under the Greenwood Tree* became one of the most popular of Hardy's novels.

The discriminating appreciation of the book by good critics in its earliest days is exemplified by the review of it in the *Athenæum* of June 15th, 1872.

It is an old commonplace to say that there is just as much romance, together with just as keen interest, in the loves of two young persons of this humble station, as in any courtship which ends at St. George's. But it is not everyone who can make as good a novel out of the one as out of the other, or produce out of such simple materials a story that shall induce us to give up valuable time in order to see the marriage fairly consummated.

Quotations were then given, particularly one from the description of the honey-taking at Geoffrey Day's; concerning whose apostrophe to the bees inside his shirt, the critic wrote 'We have seldom met anything much better.' The most serious criticism which the reviewer had to make was that the book displayed a mixture of styles, and that its rustics were not rustic enough to contrast with the other characters.

A little more observation, or rather cultivation of the

---

[1] *Random Recollections of an old Publisher*, Vol. I, p. 127.

gift which the author possesses in abundance, would show him this; and he would then give us what this book, in spite of its second title, falls short of being—a Rural Painting of the Dutch school. His present work is rather a number of studies for such a painting. The ability to paint is there; but practice only can give the power of composition.

One other review may be quoted, from the equally influential *Saturday Review* on September 28th, 1872, because it came from the pen of Horace Moule, the friend who had urged Hardy not to give up writing[1]:

This novel is the best prose idyll that we have seen for a long while past. Deserting the more conventional, and far less agreeable, field of imaginative fiction which he worked in his earlier book called *Desperate Remedies*, the author has produced a series of pictures of rural life and genuine colouring, and drawn with a distinct minuteness reminding one at times of some of the scenes in *Hermann und Dorothea*. . . . *Under the Greenwood Tree* is filled with touches showing the close sympathy with which the writer has watched the life, not only of his fellow-men in the country hamlets, but of woods and fields and all the outward forms of nature. But the staple of the book is made up of personal sketches. . . . Regarded as a whole, the book is one of unusual merit in its own special line, full of humour and keen observation, and with the genuine air of the country breathing through it.

Writing in 1912, for the issue of the book in the collected edition of his works, Hardy expressed regret that *Under the Greenwood Tree* was the work of his youth, still not sicklied o'er with the pale cast of thought, although he did not put it quite in those words:

In rereading the narrative after a long interval there occurs the inevitable reflection that the realities out of which it was spun were material for another kind of study of this little group of church musicians than is found in the chapters here penned so lightly, even so farcically and flippantly at times. But circumstances would have rendered any aim at a deeper,

---

[1] *Early Life*, pp. 115 and 120.

more essential, more transcendent handling unadvisable at the date of writing.[1]

To most readers, the great charm of *Under the Greenwood Tree*, is that it is almost the only one of Hardy's writings which does not contain a tragedy. The episode of Fancy and Mr. Maybold lies on the edge of tragedy, and that is enough. Art should not always be tragic. It has been brought as a very sound criticism against the art of Hardy that, as a whole, it insists too much upon the 'lacrimae rerum.'[2] It is no small part of the pleasure with which *Under the Greenwood Tree* can be read, and read again, that it does not end in a grave.

Under the Greenwood Tree, considered as a work of art, has a freshness about it which Hardy never again achieved. *Far from the Madding Crowd* comes nearest, as a whole; and the first part of *A Pair of Blue Eyes* achieves a spontaneous poetry which is admirable; but upon both of them there lies a deeper shadow; and both of them are clearly works of fiction; whereas *Under the Greenwood Tree* owes much of its charm to the feeling that the subject of this 'rural painting of the Dutch school' is the real life of Dorset as Hardy knew it in his youth. Out of the characters who made up the 'Mellstock' choir, out of William Leaf and Parson Maybold, Hardy took the elements from which the Wessex characters of his later novels were constructed. But here he was drawing from the life. We come across traces of 'that vanished band' occasionally in other places in his writings. They appear briefly in *Two on a Tower*; and again in the short

---

[1] A parallel passage in the 1912 Preface to *A Pair of Blue Eyes* gives Hardy's own answer: 'To the ripe-minded critic . . . an immaturity in its views of life and in its workmanship will of course be apparent. But to correct these by the judgment of later years, even had correction been possible, would have resulted, as with all such attempts, in the disappearance of whatever freshness and spontaneity the pages may have as they stand.'

[2] A review of the collected edition of Hardy's works, which appeared in the *Spectator* on September 7th, 1912, rightly said:

'Great art is representative of life, not critical of it. . . . The art of Sophocles and Shakespeare does not leave our minds impressed by a pessimistic conception of existence. It represents the flux of all things, the cessation of pain and grief as well as of joy and pleasure. It has its compensating values. . . .'

story called 'Absent-Mindedness in a Parish Choir.'[1] The bell ringers in *Desperate Remedies* are their near relatives; and rather more distant is the choir in the thirty-third chapter of *The Mayor of Casterbridge*. They appear sometimes in Hardy's poetry. 'Friends Beyond,' in *Wessex Poems*, and 'The Dead Quire' in *Time's Laughingstocks* recall their memory. The headstones of some of the men immortalized in *Under the Greenwood Tree* still stand in Stinsford Churchyard. Mrs. Hardy gives an account of the death of the man from whom the 'Tranter' was drawn.[2]

Apart from a certain debt to William Barnes, already discussed, *Under the Greenwood Tree* owes practically nothing to other writers. There are Christmas scenes in Dickens; indeed, it has been said that Dickens invented the English Christmas; but in describing the activities of the Mellstock Quire, Hardy was not borrowing suggestions from literature; he was painting from life. The music of Stinsford church had been practically created by Hardy's grandfather, Thomas Hardy the first (1778–1837), who

> played in the gallery of Stinsford Church at two services every Sunday from 1801 or 1802 till his death in 1837, being joined later by his two sons (Thomas Hardy the Second, 1811–1892, and James Hardy), who, with other reinforcement, continued playing till about 1842, the period of performance by the three Hardys thus covering inclusively a little under forty years.[3]

There is a full account of the quire and its doings in the first chapter of *Early Life*; and on p. 13 there is a plan of Stinsford Church, showing the positions of its members in the West Gallery, about 1835, which was drawn up long afterwards by Hardy under the direction of his father. Thus,

---

[1] This first appeared as one of nine 'Colloquial Sketches' in Harper's *New Monthly Magazine*, March-June 1891, and is reprinted as 'A Few Crusted Characters' in *Life's Little Ironies*.

[2] *Early Life*, p. 121. She also points out that Old Dewy was not, as has been supposed, a portrait of Hardy's grandfather. But the idea of the three generations probably came to Hardy from his own family.

[3] *Early Life*, p. 11.

although the activities of the quire in Stinsford Church came to an end while Hardy was still an infant, he grew up in the atmosphere of these departed glories. Because he had never seen or heard them, Hardy was accustomed to say that he had rather burlesqued the quire, 'the story not adequately reflecting, as he could have wished in later years, the poetry and romance that coloured their time-honoured observances.'[1] There are actually some anachronisms in the book, for Hardy describes conditions which ceased in 1841 as coexistent with events which could hardly have occurred before 1860.[2] What happened was clearly that Hardy, when he wrote the novel, made use, both of what he knew only by report and of what he knew personally; the result, even if it does contain some anachronisms, certainly justifies the means. We have other records of church choirs[3]; but the Mellstock choir lives, with the life that only art can bestow.

The Preface to the novel clearly states that it is 'intended to be a fairly true picture, at first hand, of the personages, ways and customs which were common in the villages of fifty or sixty years ago.' Hardy also there describes the music of these instrumentalists:

> Their music in those days was all in their own manuscript, copied in the evenings after work, and their music books were home-bound. It was customary to inscribe a few jigs, reels, hornpipes and ballads in the same book, by beginning it at the other end, the insertions being continued from front and back till sacred and secular met together in the middle, often with bizarre effects, the words of some of the songs exhibiting that ancient and broad humour which our grandfathers, and

[1] *Early Life*, p. 15.
[2] I am indebted to Dr. Percy Scholes for a note on this matter: he wrote to me: '*Under the Greenwood Tree* turns on the introduction of an American organ. That makes 1860 the earliest possible date, which is late for the conditions described. Even the Harmonium did not come into use much earlier or we might guess that Hardy had got a wrong name for the instrument. Note that Hardy mentions "Queen's Scholars," so the date must (I think) be subsequent to 1870.'
[3] The prevalence and importance of village orchestras is illustrated in K. R. Macdermott's *Sussex Church Music in the Past* (2nd ed., 1923). Also in *Devon and Cornwall Notes and Queries*, 1916–17.

possibly grandmothers, took delight in, and is in these days unquotable.

I owe it to the kindness of Mrs. Hardy that I have been able to inspect three manuscript music books, in her possession, which were clearly those in Hardy's mind when he wrote these words.

The first and oldest of them is a home-made volume, composed of plain paper and bound in what appears to be vellum. Inside the cover, on a slip pasted in, is written 'Thomas Hardy. Puddletown 1799,' and across is written 'Thomas Hardy, Bockhampton.' Underneath is written in the hand of Thomas Hardy the author; 'The Carol Book of T.H. 1st (1778–1837). Bass. Used at Puddletown and afterwards at "Mellstock". (Violincello).' On the first page is a table of contents, written across and downwards, containing the first lines of twenty-five sacred items (mostly, but not all, carols). At the other end of the book is written: 'Thomas Hardy. His Book. Puddletown. April 25 1800.' There follow sundry flourishes. On the second page from this end there begin the 'profane' songs, the music being ruled by hand (as throughout the book). The first six of these are:

> 'Gather ye rosebuds while ye may——'
> 'He comes, he comes, the hero comes——'
> 'The jolly bowl doth glad my soul——'
> 'What charms the heart and ear so sweet——'
> 'The dusky night rides down the sky——'
> 'Jolly mortals, fill your glasses——'

Hardy the author seems to have studied this section with particular care; in 'The Maiden's Moan' he has written three suggested emendations. As a taste of the general quality of these 'profane' items, the last four stanzas may be quoted from the last song in the book (which has words, but no corresponding music). This is entitled 'Birds of a Feather,' which concludes as follows (the original spelling is retained):

> If we meet with a female who has been gone astray
> By some artfull Villain Deluded away

Lett us pitty her weakness & sooth of her Pain
Prevent her from going the Same Road again

In all our misfortunes lett this be our plan
To bear it with patients as well as we can
In Justice love Mercy Walk humbly together
And travel through life like Birds of a feather

And when we arrive at the Inn at the Close of the Day
And have a Refreshment leave nothing to pay
And the Next Morning Journey sett all Matters Right
So hear is wishing each other good Night.

With Joyfull Assurance we will all go to Rest
No Cares of the world can trouble our breast
Awak'd by the Trumpett we will all go togeather
And Climb up to heaven like birds of a Feather

Surely a most unexceptionable ditty!

The second music book, belonging to Thomas Hardy the second, is a similar volume; it has written inside the paper binding: 'T. Hardy (Senr) from James Hook, to whose father it belonged (compiled probably about 1820).' On the opposite page, in Hardy the author's hand, is written a note describing the 'Figure of College Hornpipe as danced at Mellstock about 1840.' On an inserted page is a description of 'The Dorchester Hornpipe,' in the hand of Miss Katherine Hardy, and on the verso of this is a descriptive note, again by Hardy the author, of 'The Figure of Haste to the Wedding—as danced at Mellstock about 1840.' These call to mind the description of the dance at the Tranter's party in chapter seven of *Under the Greenwood Tree*, which opened with 'The Triumph, or Follow my Lover.' The original first page is missing, and has been replaced by Hardy the author, who gives an index in pencil of the contents. These contain a very few sacred items (such as 'Hymn 183' with the tune 'Linsted,' Psalm 117, and a Christmas Piece—'Arise and hail the sacred day'). Most of the contents are such as these:

THOMAS HARDY

Alexandria
After many moving years
By the Fountain's Flowery Side
Banks of the Dee
Beggar Girl
Bewildered Maid, etc.

The third music book is a volume bound in brown paper, measuring eight and a half by six and a half inches, bearing on the cover, in the hand of Hardy the author, 'The "Mellstock Quire" Carol Book used on the rounds on Xmas Eve.' Inside is written, in the hand of Thomas Hardy the Second, 'Thomas Hardy. Bockhampton'; and, in the hand of Hardy the author: 'The Carol Book of T.H. II. (used on the rounds on Xmas Eve in the "Mellstock Quire" down to about 1842.') This volume contains only Christmas Carols and Hymns. The great interest of this volume is that it was clearly similar to the ones which are several times mentioned in *Under the Greenwood Tree*.

For example, in chapter three:

"Better try over number seventy-eight before we start, I suppose?" said William, pointing to a heap of old Christmas-carol books on a side table.

"Wi' all my heart," said the choir generally.

"Number seventy-eight was always a teaser—always. I can mind him ever since I was growing up a hard boy-chap."

"But he's a good tune, and worth a mint o' practice," said Michael.

"He is ; though I've been mad enough wi' that tune at times to seize en an tear en all to linnit. Ay, he's a splendid carrel—there's no denying that."

"The first line is well enough," said Mr. Spinks; "but when you come to 'O Thou man,' you make a mess o't."

In the following chapter, the choir sings this redoubtable carol:

'Number seventy-eight,' he softly gave out as they formed round in a semicircle, the boys opening the lanterns to get a clearer light, and directing their rays on the books. Then

156

passed forth into the quiet night an ancient and time-worn
hymn, embodying a quaint Christianity in words orally trans-
mitted from father to son through several generations down to
the present characters, who sang them out right earnestly:—

> Remember Adam's fall,
>   O thou Man;
> Remember Adam's fall
>   From Heaven to Hell.
> Remember Adam's fall:
> How he hath condemned all
> In Hell perpetual
>   There for to dwell.
>
> Remember God's goodnesse,
>   O thou Man;
> Remember God's goodnesse,
>   His promise made,
> Remember God's goodnesse;
> How He sent His Son sinlesse
> Our ails for to redress;
>   Be not afraid!
>
> In Bethlehem He was born,
>   O thou Man;
> In Bethlehem He was born,
>   For mankind's sake.
> In Bethlehem He was born,
> Christmas day i' the morn:
> Our Saviour thought no scorn
>   Our faults to take.
>
> Give thanks to God alway,
>   O thou Man;
> Give thanks to God alway
>   With heart-most joy.
> Give thanks to God alway
> On this our joyful day:
> Let all men sing and say
>   Holy, Holy!

Having concluded the last note, they listened for a minute or two, but found that no sound issued from the school-house.

'Four breaths, and then "O, what unbounded goodness!" number fifty-nine,' said old William.

This was duly gone through, and no notice whatever seemed to be taken of the performance. . . . 'Four breaths, and then the last,' said the leader authoritatively. ' "Rejoice, ye Tenants of the Earth," number sixty-four.'

In the Carol book which is still at Max Gate, number fifty-nine is 'O what unbounded goodness, Lord.' But 'Remember Adam's Fall' is not to be found in it. Number seventy-seven is 'Awake ye drowsy mortals all'; then there is a blank page; and number seventy-nine is 'Rejoice ye tenants of the Earth.' It is clear, however, that (with the slight difference of the numeration of 'Rejoice ye tenants of the Earth') this book was one of those used by the choir and described by Hardy in the novel.

If any other exemplars of the Mellstock carol book exist, they must be in private hands, and I have not been able to see any. Miss Katherine Hardy, Hardy's surviving sister, told me that Hardy got the words of 'Remember Adam's Fall' from their mother; this suggests that he did not have access to another copy of the carol book containing them, although many must have been extant when he was born.

The first occurrence of this very beautiful carol which I have been able to discover is in *Melismata: Musicall Phansies fitting the Court Citie & Countrie Humours*. To 3, 4, and 5 *Voices*, London. Printed by William Stansly & Thomas Adams, 1611; which was edited by T. Ravenscroft. 'Remember Adam's fall,' scored for four voices, is the last of the 'Countrie Pastimes' in this volume, where it is called 'A Christmas Carroll.' As printed by Ravenscroft, it consists of nine verses; of which the second, third, eighth and ninth correspond very closely to the version given by Hardy.

The following are the only noticeable variations:

Hardy:	Ravenscroft:
He hath condemned all—	We were condemned all
He sent His son sinlesse—	How He sent His Son, doubt-less
Our ails—	Our sins—
Christmas day i' the morn—	For us that were forlorn
Our Saviour thought no scorn—	And therefore took no scorn
Our faults to take—	Our flesh to take
With heart-most joy—	With heart most joyfully
On this our joyful day—	For this our happy day

The carol is again to be found in *Cantus: Songs and Fancies.*
To 3, 4 or 5 Parts apt for Voices and Viols, compiled in
1682 by John Forbes.[1] The tune which is given by Ravenscroft is also that given by Forbes. There is no evidence to
show whether or not this was the tune found so trouble-
some by the Mellstock Quire.

The quire of Stinsford Church consisted, besides the
singers, of two violins, a viola, and a violincello or 'bass
viol' (the music book of Thomas Hardy the First being for
the latter). Puddletown boasted of eight players, and
Maiden Newton of nine, which included wood, wind and
leather, that is to say clarinets and serpents.[2] These were
the choirs alluded to in chapter four, who had been so ill
advised as to admit clarinets:

'I can well bring back to my mind,' said Mr. Penny, 'what I
said to poor Joseph Ryme (who took the treble part in Chalk
Newton church for two and forty year) when they thought of
having clar'nets there. "Joseph," I says, said I, "depend upon't,
if so be you have them tooting clar'nets you'll spoil the whole
set-out. Clar'nets were not made for the service of the Lard;
you can see it by looking at 'em," I said.'

But the serpent was no newcomer. When, in the same
chapter, another member of the Mellstock Quire says that

[1] The version and tune given in Chappell's *Old English Popular Music* (2nd ed. by
Wooldridge, 1893, Vol. I, p. 144) are those of Ravenscroft.
[2] *Early Life*, p. 12.

other choirs should have done away with serpents, Mr. Penny replies:

> 'Yet there's worse things than serpents. Old things pass away, 'tis true; but a serpent was a good old note; a deep rich note was the serpent.'

Although now a rare curiosity, the serpent was once a popular instrument. It was invented by a French Abbé at the end of the sixteenth century, and consisted of conical sections of wooden tube held together by a covering of leather, and having a cupped mouthpiece like that of the bass trombone. It somewhat resembled a serpent in shape. Its greatest vogue was in the eighteenth century, when it was introduced into the British Army by George III; and there is a part for the serpent in Handel's Water Music, now played upon the ophicleide.[1]

Besides the choir and its doings, there are other features of the country life of the very early ninteenth century in *Under the Greenwood Tree*. For example, the consultation of Mrs. Endorfield by Fancy can be paralleled in the poems of Barnes[2]; And then there is the dialect. Hardy's principles on the use of dialect in his novels were set forth in two letters to the press, one of which, in answer to a review of *The Return of the Native*, appeared in the *Athenæum* on November 30th, 1878; and the other in the *Spectator* of October 15th, 1881. The substance of the former was that 'an author may be said fairly to convey the spirit of intelligent peasant talk if he retains the idiom, compass and characteristic expressions,' and implied that Hardy's own aim was to 'depict the men and their natures rather than their dialect forms.'[3] In the second he wrote:

> The rule of scrupulously preserving the local idiom, together with the words which have no synonym among those

---

[1] There is a full account, and a picture, of the serpent in *Old English Instruments of Music* (1910), by Francis W. Galpin, p. 195 *et seq.*

[2] e.g., 'Haven Woone's fortune a-twold,' etc. There is a thorough study of Hardy's allusions to white and black witchcraft in *Folkways in Thomas Hardy*, by Ruth A. Firor (1931).

[3] See p. 178.

in general use, while printing in the ordinary way most of those local expressions which are but a modified articulation of words in use elsewhere, is the rule I usually follow.

Concerning one expression, 'Good-now,'[1] Hardy was asked in July 1892 if he could explain the origin of it. The draft of his reply is among other papers at Max Gate, and runs as follows:

The expression "good now" is still much in use in the interior of this country, though it is dying away hereabout. Its tone is one of conjectural assurance, its precise meaning being "You may be sure"; and such phrases as "I'll warrant," "methinks," "sure enough" would be used as alternatives. The Americanism "I guess" is near it.

Though I should know exactly how and when to say it, I have never thought about its root meaning. As the people who use it are those who pronounce enough in the old way "enow," it is possible that "good now " is "true enow," sure enough.

The commentators are quite in error in taking "good" to be vocative meaning "goodman," "my good fellow," as is proved by the frequency of such a sentence as this: "You won't do it my lad, good now," which would otherwise be redundant.

It may be added that Hardy was not, as has sometimes been wrongly stated, brought up to speak the Dorset dialect. Mr. V. H. Collins reports Hardy as referring to this statement in a certain book, and adding:

I did not speak it. I knew it, but it was not spoken at home. My mother only used it when speaking to the cottagers, and my father when speaking to his workmen.[2]

Under the Greenwood Tree contains the seeds of most of the Wessex novels. The Wessex folk are here. The love story is here, not yet touched to tragic issues. The Hardy heroine is instinct in Fancy. The Hardy humour is here. There are touches of the Hardy pathos; for instance, the

---

[1] In Chap. IV, 'He's clever for a silly chap, good now, sir.' The same chapter contains the expression 'chips in porridge,' to which Hardy puts a footnote that it 'must be a corruption of something less questionable.'
[2] *Talks with Thomas Hardy*, p. 73.

closing sentences. Above all, there is the power of conveying the moods of outer nature, and that deft poetic description of tiny details. There are foretastes of some of Hardy's
favourite stylistic devices, as for example the biblical
reference, so very apt, which passes between the grand-
fathers of bride and bridegroom after the wedding:

> 'Ah,' said grandfather James to grandfather William as
> they retired, 'I wonder which she thinks most about, Dick or
> her wedding raiment!'
> 'Well, 'tis their nature,' said grandfather William. 'Remem-
> ber the words of the prophet Jeremiah: "Can a maid forget her
> ornaments or a bride her attire?"'

Nevertheless, as a whole, *Under the Greenwood Tree* seems—
to one reader of it, at least—to bear, not the stamp of
fiction, but the stamp of life seen, remembered, and related
by his elders to a child.

A Pair of Blue Eyes

A Pair of Blue Eyes was written during the latter half
of 1872, in reply to a request from William Tinsley for a
serial for *Tinsley's Magazine*.[1] The first instalment appeared
in the September number, and the last in July 1873. It was
published in three volumes by Tinsley Brothers towards
the end of May 1873. Thereafter, every one of Hardy's
novels made its first appearance in the pages of some
periodical publication. The serial publication of fiction is a
feature of literary history which is of much interest, and
has not yet been adequately investigated. Nearly all the
famous novels of the later nineteenth century first appeared
as serial stories. In the years following 1850, there sprang
up an enormous crop of new periodicals whose *raison
d'être* was the publication of fiction. *Tinsley's Magazine* was
one of these. Founded by Tinsley Brothers in 1867, it ran
until 1886; and among its contributors was Mrs. Henry
Wood. Another was *Macmillan's Magazine*, in which *The*

[1] *Early Life*, p. 118.

Woodlanders first appeared. Perhaps the most notable of these magazines, called into being by the demand for serial fiction, was the *Cornhill*, founded by Smith and Elder in 1860, of which Thackeray was the first editor. It was in the pages of the *Cornhill*, during the editorship of Leslie Stephen, that *Far from the Madding Crowd* was first published, and securely established Hardy as a novelist. The history of the *Cornhill* in its first fifty years is, as its editor wrote with pardonable pride at its Jubilee, almost the history of British fiction in that period. It was for the Jubilee Number that Hardy wrote a poem (reprinted in *Satires of Circumstance*):

> Yes; your updated modern page—
> All flower-fresh as it appears—
> Can claim a time-tried heritage,
> That reaches backward fifty years
> Which, if but short for sleepy squires,
> Is much in magazines' careers.

The account which Tinsley gives of the last book which he had the chance of publishing for Hardy shows very distinct traces of pique:

I tried Mr. Hardy's third novel, called *A Pair of Blue Eyes*, as a serial in my magazine, and in book form, but it was by far the weakest of the three books I published of his. However, a good deal owing to my praise of him, and the merits of *Under the Greenwood Tree*, Mr. Hardy was engaged to write his novel called *Far from the Madding Crowd* in the *Cornhill Magazine*, and for that he found more readers than for any book I published for him. Of course Mr. Hardy was quite within his rights in not offering me his third (*sic*. i.e., fourth) book, although I had paid him rather a large sum of money for *A Pair of Blue Eyes*.[1] However, there is no doubt the Cornhill offer was a large one and started Mr. Hardy afresh on his career as a novelist, for just about that time it was by no means certain he would not return to his profession as an architect, from which he could then have obtained a good income. At all events, he told me,

[1] According to Mrs. Hardy, the sum for both the serial and three volume rights was double what Hardy could have earned by architecture in the same period (*Early Life*, p. 118), and was considered 'very reasonable.'

soon after I did business with him, that unless writing fiction paid him well, he should not go on with it; but it did pay him, and very well indeed. Since Mr. Hardy has become a noted writer of fiction, I have seen it stated that I refused more than one of his books. I never refused one of them, nor even had the chance of doing so.[1]

It is clear that we have there an authentic account of what really passed between Hardy and Tinsley, when the novelist began to feel his power, and was no longer 'much gratified' if he only lost fifteen pounds on every book he published!

The version of *A Pair of Blue Eyes* which appeared in *Tinsley's Magazine* is identical with that published in volume form, after the first half-dozen paragraphs. Hardy greatly improved his first draft; the first paragraph of the original is almost as horrible a specimen of 'journalese' as could be imagined. It is hard to realize how the same man could at the same sitting write such a paragraph, and then that describing Elfride's expression by illustrations from famous pictures; or that about her eyes—'blue as the blue we see between the retreating mouldings of hills and woody slopes on a sunny September morning.'

A Pair of Blue Eyes received more recognition in the Press than any of Hardy's previous works. It was reviewed simultaneously in the *Athenæum* and the *Spectator* on June 28th, 1873, in the *Graphic* on July 12th, in the *Saturday Review* on August 2nd, in the *Examiner* on October 10th, and in the *Pall Mall Gazette* on October 25th. The *Examiner* contrasted Hardy with George Eliot; and the *Saturday Review* wrote:

Many readers of the fresher and truer sort of fiction will be glad to welcome another story from the author of *Under the Greenwood Tree*, who now for the first time assumes his real name. . . . It is one of the most artistically constructed among recent novels. And, from considerations affecting higher matters than mere construction, we should assign it a very high place among works of its class.

[1] *Random Recollections*, Vol. I, p. 127.

This review concluded:

> The author of *A Pair of Blue Eyes* has much to learn and many faults yet to avoid. But he is a writer who, to a singular purity of thought and intention, unites great power of imagination.

Shortly after the book appeared, Hardy received a letter from Coventry Patmore—a total stranger to him—expressing the view that the story of the novel was not a conception for prose, and regretting 'at almost every page that such unequalled beauty and power should not have assured themselves the immortality which would have been impressed upon them by the form of verse.'[1] It was penetrating on the part of Patmore to have seen that the new novelist was really a poet by nature. *A Pair of Blue Eyes* was Tennyson's favourite among Hardy's novels.[2]

The framework of the story was taken from Hardy's own experience; he himself visited Cornwall on a mission of church restoration; and on that mission, in the Vicarage itself, he met the girl who became his wife. There are one or two traces of Hardy's own experience. For example, the copying of the old seat ends in the church (in Chap. VII):

> He had a genuine artistic reason for coming, though no such reason seemed to be required. Six-and-thirty old seat ends, of exquisite fifteenth-century workmanship, were rapidly decaying in an aisle of the church, and it became politic to make drawings of their worm-eaten contours ere they were battered past recognition in the turmoil of the so-called restoration.

The drawings which Hardy made of the old seat ends are preserved to this day in the present church of St. Juliot.[3] A number of incidents in the story had happened to people whom Hardy had known.[4] But further deductions on the value of the book as autobiography are not permissible. It should, in particular, be obvious that, if Hardy himself

---

[1] *Early Life*, p. 138. [2] *Ibid.*, p. 179.
[3] *Ibid.*, p. 105. [4] *Ibid.*, p. 97.

resembled any character in the novel, it was Henry Knight, and not, as has been unwisely stated, Stephen Smith. Hardy was in his thirtieth year when he went to Cornwall; he had written much poetry, and at least one novel; he had lived for years in London, and he had seen something of life.

A parallel between the relations of Stephen Smith and Knight, and those of Hardy and Horace Moule, was drawn by F. A. Hedgcock in his book *Thomas Hardy, Penseur et Artiste* (1911). In his first chapter, Dr. Hedgcock wrote: 'On ne peut s'empêcher de voir dans le récit des luttes de Stephen Smith, de Clym Yeobright et de Jude Fawley une part de souvenir personel.' That sentence alone might have been upheld. To some extent, every man's life appears in his writings; and Hardy used his experiences in his work, although he only used them as the raw material out of which he constructed different situations. But Dr. Hedgcock drew further deductions, the chief value of which was that they came to Hardy's knowledge; and produced an interesting and valuable pronouncement upon this subject of autobiography in his novels. In *Talks with Thomas Hardy*, Mr. V. H. Collins (on p. 73) reports a discussion with Hardy concerning the translation of Dr. Hedgcock's book into English, in the course of which Hardy is reported to have repudiated his self-appointed biographer, saying 'I cannot understand how he could print such stuff.'

An interesting feature of *A Pair of Blue Eyes* is that Hardy returned in it to what seems to have been a very early practice, the heading of every chapter by a quotation. In his later books, the quotations were put in the text; not but that there is a fair sprinkling of quotations and allusions in the text of *A Pair of Blue Eyes*, including ones to Adam Smith, Macaulay and Cicero; but there are far fewer than in *Desperate Remedies*. The epigraph of the book is taken from Hamlet. The scene between Smith and Knight in the Luxellian vault seems to have been suggested by the grave-diggers' scene. The number of Shakespearian allusions in

Hardy's early novels is interesting. There are five in *Desperate Remedies*, one or two in *Under the Greenwood Tree*, and three or four in *Far from the Madding Crowd*. Four of the chapter headings in *An Indiscretion* are from Shakespeare, and at least two of those in *A Pair of Blue Eyes*.

Hardy himself classed *A Pair of Blue Eyes* among his 'romances'; and, writing in 1912, he said: 'In its action it exhibits the romantic stage of an idea which was further developed in a later book.' The allusion is clearly to *Two on a Tower*. Although *A Pair of Blue Eyes* is a less satisfactory book than *Under the Greenwood Tree*, it contains passages of greater imaginative power than any which Hardy had hitherto written. The famous scene on the 'Cliff without a Name' in chapters twenty-one and twenty-two is almost too hackneyed for quotation. The early reviewers noted it, and the critic of the *Saturday Review* described it as 'worked out with extraordinary force.' The tragedy in the book is authentic Hardy; but it is not yet the searing tragedy of the later novels. The chief charm of *A Pair of Blue Eyes* is in the poetry which Patmore recognized; a poetical quality both in conception and execution which appears on nearly every page.

Far from the Madding Crowd

The genesis of *Far from the Madding Crowd* is described in *The Life and Letters of Leslie Stephen*, by F. W. Maitland (1906), to which Hardy contributed some paragraphs, as well as his poem 'The Schreckhorn' (afterwards printed in *Satires of Circumstance*). On p. 270 of that volume Hardy writes:

> It was at the beginning of December 1872, on a wet and windy morning, when in a remote part of the country, that a letter stained with raindrops arrived for me in a handwriting so fine that it might have been traced with a pin's point.

The letter was from Stephen, and led to negotiations which ended in his accepting outright the novel which Hardy was in process of writing, without having even seen the whole manuscript. Hardy came to terms with Smith and Elder, the publishers, and proofs of the first number were sent to him. When returning from Cornwall on the last day of December 1873, he bought at Plymouth a copy of the *Cornhill*, and 'there, to his surprise, saw his story placed at the beginning of the magazine, with a striking illustration.'[1]

The appearance of the story raised a great deal of interest, and the *Spectator*, during the first week of 1874, hazarded a guess that it might be from the pen of George Eliot; a similar comparison was made later in other quarters when the book appeared in volume form. Leslie Stephen wrote to Hardy:

> I am to congratulate you on the reception of your first number. Besides the gentle *Spectator*, which thinks that you must be George Eliot because you know the names of the stars, several good judges have spoken to me warmly of the *Madding Crowd*. Moreover the *Spectator*, though flighty in its head, has really a good deal of critical feeling. I always like to be praised by it—and indeed by other people! The story comes out very well, I think, and I have no criticism to make.[2]

Far from the Madding Crowd ran in the *Cornhill* from January until December 1874; it was published in two volumes by Smith and Elder in November, with the same illustrations by Helen Paterson that had accompanied it in the *Cornhill*; and it firmly established Hardy's career as a novelist. His next novel *The Hand of Ethelberta* was also to appear in the *Cornhill*; while Smith and Elder remained his publishers until 1880, and again published *The Mayor of Casterbridge* in 1886. We have seen how the friendship with Stephen deeply influenced Hardy's thought. Not the least of the results produced by *Far from the Madding Crowd* was that it enabled its author to marry Emma Lavinia Gifford in September.[3]

[1] *Early Life*, p. 128.   [2] *Ibid.*, p. 129.
[3] The serial form of *Far from the Madding Crowd* was identical with that published in two volumes, with the exception of a few words changed in chapter forty-eight. In the serial, this chapter was headed 'Doubts arise, doubts vanish.'

An incident occurred during the serial appearance of the story which was significant as a presage of what was to happen to Hardy in after years. He records it in *The Life and Letters of Leslie Stephen*. Stephen had written, warning him that the seduction of Fanny Robin must be treated in a gingerly fashion, and adding that this was necessary owing to 'an excessive prudery of which I am ashamed.' Hardy continues:

> I wondered what had so suddenly caused, in one who had seemed anything but a prude, the "excessive prudery" alluded to. But I did not learn till I saw him in April. Then he told me that an unexpected Grundian cloud, though no bigger than a man's hand as yet, had appeared upon our serene horizon. Three respectable ladies and subscribers, representing he knew not how many more, had written to upbraid him for an improper passage in a page of the story which had already been published.
>
> I was struck mute, till I said "Well, if you value the opinion of such people, why didn't you think of them beforehand and strike out the passage?"—"I ought to have, since it is their opinion, whether I value it or no," he said with a half groan. "But it didn't occur to me that there was anything to object to!"

The Grundian cloud apparently passed away without discharging its thunder further; and when the book was published in volume form, the very passage which had roused the reprobation of Stephen's lady subscribers was quoted in the review which appeared in the *Times* on January 25th, 1875. Whereupon Hardy triumphed over Stephen with: 'You cannot say that the *Times* is not respectable'; to which Stephen, being an editor and therefore infallible replied: 'You have no more consciousness of these things than a child!' Slight as it was, the incident foreshadowed the mutilation of *Tess* and the burning of *Jude*, which was to end Hardy's career as a novelist. The passage in question was in the eighth chapter, from the marvellous scene in the malthouse, where Master Coggan is describing Bathsheba's father:

"Well now, you'd hardly believe it, but that man—our Miss Everdene's father—was one of the ficklest husbands alive, after a while. Understand, a' didn't want to be fickle, but he couldn't help it. The poor feller were faithful and true enough to her in his wish, but his heart would rove, do what he would. He spoke to me in real tribulation about it once. 'Coggan,' he said, 'I could never wish for a handsomer woman than I've got, but feeling she's ticketed as my lawful wife, I can't help my wicked heart wandering, do what I will.' But at last I believe he cured it by making her take off her wedding ring and calling her by her maiden name as they sat together after the shop was shut, and so a' would fancy she was only his sweetheart, and not married to him at all. And as soon as he could thoroughly fancy he was doing wrong and committing the seventh, a' got to like her as well as ever, and they lived on a perfect picture of mutel love."

Stephen's lady subscribers must indeed have found this very terrible; but they might have found comfort from the comment of Joseph Poorgrass:

"Well, 'twas a most ungodly remedy; but we ought to feel deep cheerfulness that a happy Providence kept it from being any worse."

Far from the Madding Crowd was copiously reviewed in all the periodicals, and most of the reviews were very laudatory.[1] Several of the reviewers, including the critic of the *Times*, again made the comparison with George Eliot which the *Spectator* had first made on the strength of the opening chapter.[2] Mrs. Hardy gives an interesting passage describing Hardy's own attitude to this comparison:

Why (it was made) he could never understand, since, so far as he had read that great thinker—one of the greatest living, he thought, though not a born story-teller, by any means—she had never touched the life of the fields: her country people having seemed to him, too, more like small townsfolk than rustics; and as evidencing a woman's wit cast in country

---

[1] *Echo*, Nov. 28th, 1874; *World*, Dec. 2nd, 1874; *Athenæum*, Dec. 5th, 1874; *Examiner*, Dec. 5th, 1874; *Spectator*, Dec. 19th, 1874; *Saturday Review*, Jan. 9th, 1875; *Times*, Jan. 25th, 1875.
[2] See also L. W. Berle's *George Eliot and Thomas Hardy: a Contrast* (1917).

dialogue rather than real country humour, which he regarded as rather of the Shakespeare and Fielding sort. However, he conjectured, as a possible reason for the flattering guess, that he had latterly been reading Comte's *Positive Philosophy*, and writings of that school, some of whose expressions had thus passed into his vocabulary, expressions which were also common to George Eliot.[1]

It seems much more likely that the critics in question made the comparison on the strength of a certain occasional similarity of phrasing which had nothing to do with positivism. The *Times* critic wrote:

almost from the first page to the last the reader is never quite free from a suspicion that Mr. Hardy is, consciously or unconsciously, imitating George Eliot's phraseology and style of dealing with the rough material of words. Having thus found almost the only fault that is worth finding, we will return to a brief description. . . .

The charge is almost too indefinite either to confirm or refute. But it is true that occasionally there is a similarity of phrasing. For example:

The muddy lanes, green or clayey, that seemed to the unaccustomed eye to lead nowhere but into each other, did really lead, with patience, to a distant high road; but there were many feet in Basset which they led more frequently to a centre of dissipation, spoken of formally as the "Markis o' Granby," but among intimates as "Dickison's." A large, low room with a sanded floor, a cold scent of tobacco, modified by undetected beer dregs, Mr. Dickison leaning against the door post with a melancholy pimpled face, looking as irrelevant to the daylight as a last night's guttered candle—all this may not seem a very seductive form of temptation; but the majority of men in Basset found it fatally alluring when encountered on their road towards four o'clock on a wintry afternoon.

That, especially the sentence describing the inn, might perfectly well be Hardy. Actually, it is from the eighth chapter of *The Mill on the Floss*. To try to carry further the resemblance between the two great novelists is unnecessary;

[1] *Early Life*, p. 129.

for the critics of *Far from the Madding Crowd* carried it no further themselves; and not all of them acknowledged it. The critic in the *Athenæum*, for instance, wrote:

> How his present story could ever have been supposed to have been written by George Eliot we cannot conceive. . . . We should say, on the contrary, that some of the scenes, notably that where Sergeant Troy goes through the sword exercises before Bathsheba, are worthy in their extravagance of Mr. Reade, and of him only; while the stronger parts are Mr. Hardy's own. At least we know of no other living writer who could have so described the burning rick yard or the approaching thunderstorm, or given us the wonderful comicalities of the supper at the malt house.

The position which Hardy was making for himself can be gauged from the fact that a German translation of *Far from the Madding Crowd* was asked for.[1] Hardy was never popular in Germany,[2] so that this was the more remarkable. But it was less surprising that the novel should meet with favour in France; for the French public has appreciated Hardy more thoroughly than any outside English-speaking countries; most of his works sell in good French translations, and when he died, the Académie, at a special meeting, voted an address of sympathy to the English nation, and the *Revue des Deux Mondes* wrote of the burial in Westminster Abbey: 'Il n'y a aucune doute que l'Angleterre vient de placer là un de ses immortels. . . . La Revue se devait de saluer sa grande ombre.'[3]

The first time that Hardy was brought to the notice of the French public was in a long review of *A Pair of Blue Eyes* and *Far from the Madding Crowd* which appeared in *La Revue des Deux Mondes* on December 15th, 1875. This

---

[1] *Early Life*, p. 136.

[2] In a letter which appeared in the *New Statesman* on January 21st, 1928, it was stated that 'quite recently a German bookman of repute told me that he had time and again tried to get the novels taken up by a German publisher, but that in every case the suggestion had been turned down.' Nevertheless, *Jude* had a successful career as a serial in Germany; and *Tess* has been translated into most European languages.

[3] *Revue des Deux Mondes*, January 1928.

article was headed 'Le Roman pastoral en Angleterre,' and was from the pen of Léon Boucher.

M. Boucher gave a brief sketch of the contemporary English novel, in which Wilkie Collins occupied the chief place. After a mention of *Desperate Remedies*, he briefly reviewed *Under the Greenwood Tree*, and at much greater length *A Pair of Blue Eyes*, which he praised very highly. Most of the article was devoted to *Far from the Madding Crowd*, from which long passages were translated.

> M. Hardy a voulu rajeunir le genre antique et souvent ennuyeux de la pastorale, et il y a mis une telle vérité d'observation, une passion si profonde, une poésie si fraiche, un style si puissant, tant d'idéal et de réalité à la fois, que cette transformation peut presque passer pour une création originale.

The criticism of the more highly-coloured parts of the book was essentially sound, and has been repeated by many later critics:

> Ici commence la partie pathétique du roman. Faut-il le dire? Quoique M. Hardy y ait déployé un singulier talent, ce n'est peut-être pas celle qui lui fait le plus d'honneur. On y cotoie le bord du mélodrame, et, si l'on n'y tombe pas tout-a-fait, c'est que les situations, tout en étant violentes, ne deviennent jamais communes.

The conclusion of this article was:

> On ne saurait dire que M. Hardy appartient à une école, car par l'indépendance de son talent il ne relève que de lui-même. . . . Ceux qui aiment à trouver dans le romancier un véritable écrivain sauront lui faire une place à part et le distinguer dans la foule.

Far from the Madding Crowd has been twice adapted to the stage. In March 1882 a dramatic version by Mr. J. Comyns Carr was produced at the Prince of Wales Theatre, Liverpool, and afterwards at the Globe Theatre in London; apparently without financial success. It seems that Hardy himself, who went to Liverpool on purpose to see it,[1]

[1] *Early Life*, p. 198.

considered it too far from the novel. A play based on *Far from the Madding Crowd* was produced in the Corn Exchange, Dorchester, in the autumn of 1909, and afterwards before the Society of Dorset Men in London. Mrs. Hardy writes of this: 'Hardy had nothing to do with the adaptation, but thought it a neater achievement than the London version of 1882.'[1] Although many attempts have been made to dramatize various novels by Hardy, the most noteworthy being in the case of *Tess*, none of them have been really successful. However good in itself, the result is never Hardy; the transplantation into another form of literature cannot be effected without sacrificing almost all that makes the greatness of the novel. Had Hardy lived under Elizabeth or James I, he would probably have achieved great stage drama (which The *Dynasts* was never meant to be). As it was, he wrote fiction 'for the relief of his necessities'; and in due course produced *The Mayor of Casterbridge* and *Tess of the d'Urbervilles*. It seems best to be content with what he has given us; we already have *Othello* and *The Duchess of Malfi*.

In *Far from the Madding Crowd*, Hardy has come almost to his full stature. The sphere of experiment has been left behind; not only does he know what he wishes to do; he has the technique at command with which to do it. The humour of the Wessex rustic—and it was here that Hardy first used the word Wessex, immediately restoring it to the English language—is probably at its best in these pages. The descriptions; the opening chapter, the sheep-shearing, Gabriel Oak thatching the ricks before the storm; are worthy to stand beside any that Hardy was to write. Bathsheba is that very characteristic compound called by critics 'the Hardy woman'; but Boldwood, who has, strangely, no Christian name, is too much of a lay figure. The character of Gabriel Oak, on the other hand, is an achievement. This strong, simple and lovable shepherd is one of the most memorable figures in the Wessex novels. The 'happy

[1] *Later Years*, p. 140.

174

ending' is a concession; but even *The Return of the Native* ends with such a concession; if a final sound of wedding bells can be called a 'happy ending' when it comes after such a breaking of hearts that the peace of the grave is welcome. In *Far from the Madding Crowd*, tragedy stops short of the intensity which the later novels achieve; indeed, there is more pathos than real tragedy. The whole Boldwood episode is too artificial to grip the heart; but the episode of Fanny Robin does. It was the development of the manner in which the fortieth chapter is written that was to give us the Will of Michael Henchard, and the baptism of Tess's Sorrow. But *Far from the Madding Crowd* does not sear as *Tess* sears, or *The Mayor of Casterbridge*. Moreover, it still lacks that power—so memorably put forth in *The Return of the Native*—of enveloping the mere plot in an atmosphere more potent than any single incident. It is, in short, a work which everywhere shows the highest talent; but not yet, except perhaps occasionally in its comedy, genius. Such a novel should be highly popular; and popular *Far from the Madding Crowd* certainly was. It made Hardy's name as a novelist, and so paved the way for the greater things to come.

CHAPTER V

THE NOVELS, 1875-1891

HAVING made his name, Hardy was content to rest for a while; for *The Hand of Ethelberta* cannot be considered anything but a diversion. Editor, publishers, public and critics were all disappointed; and no wonder. To accuse them, as Mrs. Hardy does, of lack of perspicacity for failing to be enthusiastic over this frivolous departure, is unfair; for the point is not whether it was thirty years too soon for a social satire; of social satire Hardy was incapable. He was as much out of his element in a West End drawing-room as Thackeray would have been on a heath in Dorset. The Neighs, the Ladywells and the whole box of puppets are simply tiresome; and the Mountclere intrigue is tenth rate. Indeed, as the Preface shows, Hardy scarcely took the book seriously. Only occasionally a hint of the real Hardy comes through all this trumpery. Listen to the hostler in the Inn at Anglebury rebuking David Straw:

> Go home and tell your mother that ye be no wide-awake boy, and that old John, who went to school with her father afore she was born or thought o', says so. Chok' it all, why should I think there's sommat going on at Knollsea? Honest travelling have been so rascally abused since I was a boy in pinners by tribes of nobodies tearing from one end o' the country to t'other to see the sun go down in salt water, or the moon play jack o'lantern behind some rotten tower, that, upon my song, when life an' death's in the wind, there's no telling the difference!

Of the characters in the story, the only ones that memory can recall within a few hours of reading are Faith and Picotee; Ethelberta herself is rather a bag of tricks than a person. This novel gives, perhaps, a few glimpses of Hardy's early days in London; for example, in the account of Milton's grave in chapter twenty-seven; but for all that it shows of his genius it might never have been written. Perhaps it did him good to lie fallow; for two years later he wrote a masterpiece.

The Return of the Native was written during 1877 at Sturminster Newton, in the little house 'Riverside Villa' overlooking the Stour and the green meadows beyond, which was Hardy's first home after his marriage. Having been refused by Leslie Stephen for the *Cornhill*,[1] it appeared serially from June to December 1878 in *Belgravia*, a magazine founded by Mary Braddon some years before, and was published in three volumes by Smith, Elder and Co., in the autumn of that year. As the experienced Stephen had probably foreseen when he refused it, the book was not at all to the taste of the conventional. The critic of the *Athenæum* began his review with a passage which must have made the Ironic Spirit, as yet unknown to the human race whose antics cause him so much amusement, chuckle with delight:

> Now Mr. Hardy, who at one time seemed as promising as any of the younger generation of story tellers, has published a book distinctly inferior to anything of his which we have yet read. It is not that the story is ill conceived—on the contrary, there are the elements of a good novel in it; but there is just that fault which would appear in the pictures of a person who had a keen eye for the picturesque without having learnt to draw.

The real reason for condemnation, however, appears in the last paragraph, which is a significant indication of how Hardy was beginning to run counter to the conventions of his day:

> One cannot help seeing that the two persons (Eustacia and Wildeve) know no other law than the gratification of their passion, although this is not carried to a point which would place the book on the Index of respectable households. At the

[1] *Life and Letters of Leslie Stephen.*

same time it is clear that Eustacia Vye belongs essentially to the class of which Madame Bovary is the type; and it is impossible not to regret, since this is a type which English opinion will not allow a novelist to depict in its completeness, that Mr. Hardy should have wasted his powers in giving what, after all, is an imperfect and to some extent misleading view of it.[1]

This article also contained a criticism of Hardy's use of Dialect, of which the critic wrote: 'the language of his peasants may be Elizabethan, but it can hardly be Victorian.' Hardy replied in a letter in the *Athenæum* of November 30th, which has not been reprinted in England:

> An author may be said to fairly convey the spirit of intelligent peasant talk if he retains the idiom, compass and characteristic expressions, although he may not encumber the page with obsolete pronunciations. . . . In the printing of standard speech, hardly any phonetic principle at all is observed; and if a writer attempts to exhibit on paper the precise accents of a rustic speaker, he disturbs the proper balance of a true representation by unduly insisting upon the grotesque element; thus directing attention to a point of inferior interest, and diverting it from the speaker's meaning, which is by far the chief concern where the aim is to depict the men and their natures rather than their dialect forms.

The critic of the *Saturday Review* (January 4th, 1879) praised the workmanship, but compared the book unfavourably with Hardy's earlier novels, on the ground that it was less amusing: 'We maintain that the primary object of a story is to amuse, and in the attempt to amuse us Mr. Hardy, in our opinion, breaks down.' The *Times* (December 12th, 1878) confessed itself bemused, but was not ungracious:

> We seem to be transported by Mr. Hardy out of the well trodden fields of ordinary fiction into another world altogether, and that in itself is something to be thankful for. . . . We are transported, we say, into another world; and the fact is that we feel rather abroad there. . . . Yet the story is a striking one

[1] *Athenæum*, November 23rd, 1878.

and well worth reading, were it only for those graphic scenes and descriptions.

Since those days, *The Return of the Native* has come to be recognized as one of Hardy's greatest books. Lionel Johnson declared it to be his favourite among the novels. Reviewing the first part of the *Dynasts*, a critic in the *Academy* ended his article: 'We can only say with a sigh that we would give many such dramas for one *Return of the Native*.'[1] Most of the critics have contrived to make some laudatory reference to the opening chapter, and one of them compares it to 'the entry of the Gods in Wagner.'[2] The novel has been dramatised at least once.[3]

We have seen, when considering *Under the Greenwood Tree*, how Hardy could put into a novel much of what he had known in real life; so that, while the plot was purely fictitious, and the chief characters mainly products of his imagination—working, perhaps, upon suggestions taken from actual people, but not reproducing the originals— what may be called the background to the Wessex novels was very largely painted from the real. To this they owe no small part of their charm. The doings of the 'Mellstock Quire' are the making of *Under the Greenwood Tree*. The woods about High Stoy, with the moods and the voices that Hardy felt and heard among them, are the making of *The Woodlanders*. What Dorset people call the great Heath, which lives in English literature as Egdon, is very largely the making of *The Return of the Native*. Edgon Heath might almost be called the principal character of the book, for we are made to feel its 'vast impassivity' as a living presence. It provides one of the two elements which are always to be found in Hardy's art at its best. Whether we call these elements the transient and the abiding, or the human heart

---

[1] January 23rd, 1904.

[2] *Thomas Hardy: a Lecture*. A. Stanton Whitfield, 1921.

[3] A play divided into four acts and ten scenes based upon *The Return of the Native* was presented by the Hardy Players at the Corn Exchange, Dorchester, in November 1920. There is a copy of the Programme at the British Museum; and the *Graphic* of November 27th contained illustrations.

and the impersonal universe, matters little; for the fundamental meaning is the same; and in this novel Egdon Heath
is the second of them. Beside the Heath, transmuted by
Hardy's imagination into a Presence, there are also many
smaller matters introduced into the novel which are faithfully painted from the real. The most obvious of these are
the Christmas festivities at Mrs. Yeobright's house, which
bear a close relationship to those described in *Under the
Greenwood Tree*. But, while the music of the choir was the
centre of the early picture, that of the later is the Play of St.
George, which Hardy as a boy had seen acted many times.
Towards the end of his life, he reconstructed from memory
this play, which had been acted in Dorset for unremembered
generations. Twenty-five copies of his recension of it were
privately printed in 1921.[1]   The characters in it are Father
Christmas, St. George, the Valiant Soldier, the Turkish
Knight, the Doctor and the Saracen. It is about two
thousand words long, and is the play described in *The
Return*. An investigation of the origin of this apparently
very old folk-drama would be a subject for experts in folklore; but there is no doubt that it greatly fascinated Hardy's
imagination as a child; and it is fortunate that chance has
preserved further details of his impressions. Nearly twenty
years before he reconstructed it, he discussed it with
William Archer, who reported him as saying:

> The Christmas Mummers flourished well into my recollec-
> tion. . . . Our mummers hereabouts gave a regular performance
> —the Play of St George it was called. It contained quite a
> number of traditional characters. . . . Rude as it was, the thing
> used to impress me very much—I can clearly recall the odd sort
> of thrill it would give. The performers used to carry a long
> staff in one hand and a wooden sword in the other, and pace
> monotonously round, intoning their parts on one note, and

[1] The title page is: The Play of St George / As aforetime acted by the / Dorsetshire
Christmas Mummers / Based on the Version in The Return of the Native ; and
completed from other versions and local tradition / By / Thomas Hardy. In a modern
version of this by Roger S. Loomis (New York, 1929), there is a letter from Hardy
permitting reproduction of 'the recension of the Play that I managed to concoct
from my memories of it as acted in my boyhood.'

punctuating them by nicking the sword against the staff. I really don't know (what the action was), except that it ended in a series of mortal combats in which all the characters except St. George were killed. And then the curious thing was that they were invariably brought to life again. A personage was introduced for the purpose, the Doctor of Physick, wearing a cloak and a broad-brimmed beaver.

There would be twelve to fifteen actors in a company, I think. Sometimes a large village would furnish forth two sets of mummers. They would go to the farmhouses round, between Christmas and Twelfth Night, doing some four or five performances each evening, and getting ale and money at every house. Sometimes the mummers of one village would encroach on the traditional 'sphere of influence' of another village, and then there would be a battle in good earnest. (Asked if women took part) I think not—the fair Sabra was always played by a boy. But the character was often omitted. Mumming went on in some neighbourhoods until 1880, or thereabouts.[1]

The 'gypsying' at Alderworth, where Eustacia danced with Wildeve, and the festivities round the maypole in front of Thomasin's house, were both drawn from originals that must have been common enough in Hardy's youth. Less common, doubtless, was the spectacle of the frying of adders to obtain oil for the cure of snakebite; and least common of all, but most interesting, the ghastly incantation, wherewith Susan Nunsuch cursed Eustacia, mutilating and burning a waxen image of her the while.[2] Hardy's introduction of this real and ancient theme from folklore into the crescendo of his own composition, culminating in Eustacia's death, is a very clever piece of work. More significant, perhaps, and less obvious, is the artistic use to which he put the age-old custom of lighting ceremonial bonfires, described so well in the masterly third chapter. Three sentences are particularly noteworthy:

To light a fire is the instinctive resistant act of man when, at the winter ingress, the curfew is sounded throughout

---

[1] *Real Conversations.*
[2] This is discussed in *Folkways in Thomas Hardy,* by R. Firor.

Nature. It indicates a spontaneous, Promethean rebelliousness against the fiat that this recurrent season shall bring foul times, cold darkness, misery and death. Black chaos comes, and the fettered gods of the earth say, Let there be light.

The novel contains also many purely personal touches. The comical description, in the fifth chapter, of the playing of the clarinet by Thomasin's father is a humorous reproduction of the tales which Hardy had heard in his youth of the prowess of his grandfather, Thomas Hardy the First. Venn's eulogy of Budmouth, in chapter ten, is a reminiscence of Hardy's own residence at Weymouth in 1869, when part of *Desperate Remedies* was written. The mention of Scheveningen, Heidelberg and Baden, in the first chapter, recalls his visit to these places in the summer of 1876. The allusion, as an illustration of lack of sentiment, to Napoleon's refusal of terms to the beautiful Queen of Prussia (Chap. X), anticipates a scene in the *Dynasts*.

As a piece of writing alone, *The Return of the Native* holds a very high place among the Wessex novels; its construction would suffice to give it the highest. Writing long afterwards, Hardy said that it was the only one of his novels in which he had consciously striven to observe the unities[1]; the result is impressive. A sense of form was no small part of Hardy's genius. Whether or not we accept the psychological explanation so cogently advanced by Mr. Abercrombie in his study of Hardy for the importance of 'formative imagination' in art, everyone must agree with him as to Hardy's possession of it; and of all Hardy's writings, none testifies to it so clearly as *The Return*. To such shapely symmetry of construction, to so complete a blending of the setting with the story, he did not attain thereafter. Nor was he able again to maintain his own personality so completely in solution throughout the book. The later novels, to keep the metaphor, are supersaturated. *The Mayor of Casterbridge* and *Tess* are perhaps more powerful; but the greater power is gained at a heavy price of too

[1] *Later Years*, p. 235.

obvious intrusion by the author. And withal, no other of his novels better achieves upon the imagination and the emotion of the reader that peculiar mastery which it was the gift of Hardy's genius to achieve.

The advance made upon *Far from the Madding Crowd* in power of language, in intensity and in sureness of workmanship, is great. The bucolic comedy of the earlier book remains, indeed, unsurpassed. Grandfer and Christian Cantle are not what Joseph Poorgrass is. But comedy is now receding into the background with Hardy, finally to disappear altogether; and while *Far from the Madding Crowd* would be ruined by the removal of the bucolic scenes, the removal of all lighter matter would not greatly mar *The Return*. We know from a footnote that all the last part of the later book, in which the tragic tension is relaxed to a somewhat tame 'happy ending' of the secondary plot, was not in the original version. It was a concession to the editor of *Belgravia*; and Hardy ironically invites his readers to choose whatever ending they like.[1] But the true ending of the book is with Part Five; and the difference between it and *Far from the Madding Crowd* cannot be better seen than in this matter of endings. The final happy marriage of Bathsheba is at least conceivable; but for Eustacia the world could never again hold anything so sweet as the waters of oblivion. A comparison of the second chapter of the earlier novel with the first chapter of *The Return*, both descriptions of a natural scene, shows the great advance in the power of Hardy's style. The famous passage describing Egdon needs not quotation.

It has not hitherto been noticed that the origin of this deservedly celebrated chapter may possibly be found in another novel, one of the 'best sellers' of the 'seventies, *A Princess of Thule* (1874), the most popular of the novels of William Black. We know that when he was aspiring to

---

[1] The Manuscript, which is in private hands and not available for inspection, would doubtless show if the original ending was that which now concludes part five, as seems probable.

become a popular novelist in the 'sixties, Hardy studied Wilkie Collins; and there is no reason why he should not have taken a hint from Black in the 'seventies. However that may be, there is a marked and striking resemblance between the first chapter of Hardy's novel, and parts of the first chapter of *A Princess of Thule*. This chapter, called 'Lochaber no more,' chiefly describes a scene in the outer Hebrides on a dark and stormy afternoon, and is a very effective piece of writing.[1] Hardy's opening is better still, for he was by far the greater writer of the two. But it is at least interesting that the opening of a novel written in 1877 should bear a close resemblance to the very unusual opening of the most popular novel of 1874. There can, however, be no further comparison between *A Princess of Thule*, which degenerates progressively, and *The Return of the Native*, which goes from strength to strength. The fires, in the second chapter, and Eustacia's watch, in chapter six, are little less good than Egdon Heath; while the portrait of Eustacia, in chapter seven, is perhaps the best, the subtlest and the most significant that Hardy ever drew. By virtue of it she has taken her place in literature with Emma Bovary and Diana Vernon as surely as, according to her creator, she sits in heaven between the Heloises and the Cleopatras. Her mouth, long since turned to ashes, is drawn for the desire of generations unborn:

> One had fancied that such lip curves were mostly lurking underground in the South as fragments of forgotten marbles.

Her nature remains ever living in its subtlety:

> Her presence brought memories of such things as Bourbon roses, rubies and tropical midnights; her moods recalled lotus eaters and the march in *Athalie*; her motions, the ebb and flow of the sea; her voice, the viola.

It is in the person of this woman, who plays so great a part in her own undoing, but whose accusing shade might

---

[1] The paragraphs which especially suggest comparison with the description of Egdon Heath are the two beginning: 'He looked neither to the right nor the left ... as he drove away from the town into the heart of the lonely and desolate land.'

haunt the gate of paradise, crying for admission, that Hardy has created the most poignant of all his symbols, save one. From the matchless lips of Eustacia, in that scene when she goes to Rainbarrow at the eclipse of the moon to meet the man who loves her, there comes a weary burden, the burden that Hardy saw to be laid upon all life: 'Yet I know that we shall not love like this always.' Behind those words there lies the cup of tears from which the disillusioned children of the later nineteenth century drank so deeply:

> Not for me only, or son of mine—
> The Gods have wrought life and desire of life,
> Heart's love and heart's division. . . .

Beyond the crying of Eustacia in the darkness, on the night when she took her life: 'O the cruelty of putting me into this ill conceived world!' we seem to hear the Chorus of the Pities chanting:

> But O, the intolerable antilogy
> Of making figments feel!

Never again until he wrote the *Dynasts* did Hardy succeed in saying this wholly—and therefore convincingly—by art, as he says it in *The Return of the Native*. One single passage only spoils the claim that this book can make perfectly to convey its author's purpose by the legitimate means of art; and that passage does not properly belong to the book itself, for it occurs in the last part, which was added as an afterthought.[1]

The oft-debated question whether the creation of Eustacia Vye owed anything to the reading of *Madame Bovary* does not seem to merit long discussion. When the reviewer in the *Athenæum* made this comparison in 1878, he was merely using it as a stick to beat Hardy with; but more reliable critics have made the same comparison since, notably Professor Chew.[2] The similarities between Emma and Eustacia are, indeed, clear enough; the tragedy of each

---

[1] The passage is that beginning: 'Human beings, in their generous endeavour to construct a hypothesis that shall not degrade a First Cause. . . .'
[2] *Thomas Hardy* (1928).

of them consists in the disillusionment which reality brings for their romantic dreams of a happiness unconnected with reality. But this, after all, is no uncommon theme; it is as frequently met with in literature as in life; and there is no need to seek in Flaubert for an explanation of Hardy's choice of it. The aim of the two novelists is, in fact, quite different. *Madame Bovary* is a deliberately anti-romantic and most bitter satire; the whole book preaches that life is essentially small, commonplace and futile, when it is not revolting; a process that tends to give 'la croix d'honneur' to the unspeakable Homais and his kind. Now Hardy certainly painted life as tragic, but never (except perhaps at moments in *Jude the Obscure*) as disgusting and contemptible in its futility. Even *Jude* is hardly a satire upon humanity. Hardy's constant and most characteristic view of the human lot is put into the mind of Elizabeth Jane, at the close of *The Mayor of Casterbridge*:

> Her strong sense that neither she nor any human being deserved less than was given, did not blind her to the fact that there were others receiving less who had deserved much more.

It is that which Eustacia Vye exemplifies. *The Return of the Native*, while it does not attempt to preach as *Tess* preaches, is the most artistic presentation among the Wessex novels of the theme which was always present to Hardy's consciousness, the theme which he heard in the soughing of the trees in Yell'ham Wood:

> 'Life offers—to deny.'

Besides its success, artistically so complete in this vital matter, the faults of *The Return* are venial. The worst of them is an excessive and illegitimate use of coincidence. That Mrs. Yeobright was not admitted to Clym's house; that she died as she did; that Clym's letter never reached his despairing wife; these are incidents too purely fortuitous and yet at the same time too cumulative. That so great issues should be wholly hinged upon them is a fault. This excessive use of tragic coincidence until it becomes entirely unconvincing and the mind rebels against the artificial burden, is, as most of the critics have pointed out, the great weakness of Hardy's novels. That it did not succeed in marring them still more is due to the fact that, while he uses tragic accident to move on his plot, Hardy does not rely wholly upon it for conveying his sense of the tragic *fact*. The value of his novels as art depends, indeed, largely upon their power to convey this sense irrespective of fortuitous outward events. And in this respect *The Return of the Native* stands supreme. The most famous of the Wessex novels scarcely passes this test at all. Without such incredibly ill luck, Tess might have lived a happy and beautiful life. Even Jude need not have died cursing his day, had not Fate driven him into the arms of two such women as are not often found in real life. But Eustacia, had she never met either the philandering Wildeve or the dreaming Clym, would not have found happiness and peace of spirit under the sun. We feel as we read that the tragedy of the book is essentially true; and the clumsiness of the machinery detracts little from it. In this it is superior to *The Mayor of Casterbridge*, where also the tragedy is really intrinsic, but where the machinery is so bulky as not to be easily passed over. Some of the dialogue in *The Return*—to pass to another blemish—is unconvincing, notably that in the last, crucial scene between Clym and his wife; and to a lesser degree in the almost equally crucial quarrel between Eustacia and Mrs. Yeobright. But the unreality of the words does not detract greatly from the fundamental reality of both situations. And what he fails to do by dialogue in the first, Hardy does most effectively at the end of the scene, in the pathos of the tying of the bonnet. Minor excellencies of this sort are common in the book; and these happy touches add greatly to the pleasure of reading it. Thomasin looking for apples in the loft, with the pigeons flying round her head; Wildeve and Venn gambling by the light of glow-worms with the heath ponies as unwanted spectators; the creatures of the heath moving about Clym as he cuts furze, unconscious of their presence; these are all delightful remnants left over, as it were, from the fashioning of the main structure in Hardy's most enjoyable, and perhaps best, novel.

In the course of the Christmas Festivities in *The Return of the Native*, Grandfer Cantle gives one of his many reminiscences of the days when he was 'a soldier in the bang-up locals.' He says:

> In the year four 'twas said there wasn't a finer figure in the whole of South Wessex than I, as I looked when dashing past the shop windows with the rest of our company on the day we ran out o' Budmouth because it was thoughted that Boney had landed round the point.

Hardy made this the theme of his next novel. *The Trumpet Major* is really a rural painting, or series of rural paintings, of the Dutch school, after the manner of *Under the Greenwood Tree*, rather than an historical novel in the usual sense. But it has particular importance, as well as intrinsic charm; because, as Hardy tells us in the Preface to the *Dynasts*, it was the first published result of the influences which had impressed the Napoleonic wars upon his childish imagination. The second paragraph of the Preface to *The Trumpet Major* throws much light upon the matter, and must be considered also as significant to the composition of the *Dynasts*, which was taking shape when this Preface was written in 1895. While *The Trumpet Major* may be coupled with *Under the Greenwood Tree* in manner, and while the two go naturally together as the happiest of his books, a fact not unconnected with the debt that both owe to memories of childhood, they differ in this: that whereas the earlier book looks backward only, and paints a past which vanished from all save memory, the later is a prelude to the great work of Hardy's maturity. Something, at least, of the greatness of the *Dynasts* is due to his lifelong interest in the wars of the first Napoleon.

The first phase of this interest was the one described in the Preface to *The Trumpet Major*, the phase of early impressions. The second was a conscious pursuit in adult life of that which had so vividly impressed the child. The later and more advanced stages of Hardy's Napoleonic studies must be considered in connection with the *Dynasts*. It will be seen that he had begun systematic investigations by 1875, when he was already considering an 'Iliad of Europe from 1798 to 1815.'[1] There is in existence a note-book filled with details of the Napoleonic wars, written in the later 'seventies,[2] when Hardy was meditating *The Trumpet Major*. From this aspect, the novel is a first study in the imaginative use of historical material. The actual material consulted is largely enumerated in the Preface; it was at this time that Hardy bought the two massive volumes of Gifford's *History of the Wars occasioned by the French Revolution* which are still in his library; the reference made to it will be found in the sixth chapter of Book V. A large number of contemporary documents of the sort mentioned in the Preface may be seen in a volume, *Dumouriez and the Defence of England against Napoleon*, by J. Holland Rose and A. M. Broadley. Hardy knew Broad-ley; indeed, his copy of this volume is inscribed to him by Broadley; and he was doubtless very familiar with Broad-ley's unique collection of Napoleoneana long before any of it was published.[3] But the greater part of *The Trumpet Major* is indebted, not to the printed, but to the spoken word. As Hardy says in the Preface:

> The present tale is founded more largely upon testimony—oral and written—than any other in this series. The external incidents which direct its course are mostly unexaggerated reproductions of the recollections of old persons well known to the author in childhood, but now long dead, who were eye witnesses of those scenes.

Hardy is reported by William Archer to have corroborated this in a conversation some years later, when he said:

> 'Few of my longer books are so closely founded on fact as

[1] *Early Life*, p. 140. See also p. 274. [2] *Later Years*, p. 227.
[3] See p. 295.

The Trumpet Major. The incident of the people letting their cider run when Buonaparte was reported to have landed is a literal fact.'[1]

The novel ran as a serial in *Good Words* from January to December 1880; and was published in three volumes in October of that year by Smith, Elder & Co. One of the earlier of Hardy's short stories, 'A Tradition of 1804,' written in 1882, may be considered an overflow from *The Trumpet Major*. The book was very well received, being clearly more to the taste of reviewers than its greater tragic predecessor. The *Saturday Review* of November 6th devoted a long article to it:

> Mr Hardy in his latest novel has produced perhaps a finer study of character, in a certain sense, than he has before given to his readers. . . . This central character is surrounded by others, drawn for the most part with the truth and insight which have raised Mr Hardy to the high place he occupies among novelists of our time . . . such faults as these are far outweighed by the merits of the book, but it would be well in the case of a novelist of exceptional strength not to leave them unnoticed.

The *Athenæum*, on November 20th, said:

> Mr Hardy seems to be in the way to do for rural life what Dickens did for that of the town. . . . We have nothing but praise for *The Trumpet Major* . . . the author is second to no living writer in the art of making one see his scenes and know his characters.

While the critic of the *Times*, in an article on February 2nd, 1881, in which he contrived to deprecate *The Return of the Native* by implication, wrote:

> We like *The Trumpet Major* better than *The Return of the Native* and nearly as much as *Far from the Madding Crowd*.

Because it is a slighter piece of work than Hardy's tragic novels, *The Trumpet Major* has been generally passed over by the critics. With the general reader it has been a high

---

[1] *Real Conversations.*

favourite; the pocket edition, always a guide to popularity, was reprinted eleven times between 1909 and 1928. This is small wonder, for it is a charming book, even if a slight one. The slightness is due largely to lack of characterization; for, the *Saturday Review* notwithstanding, John Loveday is the only character who awakens any lively interest; his brother is unconvincing; while Festus is simply the conventional braggart. The miller and Anne's mother provide no more than the necessary background; while Anne herself, though woman enough in the Hardyan sense to choose the wrong man, is hardly a character at all, after Eustacia and Bath-sheba. But the book casts its spell, nevertheless. The life in Ower Moigne ('Overcombe') under the green downs in that far off day lives yet in these quiet pages; and, even though he be not putting forth his power, we feel the master in the writing. When he is gay, he gives us the panegyric of Casterbridge 'strong beer.' When he is grave, it is not to despair, only to a most characteristic wistfulness:

> At twelve o'clock the review was over and the King and his family left the hill. The troops then cleared off the field, the spectators followed, and by one o'clock the downs were bare again.
>
> They still spread their grassy surface to the sun as on that beautiful morning not, historically speaking, so very long ago; but the King and his fifteen thousand armed men, the horses, the bands of music, the princesses, the cream-coloured teams— the gorgeous centrepiece, in short, to which the downs were but the mere mount or margin—how entirely have they all passed and gone!—lying scattered about the world as military and other dust, some at Talavera, Albuera, Salamanca, Vittoria, Toulouse and Waterloo; some in home churchyards; and a few small handfuls in royal vaults.

When he had finished *The Trumpet Major*, Hardy took his wife to Normandy, and shortly after their return he became very ill. For nearly six months he was in bed, some of the time lying with his head lower than his body. It was in such circumstances that he dictated to his wife *A Laodicean*, upon the continuance of which the success of the newly-launched English issue of *Harper's Magazine* depended.[1] It would be stern criticism to judge by artistic standards a book written for sheer necessity under such conditions. Driven to write a novel when he was not fit to write at all, Hardy reverted to the old 'tale of mystery' which he had studied at the beginning of his career. *A Laodicean* does not pretend to be anything more than the means, as the Preface says, of whiling away an idle afternoon. The use which Hardy made of his memories of architectural training is noteworthy; as is also the extraordinary passage about paedo-baptism in the seventh chapter, already mentioned.

The novel which followed *A Laodicean* is not much more than half its length; but it is as interesting and suggestive as the other is dull and insignificant. *Two on a Tower* was written in the early months of 1882; to familiarize himself to some extent with the science of which the hero was to be an adept, Hardy, we are told, visited Greenwich Observatory, and to get permission he had to hoax the Astronomer Royal with a scientific letter about adapting an old tower in the west of England as an observatory.[2] If that letter survives, it would be an interesting document. He must also, as the novel shows, have read a few books on astronomy for the technical details used. The scene of the story, called Welland House, was really Charborough Park.[3] *Two on a Tower* first appeared as a serial in the *Atlantic Monthly*, of Boston, U.S.A., from May to December 1882; it was published in London in three volumes by Sampson, Low, Marston, Searle & Rivington in the autumn of that year.

It is not surprising that the book was frowned upon. The part assigned to a bishop in it, and the marital complications of the plot, were more than enough to ensure censure; even though Hardy was still careful to avoid, with great ingenuity, anything which could fairly be called immoral by the sensitive. It was with sardonic humour

---

[1] *Early Life*, p. 187.   [2] *Early Life*, p. 195.   [3] *Later Years*, p. 35.

that, sixteen years later, on the eve of the publication of *Jude*, he wrote in the Preface of 1895:

> I venture to think that those who care to read the story now will be quite astonished at the scrupulous propriety observed therein on the relations of the sexes.

The machinery devised to safeguard this propriety is the only tedious part of the book. It did not, however, suffice to win him favour. The *Saturday Review* (November 18th, 1882) reviewed the book very unfavourably:

> We cannot but think the work extremely disappointing, and hope that the author's next venture may be more in accordance with his former triumphs.

The critic of the *Spectator* made no attempt to conceal his feelings:

> We may be quite wrong, but in our opinion this is a story as unpleasant as it is practically impossible. . . . There is not, from beginning to end, a single gleam of probability in the plot; and what good can be served by violating all natural motives in order to produce such unpleasant results we are at a loss to see. . . . It is melodramatic without strength, extravagant without object and objectionable without truth.[1]

Two on a Tower seems to have been overshadowed, for later critics, by Hardy's greater novels, and most of them pass it over in silence, or give it but a word; Mr. Abercrombie, however, praises it highly. Professedly nothing more than a slight romance, the book may be classed with *A Pair of Blue Eyes*, which it resembles while greatly surpassing in wistful beauty; but it is, in fact, worthy of more attention than its professions would suggest.

We saw in the third chapter how the teaching of the science of his day profoundly affected Hardy's outlook; and to illustrate this, a passage from *Two on a Tower* was quoted, and placed beside some lines from *The City of Dreadful Night*. *Two on a Tower* is the only one of the Wessex novels in which the science of the nineteenth century, the implications of which lie behind all Hardy's mature work, is

---

[1] February 3rd, 1883.

allowed actually to appear; and its appearance is striking. In the first paragraph of the Preface, Hardy wrote:

> This slightly built romance was the outcome of a wish to set the emotional history of two infinitesimal lives against the stupendous background of the stellar universe, and to impart to readers the sentiment that of these contrasting magnitudes the smaller might be the greater to them as men.

These sentences, written about himself, are more pregnant than many entire volumes of criticism of Hardy. They describe in a nutshell the essential characteristic of his art. For 'the emotional history of two infinitesimal lives' and 'the stupendous background of the stellar universe,' write Eustacia Vye and Egdon Heath; or write 'shapes that bleed, mere mannikins or no' and the Immanent Will; or even Tess and 'the President of the Immortals'; it matters little what name we give to the two constants—to borrow a convenient term from mathematics—of Hardy's art. This contrast, antinomy, call it what we will, is the subject of all the forms of his art. Beside this paragraph from the Preface to *Two on a Tower* it is not inapt to place one of Hardy's best poems; that this sonnet (in *Poems of the Past and Present*) also describes the very event in nature which was the signal for the meeting of Clym and Eustacia, in the midst of Egdon, is no coincidence:

At a Lunar Eclipse

Thy shadow, Earth, from Pole to Central Sea,
Now steals along upon the Moon's meek shine
In even monochrome and curving line
Of imperturbable serenity.
How shall I link such sun-cast symmetry
With the torn troubled form I know as thine,
That profile, placid as a brow divine,
With continents of moil and misery?

And can immense Mortality but throw
So small a shade, and Heaven's high human scheme

Be hemmed within the coasts yon arc implies?
Is such the stellar gauge of earthly show,
Nation at war with nation, brains that teem,
Heroes, and women fairer than the skies?

This, the central idea of Hardy's art, provides the framework of *Two on a Tower*. The fourth chapter, already quoted, may almost be said to summarize the most important portion, from the point of view of artistic results, of Hardy's spiritual autobiography, especially in that passage where Swithin expounds the implications of science:

It is the same in everything; nothing was made for man. . . . If you are restless and anxious, study astronomy; your troubles will be reduced amazingly; but your study will reduce them in a singular way, by reducing the importance of everything. . . . It is better, far better, for men to forget the universe than to bear it in mind.

The words are placed in the mouth of Swithin St. Cleeve. But the man who placed them there wrote a poem, when he was twenty-six, in which some of these ideas are clearly to be seen. The sonnet 'In Vision I Roamed,' dated 1866, is one of Hardy's earliest surviving poems; in it he describes how

as I thought my spirit ranged on and on
In footless traverse through ghast heights of sky,
To the last chambers of the monstrous Dome,
Where stars the brightest here are lost to the eye:
Then, any spot on our own Earth seemed home!
And the sick grief that you were far away
Grew pleasant thankfulness that you were near,
Who might have been, set on some foreign Sphere,
Less than a Want to me, as day by day
I lived unware, uncaring all that lay
Locked in that Universe taciturn and drear.

This was nearly twenty years before *Two on a Tower*; twenty years after it, Hardy wrote in a private letter to a friend:

What we gain by science is, after all, sadness, as the Preacher saith. The more we know of the laws and nature of the Universe, the more ghastly a business one perceives it all to be.[1]

Two on a Tower stands midway between the awe of the young man and the despair of the old. Just before the end of that novel, we may read:

> He was a scientist. . . there is something in the inexorably simple logic of such men which partakes of the cruelty of the natural laws which are their study.

Considered simply as imaginative literature, this novel is a somewhat frail piece of work, but withal of a singular charm. The improbability of some of the story is of very small account in so frankly romantic a book; and, mere events apart, the emotional atmosphere is true enough; truer, perhaps, than in the more frequently discussed of Hardy's novels. To take an example; an otherwise discriminating critic, thinking of the latter, has written that 'Hardy's women are all of one type, differing only in degree. They are essentially Cyrenaics.'[2] And yet, mentally reviewing Hardy's women, does not Viviette stand out in the memory more strongly than these? Timid to a degree hard to believe in these days of feminine emancipation, she, at the other end of the social scale, has as much of the heroic as Marty South; if not more, for her part is an even harder one to play. Although it rather drags in the middle, the concluding chapters of *Two on a Tower* have a haunting beauty that stands out among the many beautiful pages of the Wessex novels. This climax is all the more memorable for being written in a lower key, and with much less orchestration, than is usual with Hardy. The hopeless weeping, the dry-eyed heartbreak, are absent. But the mistress who reigns sovereign here, among the sighing pines around Swithin's tower, hath her music too.

> She dwells with Beauty, Beauty that must die,
> And Joy whose hand is ever at his lips,
> Bidding adieu.

[1] See p. 64.

[2] Samuel C. Chew. Much the same is said by Arthur Symons in his *Study of Thomas Hardy* (1927).

It is rare among novelists to say so much in so few words as Hardy says, in those describing Viviette as she appeared in after years, to the eyes of the astronomer who had loved her first when she was young and he was a boy:

> The masses of hair that were once darkness visible had become touched here and there by a faint grey haze like the Via Lactea in a midnight sky.

As an introduction to Hardy's writings, which should avoid the pain of full initiation, and yet reveal the compelling charm of his sombre poetry that is so often written in prose, *Two on a Tower* is the ideal book.

In none of the three novels which followed *The Return of the Native* had Hardy put forth all his power; during these seven years he had thrown off one 'pot boiler,' and written two charming books, each of them, as we have seen, significant in its own special subject, but neither of them fully representative of his whole personality. In the summer of 1883 he and his wife moved from Wimborne to Dorchester, on the outskirts of which he bought a piece of ground and began preparations for building the house which was to be his home thenceforward.[1] Max Gate was not finished until the summer of 1885; the Hardys meanwhile lived in Dorchester, and he wrote a novel exceeding in power, although not in craftsmanship, any of its predecessors; and differing from them in some important respects. Moreover, it owes not a little to his change of home. *The Life and Death of the Mayor of Casterbridge*, to give it its full title, was being written in the summer of 1884, and was finished on April 17th, 1885.[2] It appeared as a serial both in the *Graphic* in England, and in *Harper's Weekly* in the U.S.A. from January to May 1886, in a form substantially different from that now familiar, of which more anon; and it was published in two volumes by Smith, Elder & Co. in the latter month. It is interesting and significant that, despite Hardy's now great reputation, there was some difficulty over its publication in volume

[1] *Early Life*, p. 212 *et seq.*   [2] *Early Life*, pp. 219, 223.

form, the publisher's reader reporting that 'the lack of gentry among the characters made it uninteresting.'[1] Mrs. Hardy's suggestion that this was due to the snobbishness of mid-Victorian taste seems hardly a full explanation. The reason alleged would have applied with equal cogency to every one of the books which had given Hardy his reputation; and the publishers must have known it well enough, even if they did not write this to Hardy; but the real reason was surely another one. *The Mayor of Casterbridge* exemplified what had become Hardy's personal philosophy of life with a starkness to be found in none of his previous books. In 1877 he had been willing to bow to public taste so far as to concoct a 'happy ending' to *The Return of the Native*. But in 1885 he made not the slightest concession. *The Mayor of Casterbridge* moves remorselessly to its remorseless close; and the close is the reflection concerning Elizabeth Jane, whose youth 'had seemed to teach that happiness was but an occasional episode in the general drama of pain.' It was, surely, this bitter flavour which the publisher's reader, reading the book through as a whole, caught as the readers of the weekly instalments of the doctored serial version would not; and this it was which gave him pause. His objection did not, however, finally prevent publication.

The power of the book was at once recognized. The reviewer in the *Athenæum* of May 29th, 1886, wrote of Hardy:

> He has a gift of so telling the story that it sticks by the reader for days afterwards, mixing itself with his impressions and recollections of real people, just as a very vivid dream will sometimes do, till he is not quite sure whether it also does not belong to them. He has never shown these qualities better than in his latest novel.

This review ended with an astounding sentence, worthy of quotation as showing how the chasm between Hardy's art and the public taste in fiction, or what was supposed so to be, was rapidly widening:

[1] *Early Life*, p. 235.

> *The Mayor of Casterbridge* will not be so popular as *The Trumpet Major*; nor does it deserve to be, recounting as it does the tragedy (if it may so be called) of a self-willed instead of an unselfish hero.

The still more conventional *Saturday Review* delivered itself even less perspicaciously (May 29th):

> The worst feature of the book is that it does not contain a single character capable of arousing a passing interest.

There were, however, others of a different opinion, whose opinions were more worth hearing. Stevenson wrote to Hardy:

> I have read *The Mayor of Casterbridge* with sincere admiration; Henchard is a great fellow, and Dorchester is touched in with the hand of a master. Do you think you would let me try to dramatize it?[1]

Forty years later, the book was dramatized by Mr. John Drinkwater; it had already been made into a film in 1921. During all the present century it has been very popular in England and America; and it appears to have had a certain vogue in Germany, under the title *Der Bürgermeister*.

We have seen in the third chapter how Hardy had, by the eighteen-eighties, become a profoundly disillusioned and sorrowful man. This is most obvious in *The Mayor of Casterbridge*. But there is another, hardly less interesting, background to this novel, which is provided by Hardy's move to Dorchester. The setting of the book is quite different from any which he had used before. Many critics since Stevenson have praised the picture of 'Casterbridge.' Indeed, it would probably be fair to say that Hardy's Casterbridge is familiar ground to countless people who have never seen Dorchester. The masterly picture of the little town, as it must have been in the 'fifties and 'sixties, when Hardy went to school there, and later lived there as an apprentice, arises out of these pages. The first impressions of a traveller coming to it are in the fourth chapter; then we are introduced to the Town society, both high and

[1] *Early Life*, p. 235.

low, gathered inside and outside the King's Arms[1]; next, we are taken into the more intimate recesses of The Three Mariners; there is a delightful vignette in the ninth chapter; by the end of the book we seem to have lived for many years in Casterbridge, and to know all its streets and houses, its granaries and cornfields, its courthouse and its Mixen Lane.

When Hardy returned as a man to live in the first town which he had known, it was not unnatural that he should make it the scene of the novel he was then writing. Particularly interesting is it that time has preserved what may well have been the nucleus of the whole book, although this has never been noticed. It arose directly out of his move. During the excavations which were made in the autumn of 1883 for the well and the foundations at Max Gate, the spade came upon three graves made there fifteen hundred years before. Hardy read an account of these to the Dorset Field Club, although for some reason that can only be conjectured his paper was not published in the *Proceedings* until six years later.[2] It may have been this suppression which caused him to reproduce the most striking part of this paper in the novel which he was then beginning. The most notable of many descriptive passages in *The Mayor of Casterbridge* is the first half of the eleventh chapter, describing the Roman Amphitheatre at Dorchester, known as Malmbury Rings. Before describing the Rings, Hardy gives a general description of Dorchester; the second paragraph runs:

> Casterbridge announced old Rome in every street, alley and precinct. It looked Roman, bespoke the art of Rome, concealed dead men of Rome. It was impossible to dig more than a foot or two about the town fields and gardens without coming upon some tall soldier of the Empire, who had lain there in his silent, unobtrusive rest for a space of fifteen hundred years.

[1] In the first edition this was called The Golden Crown.
[2] 'Some Romano-British relics found at Max Gate, Dorchester. Read at the Dorchester meeting, 1884; omitted from the volume of that date.' *Proceedings of the Dorset Field Club*, Vol. XI (1890), p. 78.

He was mostly found lying on his side, in an oval scoop in the chalk, like a chicken in its shell; his knees drawn up to his chest; sometimes with the remains of his spear against his arm; a fibula or brooch of bronze on his breast or forehead; an urn at his knees, a jar at his throat, a bottle at his mouth; and mystified conjecture pouring down upon him from the eyes of Casterbridge street boys and men, who had turned a moment to gaze at the familiar spectacle as they passed by.[1]

In his paper to the Field Club describing the discovery at Max Gate, Hardy had written:

On this comparatively level ground we discovered, about three feet below the surface, three human skeletons in separate and distinct graves. Each grave was, as nearly as possible, an ellipse in plan, about four feet long and two and a half feet wide, cut vertically into the solid chalk. The remains bore marks of careful interment. In two of the graves, and, I believe, in the third, a body lay on its right side, the knees being drawn up to the chest, and the arms extended downwards so that the hands rested against the ankles. Each body was fitted with one may say almost perfect accuracy into the oval hole, the crown of the head touching the maiden chalk at one end, and the toes at the other, the tight-fitting situation being strongly suggestive of the chicken in the egg shell. The closest examination failed to detect any traces of enclosure for the remains, and the natural inference was that, save their possible cerements, they were deposited bare in the earth. On the head of one of these, between the top of the forehead and the crown, rested a fibula, or clasp of bronze and iron, the front having apparently been gilt.

Before leaving the subject of the influence upon *The Mayor of Casterbridge* of Hardy's connection with the Dorset Field Club, it should be noted that the description of the amphitheatre in this eleventh chapter bears distinct traces of having been suggested by a paper on the Amphitheatre from Alfred Pope in the *Proceedings* for 1885. A number of close verbal resemblances between Hardy's description and Mr. Pope's paper, combined with the date and with

---

[1] The appearance of this passage on p. 99 of the Manuscript has nothing to suggest that it was a later addition to the chapter as originally written.

Hardy's known connection with the Club, almost rule out entire independence. Hardy had probably heard the paper read, even if he did not read it again to himself. It must, however, be remembered that he needed no one else to draw his attention to the Amphitheatre. It had been vividly impressed upon his imagination as a very small boy, when his father took him to see the burning in effigy there of the Pope and Cardinal Wiseman during some no-Popery riots.[1] This was probably the ultimate origin of the eleventh chapter in *The Mayor of Casterbridge*. The earthwork had been excavated in 1879; so that to one familiar with it from earliest childhood, writing about the town and its features in 1884, it would naturally occur to introduce some description of the ring. Hardy's description, whatever its origin, is masterly; particularly effective is the touch about old people who had, in their day dreams, 'beheld the slopes lined with a gazing legion of Hadrian's soldiery.'

In the paper which Hardy read to the Field Club in 1884, there is a passage towards the conclusion which raises interesting speculations:

> In spite of the numerous vestiges which have been discovered from time to time of the Roman city which formerly stood on the site of modern Dorchester . . . one is struck with the fact that little had been done towards piecing-together and reconstructing these evidences into an unmutilated whole—such as has been done, for instance, with the evidences of Pompeiian life—a whole which should represent Dorchester in particular and not merely the general character of a Roman station in this country, composing a true picture by which the uninformed could mentally realize the ancient scene with some completeness. It would be a worthy attempt to rehabilitate, on paper, the living Durnovaria of fourteen or fifteen hundred years ago—as it actually appeared to the eyes of the then Dorchester men and women, under the rays of the same morning and evening sun which rises and sets over it now.

Reading that passage, one cannot help asking: when first he

[1] *Early Life*, p. 27.

thought of writing a novel of which the town where he
had come to live should be the centre, did Hardy toy with
the idea that it should portray Dorchester, not of the nineteenth, but of the fourth, century? In other words, did not
The Mayor of Casterbridge come near to taking shape as an
historical romance, a second (and it would doubtless have
been a very different) *Last Days of Pompeii*? The question
can never be answered; and it is useless to speculate what
sort of a Romano-British romance Hardy would have
written. There are other indications that for some years
during the middle 'eighties his imagination remained very
much alive to the fascination of this subject, notably the
sonnet (in *Poems of the Past and Present*) written in April
1887 at the Old Theatre at Fiesole:

> I traced the Circus whose grey stones incline
> Where Rome and dim Etruria interjoin,
> Till came a child who showed an ancient coin
> That bore the image of a Constantine,
> She lightly passed; nor did she once opine
> How, better than all books, she had raised for me
> In swift perspective Europe's history
> Through the vast years of Caesar's sceptred line.
>
> For in my distant plot of English loam
> 'Twas but to delve, and straightway there to find
> Coins of like impress. As with one half blind
> Whom common simples cure, her act flashed home
> In that mute moment to my opened mind
> The power, the pride, the reach of vanished Rome.

The short story *A Tryst at an Ancient Earthwork*, republished in *A Changed Man*, but originally written in
1885,[1] is a sort of overflow, as it were, from *The Mayor of
Casterbridge*. The gigantic earthwork there called Mai Dun,
commonly known as Maiden Castle, could not fail to
attract so imaginative a man as Hardy; he mentions it

[1] Originally published in the *Detroit Post* of March 1885, its first English appearance was in a very slightly modified form in the Christmas number of the *English
Illustrated Magazine*, 1893.

briefly in the forty-third chapter of the novel; and as soon as the novel was off his hands, made it—as it well deserved —the subject of a separate story, which is certainly disappointing as a piece of literature, but doubly interesting from its subject, and which has something of the appearance of being founded on fact. The elderly gentleman in broadcloth with letters after his name, who dug all night in the storm, may well have been one of the worthies known to Hardy at the Field Club. It is to be noted that in this tale the Roman, not the Celtic, past of Maiden Castle interests Hardy.

The Mayor of Casterbridge was the first of Hardy's novels to appear in a serial version markedly different from the version afterwards published in volume form. It will be seen in the next chapter that in the case of his last two novels, Hardy, doubtless at the dictation of editors, 'bowdlerized' his work for family consumption, to such an extent that the serial versions of *Tess* and *Jude* are ridiculous. As will be seen, the Manuscripts of these two novels show very clearly that the versions now familiar were the older, the manipulations necessary to appease editors being subsequently done in different coloured ink. In the case of *The Mayor of Casterbridge*, however, the Manuscript of which has found an appropriate resting place in the Dorset County Museum, it would appear that the serial version was, in the main, the earlier. Where there are variations between the standard form of the novel (which may be taken as that of 1895) and the serial form in which it first appeared, the version in the Manuscript is that of the serial. The principal differences may be briefly summarized[1]: broadly speaking, the serial is more sensational, melodramatic and unlikely, while at the same time it keeps nearer to the proprieties demanded by the conventions of the time, which were becoming increasingly irksome to

---

[1] There is a very detailed, and in the main excellent, study of the texts of *The Mayor*, *Tess* and *Jude* in: *Thomas Hardy: from Serial to Novel*, by Mary E. Chase (University of Minnesota Press, 1927). It does not seem to have occurred to Miss Chase to refer to the MSS.

Hardy, and were violently thrown off by him in *Tess*. An excellent instance of these points is provided by Lucetta. In the serial, Henchard's meeting with her is thus described:

> For many years it has been my custom to go to Jersey in the way of business—particularly in the potato season; I do a large trade with them in that line. Well, one autumn I was there and had an accident. I fell out of a boat in the harbour, and struck my head in falling. If somebody had not fished me up instantly I should have been drowned. An account of it was in the paper at the time. . . . The person who saved me was a woman, a fruit merchant's daughter.[1]

In the early (serial) version all the relations between Henchard and Lucetta are of the very strictest propriety; to accomplish which, Hardy had not only to sacrifice verisimilitude, but also to perform some prodigious juggling. It would be tedious to relate all the absurdities at length; the chief point was that editorial pudicity was kept inviolate by making Henchard marry Lucetta at St. Helier, a fortnight before the appearance of Susan. When Lucetta comes from Jersey, Farfrae is sent to meet her at the boat at Budmouth, where a chaste scene is enacted:

> Farfrae thereupon descended to the cabin entrance, and in a moment or two a white hand and arm were stretched out behind a curtain that hung across the doorway. He murmured 'Mrs. Henchard.' The owner of the hand said 'Yes,' and he placed the letter within her fingers, which were quickly withdrawn.

There are also many minor differences between serial and volume; Elizabeth Jane's eyes, for instance, are blue in the former but black in the latter. In the Manuscript, Henchard's Christian name was first of all Giles, which later became James; there is no Michael; and Farfrae was originally, not Donald, but Alan. One of the very few significant cancels is a passage in chapter twelve:

> Henchard's voice grew hoarsely indicative of passionate revolt against human destiny, as he added: 'After eighteen years

[1] This actual passage is inserted on the verso of p. 110 of the MS., and was probably added later; but the whole chapter in the MS. is the serial version.

of caution I've compromised myself by acting a fortnight too soon.'

That is so much in keeping with the whole spirit in which the book was conceived that it is a pity Hardy erased it.

On the subject of Farfrae, there are in Mrs. Hardy's possession a number of letters from a Scotch friend of Hardy's, Sir George Douglas, in reply to letters from Hardy about Farfrae's expressions. Douglas made a list, from the serial version in the *Graphic*, of phrases which he did not think it likely a Scotsman would use; and Hardy corrected these in the second edition. This is the incident alluded to in the Preface. Of glimpses at the folk customs which Hardy had known as a child, *The Mayor of Casterbridge* affords but few. There is the weather prophet, Mr. Fall, or 'Wide-oh,' whom Henchard visits in chapter twenty-six, and is made by him to feel 'Like Saul at his reception by Samuel'[1]; and there is the fatal 'skimmington ride'; but that, despite its far-reaching results, is always kept just out of sight round a corner, and we gather its details only from allusions. Mother Cuxom's reference, in chapter thirty-six, to the practice of uneducated country girls getting a child to write their love letters for them, and paying him not to reveal the contents, is possibly autobiographical. We are told that the little Hardy was thus employed at Bockhampton.[2] Another great English novelist is also said to have had a similar experience as a boy; but young Richardson wrote out of his own fertile head the letters which his clients ordered; whereas little Hardy was supposed only to write what was dictated; a reader of his story 'On the Western Circuit' may wonder how far the dictation was adhered to.

The Mayor of Casterbridge stands by itself among the Wessex novels in several respects. It is, for instance, the only one among them in which, not love, but ambition, is the dominant tragic theme. The concentration of all the

[1] In *Tess*, this worthy is referred to as long deceased.
[2] *Later Years*, p. 38.

interest into one single character is not as great as in *Tess*. But the method of *The Mayor* clearly approaches to the method of Hardy's last two 'epic' novels; and nowhere else did Hardy so closely bind up the 'tragic mischief' with the personality of the chief character. All the critics have discussed this point; and one of them has written of Henchard:

> The warp of calamity which is spun out of the tragic character is caught up, as it were, by the weft of malign external Fate, and woven into that dire net from which there is no escape save by the way of death.[1]

The manner in which calamity is spun out of Henchard's character gives the book its title to greatness; for great it is, despite the most faulty construction to be found in Hardy's mature writings. The plot is of such a complexity, and withal so improbable, that the reader's imagination boggles and refuses to co-operate further. With all the good will in the world, we simply cannot believe that all these unlikely situations existed, and all these incredible coincidences took place. They remind us, painfully, that Hardy first learnt novel writing in the school of Wilkie Collins. Hardy was himself well aware of this weakness; on the day when the book began as a serial, he wrote in his diary:

> I fear it will not be as good as I meant; but, after all, it is not improbabilities of incident but improbabilities of character that matter.[2]

And yet, despite all the improbabilities, Hardy's genius asserted itself in the making of Michael Henchard. Among all the heroes in modern literature, he comes nearest to Aristotle's definition of the perfect tragic hero. He reminds us of the Ajax of Sophocles. The reality of this man, and the inevitability of his self-made tragedy, grip us and will not let us go. To regard him, in the words of one critic, as 'a single mortal writhing on the toasting fork of Fate,'[3] is to

---

[1] W. H. Gardner: *Some Thoughts on the Mayor of Casterbridge.* English Association Pamphlet, No. 77 (November 1930).
[2] *Early Life,* p. 231.
[3] H. C. Duffin: *Thomas Hardy: a Study of the Wessex Novels* (1916).

miss much of the poignancy of the book, and most of its greatness. He is, indeed, a victim; as, in some sense, all tragic heroes must be; but the real tragedy of Henchard is that he is the victim of himself, and he has been, not inaptly, compared with Lear.[1] Mr. Abercrombie has described more pithily than anyone else both the significance of this man, and his part in the novel:

> His is the life through which the ceaseless electricity of universal force is to be shown pouring . . . and it is his spirit that is to resist with its own desires the fatal energy of general existence, burning to incandescence with its resistance, and at last broken with its burning. . . . In the rest of Hardy's fiction, (the) tragic elements are separately provided by personality and the circumstances that have hold of personality. But the elemental antinomy which is the basis of Hardy's tragedy is entirely Henchard's own. . . . He himself appears as the symbolic counterpart of the whole tragic substance of the other dramatic novels.[2]

One of the particular contributions which Hardy made to the English novel is to be seen in greater concentration than anywhere else in the closing pages of *The Mayor of Casterbridge*. He can wring the heart as few novelists have done; and never, not even in *Tess*, did he do so more deftly or more mercilessly than in this picture of the strong man, whose proud head not the utmost extremity of contrary fortune can bow, but whose heart is broken by his severance from the only affection left to him on earth. The close, with Henchard's Will, has been praised by all the critics. Mr. Macdowall writes:

> Few tragedies in Fiction have ended on so consummate a note; it takes us into the same region as the final simplicity of *King Lear*.[3]

Had the book concluded with the words of Elizabeth Jane, without the last three paragraphs as they now stand, it

[1] W. H. Gardner: *op. cit.*
[2] *Thomas Hardy: a Critical Study* (1912), p. 123.
[3] *Thomas Hardy: a Critical Study* (1931), p. 74.

would surely have been one of the finest endings in the language. No one but Hardy would have added to the anguish of the closing pages that further, so little, and yet so significant, pain of the death of the goldfinch, brought by Henchard as a wedding gift, and forgotten in its cage. If there were a Chorus of the Pities in *The Mayor of Caster-bridge*, they would tell us, as they tell us before Waterloo, that the suffering and death of the little creature are as completely and universally tragic as the suffering and death of the strong man.

Many critics have pointed out that in its unity of treatment, *The Mayor of Casterbridge* is akin to the last two (Mr. Abercrombie calls them 'epic') novels, rather than to those whose centre lies in the dramatic relationships of a group. In another respect, also, the novel looks forward to Hardy's last period. Although it has not yet become the main theme, as it was to become in *Tess*, there is in *The Mayor* a quarrel with the general scheme of things which is that of the author, over and above whatever quarrel his characters may have with their particular destiny. In part this may be explained by the fact that Henchard, the strong man who sets his shoulders to the hurricane of adversity and says 'My punishment is *not* greater than I can bear,' provides much less opportunity for an objective indictment of Fate than does the weak Eustacia. But we have seen how Hardy himself, as he neared middle life, became rebellious against life as it is. The rebellion is very clearly to be seen in several bitter sentences in *The Mayor of Casterbridge*. In the first chapter we are told of Susan Henchard:

> When she plodded on in the shade of the hedge, silently thinking, she had the hard, half apathetic expression of one who deems anything possible at the hands of Time and Chance, except, perhaps, fair play.

At the other end of the book, in chapter forty-four, there are two very striking passages:

> Part of Henchard's wish to wash his hands of life arose from

his perception of its contrarious inconsistencies—of Nature's jaunty readiness to support unorthodox social principles.

Externally there was nothing to hinder his making another start. . . . But the ingenious machinery contrived by the Gods for reducing human possibilities of amelioration to a minimum —which arranges that wisdom to do shall come *pari passu* with the departure of zest for doing—stood in the way of all that.

Both these sentences are a clear anticipation of *Tess*; and the last paragraph of the whole book falls not far short of being a piece of propaganda. Considering the novel for a moment, not by itself as a work of art, but as the self-expression of the man who wrote it, we find *The Mayor of Casterbridge* a revealing and most poignant document. In her, perhaps natural, desire to conceal as much as possible this painful period of her husband's life, the second Mrs. Hardy does her best to let us suppose that Hardy considered his novel writing 'mere journeywork.'[1] Thirty and forty years later, under the influence of a young wife whose devotion made him as contented as he ever was in life, but who was scarcely born when his powers as a novelist were at their height, he may have come to this. But the theory accords ill with the evidence from his own diary, quoted by Mrs. Hardy, that he meant *The Mayor of Casterbridge* to be as good as he could make it; and the book itself rebuts the theory completely. It was written in those middle 'eighties when Hardy had lost all belief, not only in a beneficent First Cause, but also in all happiness and in all hope. He was turning, in sick despair, to the comfortless consolations of philosophy. In describing the sensations of Elizabeth Jane, in the eighteenth chapter, he was painting a picture of those who, like himself, had eaten of the bitter fruit of the Tree of Knowledge:

All this while the subtle-souled girl (was) asking herself why she was born, why sitting in a room and blinking at the candle; why things around her had taken the shape they wore in preference to every other possible shape. Why they stared

[1] *Early Life*, p. 235.

at her so helplessly, as if waiting for the touch of some wand that should release them from terrestrial constraint; what that chaos called consciousness, which spun in her at this moment like a top, tended to and began in.

With *The Mayor of Casterbridge* there comes to an end a period in Hardy's art, the period in which his novels are before all else works of art. Whether we consider this period to be his best depends upon personal views of the function of the artist; those who hold it to be propaganda will see the high watermark of Hardy's achievement as a novelist in *Jude*; but those who ask of the artist presentation before propaganda will think otherwise. To such, the place of the Wessex novels in our literature is assured, not by their attempted propagation of theories or doctrines, but by their portrayal of:

> sequestered spots outside the gates of the world where from time to time dramas of a grandeur and unity truly Sophoclean are enacted in the real, by virtue of the concentrated passions and closely knit interdependence of the lives therein.

That description of his own field has been bettered by none of Hardy's critics. If such be the criterion, he did his best work in *The Return* and, notwithstanding its faults, *The Mayor*. His next novel, *The Woodlanders*, from which these words are taken, shows his writing in transition. Its best part is the presentation of a simple and profoundly moving drama, upon a scene surpassed only by Egdon Heath; but interwoven with this is too much talk upon the ethics of marriage and the psychology of philandering. Giles Winterborne and Marty South hold a secure place among the men and women of English fiction who will live from generation to generation; but what are we to say of Edred Fitzpiers and Felice Charmond? It is hard to understand how one and the same hand could draw, with such sure mastery, this enduring picture of the woodlander who gave his life for a love that brought no return, and of the girl whose own fruitless love for him was stronger than the grave; and could place beside it these stilted dummies, cut out with scissors from a vulgar fashion plate. Hardy was never at his happiest when he tried to draw characters in educated 'society.' Here they are, unfortunately, an integral part of the story; but that might matter less if they simply helped to make the plot; in addition, they serve to introduce an argument about marriage, which appears as a new and unpleasing departure in Hardy's art.

The Woodlanders was being written in November 1885, and was finished on February 4th, 1887.[1] It appeared as a serial in *Macmillan's Magazine* from May 1886 to April 1887; and was published in three volumes by Macmillan on March 15th of the latter year. When correcting proofs for the Wessex edition of his novels in 1912, Hardy wrote to a friend that he liked it, as a story, the best of all.[2] He was, certainly, an accomplished story-teller by 1886, and the novel shows it; to take only a small illustration: it would be hard to find a more cleverly constructed little narrative than the story of the man trap, in chapter forty-seven; not until the very last minute is the secret given away. The technique of the book was recognized at once. The reviewer in the *Athenæum* (March 26th, 1887) wrote that in point of construction it seemed simply perfect and concluded:

> The novel is distinctly not for the Young Person of whom we have lately heard; but it should be read by all who can tell masterly work in fiction when they see it.

There was a long and laudatory notice in the *Saturday Review* (April 4th, 1887) whose critic pronounced the second volume to be the best that Hardy had ever written. *The Woodlanders* has always been a general favourite; and there are many to-day who would say that it is Hardy's best novel.

Mrs. Hardy says that Hardy was writing a woodland tale in 1875, which was then laid aside, and 'later took shape as *The Woodlanders*.'[3] It is tempting to conjecture that the original Woodlanders consisted of that part of the story

---

[1] *Early Life*, pp. 230, 243.   [2] *Later Years*, p. 151.
[3] *Early Life*, p. 135.

(doubtless incomplete) which is concerned with Giles and
Marty; Grace Melbury may well have played the part in
this story which she plays now, with slight variants; while
Robert Creedle is clearly one of the compeers of Joseph
Poorgrass. Such a story Hardy may well have written in
part between *Far from the Madding Crowd* and *The Return of
the Native*. Further evidence to support such a conjecture is
lacking. What is, however, quite certain is that Fitzpiers
and his part in the plot date from 1885, not 1875. When we
considered in the third chapter how philosophy became the
study of Hardy's middle life, some instances were given of
its exemplification in the person of Fitzpiers; others could
be added. When first he begins to covet Grace he says to
her:

> I thought, what a lovely creature! The design is for once
> carried out. Nature has at last recovered her lost union with
> the Idea![1]

But Fitzpiers not only exemplifies his creator's philosophical
studies; he has another, and much larger, part to play also.
At the end of chapter twenty-three, he tells Grace that he
does not wish to be married in a church:

> I don't see the necessity of going there. . . . Marriage is a
> civil contract, and the shorter and simpler it is made, the better.
> People don't go to church when they take a house, or even
> when they make a will.

Passing over the very remarkable resemblance of this
speech to various passages in *Jude the Obscure*, it need only
be remarked that Fitzpiers seems to graft analogous ideas
upon the girl, who could bear to hear him talk so, after she
has become his wife. When her marriage proves a failure,
Grace reads the Marriage Service to herself, and meditates:

> She became lost in long ponderings on how far a person's

[1] That such a train of thought was in Hardy's own mind at the time is clearly
shown a few pages later, when similar phraseology is incongruously put into
Winterborne's head: 'That the Idea had for once completely fulfilled itself in the
objective substance (which he had hitherto deemed an impossibility) he was en-
chanted enough to fancy must be the case at last.' But where did Giles study
philosophy?

conscience might be bound by vows made without, at the time, a full recognition of their force. That particular sentence, beginning 'Whom God hath joined together' was a staggerer for a gentle woman of strong devotional sentiment. She wondered whether God did really join them together.

The interest of this does not lie in whether it is true to its context, as it is, but in its being there at all. For it, and all that part of the book connected with it, strike a note which is wholly new in Hardy's fiction.

Unhappy marriages we have met before in his pages, but they have been quite differently treated. Hitherto, he has considered marriage only in relation, either to human nature, or to the nature of the universe, never in relation to the organization of society. Even Viviette's first marriage, which would have furnished an excellent pretext, never raises any such question. Eustacia, when her marriage has gone to wreck, rails against destiny, but not against society. There is an open quarrel with the scheme of the universe in *The Mayor*, but the opportunity offered by Henchard's entanglements is never taken in order to raise a quarrel with society over the marriage question. This point needs to be stressed; for it has become the fashion in some circles to consider Hardy primarily as a great rebel against society. Such a view, for instance, is taken by D. H. Lawrence.[1] But it is not in accordance with the facts. From his thirties onwards, Hardy, like many of his generation, was in revolt against what he considered the fundamental conditions of existence; this, the keynote of his mature work, persists. But it was only in the late 'eighties that, to this general grievance, was added a particular grievance against that part of the social system which seeks to regulate sexual relationship. Love, as many of his critics have pointed out, was always one of his favourite themes; and mostly it was love touched to tragic issues.[2] But his quarrel with human

---

[1] *Phoenix*, pp. 419–20.
[2] L. de Ridder Barzin goes so far as to say: 'C'est l'amour qui, pour lui, est l'ouvrier principal et presque unique de notre destiné.' *Le Pessimisme de Thomas Hardy* (1932), Chap. III.

society for its attitude towards sexual relationships, although it produced the two most widely known of his books, and seems, in the popular mind, to have overshadowed the more fundamental aspects of his work, was only a phase. This phase is inaugurated in *The Woodlanders*.

The trend of his thought as he approached his fiftieth year and became preoccupied with this aspect of life, is most clearly to be seen in an article, written some eighteen months after *The Woodlanders* was finished, which appeared in the *New Review* of January 1890, under the title 'Candour in English Fiction.' In the fourth paragraph of this illuminating article he wrote:

> In perceiving that taste is arriving anew at the point of high tragedy, writers are conscious that its revived presentation demands enrichment by further truths—in other words original treatment: treatment which seeks to show Nature's unconsciousness, not of social laws, but of those laws framed merely as social expedients, without a basis in the heart of things.

And in the sixth paragraph he becomes even more explicit:

> Anyhow, conscientious fiction alone it is which can excite a reflective and abiding interest in the minds of thoughtful readers of mature age, weary of puerile inventions and famishing for accuracy; who consider that, in representations of the world, the passions ought to be proportioned as in the world itself. . . . Life being a physiological fact, its honest portrayal must be largely concerned with, for one thing, the relations of the sexes, and the substitution for such catastrophes as favour the false colouring best expressed by the regulation finish that 'they married and were happy ever after,' of catastrophes based upon sexual relationship as it is. To this expansion English society raises a well-nigh insuperable bar.

The implications of the last sentence will appear in the next chapter; for this article is the Prologue to *Tess* and *Jude*. But it is also a commentary on *The Woodlanders*, where this preoccupation with the social aspect of sexual relationships begins. Whether Hardy's new departure was a fortunate one may be questioned. It has been a theme of great art in all ages that life is a tragic fact; in modern literature, Hardy is not the least of its exponents. In *The Woodlanders*, his exposition of it in Giles and Marty is convincing and moving, and fully in harmony with the deep, central theme of all his art; as Mr. Abercrombie happily expresses, when he describes these two as 'both deeply acquiescing in the process of impersonal life that has them in its power.'[1] The close of the book is great literature on this theme of life as a tragic fact. But whether great literature can be made out of 'life as a physiological fact' is questionable; that it has not been done yet has certainly not been for want of trying. Hardy tried very hard before he gave up novel-writing; and so many have followed him into the ditch, that advice might now be tendered to give this theme a rest; why not, for a change, try life as a chemical fact? The beginning of Hardy's preoccupation with the physiological fact is plain in that part of *The Woodlanders* which deals with Fitzpiers. Writing a Preface to the novel in 1895, Hardy laid the whole stress upon this one aspect, and wrote with dry sarcasm:

> It is tacitly assumed for the purposes of this story that no doubt of the depravity of the erratic heart who feels some second person to be better suited to his or her tastes than the one with whom he has contracted to live, enters the head of reader or writer for a moment. From the point of view of marriage as a distinct covenant or undertaking, decided upon by two people fully cognizant of all its possible issues and competent to carry them through, this assumption is, of course, logical. Yet no thinking person supposes that on the broader ground of how to afford the greatest happiness to the units of human society during their brief transit through this sorry world, there is no more to be said on this covenant.

He himself had a great deal more to say; and this Preface is rather a preface to *Jude*, which he was then writing, than to the *Woodlanders* to which it was prefixed. But that it *was* prefixed to that novel is enough for the present purpose.

Fortunately, *The Woodlanders* has more claims to con-

[1] *Thomas Hardy: a Critical Study*, p. 120.

sideration than as a *ballon d'essai* for the later manifesto upon marriage. Although important in considering the development of his work historically, that part of the book is the least attractive and the least representative of Hardy's genius. The *historical* significance of this part has been almost wholly ignored hitherto; but the many merits and beauties of the book have been so often praised that there is no need to do it again at length. In their enthusiasm over the little which they are shown of her, critics have tended to praise Marty South as the most memorable of Hardy's characters, forgetting the comparatively minor part assigned to her, and the infrequency of her appearances. A better claim could be made for Winterborne, of whom Lionel Johnson wrote:

> Without idealizing the man; without any dextrous enlistment of our sympathies, by hints of some finer strain in his nature than the mere facts reveal; without any shrinking from the homeliness and rusticity of his life; Mr. Hardy, through the strength of his belief in the truth and beauty of his conception, wins us without a struggle.

Marty South's elegy over Winterborne's grave is deservedly famous; it must be one of the best endings in fiction. There is another passage in the book, not quoted by critics, which, though in a lower key, is not unmemorable. It also is an elegy, spoken by Robert Creedle over his dead master:

> Forgive me, but I cant rule my mourning nohow as a man should, Mr. Melbury. I ha'n't seen him since Thursday se'night. and have wondered for days and days where he's been keeping. There was I expecting him to come and tell me to wash out the cider barrels against the making, and here was he. . . . Well, I've knowed him from table high; I knowed his father— used to bide about upon two sticks in the sun afore he died— and now I've seen the end of the family, which we can ill afford to lose, wi' such a scanty lot of good folk in Hintock as we've got. And now Robert Creedle will be nailed up in parish boards, 'a'blieve; and nobody will glutch down a sigh for he.

Hardy claims a place among our great by his power to do such things as this.

The last of Hardy's novels to be published in book form, although written before *Jude*, stands quite apart from all the others. *The Well Beloved* is a phantasy, of which the little that need be said has been said by others. To me, the best part of it is the manner in which the rocky Isle of Portland provides a changeless background to the insubstantial dreams of Pierston; as when, in London, he hears of the death of the first Avice:

> The divinity of the silver bow was not more excellently pure than she, the lost, had been. Under that moon was the island of Ancient Slingers, and on the island a house, framed from mullions to chimney-top, like the isle itself, of stone. Inside the window, the moonlight irradiating her winding sheet, lay Avice, reached only by the faint noises inherent in the isle; the tink-tink of the chisels in the quarries, the surging of the tides in the bay, and the muffled grumblings of the currents in the never-pacified Race.

Something must be said of the short stories which Hardy had been writing at intervals throughout the years covered by this chapter, and continued to write for some years more. They were reprinted in four collections, *Wessex Tales*, *Life's Little Ironies*, *A Group of Noble Dames* and *A Changed Man and other Tales*; but the dates of their first appearance are given in the list of Hardy's writings. The earliest of them to be reprinted, 'A Distracted Preacher,' was written in 1879[1]; and the latest, 'Enter a Dragoon,' in 1900. But they belong, in the main, to the late 'eighties and early 'nineties. On a general review of them, one is tempted to say that the distinguishing characteristics of Hardy's short stories are improbability and unpleasantness. The extreme nastiness of most of the contents of *Life's Little Ironies* is not redeemed by the undeniable power of the writing, and reveals how thoroughly Hardy's view of life was jaundiced when he wrote them. Gosse, if he had not admired them, might well have added these when he described *Satires of Circumstance*

---

[1] The earliest to be written has not been reprinted. This seems to have been the one called 'Destiny and a Blue Cloak' which appeared in the *New York Times* on October 4th, 1874.

as 'the Troilus and Cressida' of Hardy's work[1]; and, like those ironic verses, these ironic tales fall flat from over-statement. 'A Tragedy of Two Ambitions,' for instance, is as preposterous as it is repulsive. In none of these tales are we persuaded of the possibility of the story; it seems a misapplication of energy that so much ingenuity, and even power, should be directed merely to creating a nasty taste in the mouth. This is all that 'An Imaginative Woman' or 'The Son's Veto' leaves with its reader. *Wessex Tales* are, on the whole, better. 'The Three Strangers,' despite a leaning towards the *macabre*, is a good story. The two Napoleonic stories have obvious connections with Hardy's preparations for the *Dynasts*. *A Changed Man* contains a heterogeneous collection, ranging from the almost auto-biographical 'A Tryst at an ancient Earthwork,' to the wholly impossible, but entertaining, 'Romantic Adventures of a Milkmaid.'

This story, written as early as 1883, is the forerunner of *A Group of Noble Dames*, a curious book adding nothing to Hardy's achievement, but not without interest. The method of narration is that of the Decameron, borrowed by Chaucer in the *Canterbury Tales*. The club whose members are the narrators was, of course, the Dorset Field Club; and the Preface suggests that Hardy would have us believe the tales to be founded on the history of Dorset families. In a letter to Edward Clodd he wrote that 'most of the tales are founded on fact.'[2] However this may be, we have no diffi-culty in recognizing, in the incredible adventures of some of the noble dames, the running riot of Hardy's vivid imagination, which had never been wholly content with 'the modesty of nature.' Nevertheless, if we are prepared to part company for a while with the real world, there is much entertainment in *A Group of Noble Dames*.

The best of Hardy's short stories are those called 'A Few

---

[1] 'The Lyrical Poetry of Thomas Hardy,' in the *Edinburgh Review*, Vol. 227, p. 272; reprinted in *Some Diversions of a Man of Letters*.
[2] This letter is in the Ashley Library, Catalogue, Vol. 10.

Crusted Characters,' reprinted in *Life's Little Ironies*. Here his imagination can work upon material thoroughly familiar to him; and the fact that the narrators belong to his Wessex folk at once limits his fancy and provides the medium he loves best. 'Absent Mindedness in a Parish Choir' is a little masterpiece in the *genre* in which Hardy has no rival in English.[1] While the character of the Old Surgeon has nothing to help us swallow the tale of 'Barbara of the House of Grebe,' we are easily won over by the Master Thatcher, who, in the tale of Andrey Satchel and the Parson, tells how bride and bridegroom, having been locked in the church tower for twenty-four hours, 'busted out like starved mice from a cupboard.'

[1] In a letter to Edward Clodd, which is in the Ashley Library (Catalogue, Vol. 10), Hardy wrote, concerning 'The Superstitious Man's Story': 'All that about the Miller's soul is, or was until lately, an actual belief down here. It was told me years ago by an old woman. I may say, once for all, that every superstition, custom, etc., described in my novels may be depended on as true records of the same, whatever merit they may have in folklorists' eyes, and are not inventions of mine.'

CHAPTER VI

TESS AND *JUDE*

IT has been generally recognized that Hardy's last two
novels stand by themselves among his works. The reason
is usually considered to lie in the manifestly different construction of these two books, each of them centred upon
one human life; and this has been described by Mr. Abercrombie as fiction of an epic character, as opposed to the
dramatic fiction that went before it; but, as has been seen,
Hardy began at least to approach such a method in *The
Mayor of Casterbridge.* With their eyes upon the structural
differences, some critics have been apt to overlook a more
fundamental matter, of which the other is but an outward
symptom. *Tess of the d'Urbervilles* and *Jude the Obscure* are, in
essence, literature of another category from that to which
Hardy's previous novels belong. They are didactic; not
incidentally or occasionally, but deliberately and consis-
tently. A reader familiar with the Wessex novels as individual works, read unsystematically as novels are usually read,
will not greatly appreciate this; but let him read them in the
order of their composition, and it cannot escape him. The
previous novels, in intention as well as in execution, are
works of art; their purpose is representative. In them,
Hardy is concerned to tell a story; and such observations
as he, or we, make upon the story follow as secondary
matters. In *The Woodlanders*, as we saw in the last chapter,
the story is so manipulated that a certain aspect of it comes
in for more attention than it deserves; but still the story is
the chief concern. With *Tess* and *Jude* the whole emphasis
is shifted; they are critical, not representative. The purpose
of the story comes before the story itself. No one has
seriously disputed this except Hardy himself; when, chiefly
on the strength of these two books, critics continued for

the next twenty years to introduce the word 'pessimist' into every article they wrote about him, he became pardonably irritated, retorted that he dealt only in 'general impressions,' and claimed to be a 'meliorist.' But no one in his senses would try to found such a claim upon *Tess* and *Jude*.

It is in some ways unfortunate that Hardy's last two novels have enjoyed such immense notoriety, far exceeding the fame of his earlier books. In an address to the English Association in the year of Hardy's death, Mr. J. H. Fowler said:

> At the present time I feel there is some danger that Hardy may be regarded by a multitude of readers as a great teacher even more than as a great artist, and, if that be so, I doubt whether the influence he will exert will be altogether for the good.[1]

Anyone who has made a study of Hardy criticism since the War will testify that the fear is well founded. But it would never have been so had he not written *Tess* and *Jude*.

Tess of the d'Urbervilles is the most famous of his writings; it must be one of the most widely read novels in English. Thousands, who have never read another word from Hardy's pen, know him as the author of *Tess*. In the three years following its publication, it had been translated into French, German, Russian, Italian and Dutch. There is a version of it in Japanese. It is a prescribed book for English in American Universities. It has been twice made into an opera; it has been dramatized repeatedly; once, reluctantly, by Hardy himself in response to the demand for a play about Tess. It has been filmed; and it has given rise to imitations innumerable. Fifty years have not yet elapsed since this book was published; but already many volumes could be filled with the appreciations and depreciations, the criticisms and the rhapsodies, that have been poured forth upon it; and it would seem as if the literature of *Tess* may become in time a jungle as impenetrable as the literature of *Hamlet*.

[1] *The Novels of Thomas Hardy*; English Association Pamphlet, No. 71.

Tess was begun in the summer of 1889; there is an account in *Early Life* (p. 291 *et seq.*) of its rejection by the editors of *Murray's* and *Macmillan's Magazines*, and of its final acceptance by the editor of the *Graphic*, in which a version of it appeared as a serial from July to December 1891. But this story which came out in the *Graphic* was not the novel which we know now; it was an emasculated and meaningless monstrosity. The seduction is wholly omitted. Chapters ten and eleven of the present version are lacking, as are the last two paragraphs of chapter nine, which concludes with a paragraph made by telescoping the last three paragraphs of chapter eleven, ending thus:

> As Tess's own people down in those retreats are never tired of saying among each other in their fatalistic way: It was to be. There lay the pity of it.

The revelation by Tess to her mother, so pathetic as we know it, is replaced in the serial by this passage, placed at the end of chapter eleven:

> Her mother eyed her narrowly. 'Come, you have not told me all.' Then Tess told. 'He made love to me, as you said he would do; and he asked me to marry him, also just as you declared he would. I never have liked him; but at last I agreed, knowing you'd be angry if I didn't. He said it must be private, even from you, on account of his mother, and by special license; and foolish I agreed to that likewise, to get rid of his pestering. I drove with him to Melchester, and there in a private room I went through the form of marriage with him as before a registrar. A few weeks later I found out that it was not the registrar's house we had gone to, but the house of a friend of his who had played the part of the registrar. Then I came away from Trantridge instantly, though he wished me to stay; and here I am.' 'But he can be prosecuted for this,' said Joan. 'O no, say nothing,' answered Tess. 'It will do me more harm than leaving it alone.'

Tess does not become a mother. These omissions make this serial version meaningless; and further alterations make it ludicrous. The very pretty passage in chapter twenty-three, where Angel Clare carries the four maids across the flood on a Sunday morning, saying to the last: 'Three Leahs to get one Rachel,' is deservedly famous; in the serial, Angel makes use of a wheelbarrow. Tess does not become Alec's mistress. When Angel finds her in his rooms at Bournemouth, she explains her relations with Alec in the words: 'He has won me to be friends with him.' She then goes upstairs to the room which is hers alone; and later crosses the landing to 'another appartment . . . sometimes occupied by her cousin Mr. Durberville'; where she stabs that unfortunate and comparatively harmless gentleman with the carving knife; for what reason, heaven alone may know. Even these concessions to Mrs. Grundy, by which the whole moving story becomes fantastically absurd, did not suffice. One subscriber to the *Graphic* wrote to the editor, protesting in the name of his family of innocent daughters, against the indecency of the bloodstain in the ceiling.

In these days, when the productions of D. H. Lawrence are easily accessible to every school child, it is interesting to remember that, less than fifty years ago, this fate befell an author whose boots Lawrence was not worthy to lick. The only other comment which needs to be made was made by Hardy himself, in the article 'Candour in English Fiction,' already quoted in the last chapter. This was written at the very time that he was sterilizing *Tess* to the requirements of the editor of the *Graphic*:

> If the true artist ever weeps it probably is then, when he discovers the fearful price that he has to pay for the privilege of writing in the English language, no less a price than the complete extinction, in the mind of every mature and penetrating reader, of sympathetic belief in his personages.

Two passages which found no place in the serial version of *Tess* were published separately. A special Literary Supplement to the *National Observer* of November 14th, 1891, contained a short story called 'Saturday Night in Arcady.' This begins with a shortened version of chapter ten of *Tess*. At the words: 'Don't ye be nervous, my dear good soul,' it becomes almost verbatim the published text of the later editions, and continues until the words: 'The horse ambled along for a considerable distance.' Then the episode concludes in half a dozen short paragraphs. The description in chapter fourteen of Tess's baptism of her baby is one of the most moving in Hardy's writings. This first appeared, slightly shortened, in the *Fortnightly Review* of May 1891, under the title 'The Midnight Baptism.' It began with the words: 'The narrow lane of stubble encompassing the field grew wider with each circuit. . . .' The paragraph beginning: 'It is Tess d'Urberville'; and the eight and a half paragraphs beginning: 'A little more than persuading had to do with the coming o't' are missing. Otherwise this version is almost word for word that published in the first edition.

The Manuscript of *Tess* is in the British Museum (Add. MS. 38182). Although it contains innumerable alterations of single words and short phrases, it is substantially the story we know to-day, the alterations for the serial version having been made by Hardy later, in blue ink. We learn from it that the original title was *A Daughter of the d'Urbervilles*[1]; and that the heroine's original name was Sue; by the eighteenth chapter, Hardy discarded Sue in favour of Rose Mary; by the thirty-fifth chapter this became Tess. In the story as originally conceived, one of the main themes of the finished novel was absent. Tess's seducer was called Haunferne, and was not even a bogus kinsman; it must be agreed that Hardy's second thoughts in this matter, which came to him before he had got very far with the writing, were a great improvement. The passage describing Tess's visit to the tombs of her ancestors at Kingsbere was originally meant to go into chapter eighteen[2]; here again, second thoughts were better. The story of William Dewey and the pious bull was originally only half its present

[1] The name was clearly suggested by that of the Turberville family, many of whose graves are in the church at Bere Regis, the 'Kingsbere' of the novel.

[2] It is written on the verso of MS. p. 108. The serial, where it is in Chap. XIII, retained the early position for this passage.

length, and ended in Dewey's rescue by passing carters.[1] The most important variation between the Manuscript and the story as we know it, is in chapter eleven. Originally, Tess, like Clarissa Harlowe, was drugged before the seducer had his will of her. On page 79 of the Manuscript occurs this passage:

'Nights grow chilly in September. Let me see.' He went to the horse, took a large wicker-cased jar from under the seat, and after some trouble in opening it with a pocket corkscrew, held it to her mouth unawares. (Sue) (Rose Mary) Tess sputtered and coughed, and, gasping, 'It will go on my pretty frock!', swallowed as he poured, to prevent the catastrophe she feared. 'That's it. Now you'll feel warmer,' said (Haunferne) Durberville, as he restored the bottle to its place. 'It is only a two gallon jar of spirits that my mother ordered me to bring for household purposes, and she wont mind me using some of it medicinally. Now, my pretty, rest there; I shall soon be back.'

One passage in the Manuscript, which was cancelled and has never been printed, deserves quotation; for in it Hardy explicitly gives the reasons for which he wrote *Tess of the d'Urbervilles*. In the MS., the last chapter originally began thus:

The humble delineator of human character and human contingencies, whether his narrative deal with the actual or with the typical only, must primarily and above all things be sincere, however terrible sincerity may be. Gladly sometimes would he lie, for dear civility's sake, if he dared, but for the haunting afterthought that: 'this thing was not done honestly and may do harm.' In typical history, with all its liberty, there are as in real history, features which can never be varied with impunity and issues which should never be falsified. And perhaps in glancing at the misfortunes of such people as have, or could have, lived, we may acquire some art in shielding from like misfortunes those who have yet to be born. If truth required justification, surely this is an ample one.

The most famous sentence in the book originally ran

[1] The present ending is on a separate piece of paper, stuck on the verso of MS. p. 118.

simply: 'Justice was done.' The rest of the sentence, and the inverted commas, were added later.

The first edition of *Tess* was published in three volumes by Osgood, M'Ilvaine & Co., at the end of November 1891. It contains the story as we know it to-day, apart from a passage in chapter ten, which is missing,[1] and the account of the drugging of Tess, which, with minor variants, is as given in the Manuscript. The same chapter contains, near the end, a paragraph which was not reprinted:

> Already at that hour some sons of the forest were stirring, and striking lights in not very distant cottages; good and sincere hearts among them, patterns of honesty and devotion and chivalry. And powerful horses were stamping in their stalls, ready to be let out into the morning air. But no dart or thread of intelligence inspired these men to harness and mount, or gave them by any means the least inkling that their sister was in the hands of the spoiler; and they did not come that way.[2]

Absent from the first edition are a number of stylistic embellishments added later. As good an instance as any is to be found in chapter forty-two, describing Tess's journey to Flintcomb Ash; the words italicized are missing from the first edition:

> Towards the second evening she reached the irregular chalk table-land or plateau, bosomed with semi globular tumuli—*as if Cybele the Many-breasted were supinely extended there*—which stretched between the valley of her birth and the valley of her love.

At the beginning of her second volume, Mrs. Hardy tells how *Tess of the d'Urbervilles* became the universal topic of conversation in society, and how it brought its author innumerable private letters asking for personal advice. These he properly burnt; there are still, however, some curious letters in Mrs. Hardy's possession, one of them

---

[1] The passage beginning: 'Tess's occupations made her late in setting out . . .' as far as: 'It was a three-mile walk.'

[2] The page of the MS. on which this would occur is missing.

from South America, testifying to the great impression which the novel made upon uncritical readers. The reactions of the professional critics were very various. One extreme was represented by the *Quarterly*, which brought down upon *Tess*, as hard as it dared, the good, old-fashioned bludgeon that had once smitten *Endymion*:

> It seems only that Mr. Hardy has told an extremely disagreeable story in an extremely disagreeable manner, which is not rendered less so by his affectation of expounding a great moral law, or by the ridiculous character of some of the scenes into which this affectation plunges the reader.

The *Saturday Review* was only one degree less contemptuous (January 16th, 1892):

> There is not a single touch of nature, either in John Durbeyfield or in any other character of the book. All are stagey and some are farcical. . . . It is these suggestions (the description of Tess's figure) that render Mr. Hardy's story so very disagreeable, and *Tess* is full of them. . . . Few people will deny the terrible dreariness of this tale, which, except during a few hours spent with cows, has not a gleam of sunshine anywhere.

The opinions of those who, while disliking the book, recognized the qualities which had gone to its making, were illustrated by an article from the pen of Andrew Lang in the *New Review* (February 1892):

> It is pity, one knows, that causes this bitterness in Mr. Hardy's mood. . . . Probably bitterness is never a mark of the greatest art and the noblest thought. . . . Tastes differ so much that the blemishes as they appear to one reader may seem beauty spots in the eyes of another. He does but give of his best; and if his best be too good for us, or good in the wrong way . . . why, there are plenty of other novelists, alive and dead, and the fault may be on our side, not his.

The other extreme might be seen in the critic of the *Westminster Review* (Vol. 138, p. 655), who piled superlatives upon the book and belaboured Andrew Lang at intervals:

> One of the greatest novels of this century. . . . We trace in him (Lang) the prudishness and exclusiveness of the fashionable

preacher. Why does he attempt to deprecate a novel which is obviously outside the range, not only of his sympathies, but of his critical powers? . . . It is a monumental work. From beginning to end it bears the hall mark of truth upon every page. . . . It is the greatest work of fiction produced in England since George Eliot died.

The great bulk of educated opinion was probably expressed in a long article in the *Times* (January 13th, 1892):

> Mr. Hardy's latest novel is his greatest. Amid his beloved Wessex valleys and uplands and among the unsophisticated folk in whose lives and labours we have learned from him to find unsuspected dignity and romance, he has founded a story, daring in its treatment of conventional ideas, pathetic in its sadness and profoundly stirring in its tragic power. . . . It is well that an idealist like Mr. Hardy should remind us how terribly defective are our means of judging others.

The same note was struck by the critic of the *Athenæum* (January 9th):

> In dealing with this 'sorry scheme of things entire,' Mr. Hardy has written a novel that is not only good, but great.

The most penetrating of the contemporary reviews, in the *Academy* (February 6th), was written by William Watson:

> *Tess* is a work so great that it could almost afford to have even proportionately greater faults. . . . The great theme of the book is the incessant penalty paid by the innocent for the guilty. . . in view of the almost intolerable power with which this argument is wrought out, *Tess* must take its place among the great tragedies, to have read which is to have permanently enlarged the boundaries of one's intellectual and emotional experience.

When Lionel Johnson in 1893 wrote the first, and still one of the best, critical studies of Hardy, it was inevitable that he should consider *Tess of the d'Urbervilles* as an argument, and that he should rebut the argument in his last chapter, 'Sincerity in Art.' *Tess* is, of course, among other things, an argument; but there is no occasion at the present time to consider at length the merits of its argumentative aspect, for this has, during the last forty years, been dwelt on *ad nauseam*. Thus much may be said of it: the argument, which proceeds out of exceeding bitterness of heart, is made up of two related, but quite distinct, elements. One is a grievance against the organization of human society; the other, a quarrel with the ordering of the Universe. In both of them, it is the heart which argues rather than the mind.

In so far as it voices a grievance against human society, *Tess* is a failure. As Johnson showed, the indictment lacks both coherence and consistency; moreover, Hardy did not even clearly make up his mind what it was that he was indicting. He struck out wildly, but he hit nothing. Now he attacks human society for framing laws and conventions which run counter to Nature; and now he cries out against the cruelty of universal Nature, in whose breasts there runs none of the milk of human kindness. The famous passages have become hackneyed: had Tess been alone on a desert island, she would not have been wretched; her baby is 'that bastard gift of shameless Nature who respects not the social law'; her misery is 'based on nothing more tangible than a sense of condemnation under an arbitrary law of society which had no foundation in nature'; but for social conventions, her experience would have been simply a liberal education; and so on. What has to be said about this part of the argument in *Tess* is not, as the many who have so enthusiastically hailed Hardy as a great prophet, claim, that it is true; for it is not even convincing; but that it is something which developed very late in Hardy's art, flamed up fiercely for a little while, and then died out altogether. This indictment of human society is not to be found in *The Return of the Native*, except by the prejudice which sees what it desires to see; it is hardly to be discovered in the *Dynasts*.

With the other part of the argument in *Tess*, the matter is very different. Here, the passages are more numerous, and equally hackneyed. Before the story is well started, Hardy describes the Durbeyfield family and demands indignantly where Wordsworth gets his authority for speaking of 'Nature's holy plan.' Tess is made to tell her little brother that we live on a blighted world. There is the outburst against 'a morality good enough for divinities but scorned by average human nature.' 'In the ill-judged execution of the well-judged plan of things . . . Nature does not often say "See!" to her poor creature at a time when seeing can lead to happy doing.' Angel Clare asks Tess: 'This hobble of being alive is rather serious, don't you think so?' Tess could hear in the words of M. Sully Prud'homme (which, by the way, she would certainly not have understood) a penal sentence in the fiat: 'Tu naîtras.' Tess found in the 'Ode on Intimations of Immortality' a ghastly satire, for: 'to her and her like, birth itself was an ordeal of degrading personal compulsion whose gratuitousness nothing in the result seemed to justify.' And so forth. Considered as literature, there was nothing new in all this, as some of the most fervid admirers of *Tess* seemed to think. Twenty-three centuries before Hardy was born, a great poet had said the same thing with far more dignity:

μὴ ψῦναι τὸν ἄπαντα νικᾷ λόγον

What should be said about such passages is not, as too many would-be critics have said, that they are true; for the question of their truth can never be taken to a higher court of appeal than personal views of life; but that they are the culmination of Hardy's spiritual development during thirty years, at least. When Tess thinks that all is vanity, we are told that she thought further: 'If all were only vanity, who would mind it? All was, alas, worse than vanity—injustice, punishment, exaction, death.' Nearly twenty years before he wrote those words in the novel, Hardy had written in his private diary:

> 'All is vanity,' saith the Preacher. But if all were only vanity, who would mind? Alas, it is too often worse than vanity; agony, darkness, death also. A man would never laugh

were he not to forget his situation, or were he not one who has never learnt it.[1]

In the interval, Hardy had undergone the influences outlined in an earlier chapter, and his views had darkened as the years passed over him. The older he grew, the more ghastly a business the universe seemed to him to be.

The natural, almost inevitable, culmination of this spiritual development is the notorious sentence at the end of *Tess*: 'The President of the Immortals, in Aeschylean phrase, had finished his sport with Tess.' Mrs. Hardy rather naïvely expressed surprise that the publication of this novel started a rumour of its author's theological beliefs. It would have been surprising had it not done so. About this matter there has been too much shuffling and mealy-mouthed talk, unworthy of so brave and sincere a man as Hardy. When he became old and softened, he was naturally loth to pain those dear to him. He was also exasperated by the impertinent quizzing of half-educated critics. He therefore, nearly thirty years later, wrote a note which Mrs. Hardy prints:

As I need hardly inform any thinking reader, I do not hold and never have held, the ludicrous opinions here assumed to be mine. . . . And in seeking to ascertain how any exponent of English literature could have supposed that I held them I find that the writer of the estimate has harked back to a passage in a novel of mine, printed many years ago, in which the forces opposed to the heroine were allegorized as a personality . . . by the use of a well-known trope, explained in that venerable work, Campbell's *Philosophy of Rhetoric*, as 'one in which life, perception, activity, design, passion or any property of sentient beings, is attributed to things inanimate.'

Under this species of criticism if an Author were to say: 'Aeolus maliciously tugged at her garments, and tore her hair in his wrath,' the sapient critic would no doubt announce that Author's evil creed to be that the wind is 'a powerful being endowed with the baser human passions,' etc., etc.[2]

Now it is perfectly true that when Hardy translated μακάρων πρύτανις into 'President of the Immortals,' he did

---

[1] *Early Life*, p. 148.   [2] *Later Years*, p. 4.

not, by those words, intend to signify what believers in a personal Deity signify by the word God. At the time when he wrote *Tess* he was no longer able to conceive the Prime Cause as a personal Deity; and to accuse him of blasphemy is, therefore, altogether beside the point. At the same time, his own explanation is not very helpful; for he was, when he wrote that famous sentence, doing much more than employ a mere figure of speech. He was deliberately reviling, under the name 'President of the Immortals,' that which he afterwards came to call the Immanent Will. Contemplating the wreck of a beautiful human life which *Tess of the d'Urbervilles* depicts, he was simply exclaiming, in his own person, what, many years later, he made the Spirit of the Pities exclaim as it contemplated the plight of George III:

> The tears that lie about this plightful scene
> Of heavy travail in a suffering soul . . .
> Might drive Compassion past her patiency
> To hold that some mean, monstrous ironist
> Had built this mistimed fabric of the spheres
> To watch the throbbings of its captive lives,
> (The which may Truth forefend), and not thy said
> Unmaliced, unimpassioned, nescient Will!

Nor is Hardy the only writer who has said this. The greatest of poets have let themselves go at times. As is pointed out in the Preface to the fifth edition of *Tess*, Gloucester says much the same in *King Lear*; and so does Oedipus, in the great and awful play which Hardy studied long and lovingly:

> Ἆρ’ οὐκ ἀπ’ ὠμοῦ ταῦτα δαίμονός τις ἂν
> κρίνων ἐπ’ ἀνδρὶ τῷδ’ ἂν ὀρθοίη λόγον; [1]

Tess of the d'Urbervilles is a tragedy. It was laid down long ago by Aristotle, in the fourteenth chapter of the *Poetics*, that the object of tragedy in the form of drama is to produce

---

[1] Gilbert Murray translates (*Oedipus Rex*, 813–4):
　　　If one should dream that such a world began
　　　In some slow devil's heart, that hated man,
　　　Who would deny him?

terror and pity, τὸ φοβερὸν καὶ ἐλεεινόν. 'The plot,' he says, 'should be so constructed that even without seeing the play anyone hearing of the incidents thrills with fear and pity as a result of what occurs.'[1] Although this was written about plays, it has generally been accepted as applicable to all imaginative tragedies in literature. It is certainly true of *The Mayor of Casterbridge*. But in *Tess*, Hardy has endeavoured to provide the element of terror, less in the substance of the story itself than in the background to it; which may be called argumentative, theological, dogmatic, philosophical or what you will, but which is not intrinsic to the picture. In so far as it is not intrinsic, the book falls short of the highest artistic standards. Judged by another famous theory of tragedy, the theory that tragedy lies, not in the conflict of right with wrong, but in the conflict of right with right, the same conclusion must be reached; for in *Tess* all Hardy's powers are put forth to make us feel the right on one side only. Yet a third view, also to be found in Aristotle, but probably most familiar to-day from A. C. Bradley's application of it to Shakespeare, is that the centre of tragedy must lie in action which issues from character; in other words, the victim must be the chief cause of his own catastrophe. Whereas the whole of *Tess* is a passionate cry that the innocent pay the penalty for the guilty. One of the best critics of the book will not, therefore, have it that *Tess* is tragic:

> Upon Mr. Hardy's principles, there was no real struggle of the will with adverse circumstance, no conflict of emotions, nor battle of passions; all was fated and determined; the apparent energies of will, regrets of soul, in Tess, were but as the muscular movements of a dead body. . . . Our pity and our fear are not purified merely; they are destroyed, and no room is left for them . . . I can find no tragedy in that. I can find in it nothing but a reason for keeping unbroken silence.

Johnson wrote those words ten years before the first part of the *Dynasts* appeared; had he lived to see that drama, he

[1] Translation by W. Hamilton Fyfe.

might no longer have thought that 'the antilogy of making figments feel' was a reason for keeping silence. Were it altogether true that neither our pity nor our fear are purified by *Tess*, the book would, of course, not grip us as it does. *Jude the Obscure*, to one reader at least, comes under the condemnation of complete failure on this count. But in *Tess*, one of Aristotle's desiderata remains. We may remain unmoved by the President of the Immortals. But our pity is surely purified.

The value of *Tess of the d'Urbervilles* as literature lies in its portrayal of the heroine, and of her setting; both are drawn with the hand of a master, and are of surpassing beauty. Hardy's outbursts against 'whatever gods may be,' to use a convenient phrase made famous by Swinburne, may leave us cold; but no reader with any feeling for the art of letters can miss the subtle, sometimes exquisite, modulations by which the changes in Tess's fortunes are symbolized in her natural surroundings; for example, when she returns to the home of her childhood as a maiden no more: 'Sad October and her sadder self seemed the only existences haunting that lane.' The whole of the third part, that incomparable idyll of summer in Var Vale where for a little while Tess tasted milk and honey on the lips of Life, is partly symbolic:

> The Froom waters were clear as the pure River of Life shown to the Evangelist, rapid as the shadow of a cloud, with pebbly shallows that prattled to the sky all day long.

The inevitable happens, and the days begin to darken about Tess. On the night of her marriage, she is about to tell her secret to the husband who is so unworthy of her, as they sit before the fire:

> The ashes under the grate were lit by the fire vertically, like a torrid waste.

And in the hard, bitter days of her slavery at Flintcomb Ash, the snow comes. Towards the end of the book, the sure touch with which this symbolism has been sustained, begins to falter. Alec waits for Tess beneath the rick, and the rats within it are soon to be left shelterless, to be hunted to death. The symbol is stressed, and is a trifle commonplace. And the last sleep, on the very stone of sacrifice at Stonehenge, is too obvious.

The last part of the book, called 'Fulfilment,' is, indeed, of a quality altogether inferior to the rest, and bears unfortunate traces of Hardy's early training in the melodramatic mystery novel. The meeting between Angel and Tess in the lodging house; the murder with the carving knife; the extraordinary blood which ran through a mattress and a ceiling; the execution at Winchester; all these we should expect from an apprentice to Wilkie Collins; but they are unworthy of the hand that wrote the third part. For when he chose, Hardy wrote as only the masters write. As for mere purple passages, two of his best are to be found in *Tess*, both in the third part. One is at the end of chapter sixteen, describing the bartons where the cows had gone home as the sun was sinking. The whole paragraph is extraordinarily vivid; and it ends:

> Thus it threw shadows over these obscure and homely figures every evening with as much care over each contour as if it had been the profile of a Court beauty on a palace wall; copied them as diligently as it had copied Olympian shapes on marble *façades* long ago, or the outline of Alexander, Caesar and the Pharaohs.

The other is in chapter twenty, where Tess and Angel used to meet at their work in the very early morning:

> The mixed, singular, luminous gloom in which they walked along together to where the cows lay, often made him think of the Resurrection hour. He little thought that the Magdalen might be at his side.

The woman who is set in these surroundings ennobles her creator. As the best of Hardy's American critics has said: 'The World is not altogether wrong that has in it such a woman as Tess.'[1] In the explanatory note to the fifth

[1] Samuel C. Chew.

edition, Hardy described the novel as 'an attempt to give artistic form to a true sequence of things.' There is other evidence, not likely ever to be published, that Tess herself was painted from the life. This is not to say that everything in the novel befell in fact; what bears the stamp of truth is the woman rather than her fortunes; they, indeed, are apt to be palpable inventions. There is a sentence in chapter fourteen in which Hardy describes the voice of Tess, and speaks of: 'The stopt diapason which her voice acquired when her heart was in the speech, and *which will never be forgotten by those who knew her.*' The words italicized, which do not occur in the Manuscript, can only be one of two things; either they are literal truth, or else literary artifice. If the latter, it is one of the most cunning instances. But the important thing for us now is not whether Hardy knew a living Tess; it is that his Tess is a living woman. Whether or not he knew her, many of us have been blessed in knowing living people to whom she is akin.

All the other characters in the book are failures, with the exception of the other dairymaids, and the thumbnail portrait of Dairyman Dick; or perhaps it would be better to say that there are no other characters, only lay figures. Alec is a piece of machinery for wrecking Tess; he only becomes really human once or twice, when he is 'backsliding,' and he does not remain human. Angel Clare is wholly incredible as a living man, interesting though he may be, considered as an exposition of some of Hardy's studies in rationalism. Old Mr. Clare and the rest of his family are caricatures. Mr. and Mrs. Durbeyfield do not convince us that they were capable of having such a daughter; they also are merely part of the machinery constructed to do the girl to death. But the only phase of Tess herself which is not wholly convincing is the penultimate one, in that part of the book which shows a falling-off of power. She would not have gone back to Alec, even to save her family from starvation. There are some things in human nature upon which one can pronounce with certainty; and one of them is such love as Tess bore to the miserable Angel Clare. This is the love that seeketh not her own, that is not easily provoked, that thinketh no evil and that never faileth. Loving with that love, she would not have played it false while she lived. Here Hardy is entrapped by his desire to fling his glove in the face of Destiny. For this, it was necessary, not that Tess should die, but that she should be hounded to madness and the gallows. He forsakes the region of the possible; and he ceases to ring true. Nevertheless, so fine and so true is Tess until then that the ending detracts only in part from the achievement.

At the present day, this country girl, as she is drawn in this book, is certainly as widely familiar as any character in the whole of English fiction, if not in the fiction of any language. Between 1900 and 1930, *Tess of the d'Urbervilles* was reprinted some forty times in England alone; this leaves the large American market out of account; to say nothing of translations into other languages; and there is no indication of any decline in its popularity. We cannot doubt that this popularity is almost wholly due to the heroine herself. But the greatness of works of art is not measured by statistics. Only students now read *Clarissa*, which was once considered the greatest novel in English. A time may come when the single volume of *Tess* proves as unmanageable to our descendants as the eight volumes of Richardson's masterpiece are to us. But to anyone who disinters Clarissa Harlowe herself from those volumes, she will appear to this hour a living woman. The immortality of Clarissa, the immortality of Antigone, belongs to Tess also. Before she was taken to be hanged at Winchester, she asked her husband whether he thought they would meet again after death; and when he kissed her she cried, for she knew he meant 'No.' So often, in the course of her history, are we told that it is better never to be born, that it is fitting we be told this also. But if Tess lived and died in the flesh, she lives and does not die in Hardy's art. We bid farewell to her in the words of the greatest of Hardy's successors:

Good night. Ensured release,
Imperishable peace,
Have these for yours,
While earth's foundations stand
And sky and sea and land
And heaven endures.

Tess of the d'Urbervilles is a book passionate almost to white heat, flaming with pity, sympathy and anger; but *Jude the Obscure* is cold as ice. Alternation between major and minor was not uncommon with Hardy; witness the contrast between the mood of *The Mayor of Casterbridge* and that of *The Woodlanders*. The mood of his last novel, besides being patently influenced by his unhappy state of mind in the early 'nineties, is probably not unconnected with extensive reading, in the latter part of 1890, of the satirists, among them Martial, Lucian, Voltaire, Dryden, Smollett, Swift and Byron.[1] That Hardy was thinking of his next novel is shown by his reading of Weismann's *Essays on Heredity* at this time; the influence of heredity is one of the themes of *Jude*. The plot seems to have taken shape some time earlier; for his diary for 1888 contained this entry on April 28th:

> A short story of a young man who could not go to Oxford. His struggles and ultimate failure. Suicide. There is something the world ought to be shown, and I am the one to show it to them.[2]

The novel seems to have been written during 1893 and 1894. When he had finished it, Hardy proceeded, no doubt with sardonic humour, to make a version suitable for family consumption; and this appeared as a serial in *Harper's Magazine* from December 1894 to November 1895.

The serial version of *Jude* is even more absurd than the serial version of *Tess*, if that be possible. The method by which, in it, Arabella inveigles Jude into marriage is another lover. The incident of Sue's elopement with Jude is cut down past recognition; almost the whole of Part

---

[1] *Early Life*, p. 301.   [2] *Early Life*, p. 272.

Four, chapter five, is omitted, and even what is left has to be softened down, for Phillotson's friend Gillingham says to him:

> She'll come back again alright. I think it is only a skittish girl's freak. There's nothing between her and that cousin.

Sue and Jude do not live in the same house at Aldbrickham; Jude has a room: 'exactly opposite, the street being so narrow that they could call to each other across it'; and when Jude comes in to breakfast with Sue, he does not kiss her, he shakes hands. Instead of telling Arabella that she is Jude's, Sue says: 'He's mine in promise. The day is fixed, and everything.' Sue and Jude call each other: 'Dear Companion.' They have no child, but adopt one. The incident in the cemetery is omitted altogether. When Arabella finally gets Jude back, she makes him drunk, takes him home and—puts him in the spare bedroom!!! Nearly all the church scene between Sue and Jude is omitted, as is also, of course, Sue's penance. To chronicle all the minor absurdities of this ludicrous serial would be waste of time. Although Hardy was forced to perform this castration, it is comforting to remember that he had a highly-developed sense of humour.

The Manuscript of *Jude*, which is in the Fitzwilliam Museum at Cambridge, proves that the original version of the story was almost exactly the version now familiar, the alterations for the serial having, as with *Tess*, been made later in blue ink. In one place Hardy explicitly wrote: 'Blue Alterations are for serial only. Not for volume form' (MS. p. 262). The Manuscript contains far less alterations than does that of *Tess*; and there are no cancels of interest. Mary Green, which is, of course, Great Fawley, in Berkshire, was originally 'Fawn Green.' Hardy's paternal grandmother, whom he knew well as Bockhampton, spent many years of her youth at this place, which may account for his choice of it.[1] In chapter three in the Manuscript, Jude's suggested

[1] *Thomas Hardy*, by Clive Holland, p. 231.

comparison of Christminster with the New Jerusalem originally ran:

> I suppose it looks as the Promised Land did to Moses from Mount Nebo.

In chapter seven Jude originally began to read St. Luke's Gospel, the title of which and its opening words are given in Greek. Some of the literary allusions in the present text were added, probably in proof, after the completion of the Manuscript. To give three examples: Gibbon was not, originally, among the Christminster Ghosts; nor did Sue quote John Stuart Mill to Phillotson; nor did the dying Jude quote Job. The book originally ended thus:

> 'She may tell that to the (undecipherable). She's never found peace since she left his arms,' said Arabella triumphantly.

The book was published by Osgood, M'Ilvaine & Co. on November 1st, 1895. Its fortunes during the next twelve months have given rise to a legend, which has tended to obscure the facts. With the torrent of abuse to which Hardy was subjected by uneducated scribblers, both on anonymous post-cards and in sensation-mongering periodicals, we have no concern here. Nor need we pause over the gentleman, possibly a demented cricketer, who sent Hardy an envelope full of ashes from Australia, with an intimation that they were the ashes of his novel; nor over the lady in New York, who, when she had finished the book, opened the window to admit fresh air, turned to her bookshelf and praised God for Mrs. Humphrey Ward. The varying reactions of more responsible critics can be illustrated by some brief quotations. Feeling ran even higher over *Jude* than it had done over *Tess*. The *Athenæum* (November 23rd, 1895) wrote:

> Here we have a titanically bad book by Mr. Hardy. We have had bad books from him before, but so far his bad books have been feeble rather than anything else. In *Jude*, however, we have Mr. Hardy running mad in right royal fashion. . . . Lately so many inferior writers have stirred up the mud with this controversy (the marriage question), that one would have been

content that so great a writer as Mr. Hardy had not touched it if he were not going greatly to dignify it.

Such was probably the opinion of many admirers of Hardy, then as now. The *Saturday Review*, which seems to have received an infusion of new blood since it reviewed *Tess*, described *Jude* as:

> the most splendid of all the works that Mr. Hardy has given to the world . . . had he never written another book, this would still place him at the head of English novelists. (Feb. 6th, 1896.)

The *Westminster Review* (Vol. 145, p. 136) was hardly less hyperbolical:

> But for the miserable priggery of this end of the nineteenth century, the first part of *Jude* would be held up by critics as one of the most touching records in all literature . . . Mr. Hardy is not to blame for the brutishness of some of his readers' minds, any more than Miranda (to borrow an illustration from Mr. Ruskin) is to blame for Caliban's beastly thoughts about her . . . *Jude* is not his greatest work, but no other living novelist could have written it.

Mrs. M. O. W. Oliphant, reviewing it in *Blackwoods* (January 1896), emitted a shrill shriek in an article headed 'The Anti Marriage League.' Admitting Hardy to be a master, she wrote that *Jude*:

> unconsciously affords us the strongest illustration of what Art can come to when given over to the exposition of the unclean.

Swinburne wrote to Hardy:

> The tragedy, if I may venture an opinion, is equally beautiful and terrible in its pathos. The beauty, the terror and the truth are all yours, and yours alone. But (if I may say so) how cruel you are! Only the great and awful father of 'Pierette' and 'L'enfant maudit' was ever so merciless to his children.[1]

Six months later, Mr. Havelock Ellis wrote a long article, in which he said that *Jude* seemed to him the greatest novel written in England for many years; but even he was of opinion that the murder of the children was a blemish:

> With the opening of that cupboard we are thrust out of the

[1] This letter is in the Fitzwilliam Museum; it is quoted by Mrs. Hardy.

large field of common life into the small field of the police court or lunatic asylum, among the things which for most of us are comparatively unreal.[1]

An article which pithily expressed all that many lovers of Hardy regret in his last novel appeared in the *Fortnightly Review* (Vol. 65, No. 59):

> We cannot but hold that *Jude* represents a deplorable falling off. . . . Mr. Hardy has determined to try whether his public will accept, in lieu of a novel, a treatise on sexual pathology in which the data are drawn from imagination. . . . He has devoted five hundred pages to repeating again and again what Susarion said in three senarii.

Edmund Gosse, in a very discriminating review (in *Cosmopolis*, Jan. 1896), wrote:

> It is difficult not to believe that the author set up his four ninepins in the wilds of Wessex, and built up his theorem round them.

The most celebrated incident in the public reaction to *Jude* occurred in June 1896. On the 8th of that month, the *Yorkshire Post* of Leeds published a leading article, denouncing not only *Jude*, but also Hardy's works in general in no measured terms. Next day it printed the following letter:

> SIR,
> Will you allow me publicly to thank you for your outspoken leader in your to-day's issue denouncing the intolerable grossness and hateful sneering at all that one most reveres in such writers as Thomas Hardy?
> On the authority of one of those reviews which you justly condemn for their reticence, I bought a copy of one of Mr. Hardy's novels, but was so disgusted with its insolence and indecency that I threw it into the fire. It is a disgrace to our great public libraries to admit such garbage, clever though it may be, to their shelves.
> I am, Sir,
> Yours, etc.
> Bishopgarth,   WILLIAM WALSHAM WAKEFIELD.
> Wakefield.

[1] *Savoy Magazine*, October 1896. Reprinted in *Concerning Jude the Obscure*.

THOMAS HARDY

William Walsham How, Bishop of Wakefield, the writer of this letter, is probably best remembered as the author of the hymn 'For all the saints who from their labours rest.' He has been described to the present writer by two people who knew him as: 'a good, kind, well-meaning man, but scarcely of a literary or highly intellectual type'; and as: 'a fine old man, greatly respected and deservedly popular.'[1] Hardy said that the Bishop had doubtless burnt his novel in despair at being unable to burn its author. The journalistic world naturally received the episcopal sally with rapture, and on the evening of the same day the Bishop's letter was quoted in the *Westminster Gazette*, to the accompaniment of satiric verses entitled: 'How versus Hardy.' In the *Yorkshire Post* there ensued a resounding controversy, culminating in another leading article on June 1st. Although it was not publicly known at the time, Bishop How also wrote privately to W. F. D. Smith:

> The result was the quiet withdrawal of the book from the library (Smith's), and an assurance that any other books by the same author would be carefully examined before they were allowed to be circulated.[2]

Although Hardy was not the master of invective that Swinburne was, it is probable that, had he known of this transaction, the Right Reverend Father in God would have received a memorable trouncing.

In the midst of the uproar, there were some who asserted that *Jude the Obscure* was autobiographical. Many years later, someone wrote to ask Hardy if this was true, and the second Mrs. Hardy replied:

> To your enquiry if *Jude the Obscure* is autobiographical, I have to answer that there is not a scrap of personal detail in it, it having the least to do with his own life of all his books.[3]

This statement was very rash indeed. While it is, of course,

---

[1] I am indebted to several correspondents, and to the Editor of the *Yorkshire Post*, for information about this incident.

[2] *Later Years*, p. 48.

[3] *Ibid.*, p. 136.

true that the novel is not autobiography in the sense intended by its unmannerly critics in 1896, the events in it being purely fictitious, a large part of it reflects Hardy's own life as none of the other novels do. This is true, for example, of all that part which is concerned with the studies of Jude and of Sue. We see here, to name only outstanding instances, Hardy's own studies in Griesbach's Greek Testament, already mentioned; we see the battle over science and religion, over biblical criticism and rationalism, which so profoundly influenced Hardy as a young man. We see his reading of Swinburne and Shelley. The celebrated Christminster Ghosts are the ghosts of Hardy's own intellectual past. Insistence upon all this is needless; after what has gone before, it should be obvious enough. The personal character of the book goes even further, despite Mrs. Hardy's assertion to the contrary; as is proved by evidence which she herself unconsciously supplies. In a passage clearly reproduced word for word from what her husband told her, she describes an experience of Hardy's childhood:

> He was lying on his back in the sun, thinking how useless he was, and covered his face with his straw hat. The sun's rays streamed through the interstices of the straw, the lining having disappeared. Reflecting on his experiences of the world so far as he had got, he came to the conclusion that he did not wish to grow up. Other boys were always talking of when they would be men; he did not at all want to be a man.[1]

In the second chapter of *Jude the Obscure*, there occurs this passage about the little Jude, after his thrashing by Farmer Troutham:

> Jude went out, and, feeling more than ever his existence to be an undemanded one, he lay down upon his back on a heap of litter near the pig stye. The fog had by this time become more translucent, and the position of the sun could be seen through it. He pulled his straw hat over his face, and peered through the interstices of the plaiting at the white brightness, vaguely reflecting. Growing up brought responsibilities, he found.

[1] *Early Life*, pp. 19-20.

Events did not rhyme quite as he had thought. Nature's logic was too horrid for-him to care for. That mercy towards one set of creatures was cruelty towards another sickened his sense of harmony. As you got older, and felt yourself to be at the centre of your time, and not a point on its circumference as you had felt when you were little, you were seized with a sort of shuddering, he perceived. All around you there seemed to be something glaring, garish, rattling, and the noises and glares hit upon the little cell called your life, and shook it and warped it. If he could only prevent himself growing up! He did not want to be a man.

To anyone possessing any insight, who is at all familiar with Hardy's work as a whole, that passage plainly describes the man who wrote it. One can sympathize with Mrs. Hardy in her desire to have her husband shielded from the journalistic searchlight; everyone with a sense of decency must share her annoyance at the persons who thrust themselves upon him, and then (to take only one instance) had the impudence to publish the results as an authorized Life of Thomas Hardy. Nevertheless, when a great artist has given the best fruit of his life to the world, his life is in part a public possession. Of that inner life of the man himself out of which came the work that has enriched our literature, Mrs. Hardy's volumes give but few glimpses. Hardy wrote no autobiography; but there is more to be seen of his own inner life, by those with eyes to see, in *Jude the Obscure* than in any other novel.

It is reported that on one occasion, Lord Rosebery asked Hardy why he had called Oxford 'Christminster':

> Hardy assured him that he had done nothing of the sort, Christminster being a city of learning that was certainly suggested by Oxford, but in its entirety existed nowhere else in the world but between the covers of the novel.[1]

There is in existence a sheet of notepaper on which, in Hardy's own hand, are written most of the place-names in *Jude*, and then, after the words *approximates to*, the real

[1] *Later Years*, p. 49.

place-names in a parallel column; part of this list is as follows[1]:

Beersheba . . .	the purlieu called Jericho.
St. Silas	St. Barnabas.
Chief St.	High St.
Fourways . . .	Carfax.
Meeting place of Jude & Sue	Cross in pavement, Broad St.
Crozier Coll. . . .	Oriel?
Old Time Street . .	Oriel Lane?
Rubric Coll. . . .	Brazenose.
Cardinal Coll. . . .	Christ Church Coll.
The Cathedral . . .	Christchurch.
Cardinal Street . .	St. Aldates St.
Ch(urch) with Italian Porch	St. Mary's.
Theatre of Wren . .	Sheldonian.
The octagonal chamber (p. 141)	Cupola of Sheldonian.
Oldgate Coll. . . .	New Coll.
The riverside path . .	The towing path.

Hardy's intimate knowledge of the topography of Oxford was most probably gained when, as assistant to Arthur Blomfield, he worked for a time at the Radcliffe Chapel.[2] It is interesting to learn that in the summer of 1893, when he was planning, if not actually writing, *Jude*, he paid a private visit to Oxford, and went to see the Encænia from the undergraduates' gallery of the Sheldonian.[3] The results are to be seen in *Jude*, Part 6, chapter one. Twenty-seven years later, Hardy again stood in that venerable building; but this time he was robed in the scarlet robe, and the voice of the Public Orator sounded in his ears:

> Nunc ut homini si quis alius Musis et dis agrestibus amico titulum debitum dando, non tantum illi quantum nobis ipsis decus addatis, duco ad vos senem illustrem Thomam Hardy.

It came very late, that honour which Christminster did to herself in honouring the greatest writer of his age; but, like

---

[1] Reproduced in facsimile in *Thomas Hardy*, by Clive Holland, p. 144.
[2] According to Clive Holland, p. 54.
[3] *Later Years*, p. 22.

the memorial to Shelley, it came from a younger generation.

The reasons why Hardy chose Oxford as the university in his last novel are not far to seek. It was on the border of the country he knew best. He had visited it as a young architect's assistant, cut off from all the world of scholarship with which he had so many affinities; for it was many years before he began to have friends in Cambridge. But above all, Oxford had been the scene of the momentous struggles between theology and science which had resounded through England in Hardy's early manhood. The attacks made upon Jowett during this conflict were mentioned in the third chapter. It was not for nothing that, when he was writing *Jude*, Hardy noted in his diary:

'Never retract. Never explain. Get it done and let them howl.'
Words said to Jowett by a very practical friend.[1]

There has been much talk at cross purposes upon the subject of the alleged immorality and indecency of *Jude the Obscure*. To say, with Mrs. Oliphant, that it is 'an exposition of the unclean' is as unhelpful as to say, with Mrs. Hardy, that the unpleasantness resides in readers 'with nice minds and nasty ideas.' If it be an exposition of the unclean to portray the elemental passions of human life, much of the great literature of the world would be put on the Index. In English, both *Hamlet* and *Othello* would be damned; and among the novels of the nineteenth century, we should lose *Adam Bede* and *The Heart of Midlothian*, to mention no others. The conventions of middle and later Victorian society on the question of the treatment of sexual relationships in literature, were almost as undesirable as is the fashion of recent times in the opposite direction. When, twenty-nine years before *Jude*, *Poems and Ballads* was furiously attacked, Swinburne protested that: 'our time has room only for such as are content to write for children.'[2] It is an obvious, undeniable truth that English literature cannot be confined to: 'fit and necessary food for female infancy.' On the other hand, as Stevenson knew, the desire

---

[1] *Later Years*, p. 38.   [2] *Notes on Poems and Reviews*.

to put things plainly contains within itself a peril, the peril of 'being shoved towards grossness.'[1] This peril Hardy had successfully avoided hitherto, in novels which did not shrink from handling passion. But in *Jude* he deliberately waded in. What is to be condemned in the book is less coarseness of language, of which there is very little indeed, than an intention to wound and affront. Slight traces of such a mood are to be found in *Tess*; as, for instance, in Mrs. Durbeyfield's final remark upon the rape of her daughter: ' 'Tis Nature, after all, and what do please God.' There are many passages of this nature in *Jude*. One taken at random is Sue's description of legal marriage (one of several to the same effect); namely, that a woman must give her love 'to the chamber officer licensed by the Bishop to receive it.' It is not due to the reader's 'nice mind with nasty ideas' that this leaves a nasty taste in the mouth; it is due to Hardy's deliberate determination to create a nasty taste. Sue's return, by way of penance, to her first husband whom she loathes, is one of the most horrible things in fiction. It was, of course, meant to be horrible. Apart from sexual relationship, there are in *Jude the Obscure* more than enough deliberately horrible matters. The description of the pig-sticking is physically sickening. The murders and suicide of 'Father Time,' and the stillbirth, were intended to be a climax of horror. Whether or not these things had in them 'cathartic qualities,' as Hardy afterwards claimed, it is absurd, when he deliberately did all he could to horrify and outrage his readers, to blame the readers for being outraged and horrified. Their horror should rather have been welcomed, as a tribute to success.

Properly to understand the main subject of *Jude the Obscure*, it is necessary to glance at something that was happening in England in the early 'nineties. We have already seen Hardy beginning to dabble in practical affairs in *The Woodlanders*, where the question of incompatibility in marriage is so markedly stressed. Another aspect of

[1] *Vailima Letters.*

sexual relationships, and of society's attitude to them, is the subject of *Tess*, the first novel which Hardy wrote for a practical purpose. The whole question of marriage and divorce was brought to the forefront of public attention in 1890 by the Parnell case. In December 1889, Captain O'Shea filed a petition for divorce from his wife on the ground of her adultery with Charles Stewart Parnell, the Irish political leader. The case came into Court in November 1890; and a decree nisi, with costs against Parnell, was pronounced. Although Parnell's Irish followers publicly declared their continued allegiance to him, the English Liberal party, of which the backbone was Nonconformity, refused to overlook the matter. On November 24th, Gladstone wrote a famous open letter to John Morley, saying that:

> notwithstanding the splendid services rendered by Mr. Parnell to his country, his continuance at the present time in the leadership would be productive of consequences disastrous in the highest degree to the cause of Ireland.

A storm of controversy ensued, which cost Parnell his leadership, his reputation, his health and his life; he died in 1891.[1]

This *cause célèbre* let loose a flood of discussion and polemic upon the whole question of love, marriage and divorce; and of this *Jude the Obscure* formed a part. To consider here only two examples pertinent to this novel. With the *Fortnightly Review* Hardy had at that time close connections. In the course of 1891, that periodical published 'A Midnight Baptism,' the episode from *Tess* which the *Graphic* refused to print, as well as Hardy's short story, 'For Conscience' Sake,' a study in the results of illicit sexual relationship. The same volume of the *Fortnightly* contains an article occasioned by the Parnell case, entitled 'Public Life and Private Morals.' One paragraph discusses the grounds for regarding marriage as sacred:

[1] The whole English Press was full of this matter; see, *passim*, the *Times* of November and December 1890. It also figures more or less largely in most memoirs covering the period; there are several references, to give the latest example, in Augustine Birrell's *Things Past Redress*; see p. 123 *et seq.*

Now what are these grounds? If we say that they are merely grounds of civil contract, we entirely deceive ourselves. Marriage, merely as a civil contract is a contract which the parties concerned in it are, by mutual consent, at perfect liberty to break. But let us suppose for a moment that this was not the case. Let us suppose that this contract had something so special about it, that each party was not only bound to fulfil its conditions if the other demanded, but that each, whether they willed it or no, was bound to demand the fulfilment of them. Let us suppose further that marriage was literally a lottery—that men and women were bound to each other who had neither love nor sympathy, who were suited neither by age nor by temperament. What should we say of the sanctity of marriage then? Would it not seem hateful rather than sacred? . . . The sanctity of marriage depends, not on its being a contract, but on its being a willing contract. It depends also on the willingness of the contracting parties being the result of dispositions which will enable them to live together happily. If love and marriage were essentially incompatible, would marriage in that case have ever seemed sacred to anybody? Most of its sanctity is gone when they are bound to be incompatible practically. The legal aspect of the union is merely its husk and shell. Its real sanctity is like the sanctity of friendship; it lies far deeper than any law can reach and depends on circumstances of which no law can take account.

Later in the same year, the same periodical published another article entitled 'Marriage and Freethought,' which was a powerful plea for reasoned consideration of the whole question. A striking passage in this ran:

Could any scientific discovery in these days be discredited, even for a moment, by the authority of a biblical text? Would a text, no matter how plain, do anything towards arresting any popular reform or change? The answer to both these questions, as we are all aware, is no. . . . But the liberal and progressive thought of this country, the moment it is brought to bear on this one social question (Marriage) becomes doggedly false to every one of its boasted principles . . . while indignantly refusing to recognise the vows that bind the nun, it refuses even to consider the relaxation of those that may be killing the wife; and whilst ridiculing the idea that any other contract is inviolable . . . it treats this contract of marriage, which constantly works so miserably, as a contract which no one may violate, though every one concerned is willing, and which it is a kind of blasphemy to attempt to regulate better.

For some years past, Hardy had had strong and bitter feelings about marriage, as may be seen in *The Woodlanders*. Then the whole question became the most discussed subject in the country. When we remember that Hardy was a contributor to the periodical in which both these articles appeared, and that it was just at this time that *Jude the Obscure* was taking shape in his mind, we need no further commentary upon one aspect of that novel. Although it does not seem to have been even mentioned by any of the critics, such is the background to the book which has written upon its title-page: 'The letter killeth.'

Another matter has also to be mentioned in this connection, which also appears to have been overlooked. It was at this time that the plays of Ibsen first began to appear on the English stage. Between 1889 and 1896 there raged a bitter controversy over the Scandinavian dramatist. Hardy, Meredith and George Moore were among the first members of an Independent Theatre Association founded in 1891 to sponsor the production of Ibsen's plays. This cause was also sponsored by the *Fortnightly Review*, which published an article on the Independent Theatre Association by William Archer.[1] Edmund Gosse, a close personal friend of Hardy's at this time, was another leading spirit among the English advocates of Ibsen. The English versions of the Norwegian plays which were published by him and by Archer did much to popularize them in this country. Without going into lengthy comparisons, it is easy to see that *Jude the Obscure* owes something to Ibsen. It is not surprising to learn that in the course of 1893, when the novel was being written, Hardy went to performances of *Hedda Gabler*, *Rosmersholm* and *The Master Builder*.[2] Readers of

[1] Vol. for 1891, p. 663 *et seq.*   [2] *Later Years*, p. 20.

Jude will suspect that he also knew something of *The Doll's House* and of *Ghosts*. The less perspicacious critics accused Hardy of imitating Zola, whom they, like Mrs. Oliphant, had never read themselves. Time need not be wasted upon this comparison; nothing could well be further apart than the aims of that particular French realist, and the aims with which Hardy wrote *Jude*. But the influence of Ibsen is certainly to be seen in that novel; which is not the same thing as saying that Hardy 'imitated' Ibsen. He was in no need to imitate anybody.

In one of three letters about *Jude* which Hardy wrote to Gosse, he denied that the book was 'a manifesto on the marriage question, although, of course, it involves it.'¹ The distinction is a very fine one, if it exists at all; but there is little doubt that the ridiculous and scandalous uproar of which he became the subject made Hardy lose his head a little at the time. It may be that the 'general remarks' upon marriage only fill a few pages; but no one who has read it impartially can deny that marital relationships are one of the main subjects of the book. The horrible penance of Sue, in which that theme culminates, was deliberately contrived to sear the minds of his readers with the evil of unhappy marriage; as, indeed, was the whole plot. In the original preface dated August 1895, Hardy very clearly stated the objects of his last novel:

> to deal unaffectedly with the fret and fever, derision and disaster, that may press in the wake of the strongest passion known to humanity; to tell without a mincing of words, of deadly war waged between flesh and spirit; and to point the tragedy of unfulfilled aims.

Jude's attempt on Christminster, in all its implications, is the third of these. The deadly war waged between spirit and flesh hinges entirely upon two unhappy marriages. The facts do not admit of any denial that Hardy made it so on purpose, partly urged on thereto by the controversy raging in the country when he was planning the novel. The mar-

Privately printed by Mr. Thomas Wise; quoted by Mrs. Hardy.

riage question was both in his own heart and in the atmosphere.

The other theme of *Jude*, inextricably mixed up with the marriage question, was that of love, 'the strongest passion known to humanity' in its ruinous results upon the individual. Hardy's treatment of love has been so much discussed that it is unnecessary here to offer more than a few remarks upon it. His view of love in mature life was a part of his view of the universe. To put it more explicitly: in that wrecking of the individual, conscious, life by the unconscious, universal Process, which is the great subject of his art, the part of the universal is played by love far more often than by anything else. All his novels except two, and most of his short stories, are love stories; and the nature of them is best conveyed in the words of one of his many poems about love:

> Love is a terrible thing; sweet for a space,
> And then all mourning, mourning.

We have seen that Hardy was a student of Swinburne. In their views of love, these two great writers ran as much counter to the romantic ideas fashionable in their day as to its conventions in some other respects. Instead of the quotation from Esdras: 'Many there be that have run out of their wits for women,' etc., Hardy might well have put at the beginning of *Jude* the lines which the great god Love speaks in Swinburne's autobiographical poem 'Thalassius':

> I am he that was thy lord before thy birth,
> I am he that is thy lord till thou turn earth;
> I make the night more dark, and all the morrow
> Dark as the night whose darkness was my breath;
> O fool, my name is sorrow,
> Thou fool, my name is death.

They exactly describe the life of the unhappy Jude. But there is more to be said about the part which love plays in this novel. For here Hardy was not trying simply to write an unhappy love story; he was trying to show that love is

the inevitable instrument of the destruction of the individual. The merely physical part of love is symbolized by
Arabella, and the aspiration to wholly spiritual and intellectual companionship by Sue; and the destruction of Jude
is accomplished by them both. Here we come upon very
evident traces of Hardy's studies in philosophy. In Eduard
von Hartmann's *Philosophy of the Unconscious*, Chapter XIII,
Part 3 ('Metaphysics of the Unconscious') we may read:

> Whoever has once understood the illusory nature of success-
> ful love after union, and therewith also of that before union,
> whoever has come to see the pain outweighing the pleasure in
> all love, for that man the phenomenon of love has no more
> health, because his consciousness offers resistance to the im-
> position of means to ends which are not *his* ends; the pleasure
> of love has been for him undermined and corroded, only its
> smart remains to him unrelieved . . . he will at the same time
> be conscious that he is entangled against his will in passion
> that causes him more pain than pleasure, and with this percep-
> tion from the standpoint of individualism, the doom of love
> has been pronounced.[1]

As was seen in the third chapter, we know that Hardy
studied *The Philosophy of the Unconscious*. His poem, 'I said
to Love' (in *Poems of the Past and Present*) is on the conception that love is the imposition of means to ends which are
not the ends of the individual. And *Jude the Obscure* is, in
one of its three main themes, an exposition of this conception of love.

To some admirers of Hardy, *Jude* appears to represent
the roof and crown of his achievement. It is such an one
who writes:

> Guided by the artistry of Aeschylus, and permeated by the
> essentials of Ecclesiastes, I believe *Jude the Obscure*, in its pro-
> found and unfathomable depths of gloom and greatness, to be
> unsurpassed by any novel in the history of our literature.[2]

This can only be possible to one whose views of the nature
of art, to say nothing of the nature and meaning of life, are

---

[1] Translation by W. C. Coupland.
[2] A. Stanton Whitfield: *Thomas Hardy.*

radically different from mine. Speaking for myself, I can find *Jude the Obscure* only a terribly wearisome book, bearing undoubted marks of great power, but of power lamentably misdirected. To me, it seems false to life, and as a work of art a complete failure. It is, indeed, not a work of art at all. It is a treatise on the misery of human existence, as determined by forces within and without themselves over which human beings have no control whatever. Writing to Gosse, in one of the letters already mentioned, Hardy called Jude 'my poor puppet'; never was a truer word. Jude is, precisely, a puppet constructed for a didactic purpose, who is jerked by Hardy from the wings. We are told of him that his sensitiveness:

> suggested that he was the sort of man who was born to ache a good deal before the fall of the curtain upon his unnecessary life should signify that all was well with him again.

Just so; he is only necessary to show the antilogy of 'making figments feel.' As to Sue Bridehead, her sensitiveness, her perception, her conscience, all, in fact, that differentiate the human being from the animal, bring both her and the man she loves to agony and ruin. It could not be otherwise, for Hardy created her to this end. With Arabella, the animal, all is well. And the great blemish is, that not one of the three exists in his or her own right as an individual. They are lay figures. Many of the critics have become enthusiastic over Sue, as the subtlest of Hardy's women.[1] Endeavouring to consider her as a woman, and not as Hardy's ingeniously constructed puppet, I cannot agree with them. She is, as a woman, a psychological abnormality (which is not tantamount to saying that she is a pervert). There is no reason why art should not treat of the abnormal, but under one condition only: however abnormal the subject, the treatment must make universal appeal. If one may judge by the number of intelligent, highly educated people who 'cannot

[1] Perhaps the most notable panegyric is in the strange rhapsody by D. H. Lawrence miscalled 'A Study of Thomas Hardy.'

get through' *Jude the Obscure*, Hardy's treatment is anything but universal.

The great faults of the book appear to me to be two. To take the lesser first: it is false to art. It is ruined by continual over-emphasis; nothing is left in natural colours; nothing is allowed to speak for itself; all is 'lamp-black and light-ning'; everything is rammed down the throat of the choking reader. To give only one example: the murder of the children is about as bad as it could be. And just afterwards, the stricken parents hear the organist of a college chapel practising the anthem from the seventy-third psalm: 'Surely God is loving unto Israel.' And this stuff, we are told, is 'guided by the artistry of Aeschylus.' . . . From all the last part of the novel we can but turn away in pity. All the power of a great writer is here strained to breaking point, in the hopeless endeavour to drive home by main force the lesson which we are to be taught. The result might be beyond bearing if one could, for a single moment, forget that one was being taught; in other words, achieve the willing suspension of disbelief which constitutes poetic faith.

The greatest, fundamental, fault of *Jude the Obscure* is that it is false to life. For, to use the words of Goethe: 'Wahr-heitsliebe zeigt sich darin, dass man überall das Gute zu finden und zu schätzen weiss.' In his last novel, Hardy has deliberately turned away from 'das Gute' which, in the pages of *Tess*, he so magnificently finds, and teaches us to appreciate. In *Jude* he capitulates; and it is this capitulation which we cannot accept, for it is the negation, both of art and of life. In philosophy, the 'denial of the Will to live' may appear to some the solution of the mystery of life; as it will appear to others to be a shirking of the challenge of that mystery. In art, such denial is the betrayal which can produce nothing but stultification.

CHAPTER VII

THE POEMS AND THE *DYNASTS*

I. The Poems

THE first flowering of Hardy's genius was in poetry. The earliest of his writings to have survived is a poem called 'Domicilium,' which, according to Mrs. Hardy,[1] was written between 1857 and 1860. It was first privately printed by Mr. Clement Shorter in 1916. After Hardy's death, Mrs. Hardy printed it in the *Early Life*. The poem describes the appearance of the house at Bockhampton in which Hardy was born. Its diction and general flavour are purely Wordsworthian; so is the subject, if we consider it as only the first, descriptive, section of a Wordsworthian piece; and the conversational treatment is obviously based upon Wordsworth's practice. It seems unlikely that this poem, so clearly the result of a literary apprenticeship (leaving out of account the title, probably given to it later), was in fact the first that Hardy ever wrote, although nothing earlier has survived. But 'Domicilium' itself is the only relic of Hardy's juvenilia; between it and the poems which we know him to have written in 1865, there is a complete blank. He must certainly have written verse during those years, but it seems to have vanished without leaving a trace.

We are told of Hardy's years in London:

By 1865 he had begun to write verses, and by 1866 to send his productions to magazines. That these were rejected by editors, and that he paid such respect to their judgment as scarcely ever to send out a MS. twice, was in one feature fortunate for him, since in years long after he was able to examine those poems of which he kept copies, and by the mere change of a few words or the rewriting of a line or two to make them quite worthy of publication.[2]

[1] *Early Life*, p. 4.   [2] *Early Life*, p. 62.

The rejection of his poetry did not stop his writing. During 1866 and 1867, we are told that he wrote verses constantly, but kept them to himself. This was a matter of importance for English literature. Not only were the poems which he kept 'quite worthy of publication'; they remain to show that, while in prose the pen that was to produce *Tess* was still learning its letters, the poet who wrote the *Dynasts* was not unrecognizably far from his full stature at twenty-six, when he wrote 'Hap':

> If but some vengeful god would call to me
> From up the sky, and laugh 'Thou suffering thing,
> Know that thy sorrow is my ecstasy,
> That thy love's loss is my hate's profiting!'
> Then would I bear it, clench myself, and die,
> Steeled by the sense of ire unmerited;
> Half eased in that a Powerfuller than I
> Had willed and meted me the tears I shed.
>
> But not so. How arrives it joy lies slain,
> And why unblooms the best hope ever sown?
> Crass Casualty obstructs the sun and rain,
> And dicing Time for gladness casts a moan . . .
> These purblind Doomsters had as readily strown
> Blisses about my pilgrimage as pain.

When *Atalanta in Calydon* appeared in 1865, there were but few and feeble protests against the fourth stasimon with its denunciation of 'the supreme evil, God'; that came with 'Anactoria' in the following year. But here is Hardy, in the very year of *Poems and Ballads*, gone far beyond the idea of malignant deity. This is the doctrine of the Ancient Spirit of the Years in the *Dynasts*. And we have even some fore-taste of Hardy's later diction. 'Unblooms,' not, in itself, a happy neologism, and 'purblind doomsters,' belong to a vocabulary utterly unheard of in the eighteen-sixties.[1] To find a parallel during the third quarter of the nineteenth

---

[1] There are several surprising gallicisms in Hardy's earliest poems, e.g., in the ninth line of 'Hap.' It is possible that we are here upon the traces of Hardy's French studies at King's College, London.

century to this poem in English poetry, we should have to
go either to Fitzgerald's translation of the *Rubáiyát*, or to
Thomson's *City of Dreadful Night*. Thomson's masterpiece
first appeared in the pages of the *National Reformer* in 1874.
It is with that great and sombre poem that Hardy's sonnet
has affinities:

> And now at last authentic word I bring,
> Witnessed by every dead and living thing;
>   Good tidings of great joy for you, for all:
> There is no God; no Fiend with names divine
> Made us and tortures us; if we must pine,
>   It is to satiate no Being's gall.
>
> It was the dark delusion of a dream,
> That living Person conscious and supreme,
>   Whom we must curse for cursing us with life;
> Whom we must curse because the life he gave
> Could not be buried in the quiet grave,
>   Could not be killed by poison or by knife.

This was nine years later than Hardy's sonnet; it is the work
of a mature man; and it goes far beyond Hardy's youthful
imaginings; but in essence it is the same.

It is hardly surprising that the editors of popular magazines refused to print the poems which Hardy sent them in
the 'sixties. English poetry was then in an age of transition.
Outwardly, the reign of Tennyson was supreme; moreover
it was the Tennyson of the *Idylls of the King* (the first four of
which appeared in 1864), and of that *Enoch Arden* which
Gosse called 'an intolerable concession to commonplace
ideals'[1]; not the Tennyson of the early poems and of *In
Memoriam*, nor of the late philosophical poems. It is true
that behind the scenes a change was preparing, which was
not confined to men like Fitzgerald and Thomson, who
were under the influence of 'rationalistic' thought. There
was neither commonplace nor rationalism in Browning's
Dramatis Personæ, which also appeared in 1864; but Brown-

[1] *Life of A. C. Swinburne* (1917), p. 108.

ing did not come into his own until *The Ring and the Book* (1868–9). There was nothing commonplace, if no little rationalism, in *Atalanta in Calydon* (1865); but neither the fame of *Atalanta* nor the influence of Monckton Milnes saved Swinburne from scalding when the 'British tea kettle' boiled over on the publication of *Poems and Ballads* in 1866. The Pre-Raphaelites were beginning to make headway. William Morris, after publishing *The Defence of Guinevere* in 1858, had made considerable impression upon a small, but select and important, public with *The Life and Death of Jason* (1867). Christina Rossetti had almost had a popular success with *Goblin Market* in 1862. But the controversy over 'the fleshly school of poetry' which arose over D. G. Rossetti's *Poems* in 1870 showed how little progress had been made since Meredith's *Modern Love* had been trounced as 'modern lust' in 1862. Moreover, the magazine editors to whom Hardy sent his early poems did not belong to the circles which appreciated Browning and Morris, and discussed Fitzgerald and Thomson; they went no further than Tennyson or Jean Ingelow. The public for whom they catered did not want 'Felise' or 'The Blessed Damozel' or 'Rabbi Ben Ezra'; it wanted 'The Queen of the May.' Small wonder, therefore, that 'Hap' or 'In Vision I roamed' returned from the editorial office accompanied by the rejection slip.

It would be interesting to know how many of the poems which Hardy wrote before 1875 were destroyed; to judge from some remarks by Mrs. Hardy, who says that the sonnets 'She to Him' were part of a much larger number which perished, it would seem that those which have survived are a small minority. Of the poems later published in Hardy's first four volumes of verse which are dated before 1875, sixteen are in *Wessex Poems*, three in *Poems of the Past and Present*, eleven in *Time's Laughingstocks* and two in *Satires of Circumstance*. Very occasionally, an early poem appears in the later volumes. There are probably many other early poems among those published which are undated.

THOMAS HARDY

But dating by internal evidence is in this instance a risky matter, for Hardy's diction and sentiments did not materially alter for many years. For example: it is quite possible that 'Sapphics,' and even 'A Sign Seeker' were written before 1875; but they may equally well belong to the 'nineties. These early poems include some miscellaneous pieces; but generally speaking they can be grouped into two classes. 'Hap,' 'In Vision I roamed,' 'At a Bridal' and similar poems are of a philosophic character. They foreshadow the *Dynasts*. A much more numerous category are the love poems. The Wessex novels might almost be said to exist in embryo in the series of four sonnets 'She to Him' which are dated 1866. The group of love lyrics in *Time's Laughing-stocks*—many of which are dated between 1866 and 1871, while some undated ones clearly belong here also—is a very vital piece of literature. Few of our great poets have left such personal documents of their youth as are these poems; one thinks instinctively of Keats. But Hardy found, as most great poets have found, that his contemporaries had no use for his verses.

He was not to appear before the public as a poet until the end of the century; and even then he was before his time. When he had made a great name as a novelist, he collected what he considered the best of his early verses, added them to such others as he had written at intervals for many years, and sent them to his publishers, characteristic-ally offering to pay for their publication. This offer Mac-millans properly refused, and published *Wessex Poems* on their own account in 1898. The volume was decorated with a number of drawings by Hardy himself. These have never been reproduced, although some of them are very striking; two are given as a frontispiece to this volume.

On the whole, the reception given to *Wessex Poems* was friendly, with the polite friendliness of incomprehension due to an author indubitably great, but suffering from a tempor-ary aberration. The *Saturday Review* was frankly disgusted:

As we read this curious and wearisome volume, these many,

slovenly, slipshod, uncouth verses, stilted in sentiment, poorly conceived and worse wrought, our respect lessens to vanishing point, and we lay it down with the feeling strong upon us that Mr. Hardy has, by his own deliberate act, discredited that judgment on which his reputation rested.[1]

The *Athenæum*, however, was much more friendly:

> We do not conceal our opinion that Mr. Hardy's success in poetry is of a very narrow range . . . but within such limits his achievement seems to be considerable, and to be of a kind with which modern poetry can ill afford to dispense. There is no finish or artifice about it; the note struck is strenuous, austere, forcible; it is writing that should help to give backbone to a literature which certainly errs on the side of flabbiness.[2]

The *Westminster Review* contained a prophecy remarkable in an article written three years before the appearance of the first part of the *Dynasts*:

> Several of the poems deal with the eventful times of the first Napoleon, and their deep human interest and dramatic power suggest the reflection that, if Mr. Hardy could for once be induced to leave his beloved Wessex, he might perhaps weave a great historical romance of those stirring years.[3]

The most laudatory of all the reviews was that in the *Bookman*:

> What justifies Mr. Hardy's use of verse to the full is his gift of a peculiar intensity of expression, which could hardly find legitimate use in prose. . . . We bandy mighty names with too much lightness; but there is a quality of expression, compact equally of emotion and intellect, which we call Shakespearian; and I find it again and again in lines and phrases of these rugged and imperfect poems.[4]

Hardy wrote little else but poetry for the remaining thirty years of his life. *Poems of the Past and Present* followed in 1902. Then came the three parts of the *Dynasts*; and five more volumes of verse, the last of which, *Winter Words*, appeared after his death. *The Famous Tragedy of the Queen of Cornwall*, a play for mummers, must also be counted among

---

[1] January 7th, 1899. [2] January 14th, 1899.
[3] Vol. 152, p. 180. [4] Vol. 16, p. 139.

the poetry; its best page, the song 'Let's meet again to-night, my Fair,' is no bad love lyric for a man of eighty-two.

During the present century, Hardy has come more and more to be regarded as a poet; in this belief my own generation was educated; and after his death, a critic confidently wrote:

'It is as a poet and tragedian that he will challenge the verdict of the years.'[1]

Prophecy is always dangerous; but if by this be meant that posterity will consider the *Dynasts* the crowning achievement of Hardy's genius, as we consider *Paradise Lost* to be that of Milton's, it is probably true. If, however, it means, as some people thought a decade ago, that Hardy's lyrical poetry is a higher title to literary immortality than are the Wessex novels, it is certainly wrong. A personal friend of Hardy has written:

'Those who knew him are agreed that his great desire was to become a poet, and this was never modified or altered by the great success he won as a novelist.'[2]

The great desire of the second Mrs. Hardy was that her husband should live to see himself acclaimed as a poet, and this he did. Looking back, however, there can be no doubt that the cult for his poetry, which was so much the fashion in the nineteen-twenties, was overdone. Leaving the *Dynasts* out of account, would Hardy's place in English literature in the year 2037 be as high on the merits of his collections of lyrical poetry if he had not written the novels? No balanced critic to-day can doubt the answer to be no.

The poetry is in the nature of a commentary to the novels; for in it we see the man himself who wrote them, and something of his life. I personally am very fond of much of Hardy's verse; and would take the volume of collected poetry as companion on a holiday in preference to any of the novels, for its intimacy, its variety, and its occasionally memorable achievement. But, considered as its author's

[1] Quarterly, Vol. 253 (1929), p. 313.   [2] *Thomas Hardy*, by Clive Holland, p. 84.

chief contribution to our literature, that volume could never give Hardy a place in the first rank of English authors. This is not chiefly due to the fact that so many of the poems are trivial, and so few great; for it is an accepted canon of criticism that a poet is to be judged by his best, not his worst. It is because Hardy's poetry, taken as a whole, is of an occasional and incidental character. In comparison with the lyrical poetry of Wordsworth and of Browning, with both of which it has been compared, it does not give that consciousness of certain genius, producing what will always be peculiarly its own in the form which it has made its perfect instrument. We all know that Wordsworth could write rubbish, and that Browning could produce unparalleled combinations of obscurity and cacophony; but we are all agreed that both of them bear the hall mark of great poets: to have expressed, perfectly and for all time, that which they alone could express, that which enlarges the life of him who reads it. The *Dynasts* bears this hall mark also; but not Hardy's short poems. Perhaps, if I dare single out one where there is such bewildering abundance, the poem of his which comes nearest to producing this impression is 'A Sign Seeker' in *Wessex Poems*. This is not, in itself, a great poem; perhaps not Hardy's greatest, but probably his most individual. Both the form and the substance are his, and his only. In less than fifty lines, it imparts to its reader a consciousness of powerful and very individual personality; we seem to see, at once the soul of the poet and a vision of the whole universe as it appears to him. For a moment, through his eyes, we see 'the eyeless countenance of the mist,' the lightning blade and the leaping star; and for a moment, also, we share with him the impenetrable darkness which lies beyond:

> —There are who, rapt to heights of trancelike trust,
>   These tokens claim to feel and see,
>   Read radiant hints of times to be,
> Of heart to heart returning after dust to dust.
>   Such scope is granted not to lives like mine. . . .

THOMAS HARDY

Writing of Hardy's poetry, Edmund Gosse made a prophecy: 'When the work of Mr. Hardy is completed, nothing, it is probable, will more strike posterity than its unity, its consistency.'[1] It is, perhaps, in the poetry that this consistency is the most striking. We have already seen how some of the essential thought of the *Dynasts* is expressed in verse written nearly forty years before. One of Hardy's most characteristic poems, although not a very good one technically, and, perhaps for that reason, not quoted by any of the critics, is dated Westbourne Park Villas, 1863–7. Written long before any of the great novels, it reveals no little of that which makes both the gloom, and much of the greatness, of Hardy's work:

DISCOURAGEMENT

To see the Mother, naturing Nature, stand
All racked and wrung by her unfaithful lord,
Her hopes dismayed by his defiling hand,
Her passioned plans for bloom and beauty marred.

Where she would mint a perfect mould, an ill;
Where she would don divinest hues, a stain,
Over her purposed genial hour a chill,
Upon her charm of flawless flesh a blain:

Her loves dependent on a feature's trim,
A whole life's circumstance on hap of birth,
A soul's direction on a body's whim,
Eternal Heaven upon a day of Earth,
Is frost to flower of heroism and worth,
And fosterer of visions ghast and grim.

This sonnet is characteristic, not only of Hardy's very personal view of life, but also of his poetic technique. Here we have a strange combination of power and clumsiness. The poem is full of faults; the striving after alliteration is very bad; 'genial hour' suggests a club; 'divinest hues' and 'flower of heroism and worth' come from the cheapest

[1] *Edinburgh Review*, Vol. 227 (1918), p. 272.

magazines; 'visions ghast and grim' is a lame ending in a forced rhyme. Yet there is a certain undeniable passion about the thing; and

> Eternal Heaven upon a day of Earth

is the work, not of a poetaster, but of a poet.

'Discouragement' was a poem of Hardy's early twenties, written when the literary power that was in him was driving him to expression, but had not yet found an aim. It would perhaps only be fair, after it, to quote one of the more technically perfect poems of his maturity, from *Poems of the Past and Present*:

A BROKEN APPOINTMENT

> You did not come,
> And marching Time drew on, and wore me numb.—
> Yet less for loss of your dear presence there
> Than that I thus found lacking in your make
> That high compassion which can overbear
> Reluctance for pure lovingkindness' sake
> Grieved I, when, as the hope-hour stroked its sum,
> You did not come.
>
> You love not me,
> And love alone can lend you loyalty;
> —I know and knew it. But, unto the store
> Of human deeds divine in all but name,
> Was it not worth a little hour or more
> To add yet this: once you, a woman, came
> To soothe a time-torn man; even though it be
> You love not me?

This poem has been much praised, and, although it has avoidable blemishes, perhaps deservedly. But it has the great fault of so many of Hardy's poems, the fault of being purely occasional. It lacks the universality of Browning's shortest love lyrics. The reason, of course, is that the main current of Hardy's genius was flowing elsewhere, and this is but a pool filled in passing.

The technical aspects of Hardy's verse have been exhaustively and painstakingly, if unimaginatively, analysed in an American thesis.[1] Easily the best general critical study of the poetry is that in Mr. Macdowall's book; the chapters devoted to it are, indeed, the best parts of a very good book. There is therefore no occasion here to attempt once again what has been so well done. Mr. Macdowall goes so far as to write:

> As it was in his verse that, in spite of its inequalities, Hardy's original power affirmed itself most strongly, he was greater as a poet than as anything else. And yet not exclusively as the poet of his verse; for, as we have seen, he might be said to have created a poetry of truth there, and a poetry of beauty in the novels.[2]

It is my own belief that, had he not of material necessity harnessed his genius to another form of literature, Hardy might probably have become a considerable lyric poet. Whether he would have become greater, or as great, in lyric poetry as in the novel is an idle speculation; but I am in no doubt at all that, as it is, the novels stand as by far the greater achievement in the final reckoning. The fame as a poet which he so ardently desired has become his indeed; but it will remain his in virtue, not of his lyrical poems, but of the *Dynasts*.

II. THE *Dynasts*: GENERAL

When the first part of the *Dynasts* was given to a be-wildered world at the beginning of 1904,[3] it was generally dismissed by the critics as absurd or incomprehensible. On the appearance of the third part in 1908, some of these critics handsomely recanted; and in his book on Hardy published in 1912, Mr. Lascelles Abercrombie did not hesitate to describe it as 'one of the most momentous achievements in modern literature.'[4] This verdict has pre-

[1] *The Versification of Thomas Hardy*, by E. C. Hickson. Philadelphia, 1931.
[2] Conclusion.
[3] Only a few copies bearing the date 1903, now rarities, were distributed in the December of that year.
[4] *Thomas Hardy: a Critical Study*, p. 225.

vailed; and there is now almost universal agreement that the *Dynasts* is the greatest of Hardy's writings, and the one which most clearly reveals the full stature of his creative genius. On Hardy's eighty-first birthday, in 1921, an address was presented to him by more than a hundred of his fellow craftsmen in English letters, in which they wrote: 'We thank you, Sir, for all that you have written . . . but most of all, perhaps, for the *Dynasts*'[1]; and when he died, the writer of the leading article of the *Times* described the *Dynasts* as 'a national epic for Englishmen.'[2] It is probably fair to say that a great majority of those to whom English literature is a precious possession would, if compelled to forego all but one of Hardy's writings, choose this, for not only does it represent every aspect of Hardy's own genius; it is the most significant, as well as the most universal, of his works; and it stands head and shoulders above everything else produced in English poetry since *The Ring and the Book*.

Hardy's interest in the Napoleonic Wars began in very early childhood. Not forty years before he was born, Dorset had been stirred to its rural depths by the preparations made against Napoleon's threatened invasion of England; and in such a time and place forty years were not so long but that very vivid memories, and equally vivid romances, remained to fire the imagination of such a boy. His own grandfather had been a volunteer; and we are told that when he was eight he found in a closet a periodical, contemporary with that worthy, which greatly appealed to him.[3] The surest testimony, however, to the atmosphere of Napoleonic romance in which he grew up is that which he himself gives in the Preface to *The Trumpet Major*:

An outhouse door riddled with bullet holes, which had been extemporized by a solitary man as a target for firelock practice when the landing was hourly expected, a heap of bricks and clods on a beacon hill, which had formed the chimney and walls of a hut occupied by the beacon keeper, worm-eaten

[1] *Later Years*, p. 222.   [2] January 12th, 1928.
[3] *Early Life*, p. 21.

269

shafts and iron heads of pikes for the use of those who had no better weapons, ridges on the down thrown up during the encampment, fragments of volunteer uniform, and other such lingering remains, brought to my imagination in early childhood the state of affairs at the date of the war more vividly than volumes of history could have done.

The Trumpet Major was almost entirely written from the tales about the great invasion told to Hardy as a boy; and the *Dynasts* itself contains many scenes for which their author was not indebted to formal history, but to traditions of his own childhood; and it is significant that some of these Wessex scenes are among the most effective in the book (e.g., Pt. 1, Act ii, Sc. v, and Pt. 3, Act v, Sc. vi). In addition to *The Trumpet Major*, the short story entitled 'A Tradition of 1804' was constructed out of youthful memories. The whole matter is summed up plainly in the Preface to the *Dynasts*:

> The choice of such a subject was mainly due to three accidents of locality. It chanced that the writer was familiar with a part of England that lay within hail of the watering place in which King George the Third had his favourite summer residence during the war with the first Napoleon. . . . Secondly, this district, being also near the coast which had echoed with rumours of invasion in their intensest form while the descent threatened, was formerly animated by memories and traditions of the desperate military preparations for that contingency. Thirdly, the same countryside happened to include the village which was the birthplace of Nelson's flag captain at Trafalgar.

The last reference is significant, and must later be considered more closely.

Even without such strong personal associations, it is hardly surprising that an English poet of the nineteenth century should have chosen the subject for a poem on the grand scale from the history of the Napoleonic wars. Victor Hugo, addressing Napoleon, cried:

> Tu domines notre âge. Ange ou démon, qu'importe?

And yet, while the poetry of the early nineteenth century

naturally contains countless references to the wars which raged all over Europe from Portugal to Russia, Napoleon is not the subject of any major work. Manzoni's poem on his death, 'Il Cinque Maggio,' which Goethe declared the best of innumerable poems on that subject, is said to be the most popular lyric in Italian; but it is only an isolated lyric. Napoleon's wars are the background to the 'Freiheits-dichter' of Germany; but not their subject. An English reader at once thinks of the famous Waterloo passage in the third canto of *Childe Harold*. But this again is only an episode, not the subject of the poem. It was to be expected that, as the most stormy epoch of modern times with its epic figure passed into history, some great writer would assay to treat it imaginatively. In one of his early and most exuberant essays, the young Macaulay prophesied that in the twenty-ninth century a great epic poem, called the *Wellingtoniad*, would be written on the Napoleonic wars; and even went so far as to give a synopsis of it![1] That which had been matter for a playful skit to Macaulay became the subject of stately prophecy in the splendid poem which Tennyson wrote for the burial of the Great Duke:

> Peace, his triumph will be sung
> By some yet unmoulded tongue
> Far on in summers that we shall not see.

The tongue was moulded when those words were written, though its owner was then still a child.

The *Dynasts* is to-day the greatest imaginative representation of the Napoleonic epoch in the literature of Western Europe. As far as English is concerned, it is likely to remain without successors, as it was without forerunners. No major English poet before Hardy had cared to dedicate himself to that theme; and after Hardy none will either dare or desire to sing again the lay he sang once for all. One other great English writer only, writing while Hardy was writing, but

[1] A Prophetic Account of a Grand National Epic Poem to be entitled The Wellingtoniad and to be published in A.D. 2824. In *Knight's Quarterly Magazine*, November 1824.

surely unknown to Hardy as Hardy's drama was unknown to him, touched the Napoleonic theme. Meredith's *Odes in Contribution to the Song of French History*[1] might have become, had they been completed, a great epic poem. They are among Meredith's finest achievements; and the second of them, 'Napoleon,' rises to heights of language that Hardy never approached or attempted:

> Cannon his name,
> Cannon his voice, he came.
> Who heard of him heard shaken hills,
> An earth at quake, to quiet stamped;
> Who looked at him beheld the will of wills,
> The driver of wild flocks where lions ramped:
> Beheld war's liveries flee him, like lumped grass
> Nid-nod to ground beneath the cuffing storm;
> While laurelled over his Imperial form,
> Forth from her bearded tube of lacquey brass,
> Reverberant notes and long blew volant Fame.

That is how Meredith could write of Napoleon. But the poem is not a thousand lines long.

On the continent, leaving out of account many minor novelists in many countries, at least two writers of the first rank had given imaginative treatment to Napoleonic material. It forms the background to Tolstoi's *War and Peace*; and Victor Hugo, who has many isolated poems on Napoleon,[2] used it on a larger scale, both in *Les Misérables* and in *La Légende des Siècles*. We are told that Hardy had not read *War and Peace* when he wrote the *Dynasts*.[3] But he certainly had read at least some of the work of Hugo[4]; and he could never, if he had once read them, have forgotten the epic description of Waterloo in *Les Misérables* (one of the most notable results of Hugo's admiration for Byron), or the famous passage beginning

[1] The first of them was written in 1870, the others in 1898.
[2] e.g., 'Expiation' in *Les Châtiments*, 'Napoleon II' in *Chants du Crépuscule*, 'Lui,' etc.
[3] Arthur Macdowall: *Thomas Hardy*, p. 167.
[4] The library at Max Gate still contains *Les Religions et La Religion*.

Waterloo! Waterloo! Waterloo! morne plaine . . .

However this may be, he had in mind such works as these when he added to his first draft of the Preface to the *Dynasts* this not unimportant paragraph[1]:

The slight regard paid to English influence and action throughout the struggle by those continental writers who had dealt imaginatively with Napoleon's career had seemed always to leave room for a new handling of the theme which should re-embody the features of this influence in their true proportion.

Here we come upon a second reason for which Hardy wrote the *Dynasts*, not to be passed over as trivial because it was less compelling than the first. There can be no doubt that, as the conception of an historical poem on that Napoleonic period, which had so filled Hardy's imagination in childhood, took shape, one of the earliest of its dominant themes became that of the part played by England. Hardy, thinking of his projected 'Drama of Kings,' often had Shakespeare in mind. More must be said of this later, but the fact is beyond question. Having in his mind's eye Shakespeare's plays on English history, he cannot have forgotten their intensely patriotic purport. Even apart from famous purple passages, such as that at the end of *King John* or those in *Richard II* and *Henry V*, it is a commonplace of criticism that they are the expression of intense patriotism in the stirring age when England first knew herself to be a great nation. It is not by accident, but by design, that the chief rôle in the *Dynasts*, as has often been pointed out, is that of England. For his conception of the whole war as a duel between Buonaparte and England, Hardy received unexpected support from French authority in 1904, when the first part was already published.[2] But, as an examination of the first part clearly shows, this conception had guided the composition of the poem from the beginning.

[1] The MS. shows that this paragraph was not in the preface as first written; it was added at the bottom of a page and at the top of the following one.
[2] See p. 297.

THOMAS HARDY

The gradual growth of the *Dynasts* in the mind of its author is very clearly shown by a number of extracts from his personal memoranda, which are to be found scattered through the first volume of his biography.[1] The earliest of these is in May 1875, when he wrote:

> Mem; A Ballad of the Hundred Days. Then another of Moscow. Others of earlier campaigns—forming altogether an Iliad of Europe from 1789 to 1815.

An Iliad of Europe had, it may be noted, been Macaulay's conception of that 'Wellingtoniad' which he prophesied in his young days. Hardy was at that time already taking some serious steps towards the realization of this Iliad, for in the summer of 1875 he seems to have interviewed all the survivors of Waterloo still living at Chelsea Hospital. And in the summer of 1876 he explored the field of Waterloo, and wrote a letter to a London paper, which has not been traced, on the question of the scene of the Duchess of Richmond's famous ball in Brussels before the battle.[2] The reference in the fifth chapter of *An Indiscretion in the Life of an Heiress* to Wellington's antecedent survey of the field of Waterloo, already mentioned as the earliest reference in Hardy to Napoleonic matters,[3] is clearly to be connected with this visit in 1876. As to the Napoleonic Ballads which were the first conception of the *Dynasts*, no one appears hitherto to have noticed that four of them are actually published in *Wessex Poems*, where they are called 'Valenciennes,' 'San Sebastian,' 'Leipzig,' and 'The Peasant's Confession.' One of the dates at the foot of the first of these is 1878. Whether 'The Peasant's Confession' is as early as 'Valenciennes' is rendered doubtful by the extract from Thiers at its head; but when Hardy began to make a detailed study of Napoleonic history we do not know.

[1] The references are pp. 140, 146, 150, 188, 191, 197, 232, 256, 266, 290. The last two are in *Later Years*, pp. 57, 100.
[2] His own treatment of this ball and its sequel next morning, in the *Dynasts* (Pt. 3, Act vi, Scs. ii and iv), may owe something to reminiscences from *Vanity Fair*.
[3] See p. 125.

In June 1877, the idea of a Napoleonic epic had made a very great advance towards the realization which it finally received. Hardy's entry ran:

> Consider a grand drama, based on the wars with Napoleon, or some one campaign (but not as Shakespeare's historical dramas). It might be called 'Napoleon' or 'Josephine,' or by some other person's name.

During the severe illness which kept him in bed for several months in the winter of 1880–81, Hardy seems to have meditated at length upon his 'Great Modern Drama'; but further details are lacking. It would be interesting to know whether the appearance of the word 'Modern' denoted a turning towards ideas of philosophical drama. This seems likely; for in March 1881, a note on 'An Homeric Ballad, in which Napoleon is a sort of Achilles' is followed by this:

> Mode for a historical Drama. Action mostly automatic; reflex movement, etc. Not the result of what is called *motive*, though always ostensibly so, even to the actors' own consciousness. Apply an enlargement of these theories to, say the Hundred Days.

In a previous chapter it has been shown how the late 'seventies and early 'eighties were the period of Hardy's greatest preoccupation with philosophy. It was at this time that the original conception of a Napoleonic epic became transformed into what we see in the *Dynasts*. In February 1882 there occurs another memorandum:

> Write a history of human automatism or impulsion—namely an account of human action in spite of human knowledge, showing how very far conduct lags behind the knowledge that should really guide it.

In March 1886 these vague and rather incoherent imaginings appear to be rapidly crystallizing into what remained their final form:

> The human race to be shown as one great network or tissue which quivers in every part when one point is shaken, like a spider's web if touched. Abstract realisms to be in the form of Spirits, Spectral Figures, etc.

Here we have not only the Spirits as they appear in the *Dynasts*, but the conception of 'the anatomy of the Immanent Will,' so often made visible for the benefit of the incredulous Pities. The first of many stage directions describing it is this, in the Forescene:

> A new and penetrating light descends on the spectacle, enduing men and things with a seeming transparency, and exhibiting as one organism the anatomy of life and movement in all humanity and vitalised matter included in the display.

Having by 1886 settled the general framework of his drama, Hardy began now in his mind to work out details. The scene in Milan cathedral (Pt. 1, Act i, Sc. vi) seems to have been conceived as early as 1887, during a visit to Milan with his wife in the summer. In November, an outline scheme was drawn up, of which Mrs. Hardy writes:

> Napoleon was represented as haunted by an Evil Genius or Familiar, whose existence he has to confess to his wives. This was abandoned, and another tried in which Napoleon by means of necromancy becomes possessed of an insight, enabling him to see the thoughts of opposing generals. This does not seem to have come to anything either.

In September 1889 Hardy wrote in his diary:

> For carrying out that idea of Napoleon, the Empress, Pitt, Fox, etc., I feel continually that I require a larger canvas. A spectral tone must be adopted. . . . Royal Ghosts. . . . Title: A Drama of Kings.

During a visit to Brussels in 1896, Hardy again went to Waterloo, and also wrote in his notebook:

> Europe in Throes. Three Parts. Five Acts each. Characters: Burke, Pitt, Napoleon, George III, Wellington . . . and many others.

The *Preface* suggests that the outline of the form in which the *Dynasts* finally appeared, was drawn up in 1897, and that the composition was completed 'at wide intervals' between then and September 1903, the date of the Preface. The manuscript of the first part was sent to Macmillan at the end of that month[1]; and a number of copies, bearing the date 1903, were published in December. They were, however, very few. The larger issue appeared in January 1904, unchanged except for the date on the title-page. Both from the Preface and from the title page of the first part, it is clear that the whole must have been substantially complete by the autumn of 1903; only minor revisions of the second and third parts, not affecting the number of scenes, probably remained to be done. The second part was published in the first week of February 1906.[2] The third part appeared early in 1908. A thin paper edition in one volume has been available since 1923.

The reception generally accorded to the first part of his masterpiece can hardly have caused Hardy great surprise, after the experience of thirty years as a novelist, to say nothing of the fiasco of *Wessex Poems* five years earlier; but he would not have been human had he felt no disappointment. For the general attitude, resulting from utter incomprehension, approximated to the opinion expressed in the *New York Tribune*, that the work was so ridiculous that the second part would never be heard of.[3] No purpose would be served by dwelling here upon the critics who reviewed, or tried to review, what they did not understand. Except in so far as the condemnation was due to other causes than mere stupidity, such things have been only too common in the history of our literature. This time, even the better class of critics was nonplussed. The *Academy* of January 23rd, 1904, concluded a bewildered article headed 'A Vast Venture' with the words: 'We can only say, with a sigh, that we would give many such dramas for one

[1] *Later Years*, p. 100.
[2] In a letter to the *Times Literary Supplement* of February 14th, 1929, Richard L. Purdy, of Yale University, recorded the presence, in the library of the Phillips Exeter Academy at Exeter, New Hampshire, of a copy of the Second Part of the *Dynasts* dated 1905. He gave a collation of its title page, which differed from the title page dated 1906 in date, in the absence of a stop and in the absence of a legend on the verso. I am not aware of any other record of a copy dated 1905; only the issue of 1906 is recorded by Webb.
[3] *Later Years*, p. 114.

Return of the Native.' More common than mere bewilderment was a cordial dislike of the philosophy of the work, masquerading as literary criticism. There was a representative example of this in the *Spectator* of February 20th. The reviewer allowed that the Wessex Scenes were good, and said that the countrymen have 'the true Shakespearian ring,' a criticism which was orthodox enough, since it had first been made when *Far from the Madding Crowd* appeared thirty years before. He even conceded that in the stage directions 'Mr. Hardy attains to a kind of gruesome sublimity.' But of the Spirits he would have none. 'They conduct their espionage,' he wrote, 'in the spirit of a very young man who has just begun to dabble in metaphysics and is imperfectly acquainted with terminology.'

Even after forty years as a man of letters, Hardy was still sensitive; Mrs. Hardy quotes private memoranda made at this time in which he mused bitterly that 'by overstepping the standard boundary set up for the thought of the age by the proctors of opinion, I have thrown back my chance of acceptance in poetry by many years.'[1] The most interesting result of this obscurantist criticism was probably the answering letter which it evoked, in the *Times Literary Supplement* of February 19th:

> The truth seems to be that the real offence of the *Dynasts* lies, not in its form as such, but in the philosophy which gave rise to the form. This is revealed by symptoms in various quarters. . . . Worthy British Philistia, unlike that ancient Athens it professes to admire, not only does not ask for a new thing, but even shies at that which merely appears at first sight to be a new thing. As with a certain King, the reverse of worthy, in the case of another play, some people ask, 'Have you read the argument? Is there no offence in't?' There can hardly be, assuredly, on a fair examination. The philosophy of the *Dynasts*, under various titles, is almost as old as civilisation. Its fundamental principle, under the name of Predestination, was preached by St. Paul. 'Being predestinated'—says the author of the Epistle to the Ephesians—'according to the

[1] *Later Years*, p. 104.

purpose of Him Who worketh all things after the counsel of His own will'; and much more to the same effect, the only difference being that externality is assumed by the Apostle rather than Immanence. It has run through the history of the Christian Church ever since. St. Augustine held it vaguely, Calvin held it fiercely, and, if our English Church and its Nonconformist contemporaries have now almost abandoned it to our men of science (among whom determinism is a commonplace), it was formerly taught by Evangelical divines of the finest character and conduct. I should own in fairness that I think this has been shrewdly recognized in some quarters, whose orthodoxy is unimpeachable, where the philosophy of the *Dynasts* has been handled as sanely and calmly as I could wish.

As an example of the few more enlightened criticisms, as well as for the inimitable manner in which it is written, some extracts must be quoted from an article by Mr. Max Beerbohm in the *Saturday Review* of January 30th. Mr. Beerbohm began by referring to Hardy as a novelist:

> One assumes that he has ceased as a novelist. Why has he ceased? The reason is generally said to be that he was disheartened by the many hostile criticisms of *Jude*. To accept that explanation would be to insult him. A puny engine of art may be derailed by such puny obstacles as the public can set in its way. So strong an engine as Mr. Hardy runs straight on despite them, and stops not save for lack of inward steam. Mr. Hardy writes no more novels because he has no more novels to write.

Turning to the *Dynasts*, Mr. Beerbohm continued:

> Impossible his task certainly is. To do perfectly what he essays would need a syndicate of much greater poets than ever were born into the world, working in an age of miracles. . . . The book closes, and, so surely has it cast its spell upon us, seems quite a fugitive and negligible piece of work. We wonder why Mr. Hardy wrote it; or rather, one regrets that the Immanent Will put him to the trouble of writing it. 'Wots the good of anythink. Why, nothink' was the refrain of a popular coster song some years ago, and Mr. Hardy has set it ringing in our ears again. But presently the mood passes. And,

even as in the stage directions of the *Dynasts* we see specks
becoming mountain tops, so do we begin to realize that we
have been reading a really great book. . . . Cries Mr. Hardy's
Spirit of the Pities

> This tale of Will
> And Life's impulsion by Incognisance
> I cannot take.

Nor can I. But I can take, and treasure with all gratitude, the
book in which that tale is told so finely.

Beside the critics whose philosophy of life was outraged
by the *Dynasts*, there were some others whose objection
was based upon the liberties which Hardy had taken with
the accepted forms of literature. Typical of these was the
critic of the *Times* who, in an article in the *Literary Supplement* of January 29th, protested that 'A drama of the
Napoleonic wars in three parts, nineteen acts and one
hundred and thirty scenes is, indeed, a fearful sort of wildfowl.' It will be more convenient to consider the criticism
of the form of the *Dynasts*, and Hardy's reply to it, later in
the chapter.

By the time that the second part appeared in 1906, the
world of letters had had space in which to digest the new
and fearful sort of wildfowl; and it was beginning to dawn
upon many people that here was something very much
more important than they had at first supposed. Accor-
dingly, the second part received a much more friendly
welcome, one American periodical going so far as to ask
'Who knows that this may not turn out to be a masterpiece?'[1] But it was not until the whole work was completed,
by the appearance of the third part in 1908, that its real
scale began to be generally appreciated. The change in tone
in the four years that had elapsed since the appearance of
the first part was very well illustrated by the critic of the
Academy, who had dismissed the first part with a sigh of
incomprehension. Writing on March 14th, 1908, he began
by confessing that he still felt out of his depth:

[1] *Later Years*, p. 117.

THE POEMS AND THE *DYNASTS*

The really true and candid thing to say is, we fancy, that the work is so extraordinary in aim and energy and scope that we are almost baffled in attempting to comprehend it.

But he made handsome amends for early incredulity:

We are happy to have the completion of a work wherein a great theme is developed in the great manner of which only a mature and powerful genius is capable. And thankful as we are to the author for the vital energy and fine distinction of his drama, we are yet more thankful for the profound conception by which it is illuminated and unified—conception of a finer and loftier wisdom than any discovered by the noblest of his prose writings.

The *Times* critic, in the *Literary Supplement* of February 27th, gave special praise to Hardy's characterization:

When Mr. Bernard Shaw wishes his readers to understand a character, he prints his history, his appearance, his views on life, in a stage direction. Mr. Hardy does not; yet, if we wished to pick a character in the drama whose personal flavour and ways are not absolutely clear, we could only hit on Napoleon. . . . Not even Mr. Hardy has succeeded in seeing Napoleon without, as well as with, his destiny. But with the others the case is different. . . . Wellington is no figure-head, and Picton, Marie Louise, all the persons for whom space allowed and dramatic need demanded character, even down to the nameless mother of a nameless girl who fell in love at the Duchess of Richmond's ball, and the vicar of Durnover, who has only to speak twice and to spit twice, are as roundly human as could be.

One further article, in the *Quarterly Review* (Vol. 210, p. 193), may be quoted, for it was by Sir Henry Newbolt:

The business of the poet is to make poetry; and the adequate reception of his work, the recognition of his value as singer or seer, is the business of the public. . . From the moment when the first volume of the *Dynasts* appeared, there was, to one watcher at least, no doubt that the new light was in the sky. . . . This is not the time to criticize, to ask why Mr. Hardy has given the name of Will to that which never wills, or where he finds a place for 'chance' in his clockwork universe, or how man's evolution came to depart so far from evolutionary law as to result in the acquisition of an 'unneeded' faculty. When a man of genius formulates a system of theology in poetry, the poetry is apt to survive the theology; *Paradise Lost* is an instance in point, and the *Dynasts* is not likely to prove an exception.

It must gladden the heart of the student of literature, and restore his often sorely tried belief in an absolute and eternal scale of values, to come upon an instance of general recognition during the lifetime of a great author.

> Unto each man his handiwork, unto each his crown
> The just fate gives—

But too often there lie, between handiwork and crown, both neglect and the grave. To Hardy, the just fate gave years enough to see his crown. We have seen in these pages that he had his share, not only of neglect and incomprehension, but also of derision and abuse. The letter which he wrote on the death of Swinburne remains to show that these left their mark upon him.[1] But whatever injustice he suffered, he was generously paid at the hands of a new generation, to whom he gave his greatest work and from whom he received both understanding and homage. It was chiefly to a recognition of the stature of the *Dynasts* that he owed the Order of Merit, bestowed upon him in June 1910.[2] Thereafter, he did not lack honours, either from the sincere, or from the unconscious sycophants who compose so large a portion of civilized society. One which he is said specially to have valued was the freedom of the City of Dorchester.[3] That he became, for the last twenty years of his life, the acknowledged head of English letters, and for the last ten a figure almost legendary—so unreal seemed his physical existence beside the tremendous reality of his renown—he owed to the *Dynasts*. That he was the author of so great a poem added to the figure of the great novelist a certain

[1] *Later Years*, p. 136. See p. 71.   [2] *Later Years*, p. 142.
[3] *Later Years*, p. 143.

tinge of romantic glory which, even now, is reserved to the poet alone among artists. The very size of his achievement in this one work gave an added prestige to English letters, whose present tends always to be dwarfed by their gigantic past; it is no little thing that the literature which bore *Hamlet* and *Paradise Lost* should still have so much life that it can bear the *Dynasts*.

It is to be regretted that no material bearing upon the history of the text of the *Dynasts* has been forthcoming. Not that the study of English literature is so lacking in textual problems that we need more! Anyone who has wrestled with, say, the quartos of *Hamlet* must be thankful that in the case of the greatest English play of the last two centuries we have the manuscript of the final form, in the autograph of its author, safely in the British Museum. But it is surely a pity that no early drafts or notes of so important a work have been made available to scholars whose interest in them is not a financial one. For some such manuscripts certainly exist. A draft of the Afterscene was formerly in the possession of Mr. Howard Bliss; and Mrs. Hardy in one place speaks of 'more copious notes set down elsewhere' when quoting from the memoranda afterwards destroyed by Hardy.[1] Would it not be a service to English scholarship to deposit these beginnings of one of our masterpieces in some public library or museum?

The beautiful manuscript in the British Museum (Add. MS. 38, 183) was presented by Hardy himself, together with that of *Tess*. It is in three volumes, one part in each volume[2]; and was originally bound in brown paper covers on which, in the first volume, Hardy wrote: 'The MS. from which the book was printed.' Actually, there are minor differences between this MS. and the printed text. A complete collation would reveal a very large number of variant readings of single words and half-sentences; but scarcely

[1] *Later Years*, p. 57.

[2] Vol. 1 consists of 237 quarto sheets (written on one side only); Vol. 2 of 286 and Vol. 3 of 318.

any of these are of sufficient interest to deserve record; they were doubtless corrections in proof. Of major variations there are scarcely any. One of the most important is a paragraph in the Preface, most of which was omitted from the printed text. In view of the close parallel which it provides to Hardy's letter in the *Times Literary Supplement* of February 19th, 1904, already quoted, it is interesting. The seventh paragraph of the Preface in the manuscript reads:

> Nevertheless, the phantasmal (Abstractions) Intelligences here delineated will, without much forcing, be found to lend themselves as readily to the Predestinarianism of the Theologian as to the Determinism of the Scientist should any gentle reader so require. As already stated, the writer has no dogma herein either to enforce or to deny. The Abstractions are divided into groups of which only one—that of the Pities —represents, in the old definition, 'the Universal Sympathy of Human Nature, the Spectator Idealized,' the remainder being eclectically chosen auxiliaries that were suggested by the foregoing conclusions. But misgivings that the achievement in this feature of the drama may fall far below the original hope and intention have sadly to be confessed.

An example of an omission in the body of the text occurs in Scene vi, Act v, Part 1, where Villeneuve's first speech contains the lines:

> We are as playing cards an idiot king
> Demands for pastime in his holiday.
> Why is the world? Why man's strained sight thereof?

To such a study as this, some enquiry into the immediate literary antecedents of the *Dynasts* would seem proper. Actually, it proves to be of very little value. In the literature of the nineteenth century, after Shelley, there is nothing to which it is even remotely related. In drama which can claim to be great literature that century is almost wholly deficient. Tennyson's historical plays are certainly the least valuable portion of his writings; and the same can be said of the plays which bulk largely in the early work of Browning. Browning had much more of the dramatist than Tennyson;

but he used it to most effect in his lyrics, and in the 'submerged drama' of *The Ring and the Book*. Swinburne, with less innate dramatic gifts, wrote at least two impressive acting plays. But no one thinks first of *Bothwell* when the name of Swinburne is mentioned, any more than of *A Blot on the Scutcheon* at that of Browning,[1] or of *Becket* at that of Tennyson.

It was not, of course, only in the narrow region of historical drama that Mr. Abercrombie was thinking when he wrote:

> Hardy in the *Dynasts* attained to something that the age of Tennyson and Browning quite failed to effect (though Matthew Arnold comes near to effecting it, Swinburne also curiously near in such poems as *The Hymn of Man*).[2]

The last two allusions show that what this critic is seeking is the poetic expression of a prevailing consciousness on the issues of being and the nature of reality, in some objective, if not actually dramatic, form. This rules out portions of *The Ring and the Book* as finally—if not, perhaps, quite as justly—as it rules out *Songs before Sunrise* and *In Memoriam*. Perhaps the nearest approach, a distant one at that, to such an expression in later nineteenth-century literature is the amorphous *Festus* of Philip James Bailey. That unclassifiable poem first appeared in 1839, and provides, in its progressive conflation during fifty years, a chapter apart in literary history.[3] A kind of drama, quite lacking plot, but almost excessively devoted to the largest philosophical speculations, *Festus* certainly does provide:—

> Is thunder evil, or is dew divine?
> Does virtue lie in sunshine, sin in storm?
> Is not each natural, each needful, best?
> How know we what is evil from what good?
> Wrath and revenge God claimeth as His own.
> And yet men speculate on right and wrong,

[1] Much nearer to the core of Browning's genius is that half dramatic poem, *Pippa Passes*; but it provides no better precedent for the *Dynasts*.
[2] *A Study of Thomas Hardy*, p. 188.
[3] See an article on Bailey by Gosse, in the *Fortnightly Review*. Nov. 1902.

And good and ill as each annihilative
Of each, like day and night; forgetting both
Have but one cause and that the same—God's will;
Originally, ultimately, Him.

In this, and many other passages there is an approach to the monism which is an essential part of the philosophy of the *Dynasts*; and even an occasional suggestion of immanentism. But, despite the fact that it is cast in dramatic form, *Festus* is really only the most memorable of a whole series of rhapsodies in verse which appeared in the middle of the century, and are now only generally remembered by Macaulay's destruction of two of them, in a famous review of Robert Montgomery. Other examples, much better than *Satan* and much worse than *Festus*, are *A Life Drama* (1853) by Alexander Smith, *Balder* (1854) by Sydney Dobell, and *Night and the Soul* (1854) by J. Stanyan Bigg. All these lesser 'spasmodic' poets were concerned solely with universal problems from the point of view of the individual soul, and had nothing in common with Hardy's aim in the *Dynasts*, much less with his methods. This is essentially true, also, of Bailey.[1]

If there is no true parallel to the philosophic framework of the *Dynasts* in the middle and later nineteenth century, neither is there any parallel to its historical drama. A little earlier than Browning's first plays, George Darley published two chronicle plays, *Becket* (1840) and *Ethelstan* (1841), the subjects of which are taken from English history. In the preface to the latter, Darley even made the very interesting

---

[1] Hardy must certainly have read at least some of a poem so famous as *Festus* was when he was a young man. But it is not likely to have greatly appealed to him, either as poetry or as philosophy; and the only possible resemblances between *Festus* and the *Dynasts* are very faint. Both owed their openings to common ancestors. Some of the ditties of the Ironic Spirits have a general resemblance to the deplorable comic songs in *Festus*, e.g.

> It is sweet to hear, if fat, that we grow thinner—
> Sweet the first drop of claret after dinner—

or

> Cider may suit an old maid,
> And a young one soda water—

But Hardy did not need Bailey to teach him humour; and even the Spirit Sinister would have blushed to utter some of Bailey's enormities.

revelation that he had projected a series of such historical plays:

> These hands, unskilful as they are, would fain build up a cairn, or rude national monument, on some eminence of our Poetic Mountain, to a few amongst the many heroes of our race, sleeping even yet with no memorial stone, or one hidden beneath the moss of ages. *Ethelstan* is the second stone, *Becket* was the first, borne thither by me for this homely monument.

But when he wrote those words, he was a disappointed and disillusioned man whose work was already done,[1] and no further stones were added to the monument. Of the two which he finished, *Becket* is by far the best; and has considerable interest still. Darley's two plays on English historical subjects were written in an age already declining into purely 'poetic' drama. Darley deplored this decline, but in the preface to *Becket* expressed the fear that it was inevitable:

> Subjective composition is the natural tendency of our refined age and on this postulate founds itself an argument I fear convincing against the probable regeneration of acting drama.

The prophecy proved true; it was written sixty-three years before Hardy wrote in the preface to the *Dynasts*:

> Whether mental performance alone may not eventually be the fate of all drama other than that of contemporary or frivolous life, is a question not without interest.

The fundamental difference between Darley's plays and the *Dynasts* can best be expressed in the words of a greater playwright who preceded Darley, and who wrote what is probably the best purely historical drama of the nineteenth century. In the famous preface to *Philip van Artavelde*, Sir Henry Taylor criticized Byron for not having the philosophic mind:

> Had he united a philosophic intellect to his peculiarly poetical temperament, he would probably have been the greatest poet of the age. But no man can be a very great poet who is not also a great philosopher.

[1] See C. C. Abbott: *Life & Letters of George Darley*.

Taylor missed being a great poet; his two remarkable plays dealing with Flemish history lack that philosophy which, through history, gives glimpses of the unapparent. It was to do this that the *Dynasts* was written; all is subordinated to this intention. By this intention, and by his steadfast adherence to it, Hardy's greatest work stands apart from all the drama of the nineteenth century after *Hellas*. It is as far from *Becket* and *Philip van Artavelde* as from *Death's Jest Book* and *Joseph and his Brethren*. The Elizabethan ghosts that hovered over Darley and Taylor, and haunted Beddoes and Wells, had nothing in common with the Spirits who whispered to Hardy while he mused upon the histories of Trafalgar and Waterloo.

It appears, then, that had England in the three-quarters of a century before the *Dynasts* was written, produced no imaginative literature, Hardy's masterpiece would still be what it is. Such independence would surely be hard to parallel. But, as we have seen in a previous chapter, so remarkable and gigantic a tree did not grow without nourishment from the soil about its roots; only, this was provided by the philosophical, not the imaginative, literature of Hardy's day. To find any material debt which the *Dynasts* owes to English poetry, we must go back, beyond Hardy's contemporaries and immediate predecessors, to Shelley. It would be difficult to find two poetic dramas more widely removed from each other in spirit than *Prometheus Unbound* and the *Dynasts*; yet, as we have seen, Hardy was a student of Shelley; and there can be no doubt that the form of the *Dynasts* owes something to Shelley. Exactly what it owes cannot be concisely analysed and tabulated, but it can be felt. It was in his studies of Greek drama that Hardy became familiar with the use of the chorus. But it is a far cry, even from the *Suppliants*, that earliest surviving play of Aeschylus which seems to show that in early Greek drama the chorus played a direct part in the action, to the Spirit choruses of the *Dynasts*. It is needless to add to what has already been said on the Greek chorus and the *Dynasts*.

Hardy was indebted, not directly to Aeschylus and Sophocles, but to the amplification of the Attic chorus which Shelley introduced into *Prometheus Unbound,* and used again in *Hellas.* The whole spirit machinery of the *Dynasts* was clearly suggested by that of *Prometheus Unbound,* with its Spirits of the Hours, of Earth, of Ocean, of the Moon, its Echoes and its Faieries; to say nothing of the Oceanides, between whom and the Spirits of the Pities a resemblance has been suggested.[1] Two points alone are enough to show Hardy's debt to Shelley; The Shade of the Earth in the *Dynasts* bears a close resemblance to the Earth in *Prometheus;* and Hardy's continual use of semichoruses was clearly modelled upon Shelley's practice. The last point leads on from *Prometheus Unbound* to *Hellas.* There are distinct differences between these matchless poems; the latter, with its chorus of captive women and its introduction of the Shade of Mohamet the Second (the *ΕΙΔΩΛΟΝ ΔΑΡΕΙΟΥ* of the Persae), being much nearer to Greek drama.[2] But the *Dynasts* is equally indebted to them both. Hardy saw in *Hellas* how choral poetry might be grafted on to events in history. If there were any doubt that he had studied *Hellas* while writing his own choral drama, it would be removed by the quotation in the Preface to the *Dynasts.* Some of the lines in that same exquisite final chorus might, indeed, have come from the Spirits of the Pities:

> O cease! Must hate and death return?
> Cease! Must men kill and die?

One further debt to English poetry of the first rank Hardy owed in the writing of the *Dynasts.* It was to Shakespeare. So obvious, indeed, is it that even the critics who understood nothing else about the *Dynasts,* understood this. But it led them into further error; for, seeing that both the employment of many minor characters, and the language

---

[1] A. Macdowall: *A Study of Thomas Hardy,* p. 175.
[2] There is a detailed study of the relationship of *Hellas* and *Prometheus* to Greek drama in chapter one of my *Swinburne,* q.v.

put into their mouths, were deliberately modelled upon Shakespearian practice, they concluded that Hardy had tried to do the same with the major historical figures. They therefore judged the versified speeches of these characters (e.g., in the House of Commons scenes) as if they were intended to be like Mark Antony's oration, or the harangues of Henry V, and naturally found them wanting. Of Hardy's aim and method in representing both history and tragedy, which were utterly different from those of Shakespeare, more must later be said. But, while his main theme and his handling of it belonged wholly to his own day, Hardy used for many of his interludes the technique perfected by Shakespeare, and astonishingly successful he was in this. A certain affinity with Shakespeare in the conception of comic character of a simple type was perhaps Hardy's birthright; or possibly it was the result of an upbringing in the depths of that English countryside whose essence can hardly have changed in the centuries separating Hardy from Shakespeare, for it had not greatly changed in the centuries separating Shakespeare from Chaucer. The critics of *Far from the Madding Crowd*, even its first reviewers, have always claimed that there was something of a Shakespearian flavour about the society of which Joseph Poorgrass was the centre. To the extent to which the Wessex rustics of the *Dynasts*, and other minor characters, are relatives of Joseph Poorgrass, they are Shakespearian by nature. But they are often also, and much more obviously, Shakespearian by art. Not for nothing had Hardy studied Shakespeare and learnt the employment of minor characters at appropriate moments. The gravediggers in *Hamlet*, the countryman who brings 'the worm' in *Antony and Cleopatra*, the porter in *Macbeth*—these were such characters as he could himself create; the great dramatist showed him how to use them; and there are many of their counterparts in the *Dynasts*. No lists are needed to establish this, nor the placing of quotations side by side; it must be clear to every reader. The clearest instances of all are those scenes in the

Dynasts in which English soldiers, be they sentinels or deserters, appear in interludes of the 'dynastic moil' and illustrate what the Ironic Spirit calls

> Quaint poesy, and real romance of war.

To which the Spirit of the Pities replies

> Mock on, Shade, if thou wilt! But others find
> Poesy ever lurk where pit-pats poor mankind.
> (Pt. 2, Act iii, Sc. i.)

It is this quaint poesy, as it appears in the prose scenes of Shakespeare's Histories, particularly in the two parts of *Henry IV* and in *Henry V*, that Hardy deliberately imitated. And it is no small compliment to him that the reader of his scenes often involuntarily thinks of Pistol, Bardolph and Nym, of Poins and Gadshill, of Mistress Quickly and Doll Tearsheet, and sometimes even of the great Sir John.

III. Hardy's Use of History

Not one of Hardy's critics, not one, even, of the students who have made his work the subject of academic investigation, has considered his use of historical material in the *Dynasts*. And yet here, surely, is a matter in more need of some elucidation than Hardy's view of women, or his 'fatalism.' What is by common consent his greatest single contribution to our literature differs from all his other works in this, that he did not here create out of his own imagination the material with which he worked. The material already existed, in such abundance that its very bulk presented a formidable difficulty; and the solution of that difficulty is a measure of the greatness of his achievement. It was said of Michelangelo that in the block of marble he saw the perfect figure, which he liberated. In the vast jumble of the historical records of Napoleonic Europe, Hardy was confronted with a chaotic mountain waste, hardly yet quarried. He saw therein a stately city which was to rise from those stones. For this reason, also, some

knowledge of the materials with which he worked is indispensable to full appreciation of the *Dynasts*; for its creation lay, not in calling reality out of nothingness by the
sheer force of imagination, but in the harder task of shaping
unhewn matter to significant reality by imaginative selection and presentation.

To make a complete historical commentary to the whole
of the *Dynasts* would be a work of great labour, requiring
expert equipment of no common order; and the value of
the result would be wholly disproportionate to the labour
involved. The only purpose of such a commentary would
be to show the value, or otherwise, of the *Dynasts* as history;
and in its historical accuracy few, if any, of its readers are
greatly interested. The *Dynasts* must stand or fall by its
value as literature; in other words, it is a work, not of
science, but of art; and the interest of Hardy's sources lies
in seeing how he turned them to artistic use. This can
perhaps best be done by taking one act, and showing in
detail how it was constructed from historical raw materials.
But, although one act will serve admirably to illustrate
Hardy's methods throughout, the materials employed are
significant only for that particular act. There are nineteen
acts in the *Dynasts*. No account of the materials from which
this vast structure was raised has apparently ever been
given; and it is time that something should be known of
the raw material out of which was built one of the major
works of English literature; the detail can then be illustrated
by an example.

There is one modest paragraph in the Preface in which
Hardy refers to his use of material:

> It may, I think, claim at least a tolerable fidelity to the facts
> of its date as they are given in ordinary records. *Whenever any
> evidence of the words really spoken or written by the characters in
> their various situations was attainable, as close a paraphrase has been
> aimed at as was compatible with the form chosen.* And in all cases
> outside oral tradition, accessible scenery, and existing relics,
> my indebtedness for detail to the abundant pages of the

historian, the biographer, and the journalist, English and Foreign, has been, of course, continuous.[1]

The most significant sentence in this is that here italicized. While Hardy strove, as he says, to maintain tolerable accuracy to recorded facts, his primary concern was in artistic verisimilitude; and for this reason he sought to make his characters speak what history records them to have spoken, *when their recorded utterances happened to be artistic as well as historical.* When they did not, he had no hesitation in discarding their recorded speeches, and substituting better ones of his own. The most striking example of this is probably to be found in the divorce scene between Napoleon and Josephine, Part 2, Act v, Sc. ii; in which Hardy paraphrased *some* of the recorded words, but discarded other and far more vital ones because they did not fit in with the character which he wished to give to Napoleon. It is anticipating somewhat to say that this scene is based upon two sources, which Hardy used elsewhere: the account of the scene given by Thiers in *L'Histoire du Consulat et de l'Empire*, Vol. 11, p. 341; and that given by J. S. Memes in *Memoirs of the Empress Josephine*, Chapter VIII. The general setting was clearly suggested by Memes; the detail of the carrying of the unfortunate Josephine up the private staircase does not occur elsewhere. But the account of the colloquy between Emperor and Empress which Memes repeated from another source,[2] and which is probably genuine, having come from Josephine herself, was both too short and too romantic for Hardy. It would never do for Napoleon to tremble in his whole frame, take his wife's hand, place it on his heart, and say: 'Thou knowest if I have loved thee. To thee, to thee alone do I owe the only moments of happiness which I have enjoyed in this world. Josephine! My destiny overpowers my will. My dearest affections must be silent before the interests of

[1] In the Manuscript, there is a footnote to this paragraph which reads: 'It is intended to give a list of the chief authorities at the end of the Third Part.' The intention was never carried out.

[2] *Memoirs de Laura Junot, Duchesse d'Abrantès* (Paris 1831).

France.' It would not have provided Hardy with an excellent scene had Josephine only replied: 'Say no more. I was prepared for this—but the blow is not less mortal.' Much more in accordance with the effect which Hardy wished to produce was a hint given by Thiers:

> Napoléon, fatigué, coupa court à ses reproches en lui disant qu'il fallait du reste songer à d'autres noeuds que ceux qui les unissaient, que le salut de l'empire voulait enfin une grande résolution de leur part, qu'il comptait sur son courage et sur son dévouement pour consentir à un divorce, auquel il avait lui-même la plus grande difficulté à se resoudre.

Hardy turns this into:

> My mind must bend
> To other things than our domestic pettings:
> The Empire orbs above our happiness,
> And 'tis the Empire dictates this divorce.
> I reckon on your courage and calm sense
> To breast with me the law's formalities,
> And get it through before the year has flown.

He even ignores the hint given by Thiers that Napoleon himself had feelings on the subject. For it would have been inconsistent with the very unflattering conception of Napoleon which Hardy presents throughout the *Dynasts* that he should have been portrayed with the feelings which it would have been historically correct to give him.[1] On the other hand, when the history suited the art, Hardy asked nothing better than to be strictly historical. For after all, as so practised a novelist well knew, Nature sometimes (if rarely) gives the artistic touch; and when she does, no human effort rivals it. Such a touch was Pitt's last speech in the Guildhall. Even the Spirit of the Years is commandeered to point out how artistic is that speech!

There is evidence that Hardy conducted some research into details of Napoleonic history,[2] as indeed, he could

[1] All historical evidence suggests that the divorce cost Napoleon a severe struggle with his personal inclinations. In this matter, Hardy does violence to History.

[2] Mrs. Hardy more than once speaks of visits to the British Museum for this purpose, e.g., *Later Years*, p. 107.

hardly have failed to do in view of the vastness of the subject and of his special requirements. Nevertheless, the bulk of his material came from his own library, for he made a small collection of historical publications which is so well chosen that it embraces, in less than a hundred volumes, the whole field upon which he was working. In addition to this collection, which is still at Max Gate, and to his researches at the British Museum, he doubtless had access to the large Napoleonic collection gathered by A. M. Broadley, at Bradpole, near Bridport.[1] It is doubtful, however, whether he owed to Mr. Broadley's collection any material within the province of formal history; what he may very well have owed is an insight into such popular history as that furnished by caricature, of which there are several traces in the *Dynasts*; for example, at the end of the fifth act of Part 2, the Ironic Spirit comments upon the marriage of Napoleon with Marie Louise thus:

> The English Church should return thanks for this wedding, seeing how it will purge of coarseness the picture-sheets of that .rtistic nation, which will hardly be able to caricature the new wife as it did poor plebeian Josephine.

It must also be remembered that local Dorset traditions and memories of Napoleonic times, which had suggested *The Trumpet Major*, played their part in the conception of the *Dynasts*. In a passage already quoted from the Preface, Hardy ascribed his choice of subject to three accidents of locality; and to the local traditions which he knew in boyhood must be ascribed certain scenes in the *Dynasts*, for example, the last scene of Part I, of which hereafter.

The core of the historical material out of which Hardy constructed his great epic-drama was in his own library. A very brief account of it will show the reasons for which Hardy chose his historical books, and help to illustrate the way in which he used them. First we may take General History:

[1] Hardy's library contains the Catalogue of this Collection, *Collectanea Napoleonica formed by A. M. Broadley*, The Knapp, Bradpole, Bridport, Dorset, copies of which are in the British Museum and the Bodleian.

A. Thiers: *Histoire du Consulat et de l'Empire*. The original began to appear in Paris in 1845, and was completed in twenty volumes. The English translation by D. Forbes Campbell, also in twenty volumes, is likewise in Hardy's library. Why he should have bought an English version of a book that he could read with ease in the original is not clear.

Thiers' work is Hardy's great stand-by for the continental part of his subject. Much of the detail, and a large number of the speeches, in the *Dynasts* are based upon the text of Thiers. When Hardy departs from Thiers, it is always for some sufficient reason.[1]

Archibald Alison: *History of Europe* 1789–1815. Edinburgh and London. 1847.

This work, in twenty volumes, was the counterpart to Thiers from the English side. Hardy does not appear to have used it to the same extent that he used Thiers.

M. Capefigue: *L'Europe pendant le Consulat et l'Empire de Napoléon I*er. Paris 1840. 10 volumes.

Capefigue supplied Hardy with much greater details of certain incidents than were to be found in Thiers. To take an example, the scene between Napoleon and Madame Metternich in the first scene of Act v, in Part 2, is very closely based upon Capefigue (Vol. 7, Chapter IX), the dialogue being mostly a translation of Capefigue's account into English blank verse. The first scene of Act iii, Part 1, was also suggested partly by Capefigue, who devotes a chapter (Chapter VI of Vol. 5) to Napoleon's plans against England.[2]

C. H. Gifford: *History of the Wars occasioned by the French Revolution* 1792–1816. London 1817. 2 vols.

The reference to this work in the Preface to *The Trumpet Major* proves that Hardy knew it long before he wrote the

---

[1] An instance of an artistic reason is to be found in Ney's cavalry charge at Waterloo, for which it suited Hardy to make Napoleon responsible. Thiers makes Napoleon deplore Ney's haste.

[2] The note quoted by Hardy in Sc. i, Act iii, Pt. 1, is a footnote on p. 170, Vol. 5 of *Capefigue*.

Dynasts. It probably served him as a general introduction to Napoleonic history when, in the late 'seventies, his mind first turned to the subject with a view to imaginative treatment. It is much too general to have been of use in the writing of the *Dynasts*.

P. Lanfrey: *Histoire de Napoléon Ier*. Paris 1876.[1] 5 vols. Hardy used Lanfrey to supplement Thiers and Capefigue in certain details. Scene vi, Act v, Part 1, and some details of Trafalgar shortly to be instanced, are examples.

Edward Pelham Brenton: *The Naval History of Great Britain*, 1783–1836. London 1837.[2] 2 vols.

Hardy bought this book to help him in his reconstruction of the Trafalgar scenes, shortly to be examined in detail.

P. Coquelle: *Napoléon et l'Angleterre*, 1803–1813. Paris 1904. This book provides an extremely interesting example of Hardy's alertness in seeking historical material which suited his purpose. It first appeared in 1904, when the first part of the *Dynasts* was already published, and is a history of the diplomatic relations between England and France from 1803 to 1813 based upon documents in French and English archives which had not till then been published. Hardy used material taken from it to construct the two opening scenes of his second part. The first scene, showing the offer made to Fox by Guillet de la Gevrillière to assassinate Napoleon, which provides an excellent opening to the second part quite different from anything in the first part, was suggested by a letter first published by Coquelle. Hardy's scene follows it almost word for word. The second scene of Part 2, if scene it can be called which is an aerial chant by Rumours, is nothing but a summary of Coquelle's chapters twelve to seventeen. Apart from these concrete instances of deliberate borrowing, a case could be made for the contention that his reading of Coquelle's book

[1] This was the ninth edition.
[2] This was the second edition. The first was in five volumes and appeared in 1823, concluding at that date.

in 1904 considerably influenced Hardy's general conception of Napoleon; the influence is clearly traceable in the second and third parts.

It was an integral portion of Hardy's conception of the *Dynasts* that one of its main themes should be the part played by England. The paragraph in the Preface devoted to this matter has already been quoted. Hardy's views on this subject, already clearly visible in Part I, were not only confirmed by his reading of Coquelle in 1904; a slight twist was also given to them. To England's own prowess, nowhere so exalted as in the fifth act of Part 1, which contains Trafalgar, was added, in the second and third parts, the growing personal hatred of Napoleon for England and the conception of the whole war as a duel between them. As Napoleon says before Austerlitz (Sc. i, Act vi, Pt. 1):

> 'Tis all a duel 'twixt this Pitt and me;
> And, more than Russia's host and Austria's flower,
> I everywhere to night around me feel
> As from an unseen monster haunting nigh
> His country's hostile breath—

Very shortly after writing that, Hardy read, in the last chapter of Coquelle's book:

> Napoléon jalouse l'Angleterre plus encore qu'il ne la hait. Il a voulu dominer le continent et il y est parvenu; il veut tenir aussi le premier rang sur mer; mais il s'aperçoit bientôt que c'est impossible, et que, malgré ses efforts, les flottes britanniques seront toujours les premières du monde, et il en éprouve pour sa rivale une jalousie et une haine profondes. Napoléon ne pardonnera jamais à l'Angleterre d'être maitresse de l'océan. Au lieu de s'unir avec elle pour à deux se partager le monde, ce qu'un profond politique aurait pu tenter, il préfère éssayer de la détruire. L'échec des préparatifs de déscente, la défaite de Trafalgar surtout, sont des blessures qui ne se cicatrisent jamais. C'est cette peine cuisante qui retient la main de l'Empereur chaque fois qu'il va signer un accomodement avec l'Angleterre. Et cette paix que les Anglais lui ont proposé tant de fois, l'a-t-il jamais réelement désiré? Nous croyons avoir prouvé que non. Abaisser d'abord l'Angleterre, l'humilier et

traiter ensuite; tel était son but; mais discuter avec elle d'égal, en égal est une extrémité à laquelle il ne voulut jamais se résoudre.

This theme, already adumbrated in Part 1, becomes increasingly the *leit-motif* dominant throughout the *Dynasts*. Examples might be multiplied, but two will suffice. In the sixth scene of Act i in the second part, semichoruses of Ironic Spirits chant what is practically a versified form of the passage from Coquelle quoted above:

> Deeming himself omnipotent
> With the Kings of the Christian continent,
> To warden the waves was his further bent.
>
> But the weaving Will from eternity
> (Hemming them in by a circling sea)
> Evolved the fleet of the Englishry.
>
> *The wane of his armaments ill-advised,*
> *At Trafalgar, to a force despised,*
> *Was a wound which never has cicatrized.*
>
> *This, O this is the cramp that grips!*
> *And freezes the Emperor's finger tips*
> *From signing a peace with the Land of Ships.*
>
> The Universal-empire plot
> Demands the rule of that wave-walled spot;
> And peace with England cometh not.

And in the last scene of Part 3 the Spirit of the Years holds a parley with Napoleon at midnight in the wood of Bossu, and says:

> Thy full meridian-shine
> Was in the glory of the Dresden days,
> When well nigh every monarch throned in Europe
> Bent at thy footstool.

To which Napoleon replies

> Saving alway England's—
> Rightly dost say 'Well nigh.' Not England's—she

Whose tough, enisled, self centred, kindless craft
Has tracked me, springed me, thumbed me by the throat,
And made herself the means of mangling me.

In addition to the general works enumerated, Hardy bought the following books dealing specially with Napoleon:

L. A. F. de Bourrienne: *Memoirs of Napoleon*. An edition in English published at Edinburgh in 1830. In Constable's Miscellany Series. An instance of detail taken from this work is the sixth scene of Act v, Part 2. Hardy's account of Napoleon's first meeting with Marie Louise at Courcelles is based upon the Annexe to chapter forty-five in Bourrienne, with the addition of a few details (e.g., that Napoleon was accompanied by Murat) from the account given by Thiers (Vol. 11, p. 386).

John S. Memes: *Memoirs of the Empress Josephine*. Edinburgh, 1831: in Constable's Miscellany Series.

From this book, besides details of the divorce scene, already mentioned, Hardy took the account of the death of Josephine which is reproduced in Scene vii, Act iv, Part 3. Her last words, in particular, correspond exactly to those reported by Memes.[1]

Walter M. Sloane: *Life of Napoleon Bonaparte*. New York, 1901. Hardy probably bought this as the newest life of Napoleon, but he does not seem to have used it in the *Dynasts*.

For the purposes of depicting Trafalgar, Hardy, in addition to Brenton's Naval History, consulted Thiers, as will be seen; but he also furnished himself with Southey's *Life of Nelson*, London, 1814, in two volumes; and with a book entitled *Trafalgar* published in Paris in 1865 by a prolific and then very popular, but now almost forgotten, writer, Joseph Méry. Méry's *Trafalgar* is a novel, dedicated to a real person, Donnadieu, who was Villeneuve's 'garde-

---

[1] 'At least I shall die regretted; I have always desired the happiness of France; I did all in my power to contribute to it; and I can say with truth to all of you now present at my last moments that the first wife of Napoleon never caused a single tear to flow.'

aigle' on board the French flagship at Trafalgar, and who figures in the first chapter. The rest of the book is frankly imaginary, but the first chapter devoted to the battle is described by Méry, addressing Donnadieu, as 'écrit avec vos souvenirs, plus vrais que l'histoire.' This chapter, which has many historical inaccuracies,[1] is nevertheless stimulating to the imagination; for example:

'Autour des soixante vaisseaux, qui formaient un archipel flottant, semé de mâts, on n'entendait encore que le bruit des proues de cuivre ouvrant des sillons sur l'océan, comme les charrues de la mort.

'Tout à coup, le ciel serein sembla prêter l'arsenal de ses tonnèrres a l'Océan, et la mer trembla et se blanchit d'écume....

'La mer, si joyeuse le matin, était hideuse à voir; elle roulait d'horribles épaves dans une écume rouge, elle engloutissait les blessés et les rejetait cadavres à sa surface; elle charriait des tronçons de mâts, des lambeaux de poulaines dorées, des balcons de gaillard d'arrière, des vergues chargées de voiles, des chaloupes trouées par les boulets, et les nageurs, accrochés à ces débris, Anglais et Français, tombés des vaisseaux, continuaient la bataille en se faisant une arme de toutes les épaves qui flottaient sur l'océan.'

It was remembering this that Hardy made Villeneuve say

How hideous are the waves, so pure this dawn!—
Red frothed; and friends and foes all mixed therein.

But one remarkable touch—that of the Bucentaure's eagle —he simply translated as it stood from Méry, as will be seen.

For the history of the battles in Spain, five of which figure in the *Dynasts*, Hardy went to W. F. P. Napier's *History of the War in the Peninsula*, of which he possessed the six-volume edition published in London in 1892. These five battles, Coruña, Talavera, Albuera, Salamanca and Vitoria, are treated quite differently from other battles, artistically speaking, and must from that point of view be considered later. Historically, however, Hardy relied upon

[1] e.g., Collingwood did not take command *on board the 'Victory'* after Nelson's death.

Napier for all the information he required. His debt to Napier is conclusively proved by a small but interesting detail in the account of Salamanca—that of Colonel Dalbiac's wife riding after her husband in the battle—which Hardy can only have got out of Napier.[1]

William Siborne's *The Waterloo Campaign* (which he possessed in the edition of 1895,[2] and George Elliott's *Life of the Duke of Wellington* (London, 1816) explain by their titles the use to which Hardy put them. From Percy Fitzgerald's *Life of George IV* (London, 1881, 2 vols.) he took the material for all the scenes in which the Prince of Wales plays the chief rôle; and it was also useful to him as a source of general information upon English affairs. The presence of several books in his collection dealing with Napoleonic matters outside the period covered by the *Dynasts* shows that he read round his subject as well as in it.[3]

We shall better appreciate Hardy's workmanship if we take one section of his great creation, and examine its construction from historical sources in detail. For this purpose, the fifth act of Part the First is especially suitable, for several reasons. Hardy tells us in the Preface that his choice of the subject of the *Dynasts* was partly determined by his local connection with that Thomas Hardy who was Nelson's flag captain at Trafalgar, and by far the most illustrious scion of the family of the Dorset Hardys until it produced the author of the *Dynasts*. Nelson, Nelson's Hardy and

---

[1] Napier, Bk. XVIII, Chap. III (Vol. 5, p. 181 in the first ed.): 'Such were the soldiers, and the devotion of a woman was not wanting to the illustration of the great day. The wife of Colonel d'Albiac . . . in this battle, forgetful of everything but that strong affection which had supported her, rode deep amidst the enemy's fire, trembling, yet irresistibly impelled forward by feelings more imperious than horror, more piercing than the fear of death.'

[2] Siborne's book, which is the fullest account of Waterloo in existence, first appeared in 1844 in two volumes. After two revisions, it reached its final form in 1848 as: History | of the | War in France & Belgium | in 1815; | containing minute details of the | Battles of Quatre Bras, Ligny, Wavre and | Waterloo. | By | Captain W. Siborne, | H.P. Unattached; Constructor of the Waterloo Model | Third and Revised Edition | with | Remarks upon the Rev. G. R. Gleig's Story of Waterloo.| London | T. & W. Boone, New Bond Street | 1848.

[3] e.g., James Forbes: *Letters from France* 1803-4. (London, 1806, 2 vols.), and *Memoirs du Dr. F. Antommarchi: ou, les Derniers Moments de Napoleon.* Paris, 1825.

Trafalgar appear fleetingly in the pages of *The Trumpet Major*; and from the personal point of view it seems clear that this was the nucleus of Hardy's interest, around which the whole subject of the Napoleonic Wars gradually gathered. Hardy must have already been impressed as a child by the monument lately raised on Blackdown to his illustrious, if distant, kinsman, which he would see whenever he was taken to Weymouth from Bockhampton. The fifth act of Part 1 has particular importance in the *Dynasts* from the artistic point of view also. As has been shown, one of the main themes of the *Dynasts* is the part played by England; and of that theme, Trafalgar is at once the inception and the culmination; the inception, in that Napoleon never forgave England for it, and by his refusal to make peace with her ultimately brought about his own ruin; the culmination, in that at Trafalgar England for ever destroyed the chance of a Napoleonic world empire. Upon general grounds also, this Act stands out. For Nelson is the nearest approach to an English national hero, and Trafalgar even to this day in popular imagination the most glorious of all English victories. To the obligation thus placed upon him, Hardy responded. The fifth act of Part 1 has some claims to be the best written in the whole drama. It is very dramatic; while it has an artistic unity and an emotional force which no other battle in the *Dynasts* approaches. Its construction is masterly; for it rises through the battle and the death of Nelson to a great climax, in the debate between the Spirits of the Pities and the Years, which stands on a par with the Forescene and Afterscene as among Hardy's greatest and most characteristic achievements. The truly and deliberately Shakespearian interlude that follows, between the citizens in the Guildhall, leads to the deft introduction of the most famous words in English annals, excepting only Nelson's signal; and these are admirably set off by the Spirit of the Years. The scene of Villeneuve's suicide raises the emotional tension once again, while rounding off what may be called the plot; and the act concludes with a return to the Wessex folk who are Hardy's peculiar province, and a ballad of Hardy's composing for which so good a judge as Swinburne expressed the highest admiration.[1]

The sources upon which the first four scenes are based are these: Southey's *Life of Nelson*, vol. 2; Thiers' sixth volume; Brenton's *Naval History*, vol. 3; Lanfrey's third volume; Méry's *Trafalgar*, chapter one, provides one episode; and a few touches are taken from Alison, vol. 9. In addition, Hardy consulted the *Narrative of the Death of Nelson*, by William Beatty, surgeon of the *Victory* at Trafalgar, first published in 1807, the source upon which all accounts of the death of Nelson are ultimately based.[2] That Hardy consulted Beatty, and was not simply content with the version of Beatty provided by Southey, is proved by his introduction of the names Bligh, Pasco, Reeves, Peake, Rivers, Westphall and Bulkeley, which occur only in Beatty. The preservation of Nelson's body in spirit is also recounted by Beatty only.

A DETAILED ANALYSIS OF
THE *Dynasts*, Part the First, Act v

Scene i

The stage direction is based on information common to all the accounts. The detail of the sun shining full upon the sails of the combined fleets is given by Alison (p. 81), but the comparison with satin is Hardy's own.

The narratives of the Recording Angels are based chiefly upon the following passage in Lanfrey (p. 359):

[1] *The Letters of A. C. Swinburne*. Ed. Gosse & Wise (1918), Vol. 2, p. 266.

[2] This narrative was originally intended as part of the standard *Life of Nelson*, by J. S. Clarke and J. M'Arthur (London, 1809, 2 vols.), of which Southey's Life is a popular abridgement, but was published in 1807. The title page of the first edition runs: Authentic Narrative | of the death of | Lord Nelson | with the | Circumstances preceding, attending, | and subsequent to, that event: | the Professional Report of his Lordship's wound | and several interesting Anecdotes | By | William Beatty, M.D. | Surgeon to the *Victory* in the Battle of Trafalgar, and now | Physician to the Fleet under the command of the | Earl of St. Vincent, K.B., etc., etc. | London | Printed by T. Davison, White Friars; | for T. Cadell and W. Davies, in the Strand | 1807.|

Villeneuve avait trop souffert des reproches qui lui avaient été adressées pour s'y exposer une nouvelle fois. Sa conviction sur l'issue d'une rencontre avec la flotte anglaise n'avait pas changé, mais il avait maintenant à executer des ordres positifs, pressants, impossibles à éluder; et ce n'était plus sur lui que pouvait retomber la résponsabilité du désastre qu'il prévoyait. Avant d'obéir, il voulait toutefois, pour sa propre justification, autant que pour celle de ses compagnons sacrifiés comme lui, assembler un conseil de guerre composé des principaux officiers des deux nations. Les amiraux et contre-amiraux français et espagnoles consultés par lui sur la situation de la flotte combinée, déclarèrent à l'unanimité: 'que les vaisseaux des deux nations étaient la plupart mal armés, qu'une partie de leurs équipages ne s'étaient jamais exercés à la mer, qu'enfin ils n'étaient pas en état de rendre les services qu'on attendait d'eux.' Villeneuve expédia ce proces-verbal à Paris en y joignant une dernière supplication; 'je ne puis croire, écrivait-il à Decrès, que ce soit l'intention de Sa Majesté Impériale de vouloir livrer la majeure partie de ses forces navales à des chances si désespérées, et qui ne promettent pas même de la gloire à acquérir.' Mais Napoléon avait d'avance rendu toute rémonstrance inutile en faisant partir Rosily; car lors même que Villeneuve eût poussé l'abnégation jusqu'à attendre cet amiral pour lui remettre son commandement, avec la certitude de voir un sacrifice sublime transformé en acte de lâcheté, cette détermination n'eut point sauvé la flotte, puisque Rosily devait exécuter précisément les mêmes ordres et sans aucun delai. Averti à temps de l'arrivée prochaine de Rosily, et certain que son remplacement par cet amiral, qui lui était d'ailleurs très inférieur à tous égards, ne changerait rien au dénouement, Villeneuve n'hésita plus dès lors à se précipiter dans le gouffre où il devait trouver tout au moins la réhabilitation de son honneur outragé.

The details of the orders given to Villeneuve are slightly altered by Hardy, from those related by Lanfrey (p. 357):

Le 14 Septembre, il (Napoleon) lui expédia l'ordre direct et formel de sortir de Cadix avec l'escadre combiné, de toucher à Carthagène pour rallier les vaisseaux espagnols qui s'y trouvaient, de se rendre ensuite à Naples pour appuyer le corps de St. Cyr et faire aux croisières anglaises de Malte le plus de mal qu'il se pourrait, et enfin de se retirer sur Toulon.[1]

Out of Thiers' account of these transactions, Hardy took a touch in Scene iii, when Villeneuve says

> If it be true that, as *he* sneers, success
> Demands of me but cool audacity,
> To-day shall leave him nothing to desire.

This is from a letter, quoted by Thiers, written by Villeneuve to Decrès some time earlier, in which he says

> Au reste, si la marine française n'a manqué que d'audace, comme on le prétend, l'Empereur sera prochainement satisfait, et il peut compter sur les plus éclatants succès.

The scene upon the deck of the *Bucentaure* is based mostly upon information from Thiers (pp. 147–8), who relates the nocturnal signals of the English frigates, Villeneuve's signal to Gravina, and suggests Hardy's 'officers murmur' by writing that Rear Admiral Magon, when he saw the signal, 's'écria que c'etait une faute et en exprima vivement son chagrin, de manière à être entendu de tout son état major.' That Villeneuve says they must not look for his signals seems to be Hardy's enlargement of a hint given by Brenton.[2] Villeneuve's signal: 'Tout capitaine n'est pas à son poste s'il n'est pas au feu' is given by Thiers (p. 156) as later in the action, when the head of the French line became useless by reason of its distance from the combat.

In the stage direction, the detail that the interspaces of the first column were opposite the hulls of the second, is taken from Alison (p. 80). The colloquy on 'slaughter day' is, of course, Hardy's own. Nelson's signal is given in all the English sources; Hardy has beautifully touched up the detail—given in all the English accounts—that it was received with cheers, by making the sound of these, 'undulating on the wind,' to be heard from the French fleet.

---

[1] There is no mention of Toulon in Thiers.

[2] p. 468: 'The Comte de Dumas says the French admiral neglected to give to the officers under his orders particular instructions relative to the various positions in which the fleet might find itself.'

The detail, in Villeneuve's next speech, that the French displayed no flags during the action, is taken from Brenton (p. 451). The details of the beginning of the action are common to all the sources. Magendie's speech about Lucas is based on Brenton (p. 453):

> As they approached very near the *Bucentaure*, the French admiral's flagship, the *Redoutable* commanded by Captain Lucas gallantly resolved to interpose between his own admiral and the *Victory*, and ran upon the weather quarter of the French flagship.

This is also mentioned by Thiers (p. 155). The close of the scene provides a poetic touch different from the historical details so far given, which is of special interest in that Hardy found it in Méry's novel, *Trafalgar*, the only place where it occurs, and translated it bodily into English.

> VILLENEUVE:
>> Your grapnels and your boarding-hatchets ready!
>> We'll dash our eagle on the English deck,
>> And swear to fetch it!
> CREW:
>>> Aye! We swear. Huzza!
>> Long live the Emperor!

In the original this runs:

> A bord du *Bucentaure*, les grappins d'abordage étaient tendus vers le *Victory*; toutes les mains brandissaient la hache. 'Enfants, cria Villeneuve, je vais jeter notre aigle à bord de l'Anglais et nous jurons d'aller le reprendre. Nous le jurons, répondit l'équipage: Vive l'Empereur!'

Hardy's closing stage direction is not so close to Méry, but it follows it:

> Le *Victory* tourna sur sa quille, fit feu de babord et de tribord, évita l'abordage et vint manœuvrer dans les eaux du *Redoubtable*, commandé par l'intrépide Lucas.

Scene ii

The substance of the stage direction is common to all the sources. Pasco occurs only in Beatty. Nelson's 'See that noble fellow Collingwood' is given by both Southey (p. 257) and Brenton (pp. 451–2), who also both mention Blackwood's departure, but earlier. The reference to 'the Great Disposer of events' is taken from Southey (p. 253), who gives it as earlier in the action, just after Nelson's famous signal: ' "Now," said Lord Nelson, "I can no more. We must trust to the great Disposer of events, and the justice of our cause!" ' This detail, not given in Beatty, would alone prove Hardy's debt to Southey. The stage direction is from Southey (p. 259):

> Presently a double-headed shot struck a party of marines, who were drawn up on the poop, and killed eight of them; upon which Nelson immediately desired Captain Adair to disperse his men round the ship.

The detail of Burke's being ordered below is given by Beatty. Nelson's further comment

> Ah, yes; like David you would see the battle!

is typical of Hardy, with his fondness for Biblical allusions.

The episode of Scott's, and later Captain Hardy's, remonstrance with Nelson to take off or hide his stars, is worthy of comment. The version given in the *Dynasts* was clearly suggested by a paragraph in Southey (p. 254), who writes of Nelson before the action began:

> He wore that day as usual his admiral's frock coat, bearing on the left breast four stars, of the different orders with which he was invested. Ornaments which rendered him so conspicuous a mark for the enemy were beheld with ominous apprehensions by his officers. It was known that there were riflemen on board the French ships; and it could not be doubted but that his life would be particularly aimed at. They communicated their fears to each other, and the surgeon Mr. Beatty spoke to the chaplain Dr. Scott, and to Mr. Scott, the public secretary, desiring that some person would entreat him to change his dress or cover the stars; but they knew that such a request would highly displease him. 'In honour I gained them,' he had said when such a thing had been hinted to him formerly, 'and in honour I will die with them.'

In the appendix to Beatty's Narrative, there is a note on this:

> It has been reported, but erroneously, that his Lordship was actually requested by his officers to change his dress, or cover his stars.

Whether or no his officers did speak to Nelson about his stars is a matter which primarily concerns the historian. There can be no two opinions about the dramatic aptness of the dialogues in the *Dynasts*. At first, when Scott and Captain Hardy both try to persuade him to make himself less conspicuous, Nelson is pictured as putting them off good humouredly, 'Thank'ee, good friend. But no, I haven't time.' Later, when Hardy tries again, Nelson answers

> Faith, I have had my day. My work's nigh done.

In that one line the dramatist achieves three purposes. He strikes the string which is the dominant of tragedy—that for the greatest there comes an end, as for the least; he suggests, although it is no more than a suggestion, that Nelson is but playing the part for which the Immanent Will cast him, the exit being predetermined with the entry; and he offers an explanation of the otherwise inexplicable. For, returning to the common belief that man has some free will and is not wholly a puppet jerked by Fate, a belief that Hardy himself despite philosophy has to maintain at the peril of making his drama utterly uninteresting, Nelson can only have courted death at the hands of enemy snipers because he cared nothing for life. That death, had Nelson cared to live, would have been so easy to escape. As it was, he came to 'his full refulgent eve' for which his enemy so envied him; and became the greatest example in history, to borrow the words of Thiers, of 'le chef triomphant enséveli dans son triomphe.' In the *Dynasts* it is suggested that this consummation, if he did not devoutly wish it, he partly desired.

The stage direction concerning the shooting of Scott is

based on Southey (pp. 259–60). The detail of the bullet taking off the buckle of Captain Hardy's shoe and tearing the instep is given by Beatty. The further conversation between Nelson and Hardy is based first on Southey, then on this passage from Brenton (p. 454):

> The *Victory* for a time had ceased firing her great guns into the *Redoutable* under an impression that that ship had surrendered; but the small arm men from the tops still keeping up their fire, the great guns of the *Victory* began again, and were discharged into the side of the *Redoutable* with a diminished quantity of powder and three round shot; the officers on the middle and lower decks taking every precaution, by the depression of their guns, to avoid injuring the *Temeraire* as she lay on the opposite side of the enemy. While the *Victory* was thus occupied with the *Redoutable* on her starboard side, she engaged for a considerable time the *Santissima Trinidad* and the *Bucentaure*, who were to windward of her on the larboard side.

The stage direction put in by Thomas Hardy needs no comment. The detail of the firemen is mentioned by Brenton:

> The firemen of the *Victory* stood ready with their buckets, and at every discharge of a gun dashed a quantity of water into the holes which the shot had made in the side of the *Redoutable*.

This is taken from Beatty, and is also repeated in Southey. The next six speeches are Hardy's own, except the details about setting their own sails afire, mentioned as Nelson's opinion by Southey and Brenton, and that of the *Redoutable's* continuing to fight only with her small arms, which is Brenton (p. 456), who refers to 'the singular spectacle of a French seventy-four gun ship engaging a British first and second rate with small arms only.' The remainder of the scene is taken from Beatty's narrative, except for three small details. Captain Hardy's sending of the news to Collingwood by Hills, not mentioned by Beatty, is related by Brenton (p. 459). The shooting of Nelson's slayer is related by Southey and Brenton. From the former comes the detail that he was 'white-bloused,' from the latter that he fell dead on the poop.

Scene iii

This scene is in the main based on Thiers (p. 158 *et seq.*), from whom nearly all the details are taken. Lanfrey (pp. 367–8) also relates the attempted boarding by Lucas. Villeneuve's speech—'Now that the fume has lessened, code my biddance'—is Thiers:

> Plongé dans un épais nuage de fumée, l'amiral ne distinguait plus ce qui se passait dans le reste de l'escadre. Ayant apperçu à la faveur d'une éclaircie les vaisseaux de tête toujours immobiles, il leur ordonna, en arborant ses signaux au dernier mât qui lui restait, de virer de bord tous à la fois, afin de se porter au feu.

The other half of this speech, as has been said, is based on an earlier passage in Thiers. The touch about the red-frothed sea, taken from Méry, has also been mentioned. 'This dawn' must be taken as purely poetic, for the time was much later, the action having begun between eleven and twelve. Villeneuve's surrender is thus related by Thiers:

> Le *Bucentaure*, avec son flanc droit déchiré, sa poupe démolie, ses mâts abattus, était rasé comme un ponton. 'Mon rôle sur le *Bucentaure* est fini, s'écria l'infortuné Villeneuve, je vais essayer sur un autre vaisseau de conjurer la fortune.' Il voulait alors se jeter dans un canot et se transporter à l'avant garde pour l'amener lui même au combat. Mais les canots placés sur le pont du *Bucentaure* avaient été écrasés par la chute successive de toute la mâture. Ceux qui étaient sur les flancs avaient été criblés de boulets. On héla à la voix le *Santissima Trinidad* pour lui demander une embarcation; vains efforts! Au milieu de cette confusion aucune voix humaine ne pouvait se faire entendre. L'amiral français se vit donc attaché au cadavre de son vaisseau prêt à couler, ne pouvant plus donner d'ordre, ni rien tenter pour sauver la flotte qui lui était confiée. . . . Il ne resta à l'amiral qu'à mourir et l'infortuné en forma plus d'une fois le voeu. Son chef d'état major, M. de Prigny, venait d'être blessé à ses côtés. Presque tout son équipage était hors de combat. Le *Bucentaure*, entièrement privé de

mâture, criblé de boulets, ne pouvant se servir de ses batteries qui étaient demontées ou obstruées par les débris de gréement, n'avait pas même la cruelle satisfaction de rendre un seul des coups qu'il recevait. Il était quatre heures un quart; aucun secours n'arrivant, l'amiral fut obligé d'amener son pavilon.

The comparison with 'the bliss of Nelson's end' is Hardy's own apt embellishment. The stage direction is from Brenton (p. 467):

The *Bucentaure* . . . was taken possession of by the *Conqueror*; but the boat which took out the French admiral, unable to regain her own ship, was picked up by the *Mars*.

Thiers simply has 'Une chaloupe anglaise vint le chercher et le conduire à bord du vaisseau le Mars'; here is another proof of Hardy's meticulous attention to detail in his sources.

Scene iv

The basis of this most important scene is Beatty's narrative. Several names which occur in it, already enumerated, occur only in Beatty. The following touches are not to be found in Beatty: The list of ships captured is from Thiers (who is the only source to mention the *San Augustineo* and the *San Francisco* (pp. 163–4)). The *Swiftsure*, also incidentally mentioned later by Beatty, is specially referred to by Thiers: 'Le *Swiftsure*, que les ennemies tenaient à reconquérir parce qu'il avait été anglais, se comportait bravement et ne cédait qu'au nombre' (p. 170). The detail that several ships of the French van were bearing on to the *Victory*, and that Hardy told Nelson

Three of our best I am therefore calling up,
And make no doubt of worsting theirs, and France

is based upon Southey, who (p. 265) reports Hardy as saying:

'Five of their van have tacked and show an intention to bear down upon the *Victory*. I have called two or three of our best ships round, and have no doubt of giving them a drubbing.'

The boarding of the *Algeciras* by Captain Tyler is related by Thiers (p. 168). All the remaining historical detail is taken from Beatty. This makes it the easier to compare the finished work of the dramatist, as we have it in this fourth scene of the fifth act, with the raw material out of which it was constructed. The result of such a comparison is remarkable. To compare a finished work of art with that which inspired the artist is always fascinating, for it brings us close to the mystery of creative genius; and that mystery seems to hold the central secret of the Universe. Here is the bringing of order out of chaos; the making of something out of nothing. And this alone among men the artist can accomplish; all others are bound by the principle of the conservation of matter—they can but work with that with which they began; but the artist, taking that which is without form and void, makes thereof a living world. In more general language, out of the insignificant, the trivial, the occasional, the artist fashions that whose significance is universal and perdurable. Out of a chapter in the Book of Judges, Milton made *Samson Agonistes*; out of a chronicle of Saxo Grammaticus, Shakespeare made *Hamlet*. Out of history that is being forgotten and Memoirs that are no longer read, Hardy made the *Dynasts*. In this fourth scene of Act v in the first part we have as good an example as can be found of this process in little. Beatty's narrative of Nelson's death is interesting reading; but there is nothing in it, beyond its subject, which the reader remembers. The scene into which Hardy made it is the most memorable in the *Dynasts*. Beatty's facts are given unity and cogency; they are translated into Hardy's art, and so transmuted.

The transmutation cannot be adequately illustrated by showing what additions of his own Hardy added to the details which he found in Beatty; it can only be fully appreciated by reading Beatty's narrative, and then reading Hardy's scene. Only a part of the difference lies in Hardy's additions, for his imagination has also done its work by selection and presentation. The actual additions are these:

(1) The stage direction, which is a masterpiece. In less than a hundred and fifty words, the cockpit of the *Victory* is brought not only before our eyes, but also, by the subtler senses of hearing and smell, into our inmost consciousness.

(2) The first short dialogue between Nelson and Hardy, beginning 'We'll have 'em yet.'

(3) Nelson's 'Poor youngsters! Scarred old Nelson joins you soon.'

(4) Nelson's speech beginning ' 'Twas not worth while——' The dramatist had no opportunity to introduce the prayer which Nelson wrote before the battle, concluding with the petition that the English victory might be marked by the humanity of the victors. He therefore showed the same trait of character thus.

(5) The grotesque details about the woman who climbed out of the *Achille*, and Burke's comment. If these were not pure invention, they may have been founded upon some local tradition of Trafalgar (as are parts of Scene vii) which Hardy had heard as a boy.

(6) Nelson's speech 'By God, if but our carpenter——'

(7) The artistic climax of the scene, the twenty-five lines beginning 'What are you thinking, that you speak no word' are essentially the poet's own addition. The historical justification for them is the information, given by Beatty, of such a parting scene, and Southey's statement that Nelson's last thoughts were of Lady Hamilton. 'Next to his country,' says Southey, 'she occupied his thoughts' (p. 267). The codicil to Nelson's will is reproduced by Beatty and Southey; the injunction that she was to have his hair, and that Captain Hardy was to take care of her, are mentioned by Southey (pp. 266, 268). The best lines in the whole act, perhaps the best passage in the *Dynasts*, have—and need—no historical justification. We know that in actual life, John of Gaunt gave voice to no superb piece of rhetoric about 'This realm, this England,' nor Henry V to 'We few, we happy few, we band of brothers'; but of Shakespeare, writing poetry and not history, we ask—above all—poetic

aptitude. Hardy, writing his epic-drama for performance in the mind's eye, remains mostly very close to history; but he is writing a work of art, not a chronicle, and the art is achieved by showing the inner significance of his material. Mostly this is done by the Spirits. Here it is done by Nelson's flag captain, who replies to the question by the dying Nelson as to what he is thinking

> Thoughts all confused, my lord:— their needs on deck,
> Your own sad state, and your unrivalled past;
> Mixed up with flashes of old things afar—
> Old childish things at home, down Wessex way,
> In the snug village under Blackdon Hill
> Where I was born.

The method is that of Elizabethan drama, but the manner is another. The writer of those lines had passed through the school of Wordsworth. (cf. *Prelude*; 2, 432 et seq.)

(8) The chaplain's comment upon Nelson's death is highly characteristic of Hardy, so steeped in the English Bible:

> he has homed to where
> There's no more sea.

The conclusion of this fourth scene, the passionate debate between the Pities and the Years upon the problem of suffering, must be considered one of the most significant utterances in the literature of the last fifty years. In less than fifty lines, Hardy here not only expresses the central theme of the *Dynasts*, the theme for the sake of which the whole drama was written; he also reveals the history of his own soul; how his revulsion from the intolerable injustice of useless suffering drove him to seek in philosophy an intellectual explanation which yet explained nothing; and how his final solution could but be to suspend judgment. This passage would be interesting to the student of Hardy if it did nothing more than illustrate his studies in Schopenhauer and John Stuart Mill. As it is, the significance of this page far transcends that of any one school of thought, and even that of Hardy himself; because it is universal. 'Hinc indignatur se mortalem esse creatum.' Upon the one hand, we reach out to Sophocles who marked 'the vast injustice of the gods' in the dawn of human thought; upon the other to the poet, lately gone down into silence, who cried:

> Aye, look. High heaven and earth
> Ail from the prime foundation—

Scene v

The historical basis of this scene is a passage in Earl Stanhope's *Life of the Right Honourable William Pitt*, to which Hardy was also indebted for the material of the sixth and eighth scenes in Act vi. In the edition of 1862, it is to be found on pp. 345–6 of volume 4:

> On the ninth of November, the Lord Mayor's Day, there was, as usual, a great dinner at Guildhall. Pitt, as Prime Minister, had accepted the invitation, and went with some of his colleagues. His popularity, which had waned in these latter times, appeared on that day to shine forth in all its pristine lustre. On his way to the Mansion House he was greeted with loud acclamations. In Cheapside the multitude took off the horses from his carriage, and drew him exultingly along. At the banquet the Lord Mayor proposed his health as 'the Saviour of Europe.' Then Pitt rose and spoke nearly as follows: 'I return you many thanks for the honour you have done me; but Europe is not to be saved by any single man. England has saved herself by her exertions, and will, as I trust, save Europe by her example.' With only these two sentences the Minister sat down. They were memorable words. They sank deep into the minds of his hearers. For, beside their own impressive beauty, they were the last words that Mr. Pitt ever spoke in public.

Hardy dramatized that passage, with the aid of his imagination, his recollections of Shakespeare, and his sense of humour. It is well done. We pass in two pages from the economical citizen, gaping in dumbshow like a frog in Plaistow Marshes, to the Ancient Spirit of the Years, whose variations upon Stanhope are sonorous—

For words were never winged with apter grace,
Or blent with happier chance of time and place
To hold the imagination of this strenuous race.[1]

Scene vi

This scene, which, as Hardy points out in a footnote, is antedated to round off the Act artistically, is wholly based upon the account of Villeneuve's suicide in the third volume of Lanfrey's *Histoire de Napoléon Ier*, p. 373 *et seq.* The intervention of the Spirits of the Years and the Pities is dramatically effective; but philosophically incongruous, like the other interventions by Spirits elsewhere in the *Dynasts*; for if, as we are repeatedly told, every detail of the action is part of the predetermined mechanics of Immanent Will, the Phantoms described as personifications of Sympathy and Passionless Insight have no business to interfere with them; nor, by the premises, have they any power to do so.

Scene vii

This scene is just such a one as we should expect from Hardy; it is one of those felicitous parts of the *Dynasts* which seem to have come straight out of a Wessex novel, and its actors are of the lineage of Joseph Poorgrass and his cronies. The introduction of allusions to Captain Hardy, and to that Bob Loveday who is one of the chief characters of *The Trumpet Major*, remove it, however, from the realm of pure fiction and suggest that Hardy was using memories of his boyhood as well as his imagination. The tale of 'broaching the Admiral,' for example, may well have been a local tradition. As for the preservation of Nelson's body in spirits, there is a detailed scientific account of it at the end of Beatty's Narrative. The Ballad of Trafalgar fully merits the commendation of so expert a judge as Swinburne. The three lines of Chorus of the Years which conclude the scene are not good, and, although perhaps necessary to maintain the convention of 'a play within a play,' are an anticlimax.

[1] It may be added that the allusion in this scene to the French contention that England's loss of Nelson was greater than France's loss of ships, was taken by Hardy from Méry's *Trafalgar*.

THOMAS HARDY

IV. The *Dynasts*: Conception and Execution

The *Dynasts* might well give pause to any critic. It is, indeed, a work of so unorthodox a character that the classic methods of criticism require some modification before they will yield any result at all. This is what any educated English reader, taking up the *Dynasts* for the first time, is likely to feel. Let us even suppose our reader to be an avowed lover of literature. It was once his duty, and later became his pleasure, to study Shakespeare, and to read A. C. Bradley on Shakespearian Tragedy. With such a training, considering the *Dynasts* as a drama, he will at once begin to think of its construction, and of such matters as characterization, diction, versification, construction of plot, and the rest. And here his difficulties will begin, and will soon become insurmountable. For he will find that the *Dynasts* contains very little, if any, characterization of the Shakespearian variety; he will feel its language to be generally stilted and unpoetical, while that of the parts printed in italics will seem very unfamiliar. The versification he will often find deplorable, and also a queer hotch potch which even includes bad Sapphics. Of plot in the proper sense there is scarcely a vestige; and the action is not amenable to any canons of unity ever drawn up. At the same time, our reader, if he have any perception at all, will be conscious of great power. If he be not a man of mettle as well as judgment he will, in his bewilderment, seek a simplification; and may perhaps adopt the obvious one of skipping everything printed in italics, which is the most puzzling part, and try to read the rest as a chronicle play. This has been done many times. The result, it is safe to predict, will be disappointment. And no wonder! As well try to appreciate the last movement of the Ninth Symphony from a simple reading of the libretto without the score, as try to appreciate the *Dynasts* without the Spirits and their choruses! But if our hypothetical reader has determination, he will persevere in this strange country where all his maps are useless and his

compass ceases to point true. He will come upon scenes
that take away his breath. He will gradually learn his way
about; and ultimately, what was once so strange will become
familiar and delightful. To leave an inadequate metaphor;
the appreciation of the *Dynasts* demands an approach along
lines that do not correspond to the beaten highways of
established criticism. We must not start with our categories,
and submit it to their measure. We must first see what it
achieves in its own way; and then whether that way is good,
judged by the results. Does Hardy accomplish what he set
out to accomplish? It was once said by Galsworthy, writing
of novelists, that the business of style is to remove all
barriers between the writer and his readers. This penetrating
remark can be transposed so that it applies to the dramatist.
It is the business of dramatic technique to remove all
barriers between the spectator, and the illusion of reality
which the dramatist seeks to project. Or, in the words of
Coleridge which are quoted in the Preface to the *Dynasts*,
to procure 'that willing suspension of disbelief for the
moment which constitutes poetic faith.'

The first and obvious characteristic of the method employed by Hardy to this end is his creation of a form new
in literary technique. He places a drama within a drama.
The rudiments of such a method are perhaps to be found in
Goethe's *Faust*, with its 'Prolog im Himmel,' and the mystic
close to the second part. Goethe was indebted for the idea
of the Prologue to the Book of Job; and of that great poem
Hardy also was a lifelong student. But Goethe's drama, save for
its beginning and ending and such an adaptation of the 'deus
ex machina' as the voice from heaven before Gretchen's
death, is all actually played out upon the material
stage by its human characters (among whom for this purpose, we may include Mephistopheles). Its incidents really
are what they appear to be, not something totally different.
Whereas all the incidents on the human stage in the
Dynasts are but 'one flimsy riband' of the whole Web of
Being:

THOMAS HARDY

> Web enorm
> Whose furthest hem and selvage may extend
> To where the roars and plashings of the flames
> Of earth-invisible suns swell noisily
> And onwards into ghastly gulfs of sky—
> (Afterscene.)

This conception, whereby the actions and fates of human beings, and even of the lower forms of life, are presented in scale as portions of the whole universe, can only be called great. It is as remarkable in its simplicity as in its range. And the execution is almost as unusual as the conception; not because it is flawless—it has many lapses of detail—but because it succeeds in actually conveying this conception; and it does so, not by intellectual suggestion, but by artistic evocation. So remarkable a feat Hardy accomplished by writing a drama whose stage is neither on earth, nor in heaven, nor under the earth, but in the imagination of him who reads it.

The difference between this and other dramatic methods can be put quite briefly. In the process by which the dramatist establishes the relationship between himself and his audience, there are normally three stages. First of all, the play is mentally enacted in the imagination of its author. It is then, by the aid of directions supplied by him, actually played by living actors on a material scene. The third stage is when the sight and sound of this material representation produce in the mind of the spectator an imaginative enactment corresponding to the dramatist's conception. It must naturally happen that the second stage is sometimes the weak link in the chain, no material representation being adequate to convey all that the dramatist imagined; for this reason Lamb wished *King Lear* to be read rather than seen.[1] In the *Dynasts*, Hardy dispensed with the second stage entirely. This drama can only be enacted in the imagination of him who reads it, as it was enacted in the imagination of its author.

[1] The other reason, namely that the *King Lear* which was acted throughout the eighteenth century was mostly Nahum Tate's version with a happy ending, does not affect the argument.

THE POEMS AND THE *DYNASTS*

Here for a moment our consideration of the conception and structure of the *Dynasts* must be interrupted in order to dispose first of a smaller, but not unimportant, matter; that of Hardy's technique in the use of language. The unfamiliarity of much of the language was one of the great obstacles to immediate appreciation of the *Dynasts*. This has now largely been overcome; but there are still critics who deny that the drama is poetry. They point to the extreme baldness of much of the historical portions, and, mentally contrasting them with Shakespeare, ask 'Do you call this poetry?' At the kind of poetry which Shakespeare put into the mouths of Hamlet and Othello and Lady Macbeth, or even into those of Richard II and Henry V, Hardy never aimed. He was a poet; but he was also a novelist of the school called realist; and the historical portions of the *Dynasts* seek to create the illusion of a certain kind of reality rather than poetry. The illusion of actual reality he does not desire. What he desires follows from his whole conception of the *Dynasts* as a play within a play. He wishes us to see the historical events portrayed, not, as Shakespeare wished us to see Agincourt, in an emotional mist created by the magic of great verse, but as they actually happened *in so far as is consistent with their being at the same time scenes in the European drama of the Immanent Will.* That they should be versified was necessary to this last requirement. To illustrate by example: it would not have created the illusion of such a drama had the speeches in the House of Commons been summarized *in prose* out of *Hansard*, or had Napoleon's orders before Austerlitz been summarized in prose out of Thiers. They are therefore put into rough blank verse,

> Soldiers, your sections I myself shall lead;
> But ease your minds who would expostulate
> Against my undue rashness

cannot be called poetry. It was never meant to be. But it does create the illusion of Napoleon as an actor in the European drama; and this is all that Hardy aimed at doing. This consideration disposes of the objections of critics who quote the bad blank verse so common in the *Dynasts* and ask why it was not written as prose. Written as prose, it would cease to give the illusion of a play. This does not, of course, apply to the occasional prose scenes, of which hereafter, but to the historical scenes which make up the bulk of the work. There are in these, hundreds of lines which, considered as poetry, or even as verse, are bad. Some of them, it must be confessed, are so appalling that Hardy should never have allowed them to stand,

> The launching of a lineal progeny
> Has been much pressed upon me, much, of late

or

> Warteachben, Muger—almost all our best—
> Bleed more or less profusely

are indefensible on any grounds. It would have been so simple to have put the same thing in a way that did not outrage the ear. But Hardy was, as we saw earlier, capable of strange lapses even in prose. And, as Mr. Macdowall has pointed out,[1] blank verse was to him an alien medium. Despite this, he can compass poetry in it well enough when he wishes, as witness the dialogue between Captain Hardy and the dying Nelson, already quoted; or this speech of the Spirit of the Pities at Waterloo:

> Between the jars
> Of these who live, I hear uplift and move
> The bones of those who placidly have lain
> Within the sacred garths of yon grey fanes—
> Nivelles and Plancenoit and Braine l'Alleud—
> Beneath unmemoried mounds through deedless years.
> Their dry jaws quake; 'What Sabaoth is this,
> That shakes us in our unobtrusive shrouds,
> As though our tissues did not yet abhor
> The fevered feats of life?'

No critic will stand up to say that *that* would better be written as prose.

[1] *A Study of Thomas Hardy*, p. 182.

THE POEMS AND THE *DYNASTS*

All that part of the *Dynasts* printed in italics, from which one of the examples above is taken, does not usually come under this condemnation of being prosaic; but under that of being 'queer' and without authority in earlier English poetry. Hardy was here following a different purpose. It will later be seen that the outer drama between the Spirits is more than a frame to the history, as it is often supposed to be; it is the backbone of the whole work. The language which Hardy here used was chosen in order to evoke in his readers an imaginative response to the significance of the Spirits. For this reason, much of it is abstract and philosophical. When the Spirit of the Years says of the Immanent Will

> It works unconsciously as heretofore,
> Eternal artistries in Circumstance,
> Whose patterns, wrought by rapt aesthetic rote,
> Seem in themselves Its single listless aim,
> And not their consequence

he is giving an extreme example. But it at once conveys, by its phraseology, both his character and his part in the drama. Insistence upon this point is needless, for it is clear enough. A detail worth noting is the number of images, in the italic parts, directly derived from science. There are at least four striking examples in the Forescene alone.[1] Another peculiarity of the diction is the frequent use of rare or obsolete words and phrases, for instance 'Byss' (in the fourteenth line). This, as has been pointed out by others, was characteristic of Hardy and is not confined to the *Dynasts*.[2]

[1] They recall the saying of Coventry Patmore to Robert Bridges, that the only use of science is to provide fresh images for poetry. The examples in the Forescene are:

(1) 'germ of being.' (2) 'Flesh-hinged mannikins Its hand upwinds | To click-clack off Its preadjusted laws.' (3) 'made gyrate like animalcula | In tepid pools.' (4) 'Their sum is like the lobule of a brain | Evolving always that it wots not of.' Many others can be found elsewhere in the *Dynasts*.

[2] With special reference to the *Dynasts*, a careful examination of its diction has been made, the results of which are recorded in a letter from Mr. G. S. Loane in the *Times Literary Supplement* of February 14th, 1929. This revealed the employment of twenty-one words in senses not given in the *New English Dictionary*; and the resurrection or reinvention of six others, none of which are recorded in the *New English Dictionary* later than the seventeenth century. One of them, 'inkle' (to hint at) is not recorded after 1370.

An excellent illustration in small compass of Hardy's use of different dictions, and of the results produced, is to be found at the end of Scene v, Act v, Part 1. Pitt's famous speech at the Guildhall is turned into blank verse, retaining as nearly as possible the words which he is reported actually to have used. This is so that he may appear to the reader, as he appears to the Spirits, as an actor in the European drama. And when his voice has ceased and the scene has faded into darkness, the voice of the Spirit of the Years is heard, speaking in the stately language of prophecy:

PITT:
> My lords and gentlemen; you have toasted me
> As one who has saved England and her cause.
> I thank you, gentlemen, unfeignedly.
> But—no man has saved England, let me say;
> England has saved herself by her exertions;
> She will, I trust, save Europe by her example.

SPIRIT OF THE YEARS:
> Those words of this man Pitt—his last large words,
> As I may prophesy—that ring to night
> In their first mintage to the feasters here,
> Will spread with ageing, lodge and crystallize,
> And stand imbedded in the English tongue
> Till it grow thin, outworn and cease to be.
> So is't ordained by That which all ordains;
> For words were never winged with apter grace,
> Or blent with happier chance of time and place,
> To hold the imagination of this strenuous race.

There are in the *Dynasts* a large number of Lyrics, very various in metre and character. Some of them are songs by human beings; at least two of these, the Ballad of the Night of Trafalgar (Sc. vii, Act v, Pt. 1) and the Madman's Song (Sc. xi, Act 1, Pt. 3), are most effective. But the great majority are choruses sung by the Spirits. Some of these are, by common consent, magnificent. For instance, the chorus describing Eylau: 'Snows incarnadined were thine, O Eylau, field of the wide white spaces'—and the chorus before

Waterloo, later to be quoted. Hardy's liability to lapse into bathos or doggerel is occasionally evident. The worst example is probably that in Scene i, Act v, Part 3, describing Napoleon's escape from Elba, when the Spirits of Rumour sing:

> Should the corvette return
> With the anxious Scotch colonel,
> Escape would be frustrate,
> Retention eternal.

For such a lapse there is no excuse. But a liability to descend even to such depths does not disqualify a writer from being a great poet, as Wordsworth has amply proved. And we forget his doggerels when Hardy's genius for lyric asserts itself:

> O Immanence, That reasonest not
> In putting forth all things begot,
> Thou build'st Thy house in space—for what?

It is only the lyric that can soar thus; and its lyric choruses are perhaps the most memorable details in the *Dynasts*. Nor do they give us of their best if we consider them in isolation. We have said that in the *Dynasts* Hardy wrote a drama whose stage was set in the imagination of its reader. The lyric choruses of the Spirits play a vital part in working upon the imagination as only lyric poetry can work.

At the other extreme, there are many prose scenes, some of them justly famous: for example, Scene v, Act ii, Part 1; Scene i, Act iii, Part 2, and Scene vi, Act v, Part 3. These were the first parts of the *Dynasts* to be accepted by the critics; not only because there was Shakespearian precedent for them in drama, but also because similar scenes were already familiar in the Wessex novels. Their merits, indeed, are clear enough. But they have a subtler dramatic purpose than that of providing interludes, and are as much a part of the drama of the Immanent Will which we are called to witness as are the historical scenes. They can often stir our imagination more deeply than the formal history, and almost as effectively as the lyric choruses; as witness this, from one of the deserters in that cellar near Astorga (Sc. i, Act iii, Pt. 2):

> Would that I were at home in England again, where there's old fashioned tipple, and a proper God A'mighty instead of this eternal 'Ooman and baby;—ay, at home a-leaning against old Bristol Bridge, and no questions asked, and the winter sun slanting friendly over Baldwin Street as 'a used to do!

When Hardy wrote the *Dynasts* he tried to make us see a vision of the universe, and of all living things striving and suffering, appearing and vanishing ceaselessly therein. To this end he summoned all the resources of his technique, both as lyric poet and as realistic novelist; and his work owes no small part of its greatness to the persistent concentration of all these means to this one end.

Whether such a work, whose stage is set in the imagination, can legitimately be called a drama, is, as Hardy says in the Preface, an unimportant matter of terminology; and the controversy of 1904 on this question is not worth reviving. Its only useful result was that the title was changed to the more accurate one of 'epic-drama.' The convincing justification for his drama is given in a letter in which Hardy defended himself against the critic of the *Times*. He wrote, in the *Times Literary Supplement* of February 2nd, 1904:

> The methods of a book and the methods of a play, which your critic says are so different, are fundamentally similar. It must be remembered that the printed story is not a representation, but, like the printed play, a means of producing a representation; which is done in one case by sheer imaginativeness, in the other by imaginativeness pieced out by material helps.

Those sentences are the complete explanation of the form of the *Dynasts*; it is the means of producing a representation in the mind.

We must not look in the *Dynasts* for a complete structure of action. As we are told in the Preface, the author assumed beforehand the completion of the action by the spectator already familiar with the fable.[1] The action, indeed, using the word in its usual sense, is not his primary concern at all. For the representation in his reader's imagination which he seeks is that of a spectacle of which *human* action is only a part, if an essential, because illustrative, part. We must also remember that the various settings of his scenes are to be considered, not, as in ordinary drama, simply accessories of the action; but as an integral part of the drama, often as important as the speeches and sometimes much more important. The best example of this is to be found in what, if we retain the inadequate terminology of acting drama, we must call the stage directions. Hardy's stage directions are, after the Spirits, his most successful innovation in the *Dynasts*. They are among his most powerful means of promoting imaginative representation. Perhaps the most original of them all is in the Forescene. We have been listening to the debate of the Spirits upon the eternal problems of suffering and freewill; and then we are called to see a vision:

> The nether sky opens, and Europe is disclosed as a prone and emaciated figure, the Alps like a backbone, and the branching mountain chains like ribs, the peninsular plateau of Spain forming a head. Broad and lengthy lowlands stretch from the north of France across Russia like a grey-green garment hemmed by the Ural mountains and the glistening Arctic Ocean.

To take a completely different instance, already mentioned, here is the stage direction at the beginning of Scene iv, Act v, Part i, describing the cockpit of the *Victory* where Nelson is dying:

> A din of trampling and dragging overhead, which is accompanied by a continuous ground-bass roar from the guns of the

---

[1] The allusion to Aeschylus in the Preface is not very helpful. What Verrall actually wrote in the Introduction to his edition of the Choephoroi was, not that it would be unintelligible without supplementary scenes of the imagination, but: 'Some indispensable parts of it are represented only by allusions . . . the author presumes us to be familiar with his conception (of Pylades and Strophius), and as a fact we are not.'

> warring fleets, culminating at times in loud concussions. The
> wounded are lying around in rows for treatment, some groan-
> ing, some silently dying, some dead. The gloomy atmosphere
> of the low-beamed deck is pervaded by a thick haze of smoke,
> powdered wood, and other dust, and is heavy with the fumes
> of gunpowder and candle grease, the odour of drugs and
> cordials, and the smell from abdominal wounds.

As a means of evocation, that would be hard to beat. A
third example, less well known and less striking, but equally
good as an illustration of the purpose of these stage directions, is from the closing phase of the battle at Waterloo,
when Ney's cavalry are trying madly to break the Allied
armies:

> The Allied squares stand like little red-brick castles, inde-
> pendent of each other, and motionless except at the dry,
> hurried command 'Close up' repeated every now and then as
> they are slowly thinned. On the other hand, under their firing
> and bayonets a disorder becomes apparent among the charging
> horse, on whose cuirasses the bullets snap like stones on
> window panes.

The technique of these paragraphs is interesting. Designed
to make the reader see, hear, feel and smell for himself the
scene described, they achieve their purpose by selecting a
few details, which are presented in extraordinarily vivid
phrases. Examples in which one detail is specially selected
are these: Scene vi, Act vi, Part 2, describing the evening of
the ball at Carlton House:

> It is a cloudless midsummer evening, and as the west fades
> the stars beam down upon the city, the evening star hanging
> like a jonquil blossom.

At the end of Scene vii, Act i, Part 3, describing the burning
of Moscow:

> Explosions and hissings are constantly audible, amid which
> can be fancied cries and yells of people caught in the com-
> bustion. Large pieces of canvas aflare sail away on the gale like
> balloons. Cocks crow, thinking it sunrise, ere they are burnt
> to death.

Towards the end of Scene ii, Act i, Part 3, describing the sufferings of the French soldiers abandoned by Napoleon on the dreadful retreat from Moscow:

> Exhausted, they crouch round the fire. Officers and privates press together for warmth. Other stragglers arrive and sit at the backs of the first. With the progress of the night the stars come out in unusual brilliancy, Sirius and those in Orion flashing like stilettos; and the frost stiffens.

Nothing could more vividly convey the sense of terrible cold than that detail of the stars in Orion 'flashing like stilettos.' Hardy has been classed among the realistic novelists by those who like classifications. The stage directions in the *Dynasts* show one side of his realism more strikingly than anything in the novels.

Probably the supreme example of this method, whereby the writer supplies what is necessary for the evocation, in the imagination of his reader, of the scene he desires to depict, is the scene of the burial of Sir John Moore at Coruña (Sc. iv, Act iii, Pt. 2):

> It is just before dawn, objects being still indistinct. The features of the elevated enclosure of San Carlos can be recognized in dim outline, and also those of the old Town of Coruna around, though scarcely a lamp is shining. The numerous transports in the harbour beneath have still their riding-lights burning. In a nook of the town walls a lantern glimmers. Some English soldiers of the Ninth regiment are hastily digging a grave there with extemporized tools.
>
> A Voice (from the gloom some distance off): 'I am the resurrection and the life, saith the Lord: he that believeth in me, though he were dead, yet shall he live.'
>
> The soldiers look up, and see entering at the further end of the patch of ground a slow procession. It advances by the light of lanterns in the hands of some members of it. At moments the fitful rays fall upon bearers carrying a coffinless body rolled in a blanket, with a military cloak roughly thrown over by way of pall.

The use, in that setting, of the English Burial Service, with all its associations, is the touch of a master.

The last example leads on to a more vital matter; for it introduces into the mental picture a higher order of impressions than the purely sensory. Here we come upon the central feature of the *Dynasts*, which both makes it what it is and makes it unique. This is what are called in the list of dramatis personæ the Phantom Intelligences. The Spirits are not a mere framework in the *Dynasts*; they are its vital substance. For them the human play is played; and by them, not only is the unity of action achieved, but the action is given significance. It is they who build what without them would be a mere confused welter of events, into a vast tragedy of existence. Professor Allardyce Nichol has reminded us[1] that

> Whenever a tragedy lacks the feeling of universality, whenever it presents merely the temporary and the topical, the detached in time and in place, then it becomes simply sordid. The cardinal element in high tragedy is universality.

That universality is produced in the *Dynasts* by the Spirits. The paragraph devoted to them in the Preface does not sufficiently stress their fundamental importance; but then it is not the business of the poet to explain what he has done to those who cannot see it for themselves. Hardy explained the Pities as approximating to the Greek chorus described by Schlegel as 'the Universal Sympathy of human nature.' The passage is in the fifth of Schlegel's *Lectures on Dramatic Art*:

> We must consider it (the Chorus) as a persistent reflection on the action which is going on; the incorporation into the representation itself of the sentiments of the poet.[2]

That is certainly the starting point, not only of the Pities, but also of all the other Spirits in the *Dynasts*. They were first of all conceived as personified reflection, as Ideal Spectators. The Spirit of the Years voices this conception when he says

---

[1] *An Introduction to Dramatic Theory* (1931), p. 71.
[2] The Translation quoted is that in Bohn's series (1846), which Hardy probably used.

> The ruling was that we should witness things,
> And not dispute them.

But in point of fact, if the Spirits did nothing but witness, they would be complete cyphers and there would be no drama. It is the reaction of the Spirits to what they see, and their interactions among each other, that make the play. And this brings us to the characterization of them, a far more important feature of the *Dynasts* than has hitherto been perceived.

Before we go on, however, to consider the subtler and deeper rôle of the Spirits, something must be said of their more obvious part in the structure of the epic-drama. It is they who provide Hardy with his most potent means of inducing imaginative representation. With them, he can do much more—even by way of giving purely sensory impressions—than with mere stage directions. An example too long to quote, which needs no comment, is Scene ix, Act i, Part 3. Nearly always, however, the Spirits convey much more than simple sensory impressions; what they see, and make us see, is that deeper reality which the eye cannot perceive; for example, in Scene v, Act vi, Part 3:

SPIRIT OF THE PITIES:
> I see an unnatural Monster, loosely jointed,
> With an Apocalyptic Being's shape,
> And limbs and eyes a hundred thousand strong,
> And fifty thousand heads; which coils itself
> About the buildings there,

SPIRIT OF THE YEARS:
>   Thou dost indeed.
> It is the Monster Devastation. Watch.

There are dozens of such examples, in which the Spirits provide Hardy with the means of describing, not only the external appearance of a scene and the progress of the action, but the inner significance of these, and their relationship to the other parts of the drama, and to the whole. A very striking instance, too long to quote, is the description of Walcheren by a chorus of Pities (Sc. viii, Act iv, Pt. 2).

But the best of all is provided by the treatment of the battles in the Peninsula. Only one of these, Coruña, contains any appreciable length of dialogue. There is a little speech in Salamanca. Vimiero is described wholly in stage direction. The rest, Talavera, Albuera and Vitoria, are presented wholly through the eyes of the Spirits, with a few auxiliary stage directions. The most memorable of them is Albuera, presented from the moment when the Spirit of the Years says

> A hot ado goes forward here to-day,
> If I may read the Immanent Intent
>   From signs and tokens blent
> With weird unrest along the firmament—

And the Spirit of the Pities replies

> I see red smears upon the sickly dawn,
> And seeming drops of gore.

The three and a half pages that follow are remarkably condensed writing. They convey to us, not only all the outward incidents of that murderous day, but also all the horror and all the futility of it. The climax, describing the advance of the 'astonishing infantry' immortalized by Napier, is given to semichoruses of the Pities:

> They come, beset by riddling hail;
> They sway like sedges in a gale;
> They fail and win, and win and fail. Albuera!
>
> They gain the ground there, yard by yard,
> Their brows and hair and lashes charred,
> Their blackened teeth set firm and hard.
>
> Their mad assailants rave and reel,
> And face, as men who scorn to feel
> The close-lined, three-edged prongs of steel.
>
> Till faintness follows closing-in,
> When, faltering headlong down, they spin
> Like leaves. But those pay well who win Albuera.

Out of six thousand souls that sware
To hold the mount, or pass elsewhere,
But eighteen hundred muster there.

Pale Colonels, Captains, ranksmen lie,
Facing the earth or facing sky;—
They strove to live, they stretch to die.

Friends, foemen, mingle; heap and heap—
Hide their hacked bones, Earth!—deep, deep, deep,
Where harmless worms caress and creep.

Chorus

Hide their hacked bones, Earth! deep, deep, deep,
Where harmless worms caress and creep—
What man can grieve? What woman weep?
Better than waking is to sleep! Albuera!

In this, and many other famous passages, the Spirits are a real chorus, whose part is commentary and interpretation, but not action. The choruses upon Walcheren and Albuera, with the difference that they also describe what they interpret, are artistically comparable with the lament of the Elders of Thebes over Oedipus:

$$ἰὼ \ γενεαὶ \ βροτῶν$$
$$ὡς \ ὑμᾶς \ ἴσα \ καὶ \ τὸ \ μηδὲν \ ζώσας \ ἐναριθμῶ$$

But—and this is Hardy's great innovation—the Spirits of the *Dynasts* are much more than a simple chorus. They are also the characters. Indeed, they are the only true characters, if we may use the word in such a sense. In the full, technical sense, as we use it, of Shakespeare's personages, Hardy's Spirits are hardly 'characters.' But in the sense that they alone among the dramatis personæ act as independent beings, endowed with freewill and free judgment, the Spirits are the real characters in the *Dynasts*.

It has often been pointed out that the philosophic determinism of Hardy's epic-drama excluded characterization, in the higher sense, altogether. While critics have praised the individualization of the minor personages, they have con-

curred in regretting the absence of character in the major
ones. None of the great historical figures who come upon
the stage in the *Dynasts* is convincing. Napoleon, Alexander,
Wellington and the rest are, in Hardy's hands, little better
than puppets. We feel this least, perhaps, with Nelson; for
his appearance is too brief to demand that larger characterization which we miss in the others. The great example
of Hardy's failure with historical character is Napoleon. It
has been very truly said that 'To the understanding of
Napoleon the poet of the *Dynasts* contributes nothing.'[1]
But he not only contributes nothing; he darkens counsel in
respect of him, making him almost unintelligible. He makes
us dislike Napoleon, both as an ambitious politician who
does not scruple to wade through blood to his own ends,
and as an individual who is selfish in his intimate personal
relationships, caddish, mean and even cowardly; while of
his greatness we are given no inkling. This is wholly unconvincing. Either Napoleon was a man, in which case,
like Coriolanus, he can be great as well as little, and we can
set his greatness against his littleness; or else he was a mere
puppet of the Immanent Will, and therefore no more
morally responsible for his heartless usage of Josephine
than for winning Austerlitz. Hardy cannot have it both
ways. As he himself makes Napoleon say to the Ironic
Spirit, when shown the 'little moral panorama' of all the
victims of his wars at the end of Scene iii, Act vi, Part 3:

> Why hold me my own master if I be
> Ruled by the pitiless Planet of Destiny?

This is one of the dilemmas in which Hardy's philosophy
landed him. No kind of drama, epic or any other, is possible
in the absence of character; and character is incompatible
with the doctrine that all human beings are simply lobules
of the one brain, the Immanent Will. Hardy no doubt felt
this; and tried to overcome it by introducing a convention
to disregard it. Says the Spirit of the Years:

> 'But this no further now. Deem yet man's deeds self-done.'

[1] J. Bailey: *The Continuity of Letters* (1923), p. 237

Actually, however, we cannot disregard it. We are continually reminded of it when the type becomes italic. And this
is a blot upon the *Dynasts*. At the same time—and this
redeeming feature partly reconciles us to such automatism
—it is auxiliary to Hardy's main purpose. For, though we
cannot regard the human personages as characters sufficiently individual to interest in themselves, we can, and do,
regard them as victims. They are not masters of their fate;
they even have no influence upon their fate; but they are
capable of suffering. Here is the connecting link between
the *Dynasts* and Hardy's later novels. The *Dynasts*, however,
would be a very poor affair had it no characters more significant than merely passive ones. The progress of that
deterministic philosophy which makes *Jude the Obscure*, for
all its powerful writing, so much less great than *Tess*,
continued in Hardy's mind rapidly; and the human characters in the *Dynasts* are not even remotely, as Jude was at
least partly, responsible for the sufferings they undergo.
Great literature cannot be made with mere puppets, even
sentient ones. The character essential to a significant drama
Hardy provided in the Spirits.

Although this does not appear to have been pointed out
hitherto, it is the characterization of the Spirits which carries
the whole structure. The Spirits, although described as
abstractions, are real personalities. The chief of them, in
character as well as in the part he plays, is the Ancient
Spirit of the Years. His utterances have an austere and
sometimes rugged grandeur which is not only all their own,
but also make an impression out of all proportion to their
actual length in the text. Particularly impressive examples
are to be found in those speeches which are addressed to
human beings, above whose puny intellect and limited
vision the Ancient Spirit seems to tower like a colossus.
Thus, he prophesies to Perceval during the ball at Carlton
House:

believe
Before five more have joined the shotten years

335

Whose useless films infest the foggy Past,
Traced thick with teachings glimpsed unheedingly,
The rawest Dynast of the group concerned
Will, for the good or ill of mute mankind,
Down-topple to the dust like soldier Saul,
And Europe's mouldy-minded oligarchs
Be propped anew; while garments roll in blood,
To confused noise, with burning and fuel of fire.

He has, indeed, an apt turn for literary allusion. He rebukes
the Spirit Sinister as 'Thou Iago of the incorporeal world.'
He says to Napoleon, after his stumble at the Niemen,

The portent is an ill one, Emperor;
An ancient Roman would retire thereat!

More impressively, he quotes Latin in the wood of Bossu:

'Sic diis immortalibus placet'—
Thus is it pleasing to the immortal gods,
As earthlings used to say.

Often as he rebukes them for their illogicality, the Spirit of
the Years is himself not wholly devoid of the feelings of the
Pities; indeed, in the Afterscene he confesses that in his
youth he also was an idealist! But even in his old age, when
asked if he is going to speak 'ere the close' to the dying
Pitt, he replies:

Nay, I have spoke too often. Time and time,
When all Earth's light has lain on the nether side,
And yapping midnight winds have leapt on roofs,
And raised for him an evil harlequinade
Of national disasters in long train,
That tortured him with harrowing grimace,
Have I communed with that intelligence.
Now I would leave him to pass out in peace,
And seek the silence unperturbedly.

And to the sarcastic comment of the Ironic Spirit he replies
with a dignified rebuff. Unquestionably, the significance of
the Spirit of the Years in the drama is to impart a consciousness of the transience and insignificance of all human
endeavour and suffering when seen in the scale of the vast,

impersonal universe. This he does most effectively. To the
laments of the Pities over the horrors of Walcheren, he
replies:

> Why must ye echo as mechanic mimes
> These mortal minions' bootless cadences,
> Played on the stops of their anatomy
> As is the mewling music on the strings
> Of yonder ship masts by the unweeting wind,
> Or the frail tune upon this withering sedge
> That holds its papery blades against the gale?
> —Men pass to dark corruption at the best,
> Ere I can count five score; these why not now?
> The Immanent Shaper builds Its beings so
> Whether ye sigh their sighs with them or no!

And at the very end of the earthly drama, when he and his
fellow Spirits have communed in the wood of Bossu with
the Emperor in the hour of his overthrow, he sums up the
whole thus:

> Worthless these kneadings of thy narrow thought,
> Napoleon; gone thy opportunity!
> Such men as thou, who wade across the world
> To make an epoch, bless, confuse, appal,
> Are in the elemental ages' chart
> Like meanest insects on obscurest leaves
> But incidents and grooves of Earth's unfolding;
> Or as the brazen rod that stirs the fire
> Because it must.

If, while we read the *Dynasts*, we imaginatively share that
feeling—as we do—it is not from any intellectual acceptance of Hardy's philosophy, but from the artistic presentation of it through the character of the Ancient Spirit of the
Years, which wins us to what Coleridge called 'poetic faith.'

The Pities hardly require comment, for their significance
is obvious enough. They are, in Schlegel's words, 'the in-
corporation into the representation itself of the sentiments
of the poet.'[1] Considered psychologically—and it is surprising that this does not seem to have been done—they

[1] *Op. cit.*, Lecture 5.

are the inevitable outcome of, and climax to, Hardy's growing quarrel with the 'sorry scheme of things,' which finds vent with progressive violence in the later novels. This comment, we have seen, is a blemish in the novels, where it is inartistic because intrusive; but in the *Dynasts* it is an organic part of the fabric. Moreover, and this is important, it becomes convincing in the *Dynasts* because it is presented to us, not abstractly, as in the novels, but through the medium of a personality, the personality of the Spirit of the Pities. When Hardy in his own person reviles 'a morality good enough for divinities, but scorned by average human nature,' or bursts out 'Justice was done, and the President of the Immortals had finished his sport with Tess,' he fails to carry that conviction which the Pities carry when they cry after Nelson's death

> His thread was cut too slowly! When he fell
> And bade his fame farewell,
> He might have passed, and shunned his long-drawn pain,
> Endured in vain, in vain!

The difference does not chiefly reside in the fact that what is only sporadic comment in the novels becomes persistent and ordered statement in the play. It lies in the fact that in the play, the appeal is made through the medium of a personality which we feel to be real. The unquestionably tragic effect of the later novels, is, as we have seen, also partly achieved through personality imaginatively realized. The Pities are a dramatic projection into character of the spirit which conceived the later novels. Their persistent, bitter and sometimes passionate arraignment of the First Cause is the formulation of the deepest emotion of Hardy's soul. The most persistent and inescapable theme of his art, whether in prose or verse, is put into their lips

> O, the intolerable antilogy
> Of making figments feel!

That comes home to us, as no argument can; for we feel that the speaker of it is a living and actual personality.

Because he, too, springs from the depths of Hardy's own

nature, and is strongly characterized also, the Spirit Ironic is another most successful innovation. The ironic—sometimes too bitterly ironic—side of Hardy's personality is evident enough in the novels, where it often fails from overstatement. Several instances have been mentioned in *Jude*; and the same condemnation falls upon many of his short stories, one volume of which bears the significant title, *Life's Little Ironies*. It falls also upon such verses as those which compose *Time's Laughingstocks*. Another similar title, which in this case does less than justice to the contents, is *Satires of Circumstance*. In the *Dynasts*, the Ironies never go beyond verisimilitude; and often they are very effective; as when, in the middle of the battle of Talavera, the enemies drink together at the same brook (Sc. v, Act iv, Pt. 2), and the Ironic Spirit says:

> It is only that Life's queer mechanics chance to work out in this grotesque shape just now. The groping tentativeness of an Immanent Will (as grey old Years describes it) cannot be asked to learn logic at this time of day. The spectacle of Its instruments, set to riddle one another through and then to drink together in peace and concord, is where the humour comes in, and makes the play worth seeing!

To which the Spirit Sinister replies:

> Come, Sprite, don't carry your ironies too far, or you may wake up the Unconscious Itself, and tempt It to let all the gory clockwork of the show run down to spite me!

Another very telling touch is at the famous ball in Brussels, before Waterloo, at the climax of which the Spirit Ironic remarks:

> Methinks flirtation grows too tender here!

It is difficult to see how other means could effect what that effects so vividly and neatly.

But perhaps the greatest merit of the Ironies is not their comment on the doings of the Immanent Will—there is enough such comment already, without them—but their importation into the drama of the nearest approach to artificial comedy that it affords. Comedy of the simple sort, the comedy of country folk, soldiers and so on, there is in plenty. Something of a more advanced order is also required; and it is the Ironies who supply it, as far as it is supplied at all. The chief instance is in Scene vi, Act vi, Part 2; in this, the Spirit Ironic, with the assistance of the Spirit of Rumour (a useful accessory on several occasions to his more enterprising Phantom brethren) produces a farce with Caroline of Brunswick and 'the Fitzherbert Fair,' both of whom he induces to come to the Prince Regent's ball at Carlton House. Although abjured by the Spirit of the Years to

> Cease fooling on weak waifs who love and wed
> But as the unweeting Urger may bestead!

the Ironic Spirit persists in his little comedy, goes himself to the ball, where he tells the Spirit of the Pities—whom he addresses as 'My dear phantom and crony'—that the gloom of the guests is due to their having borrowed their diamonds at eleven per cent., and finally drives the Prince Regent to exclaim:

> 'Od seize 'em, Moira; this will drive me mad!

Indeed, he only desists from his antics when he has provoked the Ancient Spirit of the Years to a generalization upon the character of women, an indiscretion which one so experienced would surely avoid in cold blood! All this is good fooling. Both here and elsewhere, it provides a needed foil to the continual tragedy.

The Spirit Sinister is a less successful figure, considered on his pretensions. He is, in fact, hardly ever sinister, and is best regarded as a grimmer and more cynical Spirit Ironic. In this rôle he often comes into collision with the Spirit of the Pities; who, Scene ii, Act i, Part 1, says to him:

> O say no more;
> If aught could gratify the Absolute
> 'Twould verily be thy censure, not thy praise!

And when, in Scene iii, Act iv, Part 1, he chuckles over the perplexities of General Mack:

> The Will throws Mack again in agitation:
> Ho-ho!—what he'll do now!

the Spirit of the Pities rebukes him again:

> Nay, hard one, nay!
> The clouds weep for him!

At the scene of the crowning of Napoleon in Milan Cathedral, he is in very good form, and quizzes the archbishop

> Do not the prelate's accents falter thin,
> His lips with inheld laughter grow deformed,
> While blessing one whose aim is but to win
> The golden seats that other b——s have warmed?

And to the complaint of the Shade of the Earth that nature is ruled by laws inexorable, he answers:

> The lady's remark is apposite, and reminds me that I may as well hold my tongue as desired. For if my casual scorn, Father Years, should set thee trying to prove that there is any right or reason in the Universe, thou wilt not accomplish it by doomsday! Small blame to her, however; she must cut her coat according to her cloth, as they would say below there.

Such obstreperousness goads the Spirit of the Years, who has already told him once to be quiet and behave himself, to a sharp retort:

> O would that I could move It to enchain thee,
> And shut thee up a thousand years—(to cite
> A grim terrestrial tale of one thy like)
> Thou Iago of the incorporeal world,
> 'As they would say below there—'

One of these unflattering comparisons raises an interesting speculation. Was the Spirit Sinister suggested to Hardy by Mephistopheles in Goethe's *Faust*? Although he had not German enough to appreciate the original, he certainly knew it in translation; and the Spirit Sinister has just the tone of Mephisto in his lighter moods; as when, for instance, after his colloquy with the Almighty in the Prologue, he says:

> Es ist gar hübsch von einem grossen Herrn
> So menschlich mit dem Teufel selbst zu sprechen!

Sometimes the Spirit Sinister can be sinister in good earnest, as when, at the beginning of the Russian campaign, he overhears Napoleon humming 'Malbrough s'en va-t-en guerre,' and concludes the last verse for him, with the observation 'It is kind of his Imperial Majesty to give me a lead':—

> Monsieur d'Malbrough est mort,
> Est mort et enterré!

Various minor Phantoms, such as the Shade of the Earth (imitated out of *Prometheus Unbound*) and the Spirit of Rumour, call for no comment; they are hardly characterized. The Rumours on several occasions follow the tradition of comical intervention in human affairs set by the Spirit Ironic. The best instance is Scene vii, Act vi, Part 1, in which the Spirit of Rumour descends to Paris, and interviews a member of the *demi-monde*, who is waiting for the return of the French armies from Austerlitz, and whose conversation pleases him so much that he says he could give ear to it all night. She naturally asks him the usual question, to which he replies:

> Thou knowest not what thy frailty asks, good dame!

Eventually, however, his intimate knowledge of European affairs appears to her uncanny, and she leaves him:

> I like not your queer knowledge, creepy man.
> Adieu. I'll not be yours to-night, I'd starve first!

This very clever scene is introduced in order that Hardy may show how the realization that Trafalgar was the naval death of France (as Southey described it), was carefully kept from the French populace.

It is the Spirits who are the only real characters in the *Dynasts*; we *feel* that they are free agents (despite sundry unconvincing reminders to the contrary, as when the Spirit of the Years says 'I am but an accessory of Its works'). We also feel that their judgment is free, and therefore worthy of respect. And this is the crux of the whole matter. For, while monism and immanentism may or may not be satisfactory as purely intellectual concepts, you can do nothing with them in art. You cannot even present the Immanent Will and Its workings unless you can succeed in getting outside It. This is what the Spirits enable Hardy to do. It is not until, with them, he can contemplate the Universe from without, that he can convey the sense of universal tragedy which makes the *Dynasts* a great work. This brings us to the heart of Hardy's masterpiece. Its universality and its significance as art lie in its vision—a vision of the whole world, and of the worlds beyond the world; and of the life that strives and suffers in them. This vision is achieved wholly through the Spirits. In them, the *Dynasts* rises at times to astonishing greatness. One such peak is the close of Scene iv, Act v, Part 1. Another is the deservedly famous chorus before Austerlitz:

> Stand ye apostrophising That
> Which, working all, works but thereat
> Like some sublime fermenting vat—

Another is that terrible and admirable scene in the King's apartments in Windsor Castle (Sc. v, Act vi, Pt. 2), which makes the Spirit of the Pities cry :

> Something within me aches to pray
> To some great Heart, to take away
> This evil day, this evil day!

And the Ironies reply:

> Ha-ha! That's good. Thou'lt pray to It:—
> But where do Its compassions sit?
> Yea, where abides the heart of It?
>
> Is it where sky-fires flame and flit,
> Or solar craters spew and spit,
> Or ultra-stellar night-webs knit?

The most famous of all, and perhaps the best, is the chorus

that comes before Waterloo. This is so good and so characteristic that it may be quoted entire:

CHORUS OF THE YEARS (aerial music):
    The eyelids of eve fall together at last,
    And the forms so foreign to field and tree
    Lie down as though native, and slumber fast!

CHORUS OF THE PITIES:
    Sore are the thrills of misgiving we see
    In the artless champaign at this harlequinade,
    Distracting a vigil where calm should be!

    The green seems oppressed, and the Plain afraid
    Of a Something to come, whereof these are the proofs—
    Neither earthquake nor storm nor eclipse's shade!

CHORUS OF THE YEARS:
    Yea, the coneys are scared by the thud of hoofs,
    And their white scuts flash at their vanishing heels,
    And swallows abandon the hamlet roofs.

    The mole's tunnelled chambers are crushed by wheels,
    The lark's eggs scattered, their owners fled;
    And the hedgehog's household the sapper unseals.

    The snail draws in at the terrible tread,
    But in vain; he is crushed by the felloe-rim;
    The worm asks what can be overhead,

    And wriggles deep from a scene so grim,
    And guesses him safe; for he does not know
    What a foul red flood will be soaking him!

    Beaten about by the heel and toe
    Are butterflies, sick of the day's long rheum,
    To die of a worse than the weather-foe.

    Trodden and bruised to a miry tomb
    Are ears that have greened but will never be gold,
    And flowers in the bud that will never bloom.

CHORUS OF THE PITIES:
So the season's intent, ere its fruit unfold,
Is frustrate and mangled and made succumb,
Like a youth of promise struck stark and cold!

And what of these who to-night have come?

CHORUS OF THE YEARS:
The young sleep sound; but the weather awakes
In the veterans pains from the past that numb;

Old stabs of Ind, old Peninsula aches,
Old Friedland chills, haunt their moist mud bed,
Cramps from Austerlitz; till their slumber breaks.

CHORUS OF SINISTER SPIRITS:
And each soul shivers as sinks his head
On the loam he's to lease with the other dead
From to-morrow's mist-fall till Time be sped!

Of that, it need only be said that its greatness as poetry lies
less in its language than in its symbolism. The agony of the
soldier and the agony of the snail are one; no more and no
less than the agony wherewith the whole creation groaneth
and travaileth together until this hour.

Comparisons are often misleading. And yet, if the critic
is properly to do his business of helping to a full understanding of the work upon which he comments, some comparison—or rather in this case contrast—is essential. For
the *Dynasts* is a great tragedy; but Hardy's conception and
presentation of the tragic fact are so different from anything
familiar in English literature that recollections of earlier
English tragedies are likely to prove a stumbling-block.
There is no space here to examine the various conceptions
of tragedy in literature; this would demand, among other
things, detailed attention to Attic drama; and one familiar
with the complexities and subtleties of that is likely to be
able to find his way into any drama unaided. But to the
reader whose principal training in such matters has been

Shakespeare, Hardy's tragic conception is likely at first to prove baffling. For it is almost the exact opposite to the conception of Shakespeare; and yet not wholly alien from it. This is best made clear by taking the chief elements of Shakespearian tragedy, as they are analysed by A. C. Bradley in the first chapter of his book, *Shakespearian Tragedy*, and comparing them one by one with what we find in the *Dynasts*. It must, of course, be added that the phrase 'Shakespearian tragedy' is here used only with reference to the *thought* of Shakespeare's tragic plays; no comparison is attempted with Shakespearian tragedy as a form of literature.

Some points of direct contrast are at once obvious; and they include the most important characteristics of Shakespearian tragedy. To Shakespeare, tragedy must be a calamity which is exceptional. To quote Bradley: 'A tale of a man slowly worn to death by disease, poverty, little cares, sordid vices, petty persecutions, however piteous or dreadful it might be, would not be tragic in the Shakespearian sense.' But this is precisely the essence of tragedy in the Hardyan sense. It is the supreme impression left by the *Dynasts* that tragedy, so far from being exceptional, is universal; and it is just the consciousness of the one overwhelming tragedy composed of all the futile, unremembered tragedies of everyday existence, that Hardy desires to impart. Then, to Shakespeare, the suffering and calamity must befall one in an exalted station. The fall of such an one, says Bradley, 'produces a sense of contrast, of the powerlessness of man and of the omnipotence—perhaps the caprice—of Fortune or Fate, which no tale of private life can possibly rival.' This, of course, is the old idea of tragedy, as 'casus virorum illustrium,' the tragedy of which Chaucer gave a famous definition, and in the main it is, as Bradley says, that of Shakespeare; though even in Shakespeare, there is tragedy outside the ranks of kings and nobles, of which the Fool in *Lear* is the famous example. But when we come to Hardy, the position is completely reversed. It is the tragedy of a man, not the tragedy of his greatness, which interests Hardy. The most famous of his writings tells the tragedy of a milkmaid; and in the *Dynasts* we are shown the tragedy of the humble ones who fight and die, rather than that of the great ones who scheme and plan, and send men to their deaths by thousands. Then again; to Shakespeare, as Bradley points out, 'the suffering and calamity must not merely befall a man, he must have a part in it. . . . The effect of such a series (of actions) on imagination is to make us regard the sufferings which accompany it and the catastrophe in which it ends, not merely or chiefly as something which happens to the persons concerned, but equally as something which is caused by them. . . . The centre of the tragedy may be said to lie in action issuing from character, or in character issuing in action.' It was in this that Shakespeare's main interest lay; and it is here that we find the greatest contrast when we read Hardy; for the two poets are at opposite poles of thought with respect to this. Hardy's main interest, not only in the *Dynasts*, but throughout his whole creative writing, lies in the tragedy which befalls human beings, but in the causation of which they have little or no part.

The conflict inseparable from tragedy—that conflict of which Hegel has given us the classic theory—is to be found, in Shakespearian tragedy, chiefly in the souls of the heroes. The great instance is, of course, Hamlet; and it is in depicting this internal conflict that Shakespeare puts forth, perhaps, his greatest power. Now, in Hardyan tragedy, and this applies as much to the great novels—with the possible exception of *The Mayor of Casterbridge*—as to the *Dynasts*, there is no such conflict; for the reason that the catastrophe is imposed from without. The tragedies of Tess and Jude, and the essentially similar tragedies of George III and Nelson in the *Dynasts*, do not arise from conflict in the hero's soul; they are dealt out by blind and merciless destiny. At first sight, indeed, it would seem that Hardy's conception of tragedy included no element of conflict at all, but was simply that of a 'President of the Immortals' or an 'Immanent Will'—whichever it happens to be called—doing men and women to death. A closer examination will, however, reveal that the sense of tragedy in Hardy does result from conflict. The essence of Hardy's presentation of the tragic fact is the conflict between the limited and fallible, but conscious and directed, will of the individual towards ordered well being; and the unlimited and all-powerful, but unconscious and senseless, urge of an 'Immanent Will' to continuing but purposeless existence. And this brings us to some aspects of Hardyan tragedy which, while different from Shakespearian tragedy, have yet affinities with it. Bradley contends that Shakespeare makes very sparing use of tragic accident, and that even when he uses it, only does so when the action is so well advanced that the impression of causal sequence is too firmly fixed to be impaired. Nevertheless, he admits Shakespeare's use of tragic accident; and his own list of examples may be given. Romeo never got the Friar's message; Juliet did not awaken a moment sooner; Edgar arrived just too late to save Cordelia; Desdemona dropped her handkerchief at the most fatal moment; the pirates' attack on Hamlet's ship enabled him to return forthwith to Denmark. Now, such a use of tragic accident is one of the outstanding characteristics of Hardy's tragedy; more especially, as we have seen, in the novels, where it is often used to the point of becoming unconvincing. It was his favourite method of producing catastrophe; and by its very fortuitousness added greatly to the feeling of 'crass casualty.' In the *Dynasts* there is one notable passage in which the Spirit of the Years is made to say:

> The cognizance ye mourn, life's doom to feel,
> If I report it meetly, came unmeant,
> Emerging with blind gropes from impercipience
> By listless sequence—luckless, tragic chance,
> In your more human tongue.

In other words, the whole tragedy of all sentient life is

simply fortuitous; fortuitous also is the greatest tragedy of all, that we should be capable of perceiving it! Reviewing the *Dynasts*, Sir Henry Newbolt suggested an inconsistency between Hardy's 'clock-work universe' and chance. But there is no inconsistency if by 'chance' we understand—as Hardy certainly did—*apparent* absence of causation. We call events accidental of which the causes are wholly unknown to, and unsuspected by, us. But causation is nevertheless present, and can have been predetermined. The question of predetermination, however, raises a much more formidable difficulty, and brings us up against a blemish in the philosophy of the *Dynasts*.

We are told, not once but many times, that everything, even to the minutest event, is rigidly determined from all eternity.

> Ere systemed suns were globed and lit
> The slaughters of the race were writ,
> And wasting wars by land and sea
> Fixed, like all else, immutably.
>
> (Sc. v, Act ii, Pt. i.)

And again:

> O Innocents, can ye forget
> That things to be were shaped and set
> Ere mortals and this planet met?
>
> (Sc. iii, Act vi, Pt. i.)

The Pities might well have replied that their innocence did not extend to the logic upon which the Years are always priding themselves, and that they could not swallow such an argument. For the freedom of the Immanent Will is logically incompatible with such determinism. We are told that everything is caused by the blind desire-to-exist of this Will. So far, so good. But if the Immanent Will simply exists, and by the process of Its existence causes all phenomena, it is clear that there can be no predetermined phenomena. Hardy cannot have it both ways. Either everything is predetermined; or else everything is caused by the gropings of the Will. Either of these propositions may be true; they cannot both be. It does not help to say, in Schopenhauer's language, that the Will is not subject to the *principium individuationis*; for predeterminism involves subjection to time. If the events of the year 1805 were, as we are told, 'fixed like all else immutably' before the sun emerged from a spiral nebula, then the unfortunate Will, so far from being free to grope comfortably, is to all eternity bound to follow the syllabus drawn up by Itself in an unspecified past. To ask us to believe that It drew up such a syllabus and is capable of adhering thereto indefinitely in the minutest particulars, while at the same time devoid of the least rudiments of intelligence, is to ask too much!

Hardy professed to be indifferent to inconsistencies in the philosophy of the *Dynasts*, on the ground that he did not advance the work as a system of thought, but as a poem.[1] And yet in the fifth paragraph of his Preface he not only shows a desire for the intellectual acceptance of his work; he also goes out of his way to tell believers in a personal Deity that they are intellectually out of date. It would have been well for one who so summarily rated all believers in God out of the order of thinkers, after the manner of the once Reverend Leslie Stephen, to look a little more carefully into his own logic.

Hardy's stature as an artist is so much greater than as a thinker that it is pleasant to return to his conception of tragedy. Bradley says that one of the strongest impressions left by Shakespearian tragedy is the impression of waste: 'We seem to have before us a type of the mystery of the whole world, the tragic fact which extends beyond the limits of tragedy. Everywhere, from the crushed rocks beneath our feet to the soul of man, we see power, intelligence, life and glory, which astound us and seem to call for our worship. And everywhere we see them perishing, devouring one another, and destroying themselves, often

[1] *Later Years*, pp. 125–6.

with dreadful pain, as though they had come into being for no other end.' Those words, though they were written of Shakespeare, are even more appropriate to Hardy. Here, in the mystery of the tragic fact of existence, which has its testimony in human experience in all times and lands, the great English poet of the seventeenth, and the great English poet of the nineteenth, century stretch out their hands to each other. And this leads us to ponder the evolution in human thought to which the successive interpretations of the tragic fact in literature bear witness. So vast a subject is clearly beyond the scope of any study devoted to a single author; but the student of so great and so recent an author as Hardy is often drawn to consider it, and especially when he reads the *Dynasts*. In Greek tragedy, the formulation of the tragic fact is, very broadly speaking, in ethical terms. Aeschylus is almost obsessed with the idea of justice and desert; and the *Oresteia*, like the Book of Job, is a statement of the problem of moral order. In Shakespeare, this question of moral order has receded into the background. In the reading of *King Lear* and *Hamlet* our imaginative experience does not include the conviction of a fixed and ultimate order of desert and justice. Bradley writes of Shakespearian tragedy: 'While we are in its world we watch what is, seeing that so it happened and must have happened, feeling that it is piteous, dreadful, awful, mysterious, but neither passing sentence on the agents nor asking whether the behaviour of the ultimate power towards them is just.' In Hardy, the further step has been taken. The whole of his most mature and significant writings are a passionate arraignment of the injustice of the ultimate power in the universe towards its creatures. Of these writings the *Dynasts* forms the great and noble culmination.

The limits of this study exclude the very interesting question of the influence of Hardy on the literature of our own day. That would furnish matter for another study of no small complexity. Reflection suggests that to Hardy, and more particularly to the *Dynasts*, may be directly traced.

much that is new and most characteristic in English letters in the post-war years. It may seem to many that this influence has not been a good one, if it is to be judged by some of the results. But of this it is yet too early to speak confidently. What matters is that thirty years since, the heritage of English letters was enriched by a work of the first magnitude. This fact in itself suggests that, despite appearances, English poetry is not dead; that the nightmares of its recent slumbers are in part due to the incomplete digestion of the *Dynasts*: and that in the fulness of time another great poet, whole in body and mind, will arise. His vision of the meaning of life may be a very different one from the great vision of gloom shown in the *Dynasts* to a disillusioned and sorely tried generation. Nevertheless, all English poets who are yet to come will owe an inescapable debt to the genius and the integrity of so great a predecessor.

APPENDIX I

LETTER FROM ALEXANDER MACMILLAN ON
THE POOR MAN & THE LADY

To THOMAS HARDY, Dorchester.   August 10th, 1868.

I have read through the novel you were so good as to send me with care and with much interest and admiration, but feeling at the same time that it has what seem to me fatal drawbacks to its success, and what, I think, judging the writer from the book itself, you would feel even more strongly—its truthfulness and justice.

Your description of country life among working men is admirable, and, though I can only judge of it from the corresponding life of Scotland, which I knew well when young, palpably truthful. Your pictures of character among Londoners, and especially the upper classes, are sharp, clear, incisive and in many respects true, but they are wholly dark—not a ray of light visible to relieve the darkness, and therefore exaggerated and untrue in their result. Their frivolity, heartlessness, selfishness are great and terrible, but there are other sides, and I can hardly conceive that they would do otherwise than what they (i.e. you?) seek to avoid, 'throw down the book in disgust.' Even the worst of them would hardly, I think, do the things that you describe them as doing. For instance, is it conceivable that any man, however base and soul-corrupted, would do as you make the Hon. Fay Allamont do at the close, accept an estimate for his daughter's tomb—*because it cost him nothing?* He had already so far broken through the prejudices of his class as to send for Strong in the hope of saving his daughter's life. Then is it at all possible that a public body would *in public* retract their award on the grounds you make them avow in the case of the Palace of Hobbies Company?

353

The utter heedlessness of *all* the conversation you give in drawing-rooms and ballrooms about the working classes, has some ground of truth, I fear, and might justly be scourged, as you aim at doing, but your chastisement would fall harmless from its very excess. Will's speech to the working men is full of wisdom (though, by the way, would he have told his own story in public, being, as you describe him, a man of substantially good taste?)—and you there yourself give good grounds for condemning very much that is in other parts of the book. Indeed, nothing could justify such a wholesale blackening of a class but large and intimate knowledge of it. Thackeray makes them not greatly better in many respects, but he gave many redeeming traits.

(Here follows a comparison, the substance of which is: 'He meant fair, you mean mischief,' but nothing is added about Hardy's novel.)

I like your tone infinitely better. But it seems to me that your black wash will not be recognized as anything more than ignorant misrepresentation. Of course I don't know what opportunities you have had of seeing the class you deal with. . . . But it is inconceivable to me that any considerable number of human beings—God's creatures—should be so bad without going to utter wreck in a week.

Of the story itself I hardly know what to say. I should fear it is very improbable, and would be looked on as a sort of Reynold's Miscellany affair, though your really admirable handling often gives a certain dignity and power that greatly redeems it. Much of the detail struck me as strained and unnatural. The scene in the church at midnight has poetical qualities—but could it happen? Then is it within the range of likelihood that *any* gentleman would pursue his wife at midnight and *strike* her? Though you give a good deal about the family life afterwards, there is nothing to justify that very exceptional scene. It is too palpably done to bring about a meeting of the lovers.

Much of the writing seems to me admirable. The scene in Rotten Row—seen as it is and described by an outsider

—is full of real power and insight. And the characters, on the whole, seem to me finely conceived and presented. The fault of the book, as it seems to me, is that it lacks the *modesty of nature* of fact. *Romeo and Juliet* and *Hamlet* have many unnatural scenes, but Shakespeare puts them in foreign countries, and took the scenes from old books. When he was nearer home and in his own time you don't find such things in his writing. King Cophetua and the beggar maid made a pretty tale in an old ballad; but will a story in which the Duke of Edinburgh takes in lawful wedlock even a private gentleman's daughter? One sees in the papers accounts of gentlemen's daughters running away with their fathers' grooms, but you are not in that region. Given your characters, could it happen in the present day? The 'modesty of nature' takes into account all conditions.

You see I am writing to you as a writer who seems to me, at least potentially, of considerable mark, of power and purpose. If this is your first book I think you ought to go on. May I ask if it is, and—you are not a lady, so perhaps you will forgive the question—are you young?

I have shown your MS. to one friend, whose judgment coincides with my own—I wish to show it to another man of a different stamp of mind, who knows more of the upper class than either, and is yet a very noble fellow, that I may get his view as to whether it would do with modifications. Would you be willing to consider any suggestions?

P.S. I have just got my friend to write his opinion in his own words, and I enclose it. I mean the one who has already had the MS.

LIST OF HARDY'S WRITINGS[1]

Items which are recorded but cannot now be traced are given in brackets.

Between 1857 and 1860. *Domicilium*. A Poem.

(*Circa* 1858. Letter from the ghost of the Alms House Clock, Dorchester.)

(Between 1858 and 1862. Accounts of Church Restorations by Hicks, in a Dorchester paper.)

(1865. 'On the Application of Coloured Bricks and Terra Cotta in Modern Architecture.' An Essay.)

1865–71. Poems, some of which were later published in the first volumes of Collected Verse.

(1868. *The Poor Man and the Lady*. A Novel.)

1871. *Desperate Remedies*. 3 vols. Tinsley Brothers.

1872. *Under the Greenwood Tree*. 2 vols. Tinsley Brothers.

1873. *A Pair of Blue Eyes*. In *Tinsley's Magazine*, Sept. 1872–July 1873. 3 vols. Tinsley Brothers, 1873.

1874. *Far from the Madding Crowd*. In the *Cornhill Magazine*. Jan.–Dec. 1874. 2 vols. Smith, Elder & Co.

1874. 'Destiny and a Blue Cloak.' A short story in the *New York Times*, October 4th, 1874.

1875. *The Hand of Ethelberta*. In the *Cornhill Magazine*, July 1875–March 1876. 2 vols. Smith, Elder & Co., 1876.

1878. *The Return of the Native*. In *Belgravia*, Jan.-Dec., 1878. 3 vols. Smith, Elder & Co., 1878. The Manuscript is in the possession of Mrs. Clement Shorter.

1878. *An Indiscretion in the Life of an Heiress*. In the *New Quarterly Magazine*, October 1878.

1878. 'Dialect in Novels.' A Letter in the *Athenæum*, Nov. 30th, 1878.

1879. Unsigned Review of *Poems of Rural Life in the Dorset Dialect*, by William Barnes. In the *New Quarterly Magazine*, October 1879.

---

[1] This List, which does not pretend to be complete, gives the most important items in a form convenient for reference. A new Bibliography is being at present compiled in the U.S.A.

APPENDICES

1880. *The Trumpet Major*. In *Good Words*, Jan.-Dec. 1880. 3 vols. Smith, Elder & Co., 1880. The Manuscript is in Windsor Castle Library.

1880. *A Laodicean*. In *Harper's Magazine* (European Edition), Dec. 1880-Dec. 1881. 3 vols. Sampson, Low, Marston, Searle & Rivington. The Manuscript was destroyed.

1881. 'On the Use of Dialect.' A Letter in the *Spectator*, October 15th, 1881.

1882. *Two on a Tower*. In the *Atlantic Monthly* (Boston, U.S.A.), May-Dec. 1882. 3 vols. Sampson, Low, Marston, Searle & Rivington.

1883. 'The Dorsetshire Labourer.' An Article in *Longman's Magazine*, July 1883.

1883. 'An Obituary Notice of T. W. H. Tolbort, in the *Dorset County Chronicle*, August 16th, 1883.

1886. *The Mayor of Casterbridge*. In the *Graphic*, Jan.-May 1886. 2 vols. Smith, Elder & Co. The Manuscript is in the Dorset County Museum, Dorchester.

1886. An Obituary Notice of the Rev. William Barnes in the *Athenæum*, October 16th, 1886.

1887. *The Woodlanders*. In *Macmillan's Magazine*, May 1886-April 1887. 3 vols. Macmillan & Co., 1887.

1888. *Wessex Tales*. 2 vols. Macmillan & Co.

Vol. 1: 'The Three Strangers' (originally in *Longman's Magazine*, March 1883).

'The Withered Arm' (*Blackwoods Magazine*, Jan. 1888).

'Fellow Townsman' (*New Quarterly Magazine*, Jan. and April 1880).

Vol. 2: 'Interlopers at the Knap' (*English Illustrated Magazine*, vol. 2, 1884–5, and 'Littel's Living Age,' Boston, U.S.A.), 1885.

'The Distracted Preacher' (*New Quarterly Magazine*, Jan. and April 1879).

The Manuscript of 'The Three Strangers' is in the possession of Sir Sydney Cockerell.

1888. 'The Profitable Reading of Fiction.' An Article in *The Forum* (New York), March 1888.

1890. 'Candour in English Fiction.' An Article in the *New Review*, Jan. 1890.

1890. 'Some Romano-British Relics found at Max Gate, Dorchester.' (In the *Proceedings of the Dorset Natural History and Antiquarian Field Club*, Vol. 11, 1890.)

1890. On the Treatment of a Certain Author. A Letter signed by Messrs. Walter Besant, William Black and Thomas Hardy in the *Athenæum*, November 17th, 1890.[1]

1891. *A Group of Noble Dames*. Osgood, M'Ilvaine & Co. Some of the contents originally appeared as follows:

'The First Countess of Wessex,' *Harper's Magazine*, Dec. 1889.

'The Lady Penelope,' *Longman's Magazine*, Jan. 1890.

(Remainder in the *Graphic*, Christmas No., 1890, with the exception of 'The Duchess of Hamptonshire' and 'The Honourable Laura'). Some of the Manuscript is in the Library of Congress, Washington, U.S.A.

1891. 'The Science of Fiction.' An Article in the *New Review*, April 1891.

1891. *Tess of the d'Urbervilles*. In the *Graphic*, July-Dec. 1891. Episodes not in the *Graphic* were 'Saturday Night in Arcady' in the *National Observer*, November 14th, 1891, and 'The Midnight Baptism' in the *Fortnightly Review*, May 1891. 3 vols. The Manuscript is in the British Museum. Osgood. M'Ilvaine & Co.

1892. 'Why I don't write Plays.' An Article in the *Pall Mall Gazette*, August 31st, 1892.

1894. *Life's Little Ironies*. Osgood, M'Ilvaine & Co. Contents originally appeared as follows:

'An Imaginative Woman,' *Pall Mall Gazette*, April 1894.

'The Son's Veto,' *Illustrated London News*, Christmas No., 1891.

'For Conscience' Sake,' *Fortnightly Review*, March 1891.

'A Tragedy of Two Ambitions,' *Universal Review*, Vol. 2, 1889.

'On the Western Circuit,' *English Illustrated Magazine*, Dec. 1891.

'To Please His Wife,' *Black and White*, June 27th, 1891.

'The Fiddler of the Reels,' *Scribner's Magazine*, May 1893.

'The Melancholy Hussar,' in *Three Notable Stories* (Spencer, Blackett & Co., 1890).

---

[1] The author was Rudyard Kipling, whose poem 'The Three Captains' refers to this incident.

APPENDICES

('A Tradition of 1804' first appeared in *Life's Little Ironies*.)

1894. 'On the Tree of Knowledge.' A Letter in the *New Review*, May 1894.

1894. *Jude the Obscure*. In *Harper's Monthly Magazine*, Dec. 1894-Nov. 1895. Osgood, M'Ilvaine & Co. The Manuscript is in the Fitzwilliam Museum at Cambridge.

1894. 'The Spectre of the Real.' A Story by Thomas Hardy and Florence Henniker, in *To Day*, Nov. 1894. Reprinted in *In Scarlet and Grey*, 1896.

1896. *The Well Beloved*. Osgood, M'Ilvaine & Co. The first two parts originally appeared in the *Illustrated London News*, Oct.-Dec. 1892.

1897. A Letter on *The Well Beloved*, in the *Academy*, April 3rd, 1897.

1898. *Wessex Poems*. Macmillan & Co.

1902. *Poems of the Past and Present*. Macmillan & Co. The Manuscript is in the Bodleian Library.

1903⎤ The *Dynasts*. Parts 1, 2 and 3. 3 vols. Macmillan & Co.
1906⎬ (The original issue of Part 1 was made at the end of
1908⎦ 1903, but a few copies only were distributed. The same volume with a title-page dated 1904 was issued in January 1904.) The Manuscript is at the British Museum. A draft of the Afterscene was formerly in the possession of Mr. Howard Bliss.

1906. 'Memories of Church Restoration.' Read at the General Meeting of the Society for the Protection of Ancient Buildings, June 20th, 1906, published in the *Cornhill Magazine*, July 1906.

1906. Letter in the *Times* on J. S. Mill on May 20th, 1906.

1908. Preface to *Select Poems of William Barnes*, Oxford University Press, 1908.

1909. *Time's Laughingstocks*. Macmillan & Co.

1913. *A Changed Man and Other Tales*. Macmillan & Co. The Contents originally appeared as follows:

'A Changed Man,' the *Sphere*, April 21st, 1900.

'The Waiting Supper,' *Murray's Magazine*, Jan.-Feb. 1888.

'Alicia's Diary,' *Bolton Weekly Journal*, 1887.

'The Grave by the Handpost,' *St. James' Budget*, Christmas No., 1897.

'Enter a Dragoon,' *Harper's Magazine*, Dec. 1900.

'What the Shepherd Saw,' *Illustrated London News*, Christmas No., 1881.

'A Committee Man of the Terror,' *Illustrated London News*, Christmas No., 1896.

'Master John Horseleigh, Knight.' *Illustrated London News*, Summer No., 1893.

'The Duke's Reappearance,' *Saturday Review Illustrated Supplement*, Christmas 1896.

'A Mere Interlude,' *Bolton Weekly Journal*, October 17th, 1885.

'The Romantic Adventures of a Milkmaid,' *Graphic*, Summer No., 1883.

1914. *Satires of Circumstance*. Macmillan & Co.

1914. 'On the Bombardment of Reims Cathedral.' A Letter to the *Times*, October 7th, 1914.

1917. *Moments of Vision*. Macmillan & Co.

1922. *Late Lyrics and Earlier*. Macmillan & Co.

1923. *The Famous Tragedy of the Queen of Cornwall*. Macmillan & Co.

1925. *Human Shows, Far Phantasies, Songs and Trifles*. Macmillan & Co.

1928. *Winter Words*. Macmillan & Co.

LIST OF HARDYANA

AAS, L. *Thomas Hardy og hans Digtnig*. 1927.

ABERCROMBIE, L. *Thomas Hardy: a Critical Study*. 1912.

ABERCROMBIE, L. 'Thomas Hardy's *The Dynasts*.' A Lecture to the Royal Institution of Great Britain. January 15th, 1937.

BEACH, J. W. *The Technique of Thomas Hardy*. 1922.

BERLE, L. W. *George Eliot and Thomas Hardy: a Contrast*. 1917.

BRAYBROOKE, P. *Thomas Hardy and his Philosophy*. 1928.

BRENNECKE, E. *The Life of Thomas Hardy*. 1925.

BRENNECKE, E. *Thomas Hardy's Universe: a Study of a Poet's Mind*. 1924.

CATALOGNE, G. de. *Le Message de Thomas Hardy*. 1928.

CHASE, M. E. *Thomas Hardy, from Serial to Novel*. 1927.

APPENDICES

CHEW, S. C. *Thomas Hardy.* 1921. (Bryn Mawr Notes and Monographs.)

CHEW, S. C. *Thomas Hardy.* 1928.

CHILD, H. H. *Thomas Hardy.* 1916.

COLLINS, V. H. G. *Talks with Thomas Hardy.* 1928.

DANIELSON, H. *The First Editions of the Writings of Thomas Hardy. A Bibliographical Handbook.* 1916.

DUFFIN, H. C. *Thomas Hardy: a Study of the Wessex Novels.* 1916.

DUFFIN, H. C. *Thomas Hardy: a Study of the Wessex Novels, with an Appendix on the Poems and the 'Dynasts.'* 1921.

ELLIOT, A. P. *Fatalism in the Works of Thomas Hardy.* 1935.

ELLIS, H. *Concerning 'Jude the Obscure.'* 1931.

EXIDEUIL, P. d'. *Le Couple humain dans l'Oeuvre de Thomas Hardy.* 1928.

EXIDEUIL, P. d'. *The Human Pair in the Works of Thomas Hardy.* 1930. (Translation of the foregoing.)

FIROR, R. A. *Folkways in Thomas Hardy.* 1931.

FOWLER, J. H. *The Novels of Thomas Hardy.* 1828. (English Association Pamphlet No. 71.)

GARDNER, W. H. *Some Thoughts on 'The Mayor of Casterbridge.'* 1930. (English Association Pamphlet.)

GARWOOD, H. *Thomas Hardy: an Illustration of the Philosophy of Schopenhauer.* 1911.

GRIMSDITCH, H. B. *Character and Environment in the Novels of Thomas Hardy.* 1925.

GUNTHER, H. *Das Verheimlichungs-Hochzeits und Briefmotif in den Romanen Thomas Hardys.* 1933.

HARDY, F. E. *The Early Life of Thomas Hardy.* 1928.

HARDY, F. E. *The Later Years of Thomas Hardy.* 1930.

HARPER, C. G. *The Hardy Country: Literary Landmarks of the Wessex Novels.* 1904.

HARTMANN, J. *Architektur in den Romanen Thomas Hardy's.* 1934.

HEDGCOCK, F. A. *Essai de Critique: Thomas Hardy penseur et artiste.* 1911.

HICKSON, E. C. *The Versification of Thomas Hardy.* 1931.

HILLER, H. *Thomas Hardy: seine Entwicklung als Romancier.* 1933.

HOLLAND, C. *Thomas Hardy. The Man, his Work and the land of Wessex.* 1933.

HOPKINS, R. T. *Thomas Hardy's Dorset.* 1922.

JOHNSON, L. *The Art of Thomas Hardy.* 1894.

THOMAS HARDY

LEA, H. A. *Handbook to the Wessex Country of Thomas Hardy's Novels and Poems.* 1906.

LIRON, A. *La Femme dans le Roman de Thomas Hardy.* 1919.

MACDONNELL, A. *Thomas Hardy.* 1894.

MACDOWALL, A. *Thomas Hardy: a Critical Study.* 1931.

MAXWELL, D. *The Landscape of Thomas Hardy.* 1928.

OLIVERO, F. *An Introduction to Hardy.* 1930.

PARKER, W. M. M. *On the Track of the Wessex Novels; a Guide to the Hardy Country.* 1924.

PURDY, R. L. *Thomas Hardy.* Catalogue of a memorial edition of first editions, autograph letters and MSS. 1928.

RIDDER-BARZIN, L. de. *Le Pessimisme de Thomas Hardy.*

RUTLAND, W. R. *Thomas Hardy: Conférence Inaugurale.*

SALBERG, G. *Thomas Hardy's Frauen im Lichte seiner Weltanschauung.* 1927.

SAXELBY, F. O. *A Thomas Hardy Dictionary.* 1911.

SWANN, G. R. *Philosophical Parallelisms in six English Novelists.* 1931.

SHERREN, W. *The Wessex of Romance.* 1908.

SYMONS, A. *A Study of Thomas Hardy.* 1927.

TOMLINSON, H. M. *Thomas Hardy: a Study.*

UFER, A. A. MK. *Uber die kompositionelle Bedeutung der Natur bei Thomas Hardy.* 1930.

VOGT, F. *Thomas Hardys Naturansicht in seinen Romanen.* 1932.

WEBB, A. P. *A Bibliography of the Works of Thomas Hardy.* 1916.

WHITFIELD, A. S. *Thomas Hardy: a Lecture.* 1921.

WILLIAMS, R. *The Wessex Novels of Thomas Hardy.* 1924.

WINDLE, B. C. A. *The Wessex of Thomas Hardy.* 1901.

ZACHRISSON, R. E. *Stil och personlighet i T. Hardy's diktining.* (No date. Upsala.)

ZACHRISSON, R. E. *Thomas Hardy's Twilight View of Life.* 1931.

INDEX

INDEX

364

INDEX